Stewart Clark   Graham Pointon

wordfor
word

effect·brake break·ma
quiet·desert dessert·pe
cautious·high tall·wait

*'Make the right choice,
Get the right meaning.'*

UNIVERSITY PRESS

OXFORD
UNIVERSITY PRESS

Great Clarendon Street, Oxford OX2 6DP

Oxford University Press is a department of the University of Oxford. It furthers
the University's objective of excellence in research, scholarship, and education
by publishing worldwide in

Oxford New York

Auckland Bangkok Buenos Aires Cape Town Chennai Dar es Salaam Delhi
Hong Kong Istanbul Karachi Kolkata Kuala Lumpur Madrid Melbourne
Mexico City Mumbai Nairobi São Paulo Shanghai Taipei Tokyo Toronto

ISBN 0 19 432755 8

Illustrated by Roger Penwill

Printed in China

Contents

Introduction

Words are your tools to express your ideas, thoughts, feelings, and reactions. It is sometimes difficult even in your own language to find words that are precise enough to get your exact message across to others. When we use English, we are faced with a language where the spelling of words often has little to do with their pronunciation, where slang and idiom are intertwined with standard phrases, and where most words have multiple meanings. English is full of traps which are easy to fall into. As Bill Bryson said: 'Any language where the unassuming ... word *fly* signifies an annoying insect, a means of travel, and a critical part of a gentleman's apparel is clearly asking to be mangled'. (*Mother Tongue*, Penguin Books, 1990)

Word for Word will guide you around many of the potential pitfalls in English. There are enough of them. About 3000 of the most common problem words have been collected in this book. Using *Word for Word* will increase your confidence and skill in writing or speaking English both as a working language and for study. Unlike a dictionary, *Word for Word* presents groups of words that are often confused. So *job* comes with *position*, *situation*, and *post*. *Sensible* is together with *sensitive*, *insensible*, and *insensitive*. Each explanation is straightforward and is illustrated by an example. *Insensible*, for example, points out that even though it contains the prefix *in-*, it is not the opposite of *sensible*: 'The boxer was knocked insensible'.

Some words are confused because they are soundalikes, and even native English speakers can mix up *reigns* and *reins*, even though they mean very different things, just because they are both pronounced 'rains'. Other words are included because they are lookalikes, such as 'suit' and 'suite', or 'recover' and 're-cover'. Cultural sensitivities are also considered, so that *Asian* and *Asiatic* are in a group that explains that *Asian* is used for people, *Asiatic* for geography. As it is racially offensive to use Asiatic for people, these words must not be confused.

This book also includes about 100 tinted boxes, which advise on issues such as how to write letters and emails in American and British English, as well as on language matters like when to use the 's'-genitive. *Word for Word* does more than explain the differences between words, it also helps with the pronunciation, spelling, and usage. It is a book that you can use with confidence, as it is based on modern British English style and usage.

Here is a book you will enjoy having on your desk. We all know that English is a funny language. *Word for Word* includes a few jokes that will help you remember to avoid the pitfalls. No one wants to make their English even funnier than it is already, although thousands unknowingly do just this every day.

How to use this book

Word for Word helps you use words and expressions correctly. Example sentences reinforce the meaning and show you how the word is used in context. There is also help with the pronunciation and spelling of difficult words as well as references to related terms. If you do not find a word immediately, the index will help you locate it more quickly.

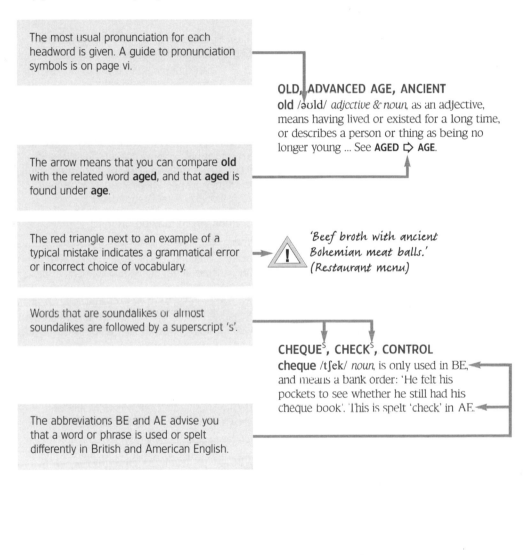

The most usual pronunciation for each headword is given. A guide to pronunciation symbols is on page vi.

OLD, ADVANCED AGE, ANCIENT
old /əʊld/ *adjective & noun,* as an adjective, means having lived or existed for a long time, or describes a person or thing as being no longer young ... See **AGED** ⊏〉 **AGE**.

The arrow means that you can compare **old** with the related word **aged**, and that **aged** is found under **age**.

The red triangle next to an example of a typical mistake indicates a grammatical error or incorrect choice of vocabulary.

⚠ *'Beef broth with ancient Bohemian meat balls.'*
(Restaurant menu)

Words that are soundalikes or almost soundalikes are followed by a superscript 's'.

CHEQUE⁵, CHECK⁵, CONTROL
cheque /tʃek/ *noun,* is only used in BE, and means a bank order: 'He felt his pockets to see whether he still had his cheque book'. This is spelt 'check' in AE.

The abbreviations BE and AE advise you that a word or phrase is used or spelt differently in British and American English.

Guide to pronunciation

The pronunciation of headwords, and of some other words, has been given in the alphabet of the International Phonetic Association (IPA). Except where specified, only British English pronunciations are shown. The following list shows the IPA symbols, followed by sample words illustrating the sound. As the English spelling system is so complex, the same *written* letters may often be *pronounced* in different ways, depending on the word concerned.

Vowels

iː	m**ee**t, mach**i**ne
i	happ**y**, th**e** (before a vowel)
ɪ	p**i**t, d**e**part
e	m**e**t
æ	m**a**t
ɑː	f**a**ther
ɒ	h**o**t
ɔː	th**ou**ght, l**a**w
ʊ	w**oo**l, p**u**t
uː	b**oo**t, r**u**de
ʌ	h**u**t, c**o**me
ɜː	h**er**d, b**ir**d, w**or**d, c**ur**d, c**o**lonel
ə	**a**bove, th**e** (before a consonant), c**o**mpare

Diphthongs

eɪ	m**ay**, **eigh**t, m**a**te
aɪ	m**igh**t, m**i**te, b**y**
ɔɪ	b**oy**
əʊ	n**o**
aʊ	n**ow**
ɪə	h**ere**, id**ea**
eə	th**ere**
ʊə	p**oor**, sk**ua**

Consonants

p, b, t, d, k, g, f, v, s, z, h, m, n, l, r, w all have the values normally associated with them in English: [g] is always as in *get*, never as in *general* ['dʒenərəl]; [f] is always as in *fit*, never as in *of* [ɒv]; [s] is always as in *soft*, never as in *rose* [rəʊz].

θ	**th**in, **th**igh, e**th**er
ð	**th**ere, **th**y, ei**th**er
ʃ	**sh**in
ʒ	mea**s**ure
tʃ	**ch**ur**ch**, ma**tch**
dʒ	**j**u**dg**e
ŋ	si**ng**
j	**y**acht

The following sound, not part of most British English accents, also appears:

ã	fia**ncé** (a nasalized vowel sound, used by those who know French)

Stress

The main stress is marked by the symbol ['] placed immediately before the stressed syllable: *important* [ɪm'pɔːtənt]. If a second syllable in a word carries some smaller degree of stress, then it is shown by [ˌ] placed immediately before it: *co-respondent* [ˌkəʊrɪ'spɒndənt].

Sounds which may be omitted

These are shown in italics:

allocate ['æləʊkeɪt] where the second syllable may contain either the neutral vowel [ə] or the full diphthong [əʊ];

competitor [kəm'petɪtə*r*] where the final -r will be pronounced only if the following word begins with a vowel;

postpone [pəʊs*t*pəʊn] where the -t- may be pronounced or omitted, depending on the speaker, and on the rate of speech (the faster, the more likely it is to be omitted).

Consonants which fill the whole syllable are shown with [ˌ] beneath them: *angle* ['æŋgl̩].

On rare occasions, when syllables need to be separated within a word, [.] is placed between the syllables: *coincide* [ˌkəʊ.ɪn'saɪd].

Weak forms

Many short words (prepositions, articles, determiners) have a 'strong' form, containing a full vowel, and one or more 'weak' pronunciations, depending on their position in the sentence, and the amount of stress placed on them. The strong forms occur most frequently when the word comes at the end of a sentence, or when the speaker is deliberately emphasizing it. A common fault of non-native speakers of English is to use too few weak forms. Where appropriate, we have included both the strong and weak forms.

Aa

ABIDE, ABODE

abide /əˈbaɪd/ *verb*, when combined with 'by', means to accept or obey something: 'We have to abide by the rules'. In this sense, the past form is 'abided' [əˈbaɪdɪd]. 'Abide' used with the negative of 'can' or 'could' means that the speaker cannot tolerate a person or idea: 'I can't abide the thought of living so near to his family'. An archaic meaning of 'abide' is 'to live with'. The past tense for this meaning was 'abode'.

abode /əˈbəʊd/ *noun*, means a dwelling, and is used in the legal phrase for someone who is homeless: 'A person of no fixed abode'. It is a formal word that is used in poetry or in the humorous expression: 'My humble abode'. More neutral alternatives are 'residence', 'house', and 'address'.

ABILITY, CAPACITY

ability /əˈbɪlɪti/ *noun*, means the skill and human power to do something: 'He is a negotiator of immense ability'.

capacity /kəˈpæsɪti/ *noun*, means the ability to produce something, or to have a talent for doing something when referring to skill. One distinction is that 'ability' is something acquired and 'capacity' is something inborn: 'His ability as a negotiator was helped by his capacity for remembering faces'. 'Capacity' also means the maximum amount that can be produced by a machine: 'This photocopier has the capacity to print fifty pages a minute'.

ABNORMAL, SUBNORMAL

abnormal /æbˈnɔːməl/ *adjective*, means something that differs from what is considered normal: 'Many consider that global warming has resulted in abnormal weather conditions'.

subnormal /sʌbˈnɔːməl/ *adjective*, means something below what is considered normal: 'Many winters had subnormal temperatures'.

ABOLISH, EXTINGUISH

abolish /əˈbɒlɪʃ/ *verb*, means to end or destroy customs, practices and institutions completely: 'Slavery was abolished by law in the 19th century'.

extinguish /ɪksˈtɪŋgwɪʃ/ *verb*, means to put out a fire: 'Three weeks of heavy rain extinguished the forest fires'. It also has the figurative meaning of to destroy: 'When the talks broke down, all hope of peace was extinguished'. The related adjective and noun forms 'extinct' and 'extinction' refer specifically to an animal or plant which no longer exists.

absolutes and fuzzy absolutes

- One of the best examples of an absolute is *unique*, which means that there is only one of its kind, and thus, logically, should never be qualified by 'more', 'most', or 'very'. There are other words in this category such as: *absolute, complete, entire, equal, excellent, extreme, full, horizontal, ideal, impossible, infinite, parallel, perfect, perpendicular, round, square, thorough, total, utter, vertical*. Careful writers accept that if something is *horizontal* or *parallel*, it is simply that, and constructions like 'this is the more perpendicular line', 'the most horizontal line', or 'the most parallel line' should be rewritten.

- However, English as a living language often defies the laws of logic. As *The New Oxford Dictionary of English* points out, most of these absolutes have a precise core meaning but also a secondary fuzzy meaning, so that *unique* also has the fuzzy meaning of 'very remarkable,' and *infinite* also means 'very great'. It is here when we indicate approximation that constructions with 'nearly', 'almost', 'close to' are used to convey approximation to the ideal/perfection: *This result was nearly ideal/perfect*.

- If comparatives are linked to such fuzzy absolutes, sometimes the result unintentionally sounds like advertising, such as: 'more perfect results', 'more excellent performance'.

ABSTRACT, ABSTRACTEDLY

abstract /ˈæbstrækt/ *noun & adjective*, as a noun, means a summary of a report or paper, usually in about 250 words. As an adjective, 'abstract' means existing in thought or just as an idea: 'Enough abstract thought; give me one concrete example'. 'Abstract' can also refer to a direction in art and artistic expression. Note that the stress is on the first syllable.

abstract /əb'strækt/ *verb*, means to take away, or remove a part from a larger entity: 'The hydropower scheme meant abstracting millions of litres of water from the river'. Note that the stress is on the second syllable. This is a formal term.

abstractedly /əb'stræktɪdli/ *adverb*, means deep in thought and not paying attention to what is going on: 'He walked right past me, gazing abstractedly at the sky'.

ABUSE, MISUSE

abuse /ə'bjuːs/ *noun*, /ə'bjuːz/ *verb*, means poor treatment or violent and improper use of something: 'He was imprisoned after being found guilty of repeated child abuse'. 'Alcohol abuse' is the excessive consumption of alcohol. Note that as a noun, 'abuse' rhymes with 'juice', but as a verb it rhymes with 'news'.

misuse /mɪs'juːs/ *noun*, /mɪs'juːz/ *verb*, means the use of something dishonestly, or for a purpose that it was not designed for: 'Using that expensive Burgundy to make a gravy is a clear case of alcohol misuse'. Note that as a noun, 'misuse' rhymes with 'juice', but as a verb it rhymes with 'news'.

ACADEMIC, SCHOLARLY, SCHOLAR

academic /ækə'demɪk/ *adjective & noun*, as an adjective, normally means matters associated with university education such as 'academic standards'. In this sense, it is a positive word. 'Academic' also refers to something that is without practical application and of no immediate relevance: 'We have already won the overall competition, so the score of this match is academic'. As a noun, 'academic' is used to mean a teacher or researcher in higher education.

scholarly /'skɒləli/ *adjective*, refers to serious academic study: 'His theories have been printed in a scholarly paper'. This is used only in a positive sense. 'Scholarly' can also be used for a person who is studious, learned or engaged in university research.

scholar /'skɒlər/ *noun*, means a learned person, teacher or researcher in the classics, arts, and humanities, or other non-scientific disciplines: 'She was a distinguished Latin scholar'. It can also mean the holder of a scholarship such as 'a Rhodes Scholar'.

ACCEPT[S], EXCEPT[S]

accept /ək'sept/ *verb*, means to receive something: 'He was pleased to accept the award from the Design Council'. 'Accept' also means to agree to something willingly: 'After twenty years the director accepted the need to modernize the company'.

except /ɪk'sept/ *preposition & verb*, as a preposition, means not including, or omitting something: 'Except for the teacher, the rest of the villagers were illiterate'. As a verb, 'except' means to leave out, but is less common than 'to exclude'. See **EXCLUDE**.

ACCESS, EXCESS

access /'ækses/ *noun & verb*, means entry or admittance: 'There is no right of access for the public'. As a verb, 'access' can mean to open a computer file: 'She double-clicked and accessed the file'. It also means to reach or enter something, and the related adjective is 'accessible': 'The Open University has made university education accessible to the general public'. See **ADMIT** ⇨ **ACKNOWLEDGE**. See **ENTRY**.

excess /ɪk'ses/ *noun*, /'ekses/ *adjective*, means something more than is permitted or desirable: 'He had 20 kilos of excess baggage'. The related adjective is 'excessive' /ɪk'sesɪv/: 'Excessive drinking is very bad for your health'.

ACCIDENT, MISHAP, DISASTER, CATASTROPHE

accident /'æksɪdənt/ *noun*, means an unintentional incident that results in damage or injury: 'There was another serious accident on that road last night'. The phrase 'by accident' means the same as 'accidentally' or 'unintentionally': 'I took the wrong coat home by accident'.

mishap /'mɪshæp/ *noun*, means an unlucky accident: 'Delivery was delayed by a minor mishap in our factory'. The word 'mishap' is used for accidents that are not very serious.

disaster /dɪ'zɑːstər/ *noun*, means a sudden event or serious accident that results in great damage or loss of life: 'The train crash was one of many such disasters in India'. Note that English often uses 'disaster' where other languages would use the equivalent of 'catastrophe', for example 'disaster area' and 'disaster fund'.

catastrophe /kə'tæstrəfi/ *noun*, means an event that results in widespread and often sudden damage or suffering: 'The earthquake was a catastrophe for the whole nation'.

ACCOMMODATION, ACCOMMODATIONS

accommodation /əkɒmə'deɪʃn̩/ *noun*, means a room or building where someone can live or stay: 'Student accommodation in town is always hard to find at the beginning of term'. Note the double 'c' and 'm'. 'Accommodation' is uncountable when used in this sense. This is also a very formal term meaning a settlement, agreement or compromise: 'The two sides came to an accommodation'. This word is only used in the singular in BE.

accommodations is the plural of 'accommodation', but is used only in AE: 'The cost of overnight accommodations is included in the price of the ticket'.

ACHIEVE, ACCOMPLISH, ATTAIN

achieve /ə'tʃiːv/ *verb*, means to reach an objective or standard, especially over a period of time. 'He was delighted to have achieved his ambition of becoming a rock star'. The related noun is 'achievement'.

accomplish /ə'kʌmplɪʃ/ *verb*, can mean the same as 'achieve', but has an additional sense of successfully completing something: 'They safely accomplished the task of freeing the soldiers'. The related adjective, 'accomplished', describes a person who does something with great skill: 'She is an accomplished pianist'. The related noun is 'accomplishment'.

attain /ə'teɪn/ *verb*, means to reach a certain standard, and is the word to use when comparison or measurement is involved: 'She attained the highest grades in her final exams'. The related noun is 'attainment'. A less formal alternative to 'attain' is the verb 'get'.

ACID, ACRID

acid /'æsɪd/ *adjective*, means sharp in taste and tone: 'The stand-up comedian had an acid sense of humour'. An 'acid test' means a crucial trial: 'The acid test is whether the software will actually work'.

acrid /'ækrɪd/ *adjective*, means unpleasantly bitter in taste or smell: 'The acrid smell came from the burning building'. Figuratively, an 'acrid parting' means an angry and bitter departure.

ACKNOWLEDGE, ADMIT

acknowledge /ək'nɒlɪdʒ/ *verb*, means to confirm that something has been received: 'The company sent me a letter acknowledging my complaint'. It also means to recognize or accept a truth: 'She has never acknowledged her responsibility in this matter'. 'Acknowledge' is used in formal contexts to mean to thank: 'I acknowledge the financial support from the Research Council'. The related noun 'acknowledgement' can also be spelt 'acknowledgment'. The plural form of the noun can mean a section of a book or report in which the author lists or thanks those who have made a contribution.

admit /əd'mɪt/ *verb*, means to accept responsibility: 'I admit that your complaint is justified'. It also means to enter or allow access: 'This ticket admits one'. See **ACCESS**. See **ENTRY**.

ACOUSTIC, ACOUSTICS

acoustic /ə'kuːstɪk/ *adjective*, refers to hearing, sound, or the science of sound. In anatomy, an example is the 'acoustic nerve', and in sound, an 'acoustic image'. 'Acoustic' is also found in expressions such as 'acoustic guitar'. Many technical expressions use the related adjective 'acoustical' /ə'kuːstɪkl/ in terms like 'acoustical measurement' and 'acoustical shadow'. In AE, 'acoustical' means the same as 'acoustic'.

acoustics /ə'kuːstɪks/ *noun*, has two meanings. One is the science of sound, when, like other academic subjects ending in -**ics**, it always takes a singular verb: 'Acoustics is a challenging field'. In the second sense, 'acoustics' means the acoustic properties of a room or a building, and takes a plural verb: 'The acoustics in the Greek amphitheatre are perfect'. See **–ICS**.

acronyms, abbreviations

- An acronym is a word formed from the initial letters of other words and is pronounced as a word, such as *AIDS* /eɪdz/ and *NATO* /'neɪtəʊ/. An abbreviation may be formed from the initial letters in a phrase or name and is read letter-by-letter, like I,B,M or A,S,A,P for 'as soon as possible' in BE. Note that it is normal to write the term in full the first time it is mentioned followed by the acronym or abbreviation in brackets. Then just the abbreviation can be used: *This is called Finite Element Modelling (FEM). Engineering design now uses FEM widely.*

acronyms

- An acronym is written without stops and read as a word. Some of these words are used so much that it is often difficult to remember that they are acronyms. Examples are *Aids*, also written *AIDS* (**a**cquired **i**mmune **d**eficiency **s**yndrome) and *PIN* (**p**ersonal **i**dentification **n**umber). This often leads to the mistake of writing 'PIN number'. Most acronyms are written in capital letters, but a few are in lower case and are scarcely recognizable as acronyms as they are treated as everyday words. Examples of these are *laser* (**l**ight **a**mplification by **st**imulated **e**mission of **r**adiation), pronounced /ˈleɪzər/ and *radar* (**ra**dio **d**etection **a**nd **r**anging), /ˈreɪdɑːr/. Market researchers love to produce acronyms such as *YUP* (**Y**oung **U**rban **P**rofessional) that occasionally survive and generate everyday words, written in lower case, such as the noun *yuppie* /ˈjʌpi/. Some of the acronyms that are widely adopted are carefully chosen to make catchy words like the American term *WASP* (**W**hite **A**nglo-**S**axon **P**rotestant). Most dictionaries of computing terms are full of acronyms such as *GIGO* /ˈgaɪgəʊ/ ('**g**arbage **in**, **g**arbage **o**ut').

abbreviations

- With familiarity, an abbreviation may change into an acronym. An example is U.N.E.S.C.O., written originally as initial letters with stops, and read letter-by-letter. It has now developed into the acronym *UNESCO* /juːˈneskəʊ/. Abbreviations formed from the initial letters in the names of companies, organizations and states, such as *IBM*, *the EU* and *the USA* are written in modern dictionaries without stops. Note that there may be differences in pronunciation between English and other languages. For example, *VIP* is read as a three-letter abbreviation in English, but may be an acronym if borrowed into other languages and pronounced as a single syllable.
- Apart from names, abbreviations are also formed by writing the first letter or a few of the letters in a word, but these are to be read aloud as if the whole word was written. Examples: *dept* (department), *asst* (assistant), *Fri.* (Friday), *Mr* (Mister), *Dr* (Doctor). In BE, abbreviations which end with the final letter of the word do not have a stop, while those that do not end like that are followed by a stop. Thus 'Doctor Arthur Smith' would be abbreviated *Dr A. Smith*. In AE, stops are usual after all abbreviations, such as *Mr.*, *Ms.*, and *Dr.*

- Plurals of abbreviations are often formed with an *s* as in: *no.*, *nos.* (number/s); *fig.*, *figs.* (figure/s); *eq.*, *eqs.* (equation/s). The plural of *p.*, is *pp.* (pages). The ISO standard concerning SI units states that abbreviations such as *cm*, *h*, *kg*, *km*, *m*, and *s* are to remain unaltered in the plural and are to be written without a final stop (ISO 31-0:1992).

non-English acronyms and abbreviations

- Foreign acronyms and abbreviations usually follow the practice of the UN and elsewhere where institutions often mix their English names with an acronym or abbreviation that is from French or German. An example of this is Système International d'Unités, which in English is called the *International System of Units*, but the abbreviation *SI* is used in all languages.
- Remember that it may be difficult for the speakers of one language to understand the acronyms or abbreviations of another. Many non-Spanish speakers would find it difficult to interpret RENFE, just as non-Francophones would not immediately understand what ORTF stands for. As acronyms and abbreviations in one language often have no direct equivalent in another, it is worth checking in an authoritative English dictionary that abbreviations exist before risking confusing readers with a direct translation from another language. Typical examples of such mistakes are 'w. r. t.' (correctly, *with regard to* or *regarding*) and 'f.ex.' (correctly, *for example* or *e.g.*).

ACROSS, ABOVE, OVER (POSITIONS)

across /əˈkrɒs/ *preposition & adverb*, means from one side to the other: 'We swam across the river'. 'Across' can either express movement: 'The plane took us across the Alps', or position: 'The pub is just across the street'. The expression 'across the board' means a situation or change that affects all levels: 'The savings made by the company will bring improvements across the board'.

above /əˈbʌv/ *preposition & adverb*, means at a higher level than something else without touching it: 'We are now above the Alps'. 'Above' stresses the distance or height: 'The plane was just above the trees'. It can also mean higher than a rate or a norm: 'She is well above average in mathematics'.

over /'əʊvər/ *preposition & adverb*, means the same as 'above', when used to describe a position that is at a higher level: 'We are now over the Alps'. However, 'over' can also mean higher than a specified figure: 'Everyone over 45 will benefit from the new legislation', or covering the surface of something: 'There was a thick layer of snow over the hills'. 'Over' is also used to mean from one side to the other, in a similar way to 'across': 'We walked over the field'. See **PREPOSITIONS**.

ACT, ACTION

act /ækt/ *noun & verb*, as a noun, is usually something which is carried out once, often a deed such as a criminal act: 'The explosion was incorrectly described as an act of terrorism'. A natural disaster is often called an 'act of God' by western insurance companies. In the legal sense, an 'Act' is capitalized and means a law passed by the legislature of a country. As a verb, to 'act' means to begin a process in response to a particular situation: 'When my windows were broken for a third time I realized that I had to act'. It can also mean to perform in a film or play, or to pretend: 'He acted as if he knew nothing about the dent in the car door'.

action /'ækʃn/ *noun*, stresses the process involved in an act that is typically directed towards a defined aim: 'The hijackers were overcome by the government's prompt military action'. It may also refer to legal proceedings: 'My client is considering taking legal action against you'.

ACTUAL, TOPICAL, CURRENT

actual /'æktʃʊəl/ *adjective*, refers to a real, factual event and something which exists: 'The newspaper quoted his actual words'. 'Actual' is often contrasted with something expected or estimated: 'The actual cost was only 60% of the estimate'. 'Actual' is a word that needs to be used with care, and it must not be confused with the similarly spelt word in many other languages, which usually means 'topical' or 'current'. See **FALSE FRIENDS**.

topical /'tɒpɪkl/ *adjective*, means either 'relevant' or 'of interest at the moment'. Compare: 'This film is about a topical problem' (one that is relevant and of current general interest) with: 'This film is about an actual problem' (one that is real and not imagined).

current /'kʌrənt/ *adjective & noun*, as an adjective, means happening at the present time: 'During the current financial crisis many families cannot afford holidays'. As a noun, 'current' means a flow of liquid, gas or electricity: 'The Gulf Stream is a current of warm water'. See **CURRENTLY ⇨ NOW**. See **FLOW ⇨ FLOAT**.

⚠️ *'I would like to thank Professor Jones: his comments were very actual.'*

ACUTE, CHRONIC

acute /ə'kjuːt/ *adjective*, refers to a sudden illness or a very serious occurrence: 'Following the crash, the badly injured pilot suffered acute pain'.

chronic /'krɒnɪk/ *adjective*, refers to a serious medical or other condition that persists for a long time: 'Seven years after the accident, the pilot was still suffering from chronic pain'.

AD⁵, ADD⁵, ADVERT

ad /æd/ *noun*, is an informal short form of 'advertisement'. Both 'ad' and the plural 'ads' are typically combined with words such as 'classified' and 'small', and refer to short advertisements grouped by subject in newspaper columns: 'They went through the classified ads to find a flat to rent near the river'. Another term for 'classified ads' is 'small ads'. These are also called 'want ads' in AE.

add /æd/ *verb*, means to increase or to say something more. Note that if something is added, such as an 'added advantage', one advantage must already have been mentioned.

advert /'ædvɜːt/ *noun*, is a short form of 'advertisement'. The word is used for all sorts of adverts anywhere; on TV, in the media, on hoardings or billboards: 'The company placed adverts all over town to announce the opening of the new mall'.

AD, BC

AD /ˌeɪ 'diː/ stands for Anno Domini and is written before the year: 'Pompeii was destroyed in AD 79'. Some people argue that it is incorrect to use 'in AD 79' because in Latin, 'anno' means 'in the year'. However, this combination is in general use. Another criticism is that 'AD' should not be combined with 'century', because a century cannot be in the year of anything. Nevertheless, 'AD' often illogically follows 'century' for clarity: 'The church dated back to the fourth century AD'.

BC /ˌbiː ˈsiː/ stands for 'before Christ', and is written after the year: 'Julius Caesar was assassinated in 44 BC'. Note that 'AD' and 'BC' should be written in small capitals in printed text.

ADAPT, ADOPT, ACQUIRE

adapt /əˈdæpt/ *verb*, means to adjust to something: 'In South Africa he had to adapt to life in the southern hemisphere'. The related noun is 'adaptation'. A person who adapts something is an 'adaptor', also spelt 'adapter', and this word is also used for the piece of equipment which allows two otherwise incompatible items to be connected.

adopt /əˈdɒpt/ *verb*, means to put into practice or to borrow: 'When we moved to Australia we adopted the custom of Christmas Day beach parties'. The related noun is 'adoption', which usually means taking legal responsibility for someone else's child. A person who adopts a child is usually called an 'adoptive parent'.

acquire /əˈkwaɪər/ *verb*, means to learn or develop a skill, habit or quality: 'She acquired new habits after becoming a star in Hollywood'. The related noun is 'acquisition'.

addresses in letters

- In modern English, all addresses are written with as few stops and commas as possible. Companies and organizations have their name on the top line of a letterhead followed by the address. However, in personal letters in English only the address is placed at the top. (When the recipient does not know the writer, the writer's name should be printed underneath his or her signature.)

- The address of the recipient is normally placed under the address of the sender. Many people place both addresses against the left-hand margin of the letter/email. Note that although the street number is placed before the street name in the UK and the USA and elsewhere, there are many countries in which this order is reversed. Try to follow the practice of the country of destination.

Visclar Ltd.
33 Hill Lane
Cambridge
CB2 2QF
England
GB
and:
Clovn Corporation
3501 Market Street
Milwaukee, WI 53201
USA

- Common short forms in addresses are: *Ave* (Avenue), *Blvd* (Boulevard), *Rd* (Road), *Sq.* (Square), *St* (Street).

- ISO 3166-1 lists the international two-letter codes for about 240 countries. In many European countries this country code is placed in front of the postcode and place name and is followed by a hyphen, for example DK-1014 Copenhagen.

See **LETTERS AND EMAILS**.

ADHESION, ADHERENCE

adhesion /ədˈhiːʒn/ *noun*, means the quality of sticking or glueing: 'The new type of glue did not sell very well, due to its poor adhesion'.

adherence /ədˈhɪərəns/ *noun*, means support for a particular party or ideology: 'His adherence to the party was never in question'. This is a formal word, a more general alternative being 'support'.

ADJACENT, ADJOINING

adjacent /əˈdʒeɪsn̩t/ *adjective*, is a general word that means either 'close to' or 'nearby', and not necessarily sharing the same boundary: 'The two military aircraft landed simultaneously on adjacent runways'.

adjoining /əˈdʒɔɪnɪŋ/ *adjective*, means 'next to', and always sharing the same boundary: 'The aircraft moved off the runway on to the adjoining taxiing area'. Things that are adjoining must be joined.

adjectives

- Adjectives are words that add something to the meaning of nouns, by naming an attribute, such as a colour, or size. Examples are *green*, *large*, and *quiet*. They do not have a plural form. In English, adjectives are typically placed immediately before the noun: *a green frog*; or after verbs like *be, feel, seem*: *the water was muddy*. Some adjectives may appear in only one of these positions: *When we got there, the woman was alone*, not 'an alone woman'. Note that some adjectives end in *-ly* (*a friendly dog, a silly dog, a lovely dog*). See **ADVERBS**. See **HYPHENATION IN COMPOUNDS**.

ADJOURN, POSTPONE, DEFER, RAIN CHECK

adjourn /ə'dʒɜːn/ *verb*, means to break off a meeting that has started: 'We will adjourn the meeting until next week'. More informally, when combined with 'to', 'adjourn' can also mean to move somewhere else: 'After the wedding ceremony they adjourned to the hotel for the reception'. See **CANCEL**.

postpone /pəʊst'pəʊn/ *verb*, means to reschedule an event or meeting that has not yet started: 'The takeover negotiations were postponed because of the director's sudden illness'.

defer /dɪ'fɜːr/ *verb*, means to delay making a judgement or decision: 'The committee has unfortunately deferred its decision until its next meeting'. When combined with 'to', 'defer' means to submit to another person's knowledge or decision: 'I defer to your superior mechanical expertise'. This is a formal use of the verb.

rain check /'reɪn tʃek/ *noun*, means that a matter will be discussed or decided later. It is usually combined with 'take', as in: 'I will have to take a rain check on this'. It is an informal AE term that is used a lot in business. The expression originated as the term for a new ticket issued for a rescheduled baseball or American football match stopped because of rain or other bad weather conditions. See **RAIN**.

adverbs

- Adverbs are words that add something to a verb, an adjective, or a whole sentence, but never a noun. Many adverbs of manner end in *-ly*, such as *quickly, proudly*, but other adverbs, like *here* and *now*, do not. Some phrases where adverbs without *-ly* are preferred are: *sell cheap, run fast* and *play fair*. See **LINK WORDS**.

- It is best to avoid a string of *-ly* adverbs together. NOT: 'The email was really exceedingly badly written'. USE: *It is clear that the email was very badly written*.

- Do not use hyphens after *-ly* adverbs, because they have no purpose. NOT 'He is an equally-good man'. USE *He is an equally good man*. See **HYPHENATION IN COMPOUNDS**.

- A useful rule to remember is that when more than one adverb or adverbial phrase is used in a sentence, they tend to come in the order 'manner', 'place', and 'time', which coincidentally is the alphabetical order of these three words ('m', 'p', 't'): *He walked quickly* (manner) *down the street* (place); *I'll meet you in the market place* (place) *at five o'clock* (time); *The wind blew violently* (manner) *all night* (time).

ADVERSE, AVERSE

adverse /'ædvɜːs/ *adjective*, means unfavourable, or harmful: 'The weather report warned us of adverse weather conditions'. 'Adverse' is not used about people.

averse /ə'vɜːs/ *adjective*, means opposing or having a strong dislike for a thing or person. 'Averse' is combined with 'to', and normally follows the verbs 'be' or 'feel': 'She was averse to men with beards'.

ADVICE, ADVISE

advice /əd'vaɪs/ *noun*, means a recommended course of action. It is an uncountable noun, and therefore 'a piece of advice' or 'some advice' are often used to express amounts of advice. It always takes a singular verb and determiner: 'This advice is very important, and it should be followed carefully'. Note that 'advice' is replaced by a singular pronoun. The ending rhymes with 'ice'.

advise /əd'vaɪz/ *verb*, means to make recommendations: 'The policeman put his notebook away and advised us to keep to the speed limit'. The ending rhymes with 'eyes'.

AERIAL, SPATIAL

aerial /'eərɪəl/ *adjective & noun*, means something in the air or involving the use of aircraft, such as 'aerial surveillance'. As a noun in BE, an aerial is a wire that can transmit or receive radio waves. See **ANTENNA**.

spatial /'speɪʃl/ *adjective*, means relating to space and the position and shape of things in it: 'His spatial awareness was not very good, and he was always bumping into things'.

AFTERWARDS, SUBSEQUENTLY

afterwards /'ɑ:ftəwədz/ *adverb*, means later or after something that has been mentioned: 'The car hit a tree and the driver said he was very shaken up afterwards'. This is the normal BE spelling. 'Afterward' /'ɑ:ftəwəd/ is the AE alternative.

subsequently /'sʌbsɪkwəntli/ *adverb*, can mean the same as 'afterwards', but may refer to something that happens much later: 'He recovered from his injuries, but subsequently the doctors discovered symptoms of whiplash'. This is a formal word.

AGE, AGED, ELDERLY

age /eɪdʒ/ *noun & verb*, as a noun, means the duration of a life: 'He lived happily to a great age'. When capitalized, it can also refer to a period in history: 'The Elizabethan Age will be remembered for its poets and playwrights'. As a verb, 'age' refers to people or things becoming older: 'Because of regular exercise, the couple were aging more slowly than other pensioners'. The present participle is spelt 'aging' in AE and BE, and may also be spelt 'ageing' in BE.

aged /eɪdʒd/ *verb & adjective*, /'eɪdʒɪd/ *noun*, as the past tense of the verb 'age', refers to people getting older: 'The health service was expanded as a large percentage of the population aged'. It also refers to things developing in flavour over time: 'The brandy was aged in special casks'. As an adjective, 'aged' expresses how old a person is: 'The children in the class were aged between 8 and 10'. Note that as a verb or adjective, 'aged' is pronounced as one syllable. As a noun, this means old people collectively: 'They gave away their savings to help the aged'. The noun 'aged' is used with the definite article and is pronounced as two syllables. See **OLD**.

elderly /'eldəli/ *adjective & noun*, as an adjective refers to people who are old: 'Elderly people in the town were looked after very well'. This is a more polite term than calling people 'old'. As a noun, 'elderly' is used with the definite article: 'The elderly were allowed free taxis to the hospital and back'. See **ELDER/ELDEST**.

AGGRAVATE, EXACERBATE, ANNOY

aggravate /'ægrəveɪt/ *verb*, means to make a situation worse; for instance, by scratching an open wound, or by saying something to make someone more angry than they already were: 'The press comment seriously aggravated the problems of the socialist party'.

exacerbate /ɪg'zæsəbeɪt/ *verb*, means 'aggravate', but is used for situations, diseases or problems: 'Unfortunately her reaction to the story in the press only exacerbated the situation'. This is a formal word.

annoy /ə'nɔɪ/ *verb*, means to make a person angry. 'Aggravate' is often used in this sense, but careful writers still distinguish between aggravating a situation, and annoying a person.

AGO, SINCE, FOR

ago /ə'gəʊ/ *adverb*, always refers to a specific time in the past, whether five minutes ago or two thousand years ago: 'The Romans were using central heating two thousand years ago'. When a clause is introduced by 'ago', add 'that', not 'since': 'It was nearly 450 years ago that Shakespeare was born'. Note that it is incorrect to combine 'for' and 'ago' in the same phrase. It is also incorrect to use present perfect tenses before 'ago'.

since /sɪns/ *preposition, conjunction*, refers to a continuous period between the time considered and the present: 'It is nearly 450 years since Shakespeare was born'. As 'ago' refers to the past, and 'since' refers to the present, never combine the two time expressions in the same clause.

for /fər, fɔ:r/ *preposition*, refers to a continuous period of time which may or may not still be going on, depending on which verb tense is used in the main clause: 'He was president for eight years until 1980'. The strong form /fɔ:r/ is only used when 'for' is the final word of a sentence.

AGREE, APPROVE, CONSENT, ACCEDE

agree /ə'gri:/ *verb*, means to have the same opinion as another person: 'We agreed that it would be a good idea to write a book'. To 'agree with' a person or idea means to support a theory or point of view: 'I agree with the principles underlying freedom of speech'. In a grammatical sense, to 'agree with' means to be consistent: 'You should always check that the verb agrees with its subject'. Figuratively, if food does not 'agree with' a person, it makes them ill. To 'agree to' something means to accept a suggestion made by somebody else: 'They agreed to the new pension plan'.

approve /ə'pru:v/ *verb*, means to accept someone else's proposal or actions as being satisfactory: 'He approved the publication plan'. To 'approve of' means to like or be pleased with someone else's plans or actions: 'They thoroughly approved of their daughter's choice of husband'. The phrase 'approved by' refers to the body that accepts a proposal or plan: 'The budget cuts were approved by the board'.

consent /kən'sent/ *noun & verb*, means permission or agreement to do something: 'Children need their parents' consent to buy goods by mail order'. As a verb, 'consent' is combined with 'to' when followed by a noun or verb: 'She consented to be my wife'. A less formal alternative is 'agree to'.

accede /ək'siːd/ *verb*, means to agree or consent to something: 'The government was reluctant to accede to the union's demands'. This is a very formal word: 'agree' and 'consent' are less formal alternatives.

AGREEMENT, AGRÉMENT, GENTLEMAN'S AGREEMENT, ARRANGEMENT, DEAL

agreement /ə'griːmənt/ *noun*, means a negotiated and legally binding arrangement between two or more parties. An agreement can be written or oral: 'An agreement was reached between the three computer companies'. See **TREATY**.

agrément /'ægreɪmɑ̃/ *noun*, borrowed from French, is found on a product's label to show that it has been approved by the relevant EU authority. Hence its meaning in English is 'approval'.

gentleman's agreement /'dʒentlmənz ə'griːmənt/ *noun*, means an unwritten, but binding agreement, based on trust and usually confirmed by a handshake. This may also be called a 'gentlemen's agreement'. An alternative term is a 'verbal agreement'.

arrangement /ə'reɪndʒmənt/ *noun*, means a practical agreement on a personal or commercial basis: 'The travel agents have an arrangement with several hotels in Rome'. It can also mean an agreement to settle a debt: 'They eventually came to an arrangement with the creditors'.

deal /diːl/ *noun*, means an agreement of any type. It is an informal word that refers either to a commercial transaction: 'That car was a really good deal'; or to a compromise: 'The government refuses to make any deals with terrorists'.

A well-known rally driver is reported as saying: 'For many years, Ford and I have had a gentleman's agreement - in writing of course.'

agreement between subject and verb

In most cases, it is clear that a singular subject must be followed by a singular verb, and a plural subject by a plural verb. However, there are some exceptions to this general rule, outlined below, which are dealt with in more detail under the specific entries in this book.

- Uncountable nouns are always singular, but cannot be preceded by 'a/an': *advice, bread, damage, information, transport, wheat*. They have no plural form, and are always followed by a singular verb. See **UNCOUNTABLE NOUNS**.

- Academic subjects ending in *-ics* are singular: *linguistics, mathematics, physics*. These are followed by a singular verb. See **-ICS**.

- Some nouns ending in *-s* are singular. One such group refers to diseases, such as *measles* and *mumps*. Another such group refers to games, such as *billiards, draughts* (AE *checkers*), and *dominoes*. There are a few other words that follow this pattern, including *crossroads, means*, and *news*. These are all followed by a singular verb.

- Some nouns ending in *-s* are plural, but have no singular: *antics, oats*. These are followed by a plural verb. See **PLURAL NOUNS**.

- Some nouns are plural, even though they do not end in *-s*, and must take a plural verb. Examples are: *cattle, clergy, gentry, people, police*. These words have no singular form.

- Pairs of things are plural: *binoculars, scales, scissors, trousers*. These are followed by a plural verb but if the phrase 'a pair of' is used in front, they are followed by a singular verb.

- Collective nouns may be either singular or plural in BE, but are always singular in AE. Examples are: *company, family, team*. See **COLLECTIVE NOUNS**.

- Two singular nouns joined by *and* take a plural verb except when they have become a fixed phrase: *John and David are brothers*, but *fish and chips is a good meal*.

AID[s], AIDE[s], AIDS, SUPPORT

aid /eɪd/ *noun,* means financial assistance, often at government level: 'Considerable aid is always necessary for orphans in war zones'. 'Aid agencies' distribute food, shelter and financial help to regions in need. 'Aid' is an uncountable noun.

aide /eɪd/ *noun,* means an assistant in the armed forces, government and diplomatic corps: 'The aide to the President held a press conference'.

Aids /eɪdz/ *noun,* is the acronym for **a**cquired **i**mmune **d**eficiency **s**yndrome. Although it ends in '-s', 'Aids' always takes a singular verb. An alternative spelling is AIDS.

support /sə'pɔːt/ *noun,* means practical assistance such as the 'customer support' or 'technical support' provided for computer software users: 'Customer support is included in the price of this PC package'. It can also refer to help provided by sympathetic individuals: 'She was pleased to have the support of her colleagues when she applied for promotion'. This is an uncountable noun.

AIR-, AERO-

air- /eər-/ is the prefix used in most of the words connected with aviation in BE and AE, such as 'aircraft' and 'airborne'.

aero- /eərəʊ-/ is the prefix used in a few words connected with aviation, such as 'aeroplane' (BE) and 'aerospace'.

AIRCRAFT, AEROPLANE

aircraft /'eəkrɑːft/ *noun,* means a powered flying vehicle. This includes aeroplanes and helicopters. It is often used in BE as an alternative for 'aeroplane'. Note that in BE, 'aircraft' is used for both the singular and plural forms: 'One aircraft was landing and six aircraft were on the runway'. In AE, it is the plural of 'airplane'.

aeroplane /'eərəpleɪn/ *noun,* is the usual BE form for a powered flying vehicle with fixed wings. The short form is 'plane'. 'Airplane' /'eəpleɪn/ is the AE form.

ALL[s], AL-[s]

all words are written in two words like 'all ready', 'all right', and 'all together', or with a hyphen like 'all-important' or 'all-inclusive'. Note that both words carry meaning, as in: 'Are you all ready to go?' Remember to keep the double 'l'.

al- words are written in one word like 'already', 'alright', and 'altogether'. Note that these words do not have the same meaning as 'all' words : 'She has already gone'. 'Al-' words only have a single 'l'.

ALLOCATE, ALLOT

allocate /'æləkeɪt/ *verb,* means to share or divide resources for a particular purpose: 'The university allocates most of its spare resources to Computer Science students'.

allot /ə'lɒt/ *verb,* means to assign as a whole without the idea of distribution: 'The European Commission allotted a further €50 million to medical research'.

ALLOW, LET, PERMIT

allow /ə'laʊ/ *verb,* means to accept a form of behaviour or course of action: 'Some schools allow pupils to wear their own clothes instead of a uniform'.

let /let/ *verb,* means the same as 'allow', but is a more informal word: 'My parents won't let me do anything'. 'Let' also means to rent out a property. See **RENT**.

permit /pə'mɪt/ *verb,* is a more formal alternative to 'allow', and is commonly used in the passive: 'Talking during the exam is not permitted'. Note that the second syllable is stressed.

permit /'pɜːmɪt/ *noun,* means an official authorization to do something, often in the form of a written document: 'He was fortunate to be given a permit to watch the band rehearse before their concert'. Note that the first syllable is stressed.

ALL RIGHT[s], ALRIGHT[s]

all right /'ɔːl 'raɪt/ *pronoun & adverb,* means that everything referred to is correct: 'These answers are all right'. Make certain that both words are stressed.

alright /ɔːl'raɪt/ *adjective & adverb,* means satisfactory but not excellent: 'The test result was alright'. Some guides to English consider that 'alright' is an informal spelling and is to be avoided. *The New Oxford Dictionary of English* states that the spelling 'alright' is acceptable, as it is similar to 'altogether' and 'already'. Nevertheless, many people consider it to be unacceptable in formal writing.

ALL TOGETHER[S], ALTOGETHER[S]

all together /ˈɔːl təˈgeðər/ *pronoun & adverb*, means doing something as a group: 'I like nothing better than to have my family all together on my birthday'. Make certain that both words are stressed.

altogether /ɔːltəˈgeðər/ *adverb*, means in total, completely or entirely: 'Altogether there are six bedrooms in the house'. Note that 'altogether' is often used to reduce the strength of a negative statement: 'What the politician said was not altogether true'.

ALLUDE, REFER, ELUDE

allude /əˈljuːd/ *verb*, means to refer to something indirectly: 'The reporter alluded to the president's secret fortune'. The related noun is 'allusion'.

refer /rɪˈfɜːr/ *verb*, means to state things directly : 'The reporter referred to the $350 million that the president had placed in his Swiss bank account'. The related noun is 'reference'.

elude /ɪˈljuːd/ *verb*, means to evade or escape, usually by skill: 'The fox eluded the pack of hounds for two hours by running downstream'. If something eludes a person, it means that he or she has failed to achieve or understand it: 'The championship trophy has once again eluded the town's football club'. See **DELUSION**.

ALONE, SOLITARY, LONELY, LONE

alone /əˈləʊn/ *adjective & adverb*, as an adjective used with 'be', means separate from others: 'She looked forward to being alone in the flat'. However, to 'feel alone' suggests unhappiness. 'Alone' is not used directly before a noun. More common alternatives in spoken English are on my (your, his, etc.) own and by myself (yourself etc.).

solitary /ˈsɒlɪtəri/ *adjective*, also means being separate from others. A 'solitary' person likes to be 'alone', but a 'solitary' thing or place stands on its own: 'The only sign of human occupation on the island was a solitary villa'. 'Solitary' is used before a noun, never before a verb. 'Solitude' is the state of being 'solitary'.

lonely /ˈləʊnli/ *adjective*, suggests that someone who is on their own dislikes being away from others and is unhappy. 'Lonely' can be used with the verbs 'be' or 'feel': 'She was very lonely when she moved to the island'.

Many newspapers carry personal contact columns called 'lonely hearts' columns. An informal AE term for 'lonely' is 'lonesome' /ˈləʊnsəm/.

lone /ləʊn/ *adjective*, means without other people or things: 'The lone police officer in the park had to call for reinforcements'. 'Lone' is always used directly before a noun. A parent without the support of others may be a 'lone parent' or a 'single parent'.

'This hotel is renowned for its peace and solitude. In fact, crowds from all over the world flock here to enjoy its solitude.'
(Hotel brochure)

ALTERNATE, ALTERNATIVE

alternate /ˈɔːltəneɪt/ *verb*, means to vary regularly between two or more things: 'To make lasagne, you need to alternate layers of meat sauce and pasta'. Note that the stress is on the first syllable.

alternate /ɔːlˈtɜːnət/ *adjective*, refers to two things that follow each other in a repeated pattern: 'I usually see my sister on alternate weekends, which means that I see her about twice a month'. Note that the stress is on the second syllable. In AE, 'alternate' is also used instead of the BE sense of 'alternative'.

alternative /ɔːlˈtɜːnətɪv/ *adjective*, originally meant providing a choice between two options. Though 'alternative' is derived from the Latin *alter* (other of two), it is increasingly common to see references to 'several alternatives'. An 'alternative lifestyle' means a way of life that is unconventional. Note that the stress is on the second syllable.

ALTHOUGH, EVEN THOUGH, THOUGH

although /ɔːlˈðəʊ/ and **even though** /ˈiːvn ˈðəʊ/ *conjunctions*, both mean 'in spite of the fact that', or 'but', and are mainly used at the beginning or in the middle of a sentence: 'Although/Even though we ran, we did not catch the bus' and 'We didn't catch the bus, although/even though we ran'.

though /ðəʊ/ *conjunction & adverb*, as a conjunction is used at the beginning or middle of a sentence. 'Though' has the same meaning as 'although' and 'even though', but is more common in spoken English. As an adverb, 'though' may be used at the end of a sentence to mean 'however': 'We did not catch the bus, though'. Note that a sentence that starts with one of these words should not contain the word 'however'. See **HOWEVER**.

ALUMINIUM, ALUMINUM

aluminium /ˌæljʊˈmɪnjəm/ *noun*, is a lightweight metal with the chemical symbol Al. This is the BE spelling and pronunciation, with stress on the third syllable.

aluminum /əˈluːmɪnəm/ is the AE spelling and pronunciation of 'aluminium'. Note that there is only one 'i' in the AE spelling, and that the stress is on the second syllable.

AMERICA, (THE) AMERICAS

America /əˈmerɪkə/ means either the political unit: the United States of America, or the geographical land mass comprising North and South America joined by Central America.

(The) Americas /ði əˈmerɪkəz/ means the geographical land mass comprising North and South America joined by Central America. This is usually preceded by the definite article.

AMIABLE, AMICABLE

amiable /ˈeɪmɪəbl̩/ *adjective*, describes people and expressions that appear friendly: 'She has an amiable face'.

amicable /ˈæmɪkəbl̩/ *adjective*, is used to describe an agreement or a friendly relationship: 'The children and the teacher got on well together. It was an amicable class'.

AMONG(ST), AMID(ST), MID, BETWEEN

among /əˈmʌŋ/ *preposition*, is used about people or things in a group: 'She shared the food among the passengers'. 'Among' is used when there are more than two people or things in the group. See **PREPOSITIONS**.

amongst /əˈmʌŋst/ *preposition*, is an alternative form for 'among' and is mainly used in BE.

amid(st) /əˈmɪd(st)/ *preposition*, means in the middle of, or surrounded by. There is no difference in usage or meaning between 'amid' and 'amidst'.

mid- /mɪd/ *prefix*, means in the middle of: 'mid-20th century politics', or halfway between two extremes: 'The angler stood midstream'. 'Mid-' is either hyphenated or written as part

of a combined word without a hyphen, for example 'mid-morning' and 'midnight'. It is best to consult an authoritative dictionary for individual examples.

between /bɪˈtwiːn/ *preposition & adverb*, generally refers to two people or things. However, 'between' is increasingly used when something is divided between more than two people or things: 'She shared the food equally between her six cats'. If there are measurements or dates etc. after 'between', these should be linked by 'and'. Example: 'Voters born between 1975 and 1979'. Avoid using 'between 1975-1979' or 'between 1975 to 1979'.

ANALYSIS, ANALYSES, ANALYSE, ANALYST

analysis /əˈnælɪsɪs/ *noun*, means the detailed examination of the elements or structure of something. This is the singular form. Note that the stress is on the second syllable.

analyses /əˈnælɪsiːz/ *noun*, is the plural of 'analysis'. Note that the stress is on the second syllable, and that the final syllable is pronounced as 'seas'.

analyse /ˈænəlaɪz/ *verb*, means to examine carefully and in detail. This is the BE spelling. Note that the only stress is on the first syllable. The AE spelling is 'analyze'. See **-YSE**.

analyses /ˈænəlaɪzɪz/ *verb*, is the third person singular of 'analyse'. Note that the stress is on the first syllable and that the third syllable rhymes with 'size'.

analyst /ˈænəlɪst/ *noun*, is a person who analyses material or compounds: 'She is a chemical analyst at ICI'.

AND, AMPERSAND

and /ənd, n̩d, ænd/ *conjunction*, The most common use of 'and' is to connect two elements or things: 'Her brother and sister were at the party'. Note that it is not necessary to repeat the determiner (her) after 'and' if they are two closely connected terms. Another use of 'and' is in mathematics to mean plus: 'Two and two equal four'. The pronunciation of 'and' can vary: the one with a full vowel rhyming with 'hand' only occurs if 'and' is used emphatically. See **COMMA**.

ampersand /'æmpəsænd/ *noun*, is the symbol '&'. This is used informally to replace 'and' in short notes and in set phrases like 'R&D' (research and development). It is also used formally in the names of companies: 'Procter & Gamble'. Note that 'ampersand' is used for two things only, being always read as 'and'.

ANGEL, ANGLE

angel /'eɪndʒəl/ *noun*, means a heavenly being or a person with exemplary behaviour: 'She is a real angel'.

angle /'æŋgl/ *noun*, means the space between two lines that meet in mathematics or a means of describing the steepness of a surface. An 'angle' also means a way of considering an issue in informal English: 'We could not understand what his angle was'. A formal alternative is 'line of argument'.

'The pipeline has minor bending angels.'

ANGRY ABOUT, ANGRY WITH

angry about /'æŋgri əbaʊt/ *adjective & preposition*, means having strong feelings of irritation about an issue or situation: 'They were angry about the bank's decision not to extend the loan'.

angry with /'æŋgri wɪð/ *adjective & preposition*, means having strong feelings of irritation about a person or group of people: 'They were angry with the bank manager for not extending the loan'.

ANNEX⁵, ANNEXE⁵

annex /ə'neks/ *verb*, is used for a dominant power acquiring territory: 'In 1939, Germany and the Soviet Union each annexed part of Poland'. Note that the verb is stressed on the second syllable.

annex /'æneks/ *noun*, refers to an addition to a document or report. 'Annex' in AE is also an alternative spelling of the BE 'annexe'. Note that the noun is stressed on the first syllable. See **APPENDIX**.

annexe /'æneks/ *noun*, means an additional part of something, such as an extra hotel building: 'The hotel annexe is across the road'. This spelling is mainly used in BE.

ANNUAL, PERENNIAL

annual /'ænjʊəl/ *adjective & noun*, as an adjective, means something that happens each year. In business English, 'annual' is often used in phrases such as 'annual report' and 'annual general meeting' (AGM). In the noun form, an 'annual' is a plant that has a one-year life cycle. An 'annual' can also be a special kind of book, usually for children, published once a year as a series: 'He bought the children an annual for Christmas'. See **BIANNUAL**.

perennial /pə'reniəl/ *adjective & noun*, means lasting or recurring: 'Hurricanes in the Caribbean are a perennial problem'. As a noun, a 'perennial' is a plant that flowers annually and may live for many years.

⚠ 'The British Medical Association urges that you undergo your annual examination at least every five years.'

ANTE-⁵, ANTI-⁵

ante- /ˌænti-/ *prefix*, means both before and in front of. In the before sense, there are words such as 'antenatal' meaning prior to birth and also 'antedate' which means before in date. 'Antediluvian' means before the Biblical flood and is sometimes used to describe very antiquated concepts. 'Ante-' can be used to mean 'in front of', for instance 'antechamber', a minor room leading to a more important one. Note that in BE 'ante-' and 'anti-' are pronounced the same and rhyme with 'scanty'.

anti- /ænti-/ (BE), /æntaɪ-/ (AE) means against or opposed to. An 'antiseptic' is an agent which destroys bacteria. Other words with 'anti-' are: 'antibiotic' and 'antibody'. 'Anti-' in the sense of 'opposed to' is the basis of words like 'Antichrist' and 'anti-hero'. There are also a very few words that are stressed on the second syllable, such as: 'antipathy' /æn'tɪpəθi/ and 'antipodes' /æn'tɪpədiːz/. See **HYPHENATION IN INDIVIDUAL WORDS**.

ANTENNA/ANTENNAE, ANTENNA/ANTENNAS

antenna /æn'tenə/ *noun*, refers to the sense organ on the heads of insects (or people in a figurative sense). The plural form 'antennae' is pronounced /æn'teniː/ in both BE and AE: 'Her antennae were alerted by the mention of a certain woman'.

antenna /æn'tenə/ *noun*, in technical use means an arrangement of aerials. In this sense, the plural is 'antennas' /æn'tenəz/: 'All the masts and antennas were blown down during the gale'. In AE, 'antenna' is synonymous with 'aerial'. See **AERIAL**.

ANTICIPATE, EXPECT, LOOK FORWARD TO, HOPE

anticipate /æn'tɪsɪpeɪt/ *verb*, means to act, or make a decision, in the belief that some other action will take place: 'He anticipated the fall in the stock market by selling all his shares'.

expect /ɪks'pekt/ *verb*, means to believe that something will happen in the future: 'She expected him to arrive on the next train'. See **ATTEND**.

look forward to /lʊk 'fɔːwəd tə/ *verb*, means to expect something in the future with pleasure: 'He was looking forward to a long holiday once the contract was signed'.

hope /həʊp/ *verb*, means to want a particular event to happen: 'He hoped that his favourite TV programme would not be cancelled'.

ANTIQUE, ANTIQUATED

antique /æn'tiːk/ *adjective & noun*, means things made valuable by age: 'This is an antique table'. 'Antique' is used for things that are not as old as ancient objects. See **OLD**.

antiquated /'æntɪkweɪtɪd/ *adjective*, means ideas and things that are out of date and are not in favour: 'His ideas about marriage are as antiquated as his vintage car'.

'For sale, 4-poster bed, 101 years old. Perfect for an antique lover.'

ANTISOCIAL, UNSOCIAL, UNSOCIABLE

antisocial /ænti'səʊʃl̩/ *adjective*, means hostile to society: 'The graffiti and vandalism are just two examples of their antisocial behaviour'.

unsocial /ʌn'səʊʃl̩/ *adjective*, means outside normal working hours: 'Allowance for unsocial working hours'. It can also mean causing annoyance to others, but is less common than 'antisocial' in this sense.

unsociable /ʌn'səʊʃəbl̩/ *adjective*, refers to someone who is unfriendly or badly mannered: 'He's too unsociable to work as a waiter'.

ANXIOUS, CONCERNED

anxious /'æŋkʃəs/ *adjective*, refers to being worried or nervous about a particular matter: 'Maria is anxious about the result of her pregnancy test'. Note that 'anxious' is typically used where a decision is about to be made or where the result is uncertain. The related noun is 'anxiety' /æŋg'zaɪti/.

concerned /kən'sɜːnd/ *adjective*, refers to being worried or nervous about something. It refers to general and ongoing worries and issues: 'The family is concerned about Maria's ill temper'. Note that 'concerned' does not have the pressing urgency that is found in 'anxious'. The related noun is 'concern'.

ANYONE⁵, ANY ONE⁵

anyone /'eniwʌn/ *pronoun*, means any person, and is interchangeable with the more informal 'anybody'. The question 'Is anyone there?' suggests that the speaker expects or encourages a negative answer. If the answer is expected to be positive, the speaker would ask: 'Is someone there?' Note that 'anyone' or 'anybody' always takes a singular verb, because it refers to any single person. See **SOMEONE**.

any one /'eni 'wʌn/ *determiner & pronoun,* means no matter which person or thing is selected from a fixed number: 'I would like any one of those chocolates'. Note that 'any one' always takes a singular verb, because it refers to 'any single person/thing'. Both words are stressed.

ANYWHERE, ANYPLACE

anywhere /'eni*h*weər/ *adverb,* means in, at or to any place: 'They now had the money to travel anywhere in the world'. 'Anywhere' can also refer to a range of time, distance, etc.: 'The ship could be anywhere between England and Denmark', meaning that the ship's position is completely unknown. Note that 'anywhere' is used in negative sentences and questions where the expected answer is no, unlike somewhere, which occurs in positive sentences and questions. See **SOMEWHERE**.

anyplace /'enipleɪs/ *adverb,* means the same as 'anywhere', but is only used in AE.

apostrophe (')

contractions and pronouns

• Contractions such as *I'm* and *don't* should only be used in informal, conversational writing and when reporting speech. Although it is correct to use an apostrophe to indicate a missing letter and write: *aren't, can't, isn't, it's* etc., contractions are to be avoided in official letters, reports, academic papers or theses and other types of formal English. Here, the expected forms are: *are not, cannot* (one word), *is not, it is*. Using contractions wrongly not only looks very informal, it also leads to mistakes like confusing *it's* with the possessive pronoun *its*, which both sound the same. Also, *us* is sometimes contracted with verbs like *let,* as in *Let's go.*

• A few pronouns take an apostrophe in the genitive ('s'-genitive): *some, any, every* and *no* when combined with *-body, -one* and *-other.* Example: *Someone's life is at stake.* See **CONTRACTIONS**. See **GENITIVE FORMS**.

 'Beauty care that let's me be me.' (Cosmetics advert)

nouns

Apostrophes are used to form the genitive when the noun refers to people and animals, as well as things we are fond of and feel close to. Two general rules are:

• Place *'s* after singular nouns that end in *-s,* or after a noun (singular or plural) that does not end in *-s*. (Examples: *the class's teacher, dog's dinner, a child's toys, the children's toys.*)

• Place an apostrophe after plural nouns that end in *-s*. (Examples: *the classes' teacher* and *the dogs' dinner.*)

These rules make it clear whether Fido has his own dinner (*dog's dinner*) or has to share with others (*dogs' dinner*). See **GENITIVE FORMS**.

dates and abbreviations

• A useful rule is to use *'s* to form genitives (*1930's* and *IBM's*), and *s* without an apostrophe to form plurals (*1930s* and *PCs*). Thus *the 1930's fashions* means 'the fashions of the 1930s'. Similarly, *the PC's future* means 'the future of the PC'. It is recommended to use *'s* with single letters (such as in a formula) that might be confusing to read. Example: *Dot your i's and cross your t's, please* (meaning 'tidy up what you have written').

APPEAL, PROTEST

appeal /ə'pi:l/ *verb & noun,* as a verb in a legal sense, means to call on a higher authority to review a decision. In BE, this use is always followed by against: 'He appealed against his sentence'. In AE, the word against may be omitted. When using 'appeal' as a noun, a common expression is to 'lodge an appeal against' a decision.

protest /prəʊ'test/ *verb &* /'prəʊtest/ *noun,* as a verb in AE, means to show strong public disagreement with a decision or issue. In BE, to 'protest about/against' something has the same meaning. In both AE and BE, a person who protests their innocence is claiming very forcefully that they are innocent. Note that as a noun, the stress is on the first syllable.

APPENDIX/APPENDICES, APPENDIX/APPENDIXES

appendix (1) /ə'pendɪks/ *noun,* is an annex or an addendum to a report. In this sense it has the plural 'appendices' /ə'pendɪsi:z/: 'The appendices to this report provide the detailed data'. Many style guides suggest that 'appendices' are numbered A, B, C and D. If there are sections within an 'appendix', these are numbered A.1, A.2 etc. A neat way to refer to Table 2-1 in Appendix B is 'see Table B.2-1'. Similarly, Figure 2-2 in Appendix C is referred to as 'see Figure C.2-2'. See **ANNEX**.

appendix (2) is an internal bodily organ: 'He had his appendix removed at the age of three'. This meaning of 'appendix' has the plural 'appendixes' /ə'pendɪksɪz/. The 'k' sound in this plural should be pronounced.

approximation

- **about** /ə'baʊt/ *adverb*, is a term of approximation that is often used in front of quantitative amounts and numerals: *This is about 50% cheaper; He is about 45*. See **SOME**.
- **roughly** /'rʌfli/ *adverb*, is a term of approximation that is often used before fractions: *This is roughly half the original price*, or informally for an estimate of an amount: *It is roughly 50 km from here to Paris*.
- **approximately** /ə'prɒksɪmətli/ *adverb*, is used in front of quantitative amounts: *It weighs approximately 25 kilo; approximately €2 million*.
- **approx.** is usually written after the approximation and is often in brackets: *The price is €2 million (approx.)*. Although the abbreviation is acceptable in formal written English, read this as 'approximately'. The pronunciation /ə'prɒks/ should only be used in informal contexts, not in formal presentations.
- **circa** /'sɜːkə/ *preposition*, is used in restricted contexts for dates or amounts: *The cathedral is circa 1450*. See **C**.
- **-ish** /-ɪʃ/ *suffix*, is an informal ending that is added to numerals for approximation: *I will see you about tenish* (meaning about 10 o'clock). Note that a person or the temperature is *in their/the thirties*, but only a person is *thirtyish*.
- **-odd** /-ɒd/ *suffix*, is another informal approximation. This must be used with a hyphen as in *The class had twenty-odd students* (meaning a few more than 20 students), to distinguish the phrase from *twenty odd students* (i.e. strange students). *Twenty-odd* has only one stress: /'twenti ɒd/, while *twenty odd* has double stress: /'twenti 'ɒd/. See **FUNNY**. See **HYPHENATION IN COMPOUNDS**.
- **umpteen** /ʌmp'tiːn/ *determiner*, is an informal word meaning very many, or indefinitely many: *I've told you umpteen times before: that door must be kept closed*. See **NUMBERS IN WORDS**.

'Since we have been on television, we have had fifty odd Senators and Representatives on our programme.'

ARAB, ARABIA, ARABIC

Arab /'ærəb/ *noun & adjective*, means a member of one of the Semitic peoples inhabiting parts of the Middle East and north Africa: 'An Arab sheikh has just bought our local race track'. See **NATIONALITY WORDS**.

Arabia /ə'reɪbɪə/ *noun*, means the geographic area between the Red Sea and the Persian Gulf. This is also called the Arabian /ə'reɪbɪən/ peninsula. See **FOREIGN PLACE NAMES**.

Arabic /'ærəbɪk/ *adjective & noun*, refers to the language and literature of the Arabs. Arabic also means a way of writing numbers: 'Write this in Arabic numerals (1, 2, 3)'.

ARE NOT, AREN'T, AIN'T

are not /ɑː 'nɒt/ is part of the verb 'to be'. This is the standard written form. 'We are not amused' is a phrase associated with Queen Victoria who ruled Britain from 1837 to 1901.

aren't /ɑːnt/ is a contraction for 'are not'. This is used in dialogue to represent standard spoken English. It may also stand for 'am not' in the interrogative form 'aren't I?'

ain't /eɪnt/ is a contraction for 'are not', or 'am not'. It is only used in non-standard English. See **CONTRACTIONS**.

ARMED FORCES, MILITARY

armed forces /ɑːmd 'fɔːsɪz/ *noun*, is the BE term for the Army, Navy and Air Force: 'The Commander-in-Chief of the armed forces met NATO leaders in Brussels'.

military /'mɪlɪtri/ *noun & adjective*, is a term for the armed forces that is commonly used in AE: 'The news of the attack was given by the US military'. As an adjective it refers more generally to activities connected with the armed forces.

ART, FINE ARTS

art /ɑːt/ *noun*, refers to skill as a result of knowledge or practice and its application in aesthetic creativity: 'He studied perspective when he took art at school'.

fine arts /'faɪn 'ɑːts/ *noun*, means creative art, especially visual art that appeals to the intellect or sense of beauty: 'He devoted his leisure to painting and the fine arts'. This includes literature and music. To 'get something down to a fine art' is an informal expression meaning that a person has learned through experience how to perform a routine task efficiently: 'He can clean the car in two minutes. He has got it down to a fine art'.

ARTIFICIAL, SYNTHETIC

artificial /ɑːtɪ'fɪʃl/ *adjective*, means something that is not natural. An 'artificial' product imitates the real product: 'This sofa is covered in artificial leather, which is not leather at all, just plastic'. 'Artificial intelligence' is not intelligence, it is computer software that can simulate intelligent human behaviour.

synthetic /sɪn'θetɪk/ *adjective*, means the result of a man-made process to manufacture products that are often identical to the natural ones. Thus, 'synthetic rubber' is rubber that is produced by an industrial process, not by refining a natural product.

ARTIST, ARTISTE

artist /'ɑːtɪst/ *noun*, means a gifted and skilled person such as a painter, craftsperson or performer: 'Paintings by artists who died in poverty are now sold for millions'.

artiste /ɑː'tiːst/ *noun*, means a performing dancer or singer, particularly on the stage or in a circus: 'Many circus artistes belong to different generations of the same family'. Note that the last syllable rhymes with 'beast'.

ARTS, HUMANITIES, LIBERAL ARTS

arts /ɑːts/ *noun*, means subjects such as literature, language, philosophy, and history as opposed to science and technology: 'There were many arts graduates on the journalism course'.

humanities /hjʊ'mænɪtɪz/ *noun*, is a term that was originally restricted to classical studies in Latin and Greek. 'The humanities' is now used more broadly to mean all arts subjects: 'The university tried to stop so many students studying the humanities'.

liberal arts /'lɪbərəl 'ɑːts/ *noun*, is a term that sometimes has wider scope than the 'arts' or 'humanities'. In AE, where the term is frequently used, 'liberal arts' courses cover a range of arts and science subjects intended to develop students' general knowledge and cultural awareness.

–ARY⁵, –ERY⁵, –ARILY

-ary /-əri/ *noun & adjective suffix*, means connected with. This ending appears in more words than the '-ery' spelling. Typical examples of nouns and adjectives with this ending are: 'military' and 'stationary' (meaning 'not moving').

-ery /-əri/ *noun suffix*, refers to a place, condition, or class, but there are fewer words with this spelling than with '-ary'. Some common nouns ending in '-ery' are: 'cemetery' and 'stationery' (meaning 'writing material').

-arily /-ərɪli/(BE) /-'erɪli/(AE) *adverb suffix*, means connected with. The traditional BE pronunciation of adverbs formed from adjectives ending in '-ary' carries no stress on the suffix, whereas the typical AE pronunciation does: 'momentarily' /'məʊməntərɪli/ (BE) /məʊmən'terɪli/ (AE), 'primarily' /'praɪmərɪli/ (BE) /praɪ'merɪli/ (AE).

ASCENT⁵, ASSENT⁵

ascent /ə'sent/ *noun*, means physical movement upwards with effort or by climbing: 'The ascent of Mount Everest'. 'Ascent' should be avoided in figurative contexts, and rise is often a better alternative: 'The dictator's rise to power was extremely rapid'. 'Ascension' is a related noun that describes the action of rising, which is only used in formal and religious contexts: 'The Queen's ascension to the throne'.

assent /ə'sent/ *noun*, means agreement or giving agreement to something: 'In many parliamentary systems, laws have to receive the assent of both Houses'.

ASHAMED, EMBARRASSED

ashamed /ə'ʃeɪmd/ *adjective*, means feeling shame because of a serious act or action that has been done. Only use 'ashamed' when someone feels guilty about doing something of importance: 'Driving that bus full of schoolchildren after you had been drinking should make you very ashamed'.

embarrassed /em'bærəst/ *adjective*, refers to a person in a difficult social situation who feels awkward following a stupid mistake: 'He was embarrassed because he had forgotten to shave'. A person who is embarrassed may also feel shy and inadequate: 'She was embarrassed that everyone else spoke French more fluently than she did'. Note the spelling.

ASIAN, ASIATIC

Asian /'eɪʃn̩/ *adjective & noun*, in Britain, refers to a person from the Indian subcontinent. In the USA, 'Asian' refers to a person from the Far East. Elsewhere, the term 'Asian' refers to a person who is a native or inhabitant of the continent of Asia. This is the term to use for both the people and the culture.

Asiatic /eɪʃɪ'ætɪk/ *adjective*, can be used to refer to geographical features in Asia: 'Oil companies are now showing increasing interest in Asiatic offshore waters'. Note that it should not be used to refer to people as this is racially offensive. Use 'Asian' or the specific nationality of the person when referring to someone from Asia. See **ORIENTAL** ⇨ **ORIENT**.

ASK, BEG, INVITE, REQUEST

ask /ɑːsk/ *verb*, can mean to express a wish politely: 'He asked the teenagers not to make so much noise'. To 'ask for' means to enquire about something: 'He asked for some advice'.

beg /beg/ *verb*, means to ask for something anxiously or meekly: 'The tramp begged for money'. 'Beg' is also found in some common expressions such as 'I beg your pardon', which is a polite way to ask someone to repeat what they said.

invite /ɪn'vaɪt/ *verb*, means to tell someone politely that they are welcome to attend a meeting or social event: 'You are invited to meet the President'. 'To invite trouble' means to do something that is likely to have an unpleasant result: 'Asking Henry to the meeting was just inviting trouble'. See **INVITATION**.

request /rɪ'kwest/ *verb*, means to ask formally and politely: 'Visitors are requested not to walk on the grass'. 'Request' is followed directly by a noun without a preposition: 'We request your attendance at the performance tomorrow evening'. This is more formal than 'invite'. See **DEMAND**.

ASSUME, PRESUME

assume /ə'sjuːm/ *verb*, means to suppose without evidence, as in: 'Let's assume that you win the football pools. What would you do with the money?' Note that if someone 'assumes' a name, this is one that has been adopted and is not that person's real name: 'He lived in Cuba under an assumed name'. The related noun is 'assumption' /ə'sʌmpʃn̩/.

presume /prɪ'zjuːm/ *verb*, means to suppose or conclude on the basis of probability: 'I presume you know why I have asked you here? It can hardly be a surprise'. This is a formal word, although it is becoming common for 'presume' and 'assume' to be used interchangeably. The related noun is 'presumption' /prɪ'zʌmpʃn̩/.

ASSURE, ENSURE⁵, INSURE⁵, SECURE

assure /ə'ʃʊər/ *verb*, means to be certain and convinced: 'They were assured that the painting was an original'. 'Assure' also means inform in a positive way: 'He assured me that I would receive the cheque very soon'.

ensure /ɪn'ʃʊər/ *verb*, means to make sure or certain: 'He ensured that all the doors were locked'. An alternative spelling in AE is 'insure'. Note that in spoken English 'ensure' and 'insure' are often pronounced the same.

insure /ɪn'ʃʊər/ *verb*, means to take out insurance either on something: 'It is illegal in Britain not to insure your car', or against an unexpected and unwelcome event: 'The house is not insured against flooding'. In AE, 'insure' is an alternative spelling of 'ensure': 'He insured that the window was closed'. See **INSURANCE**.

secure /sɪ'kjʊər/ *verb & adjective*, as a verb, means to obtain something as a result of effort: 'He secured tickets for the cup final'. It can also mean to protect something: 'All the doors in the prison were secured with extra locks'. In this sense, the opposite is 'not secured'. As an adjective, it means safe: 'Children need to feel secure'. 'Secure' can also mean firmly fastened: 'He shook the ladder to make certain it was secure before he climbed it'. The opposite of 'secure' as an adjective is 'insecure'.

AT, IN, ON, TO (*PREPOSITIONS OF PLACE*)

at /ət, æt/ refers to the position of an area or space: 'We met at the cinema' (either inside or near to it). 'At' is also focused on where an event or activity takes place, rather than on the building or place itself: 'She is at the gym'

(= doing some exercise). 'At' is also used with a specific address: 'He lives at 16 Vernon Road'. The strong form /æt/ is only used when this is the final word of a sentence. See **PREPOSITIONS**.

in /ɪn/ means inside an area or space: 'We met in the cinema' (inside the building), and focuses on the place or building itself, rather than the activity: 'I saw her in the gym' (= she was somewhere in the building). 'In' is also used with countries, regions, towns and villages, and names of streets: 'He lives in Vernon Road'.

on /ɒn/ means touching a surface, rather than being within or near an area: 'He was sitting on a stool'. Note that the phrase 'on the TV' can refer to something placed on the top of the TV set or to a particular programme being shown: 'Is there anything interesting on TV tonight?' 'On' is also used with mountains and small islands: 'She lives on the Isle of Wight'. 'Upon' /əˈpɒn/ is the formal version of 'on'. It is also used in fixed phrases such as 'once upon a time'.

to /tə, tʊ, tuː/ is used with verbs of movement to mean in the direction of a person or place: 'He threw the ball to me but it was too high for me to catch'. The strong form /tuː/ is only used when this is the final word of a sentence. See **PREPOSITIONS**.

AT, IN, ON (*PREPOSITIONS OF TIME*)

at /ət, æt/ refers to a specific time of the day: 'Come back at 3 p.m.' It is also used for named occasions: 'I saw him at Christmas'. See **DATES**. See **PREPOSITIONS**. See **TIME OF DAY**.

in /ɪn/ refers to a length of time: 'Come back in three days'. The exact duration is not always given, as in: 'I have not seen her in years'. 'In' is also used for parts of a day: 'She is arriving in the afternoon'.

on /ɒn/ refers to a particular day or date: 'Come back on 25 September', 'I saw him on Friday'.

ATTEND, ATTENDANT, ASSIST, ASSISTANT

attend /əˈtend/ *verb*, means either to be present at: 'Six hundred people attended the meeting in the Town Hall'; or to go somewhere regularly: 'She attended the same school from the age of 11 to 18'. The related noun is 'attendance' /əˈtendəns/. 'Attendance' is also a normal word to use for the number of people present at an event: 'The club expects a high attendance at the next home match'.

attendant /əˈtendənt/ *noun*, means a person whose job is to help those visiting a public place such as a 'museum attendant' or a 'cloakroom attendant': 'The cloakroom attendant amused us with the stories of things people had forgotten to collect'. In another sense, an 'attendant' is someone who serves and accompanies important people or dignitaries.

assist /əˈsɪst/ *verb*, means to help: 'He assisted his mother by holding the torch while she searched under the bed'. The related noun is 'assistance'. Note that 'Can you lend me some assistance?' is a formal way of saying 'Can you help me?'

assistant /əˈsɪstənt/ *noun*, means someone who ranks below a senior executive or manager, and helps them carry out their duties. On a business card, the word should be written in full if there is enough space, or the abbreviation 'Asst' should be used: Asst Manager. See **SALES PERSON**.

AUTHENTIC, GENUINE

authentic /ɔːˈθentɪk/ *adjective*, means that something is true to life and reliable: 'An authentic account of the Russian Revolution'.

genuine /ˈdʒenjʊɪn/ *adjective*, emphasizes that something is an original. 'The old lady said that the sketch was a genuine Picasso. Experts argued about this for years'.

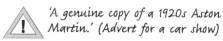

'A genuine copy of a 1920s Aston Martin.' (Advert for a car show)

AUTHOR, AUTHORESS

author /ˈɔːθər/ *noun & verb*, as a noun, means a writer of books or articles. An author can be either male or female. Writers of poems and plays are called poets and playwrights, respectively. The verb form is used much less commonly than the verb 'write'. See **WE – TIPS FOR AUTHORS**.

authoress /ˈɔːθəres/ *noun*, means a female author. Most women writers prefer to be called 'author'. See **SEXIST LANGUAGE**.

AUTHORITARIAN, AUTHORITY, AUTHORIZED, AUTHORITATIVE

authoritarian /ɔːθɒrɪ'teərɪən/ *adjective*, means demanding that others show obedience to authority: 'An authoritarian system of government'. As authoritarian refers to something that hinders personal freedom, it is now considered a negative word in western democracies.

authority /ɔː'θɒrɪti/ *noun*, is a positive word for the official power to rule or to influence others: 'He was a teacher with authority in the class'. Someone who is 'an authority' on a specific subject is an expert. When a signature on a letter is followed by 'By authority', this indicates that the writer is responsible for the letter's contents.

authorized /'ɔːθəraɪzd/ *adjective*, means having official permission to be an agent: 'As the car was still under warranty, we took it to an authorized dealer for its service'.

authoritative /ɔː'θɒrɪtətɪv/ *adjective*, means having authority in the sense of being trustworthy and reliable: 'The latest French dictionary has been widely acclaimed as the authoritative version'.

AUTUMN, FALL (SEASON)

autumn /'ɔːtəm/ *noun*, is the BE term for the season between summer and winter: 'The summer ended in a spell of autumn showers'. Autumn is only capitalized in initial position. In figurative use, autumn means a period of mellowness, often with reference to the later period of a person's life: 'The politician became more tolerant in the autumn of his life'.
See **SEASONS**.

fall /fɔːl/ *noun*, is the AE term for 'autumn'. It is only capitalized in initial position.

AUXILIARY, ANCILLARY

auxiliary /ɔːg'zɪljəri/ *adjective & noun*, means having an additional position, that is of equal status to a main group of workers: 'The hospital called in the auxiliary nursing team'. The standby engine on a boat is called the 'auxiliary engine'. Note the pronunciation.

ancillary /æn'sɪləri/ *adjective*, means having a secondary or minor role, or helping someone more highly qualified: 'The hospital employed many ancillary workers'.

AVERAGE, MEAN, MEDIOCRE

average /'ævərɪdʒ/ *noun & adjective*, as a noun, means the result of the addition of mathematical units and the division of the total by the number of units. For example: 3 plus 6 plus 12 equals 21, 21 divided by 3 equals 7. Thus 7 is the 'average' of 3, 6 and 12. As an adjective, this word means a person who does not demonstrate any special skill or talent: 'His performance could best be described as average'.

mean /miːn/ *noun & adjective*, as a noun, means the figure halfway between the highest and lowest: 'The mean of 3, 6 and 12 is 7.5'. In its adjective form, 'mean' describes someone who is not generous with money or feelings: 'He was very mean, even though he was wealthy'.

mediocre /miːdi'əʊkər/ *adjective*, means of moderate quality, generally in a negative sense: 'The film critics had all called the Oscar-winning film mediocre, but the public disagreed and flocked to see it'. As things are either 'mediocre' or not, phrases like 'more mediocre' and 'most mediocre' should be avoided. This is the spelling in both BE and AE.

AVOID, EVADE

avoid /ə'vɔɪd/ *verb*, means to keep away from something: 'He avoided paying taxes, which is legal'. The related noun is 'avoidance' /ə'vɔɪdəns/.

evade /ɪ'veɪd/ *verb*, means to escape from something by deception: 'He evaded the tax authorities for years, but was finally imprisoned'. The related noun is 'evasion' /ɪ'veɪʒn̩/.

AXE, AXIS, AXES

axe /æks/ *noun*, means a tool used for chopping wood. This is the BE spelling. 'Ax' is the normal AE spelling for 'axe'.

axis /'æksɪs/ *noun*, means a line that a body rotates around: 'The earth revolves on its axis every 24 hours'. There are numerous other mathematical and scientific uses of this word.

axes *noun*, is the plural spelling of both 'axe' and 'axis'. However they are pronounced differently: 'axes' meaning chopping tools is pronounced /'æksɪz/, to rhyme with 'Max is', while the mathematical term 'axes' is pronounced /'æksiːz/, which rhymes with 'Jack sees'.

Bb

bachelor's degree, BA, BSc

A bachelor's degree is the first degree from a university or equivalent institution. In universities which are within or based on the UK/US higher education systems, the most normal types are *Bachelor of Arts* (abbreviated *BA* in BE and *B.A.* in AE) and *Bachelor of Science* (abbreviated *BSc* in BE and *B.Sc.* in AE). Although it may seem useful to 'translate' a qualification into its apparent English-language equivalent, this is not recommended as no two degrees are identical. On the English language version of a CV or business card, it is always best to write degrees in their original language. If necessary, this can then be followed by an approximate translation, in brackets, such as *(BA History)* or *(BSc Biology)*.

BACKSIDE, BACK

backside /bæk'saɪd/ *noun*, written as one word means only 'buttocks' in BE: 'He planted his backside in the director's chair, and refused to move'. In AE, 'backside' can also mean the rear of an object, like the 'backside' of a mountain. If this is spelt as two words, it means only the other side of something.

back /bæk/ *noun*, means the other side of something: 'The safety instructions are on the back of this folder'. In a building such as a cinema, the 'back' is the rear part: 'There are seats available at the back'. See **REVERSE**.

 'The young leaves have a hairy backside.' (Notice by a tree in an arboretum).

BACKWARD, BACKWARDS

backward /'bækwəd/ *adjective*, means towards the rear: 'A backward glance in his mirror'. 'Backward' also refers to a lack of progress: 'She feels that returning to live with her parents would be a backward step'. 'Backward' was formerly used about people who are slow at learning or developing, but this is no longer considered acceptable.
See **LEARNING DIFFICULTY**.

backwards /'bækwədz/ *adverb*, means a reverse direction of movement: 'He drove backwards'. This is the BE spelling. 'Backward' is an alternative spelling, especially in AE.

BAD, POOR

bad /bæd/ *adjective*, refers to something of inferior quality or that is unpleasant: 'Bad weather, such as storms and floods, has caused a lot of damage recently'. 'Bad' can also be used to intensify the force of something, such as 'a bad cold' or 'a bad storm'. When 'bad' is used about a person, it can convey moral judgement: 'He is a thoroughly bad person'.

poor /pʊər/ *adjective*, means not good enough: 'This is a poor excuse for failing your exam'. In another sense, poor means having insufficient money or resources: 'Looking at the houses, you can see that this is a poor part of the country'. Note that although a 'poor person' means an individual with little or no money, an expression such as 'poor John' expresses sympathy.

BALL GAME, STATE OF AFFAIRS

ball game /'bɔːl geɪm/ *noun phrase*, means any game played with a ball, but especially baseball in AE. 'A whole new ball game' has also become an informal phrase in AE and BE to mean a situation that is entirely different to a previous one: 'She had been working as an office manager, so running a large department would be a whole new ball game'. It tends to be used towards the end of a sentence.

state of affairs /'steɪt əv ə'feəz/ *noun phrase*, also refers to a situation but is a more formal word than 'ball game'. It can be used at the beginning, middle or end of a sentence: 'This state of affairs is extremely damaging'.

BANK CARD, CASH CARD, CHARGE CARD, CREDIT CARD, DEBIT CARD, STORE CARD

bank card /'bæŋk kɑːd/ is sometimes called a cheque card or bankers card and is frequently used in connection with a cheque, as a guarantee of payment. This is a more general term than the others in this group.

cash card /'kæʃ kɑːd/ is a type of bank card which is used to withdraw money from a cash machine. These are called ATM cards in AE. See **CASH MACHINE**.

charge card /'tʃɑːdʒ kɑːd/ is used to purchase goods or services on credit, but the bill, once received, must be paid in full. American Express and Diners Club issue charge cards.

credit card /'kredɪt kɑːd/ is used to purchase goods on credit. Only a percentage of the bill has to be paid each month, but interest is charged on the outstanding balance.

debit card /'debɪt kɑːd/ is used like a charge card or credit card, but the money is taken direct from the user's account, with no period of free credit.

store card /'stɔː kɑːd/ is a restricted type of credit card, which is valid only in outlets of the retail store that issues the card.

BANKNOTE, BILL

banknote /'bæŋknəʊt/ noun, means paper money issued by a bank: 'The police asked where the man got the ten forged banknotes from'. 'Banknote' is usually shortened to 'note': 'I paid with a twenty pound note'. This is the normal BE term. See **NOTE**. See **PIECE** ⇨ **PEACE**.

bill /bɪl/ noun, is the AE term for 'banknote': 'All dollar bills are the same size'. Note that 'bill' in BE refers to an invoice sent by a company, or a piece of paper showing the cost of food and drink consumed in a cafe or restaurant. In AE this is called a 'check'.

BASIC, BASICS, BASIS, BASE^S, BASS^S

basic /'beɪsɪk/ adjective, means forming an essential part: 'It is important to grasp the basic principles of science'. An alternative in this sense is 'fundamental'. Another meaning is 'at the simplest level': 'The campsite is pleasant but the facilities are a bit basic'. Sometimes 'basic' is redundant, as in the sentence 'The basic performance of this car is good'.

basics /'beɪsɪks/ noun, means either the most essential facts, ideas, skills etc.: 'It was a long time before he grasped the basics of mathematics'; or material objects that are needed by people in a given situation: 'The floods left a million people without the basics - food, clean water, and shelter'. The phrase 'get back/down to basics' means to focus on the simple and most important issues, not complex details: 'That football team needs to get back to basics and start scoring goals'.

basis /'beɪsɪs/ noun, means the principles that provide a foundation for something: 'Love should be the basis of family life'. The plural of 'basis' is 'bases', pronounced /'beɪsiːz/. Note that the second syllable is pronounced 'seas'.

base /beɪs/ noun, adjective & verb, as a noun, is a physical foundation or support: 'The base of the statue'. It is also a military camp: 'They did not wear uniform off base'. The phrase 'off base' also means off target, especially in AE. The plural of 'base' is 'bases', pronounced /'beɪsiz/. Note that this rhymes with 'faces'. As an adjective, 'base' means low in morality: 'She was a base liar who did not know right from wrong'. As a verb, 'base' means to select a specific location as the centre for an activity such as a holiday or business: 'The company is based in Brussels'.

bass /beɪs/ adjective & noun, means low, but is only used in musical terms: 'Bass guitar, bass voice'. As a noun, 'bass' refers to musical instruments or singers. Note that this rhymes with 'face'.

BATH, BATHTUB, BATHE

bath /bɑːθ/, noun & verb, as a noun, means a long narrow container that people sit or lie in to wash themselves, and is normal BE usage. 'Bath' can also refer just to the water: 'Would you mind running a bath for me, please?' As a verb, 'bath' means to wash someone else in a bath. 'Will you bath the boys tonight, please?' In BE, people 'have a bath', in AE they 'take a bath'. Figuratively, 'to take a bath' means to suffer a large financial loss, as in: 'We took a bath in Hong Kong last year'.

bathtub /'bɑːθtʌb/ noun, or 'tub' are alternatives to 'bath'. These words are especially used in AE.

bathe /beɪð/ verb. In BE, this means to swim in a pool, river, lake or the sea. In AE, 'bathe' and 'swim' are used as in Britain, but 'bathe' also means to wash in a bathtub. 'Bathe' is also used in both BE and AE for washing something carefully: 'bathe a wound' or 'bathe your eyes'. Note that 'bathe' has the same vowel sound as 'bay'.

*'If the weather is warm, you can
have a bath in the lake.'*
(Tourist brochure)

BATTLE, STRUGGLE, FIGHT

battle /'bætl̩/ *noun & verb*, as a noun, means a
major military action like the Battle of
Waterloo. 'Battle' can also refer to less physical
confrontations: 'You'll have to deal with this
yourself. I can't fight all your battles for you'.
As a verb, 'battle' means to make a great effort
to achieve something: 'They battled against the
blizzard for three hours'.

struggle /'strʌgl̩/ *noun & verb*, as a noun, means
efforts made to get free of someone's grasp:
'There was a struggle and then one of the men
ran away'. It can also be used in a figurative
sense meaning an attempt to achieve justice or
freedom under difficult circumstances: 'The
struggle for independence went on for ten
years'. As a verb, 'struggle' means to attempt to
get free of someone's grasp or to attempt to do
something despite difficulties: 'They struggled
to keep dry in the heavy rain'.

fight /faɪt/ *noun & verb*, as a noun, has a similar
meaning to 'struggle', although 'fight' suggests a
more physical confrontation: 'There was a fight
outside the school yesterday, but luckily no-one
was hurt'. 'Fight' is also used in fixed phrases
where there is little direct violence, for example,
the 'fight for survival', and the 'fight against
poverty'. As a verb, 'fight' means to take part in
a battle or struggle: 'The youths were still
fighting when the police arrived'. It also has the
less physical meaning of the noun form: 'He
fought against his illness for many years'.

BEACH⁵, BEECH⁵, SEASIDE

beach /biːtʃ/ *noun & verb*, as a noun, means a
shoreline, which can be sandy or rocky. As a
verb it means to bring something, usually a
boat or ship, on to the shore: 'The tanker was
beached to avoid the risk of an oil spill'. A
'beached whale' is one that is stranded on the
shore and unable to return to the sea.

beech /biːtʃ/ *noun*, is a type of hardwood tree:
'The leaves on the beech trees turn golden at
this time of year'.

seaside /'siːsaɪd/ *noun*, means the coastal area
that is used by people for holidays. The phrase
'the seaside' is typical of BE: 'We weren't the
only ones to decide on a day at the seaside'.
'Seaside' is often combined with resort to refer
to a place where people go on holiday: 'Sussex
is full of seaside resorts'. In modern BE and AE,
the term 'sea' is being increasingly used, and
the phrase 'day by the sea' is a common
expression. See **COAST**. See **SEA**.

BEAR, CARRY

bear /beər/ *verb & noun*, as a verb, means to
support: 'The rope cannot bear the weight of
two adults'. It can also mean to endure: 'She
could not bear the pain and went to the
dentist'. 'Bear' is often used in figurative
contexts such as 'bear arms' (to carry weapons)
or 'bear a grudge' (feel resentment against
someone for a time). The noun 'bear' means a
large furry mammal of the family *ursidae*, for
instance, a 'polar bear'.

carry /'kæri/ *verb*, means to support and move:
'The firefighter carried the woman out of the
house'. It can also mean to transport: 'This
plane carries 165 passengers'. 'Carry' is also
used in many figurative expressions, as in to
'get carried away', meaning to lose self-control.

BEAR MARKET, BULL MARKET

bear market /'beə maːkɪt/ is a market in
which share prices are falling: 'The bear market
at the beginning of the 21st century surprised
many analysts'. The related adjective is 'bearish'.

bull market /'bʊl maːkɪt/ is a rising market.
'The savings of many people depend on
continuing bull markets'. The related adjective,
'bullish', also has a general meaning of feeling
confident about the future.

BEER, ALE

beer /bɪər/ *noun*, is an alcoholic drink made from fermented malt and hops. In this sense it is uncountable: 'Consuming too much beer on a regular basis is a health hazard'. 'Beer' used as a countable noun means a 'glass of beer': 'Two beers, please'.

ale /eɪl/ *noun*, is a general type of beer. It is now used in names like 'brown ale' and 'mild ale'. In AE, the terms 'beer' and 'ale' are used to distinguish different fermentation processes. See **FERMENT**.

BEET[S], BEAT[S], BEATEN

beet /biːt/ *noun*, is a type of plant that is cultivated for human or animal food: 'Fields of sugar beet are found all over this part of the country'.

beat /biːt/ *verb & noun*, as a verb, means to hit someone or something repeatedly. It also means to defeat. The informal expression 'dead beat' means to be exhausted: 'The footballer said that he was dead beat'. The past tense has the same form as the infinitive. As a noun, 'beat' means the main rhythm in music: 'They were all tapping out the beat with their feet'. It also means the striking of something such as a drum: 'The six beats on the drum was the signal they were waiting for', or the regular movement of something such as a heart: 'His heart beat was very strong'.

beaten /biːtn/ *verb & adjective*, is the past participle of 'beat': 'He was badly beaten up by a gang'. It is also used in the expression 'off the beaten track' to describe a path or place that is remote.

'Clear soup with beef rashers beaten up in the country people's fashion.' (Hotel menu)

BEGIN, COMMENCE, START

begin /bɪˈgɪn/ *verb*, means to initiate something gradually: 'He was beginning to go bald'. It is often used at the start of a process: 'We begin teaching at 8.30 every morning'. The related noun is 'beginning'.

commence /kəˈmens/ *verb*, means to originate, and tends to be used in official contexts: 'The awards ceremony will commence at 5 p.m.' This is a more formal alternative to 'begin'. The related noun is 'commencement'.

start /stɑːt/ *verb & noun*, as a verb, is often used interchangeably with 'begin'. However, 'start' can mean either to cause a machine to move or work: 'I'll start the car while you lock the front door'; or to cause something to begin. 'It was those children who started the fire'. As a noun, 'start' means a quick beginning: 'The Formula 1 drivers were all trying to get a fast start'. It also features in expressions such as 'make a start' (on something), meaning to begin a task.

BEHAVIOUR, CONDUCT

behaviour /bɪˈheɪvjər/ *noun*, means the way a person acts: 'The newspaper reported the violent behaviour of the footballers off the field'. 'Behaviour' can also be applied to animals, plants and chemicals: 'The behaviour of the horse was studied carefully before the race'. For machines, it is more usual to use the word performance. 'Behavior' is the AE spelling.

conduct /ˈkɒndʌkt/ *noun*, means the way a person acts in a particular situation. It is a more formal word than 'behaviour', and is often used in fixed expressions such as 'professional conduct' and 'code of conduct'. Note that the stress is on the first syllable.

conduct /kənˈdʌkt/ *verb*, means to lead: 'The guide conducted the tourists around the castle'. It is also used reflexively to mean the same as behave: 'The crowd conducted itself well'. Note that the stress is on the second syllable.

BELOW, UNDER, BENEATH, UNDERNEATH, BEHIND

below /bɪˈləʊ/ *preposition*, means either physically lower than something else: 'The town is below sea level'; or lower on a scale: 'It is 10 degrees below freezing today'. Note that 'below London Bridge' means on the seaward side. In a report, a figure that comes later can be described as 'below': 'See Figure 6.1, below'. See **PREPOSITIONS**.

under /ˈʌndər/ *preposition*, means directly below something: 'The ship was directly under London Bridge'. 'Under' can also be used with price to mean less than: 'This PC is under €1000'. 'Below' can never be used in this context. 'Under' is also used to mean 'in the course of': 'The bridge is under construction'.

beneath /bɪˈniːθ/ *preposition & adverb*, means both 'under' and 'lower than': 'She swam beneath the waves'. 'Beneath' also means not good enough for someone: 'Doing the secretarial work was beneath her'.

underneath /ˌʌndəˈniːθ/ *preposition & adverb*, means under or below something, or covered by the object on top: 'They sheltered underneath the tree'. 'Beneath' may be used as a formal alternative in this sense.

behind /bɪˈhaɪnd/ *preposition*, means towards the back of something and possibly hidden by it: 'The moon disappeared behind the clouds'. Note that if something is 'behind' an object, it is separate from it, so that a cafe 'behind' the station is not part of the station. However, a cafe 'under' the station would be on the station premises.

BERRY⁵, BURY⁵

berry /ˈberi/ *noun*, means a small fruit that grows on a plant: 'The berries were delicious with cream'. This word is used as part of the name of numerous fruits, such as 'strawberry' and 'raspberry'.

bury /ˈberi/ *verb*, means to cover something with earth, sand or snow: 'Their car was buried in the landslide'. It is also used figuratively: 'The government is hoping to bury the bad news about the economy'. See **BURIAL**.

BERTH⁵, BIRTH⁵

berth /bɜːθ/ *noun*, means a place to sleep on a ship or train: 'As we were only given seats for the night, we paid extra for a berth on the ferry'. It also means a mooring for a ship. See **DOCK**. See **PORT ⇨ HARBOUR**. See **QUAY ⇨ KEY**.

birth /bɜːθ/ *noun*, means when a baby is born, or the start of an age: 'The twentieth century saw the birth of the computer age'. 'To have a child' means to give birth.

 'Ladies are requested not to have children in the bar.' (Cocktail lounge notice)

BESIDE, BESIDES

beside /bɪˈsaɪd/ *preposition*, means 'alongside', or 'at the side of': 'The dog slept beside his master'. 'Beside' is also used to make physical comparisons: 'My car looks really small beside yours'. It is found in phrases like 'beside the point', meaning irrelevant, or 'beside oneself', meaning in a state of distress. See **PREPOSITIONS**.

besides /bɪˈsaɪdz/ *adverb*, means 'apart from' or 'in addition to': 'Besides all that, he is a respectable member of the church'.

BI-, DUO

bi- /baɪ-/ *prefix*, means two, or having two. Note the ambiguity in measurements of time such as 'biweekly' and 'bimonthly', which can mean once every two weeks/months or twice a week/month. It is recommended to avoid such combinations, and use 'every two weeks/months' or 'twice a week/month'. See **BIMONTHLY**. See **DUAL**.

duo /ˈdjuːəʊ/ *noun*, means two people or things acting together, especially in entertainment or sport: 'That TV duo are as hopeless as their jokes'.

BIANNUAL, BIENNIAL, BIENNALE

biannual /baɪˈænjʊəl/ *adjective*, means twice a year. Potential confusion with 'biennial' can be avoided by replacing 'biannual' with 'semi-annual', 'half yearly', or 'every six months'. See **ANNUAL**.

biennial /baɪˈeniəl/ *adjective & noun*, as an adjective, means once every two years: 'As this course is biennial, it will not be taught next year'. Potential confusion with 'biannual' can be avoided by replacing 'biennial' with 'every second year' or 'every other year'. As a noun, 'biennial' refers to a plant that lives for two years, and flowers only in the second, before dying: 'This plant did not flower this year as it is a biennial'.

Biennale /ˌbiːeˈnɑːleɪ/ *noun*, means a large exhibition or music festival held on a 'biennial' basis: 'The first Biennale was held in Venice in 1895'.

BICENTENARY, BICENTENNIAL

bicentenary /ˌbaɪsenˈtiːnəri/ *noun*, means a two-hundredth anniversary. This is the common term in BE: 'The bicentenary of the French Revolution was in 1989'. Note that the third syllable rhymes with 'teen'.

bicentennial /baɪsen'teniəl/ *noun*, is the common term in AE for 'bicentenary': 'The bicentennial of the Declaration of Independence was celebrated in 1976'. Note that the third syllable rhymes with 'ten', and that 'bicentennial' has three 'n's.

BILLION, BILLIONS, MILLIARD, TRILLION

billion /'bɪljən/ *noun*, is used today in both BE and AE to mean a thousand million (10^9). Formerly in BE, 'billion' used to mean a million million (10^{12}), but this is now old-fashioned. When 'billion' is used with a unit of time, distance, temperature, money, etc., it takes a singular verb: '2.5 billion dollars is required'. Otherwise, a plural verb is used: 'One point two billion people were watching the match on TV'. Note that when 'billion' follows an exact number or the words 'a', 'a few', or 'several', it takes a plural verb: 'There are several billion stars in our galaxy'. The abbreviation is 'bn'.

billions is the plural of 'billion' and refers to an inexact very large number. Often it has 'tens of' or 'hundreds of' in front. Thus 'billions' can range from a few billions to many billions: 'The budget deficit is likely to increase into the billions'. It is often followed by 'of' and informally, it can mean 'very many': 'He has done this billions of times'.

milliard /'mɪljəd/ *noun*, means a thousand million (10^9) and is used so rarely in English that it is best avoided. Use 'billion' instead.

trillion /'trɪljən/ *noun*, means a million million (10^{12}). This is the standard meaning of 'trillion' in international scientific English and modern BE and has always been the meaning in AE. The meaning of 'trillion' in BE used to be a million million million (10^{18}), but this is now considered old-fashioned.

BIMONTHLY, BIWEEKLY, FORTNIGHTLY, SEMI-MONTHLY, SEMI-WEEKLY

bimonthly /baɪ'mʌnθli/ *adjective & noun*, means either twice a month or every two months. Because of the ambiguity about its meaning, it is best to avoid this word. Depending on the context, use the less confusing 'fortnightly' or 'semi-monthly', or 'every second month'. In publishing, however, 'bimonthly' means every two months.

biweekly /baɪ'wiːkli/ *adjective & noun*, means either twice a week or every two weeks. Avoid this ambiguous word and use either 'semi-weekly' or 'fortnightly'.

fortnightly /'fɔːtnaɪtli/ *adjective & noun*, means every two weeks.

semi-monthly /semi'mʌnθli/ *adjective & noun*, means twice a month. Note that the pronunciation /semi-/ is normal in BE, while /semaɪ-/ is standard in AE.

semi-weekly /semi'wiːkli/ *adjective*, means twice a week. Note that the pronunciation /semi-/ is normal in BE, while /semaɪ-/ is standard in AE.

BIRTHDAY, DATE OF BIRTH

birthday /'bɜːθdeɪ/ *noun*, is the anniversary of a person's birth. In AE, 'birthday' may also mean a person's date of birth, as in 'State your birthday on the form'.

date of birth /'deɪt əv 'bɜːθ/ *noun*, is the date on which a person was born. This is abbreviated to 'dob' or 'DOB' on some forms.

BISECT, DISSECT

bisect /baɪ'sekt/ *verb*, means to divide something into two parts, which are usually equal: 'The transport plan of the new town was based on an overhead railway that bisected the entire urban area'.

dissect /dɪ'sekt/ *verb*, means to cut something up in order to examine its structure, or figuratively to examine something in detail: 'The pupils had to dissect a frog in class'. Although many people pronounce this word to rhyme with 'bisect', it is recommended to make the first syllable rhyme with 'miss', not 'my'.

BLACK, AFRICAN AMERICAN, NEGRO, COLOURED

black /blæk/ *adjective & noun*, means relating to a race of people with dark skin, especially of African and Australian aboriginal origin. Among Black Africans or West Indians in Britain, 'black' is the most acceptable word to describe their appearance. This can be capitalized for a group but not for an individual: 'A black police officer was promoted to inspector'. See **NATIVE AMERICAN**.

African American is the currently accepted term in the US for Americans of African origin.

Negro /'niːgrəʊ/ *noun*, is an ethnic or historical term for Black Africans and is only used today in contexts like 'Negro spirituals'. 'Negro', together with the female form 'Negress', should be avoided elsewhere.

coloured /'kʌləd/ *adjective & noun,* means wholly or partly of non-white descent. This is an offensive term and 'black' is a safer alternative. However, in South Africa 'coloured' is a technical term for those of mixed race. 'Colored' is the AE spelling. In the US, the term is disliked by most blacks and it is mainly found today in organizational names.

blend words

Blends are words formed by combining parts of other words. Some of these are firmly established in English and are found in larger dictionaries, so they can be used freely. Examples include:

breathalyser /'brɛθəlaɪzər/ (breath, analyser)

brunch /brʌntʃ/ (breakfast, lunch)

cheeseburger /'tʃiːzbɜːgər/ (cheese, hamburger)

moped /'məʊped/ (motor, pedal)

motel /məʊ'tel/ (motor, hotel)

Oxbridge /'ɒksbrɪdʒ/ (fictitious place, from Oxford and Cambridge universities)

paratroops /'pærətruːps/ (parachute, troops)

smog /smɒg/ (smoke, fog)

workaholic /wɜːkə'hɒlɪk/ (work-addiction, alcoholic).

BLOC^S, BLOCK^S, QUARTER

bloc /blɒk/ *noun,* is usually a political or ideological group: 'The large bloc of voters showed little party loyalty'. It can also be used for a group of countries with common interests: 'The former Soviet bloc was a world force'. 'Bloc' is also used in the expression 'en bloc', which means 'as a whole': 'The police moved the refugees en bloc'.

block /blɒk/ *noun,* has many meanings. One is as a quantity of something that is regarded as a unit: 'a block of ice' or 'a block of shares'. In BE, it is used to mean a building that is part of a hospital or school: 'Our next class is in the science block'. The terms 'tower block' and 'block of flats' both relate to housing. In AE, 'block' means a group of buildings surrounded by roads on all sides. Note that distance in urban areas in the US is often indicated in 'blocks': 'Walk three blocks, then take a left'.

quarter /'kwɔːtər/ *noun,* means a part of a town or city with a special character: 'The Latin Quarter of Paris'. See **FOURTH ⇨ FORTH**. See **MEASUREMENTS**.

BLOND^S, BLONDE^S, BROWN, BRUNETTE

blond(e) /blɒnd/ *adjective,* refers to a fair-haired person: 'He is a blond youth'. Some people distinguish between 'blond' for males and 'blonde' for females. Both spellings are correct. See **GREY**.

blonde /blɒnd/ *noun,* means a fair-haired woman: 'He's over there talking to the blonde'. However, this may be regarded as a negative stereotype and can be replaced by 'blond(e)' as an adjective: 'He's over there talking to the blonde-haired woman'.

brown /braʊn/ *adjective,* is used for both males and females to describe hair which is dark but not black: 'He had a magnificent mane of chestnut brown hair'.

brunette /bruː'net/ *noun,* is used to describe a woman with dark brown hair: 'Before she dyed her hair she was a brunette'. Although not considered as unfavourably as the noun 'blonde', many people prefer to use the adjective phrases 'with dark hair' or 'dark-haired'. An alternative AE spelling is 'brunet'.

BOAT, SHIP

boat /bəʊt/ *noun,* usually means a small vessel for travelling on water: 'They had two motor boats and a sailing boat on the lake'. It can also be used to describe travel in larger vessels such as ferries: 'They crossed the Baltic by boat'. Submarines are also termed 'boats'.

ship /ʃɪp/ *noun & verb,* as a noun, means a large vessel for transporting passengers or goods. It is also possible to travel 'by ship'. As a verb, 'to ship' usually means to transport goods or people. Some people only use this verb for ships. Nevertheless, 'shipping' by air, road or rail is widely used: 'Ship this consignment by air'. See **FREIGHT**.

BOLDER^S, BOULDER^S

bolder /'bəʊldər/ *comparative adjective,* refers to a person or animal that is braver than another: 'His youngest brother was always bolder than the rest of the gang'.

boulder /'bəʊldər/ *noun,* means a large rock: 'Among the rocks were boulders as large as a car'.

BONA FIDE, BONA FIDES

bona fide /'bəʊnə 'faɪdi/ *adjective,* means genuine and real: 'Only bona fide members are allowed to bring guests'.

bona fides /'bəʊnə 'faɪdiːz/ *noun*, means good standing. Though it ends with 's', it is not a plural and takes a singular verb: 'His bona fides was questioned'.

BORDER, BOUNDARY, FRONTIER

border /'bɔːdər/ *noun*, means the edge of something: 'The border of the garden bed was lined with stones'. 'Border' also means the demarcation line between two countries. This often follows a natural division, such as a river, or range of mountains. 'Border' is less formal and less menacing than 'frontier': 'The USA and Canada have a long border'. In AE, 'state line' is the term used for borders between states in the USA.

boundary /'baʊndəri/ *noun*, is a limit, or a line that marks a division, often between two administrative areas within the same country: 'Many of the county boundaries in England and Wales were changed in 1974'.

frontier /'frʌntɪər/ *noun*, means a formal border separating two countries: 'In Kashmir, there are conflicting claims about where the frontier should be in this area'. 'Frontier' is also used to refer to the limit of settled land, beyond which lies a wild and unknown territory. A 'frontier' can also be a breakthrough: 'What we are learning about the brain is pushing back the frontiers of knowledge'.

BORE, DRILL

bore /bɔːr/ *verb & noun*, as a verb, means to make a hole using a cutting tool: 'We have to bore a hole through this metal plate'. It also means to be uninteresting: 'The dull speaker bored his audience'. As a noun, it means the hollow cylinder in a gun or rifle, or an engine cylinder. Note that the adjective 'boring' /'bɔːrɪŋ/ nearly always means something that is dull and tedious.

drill /drɪl/ *noun & verb*, as a noun, means a machine with a rotating cutting tip. In the oil industry the 'drill string' is the connected lengths of pipe or casing involved in producing a 'borehole'. As a verb, 'drill' means to pierce, or make a hole using a rotating tool: 'He drilled a hole in the bathroom wall and fractured a concealed water pipe'.

BORNˢ, BORNEˢ

born /bɔːn/ *past participle & adjective*, as a past participle of the verb 'bear', means having come into the world as a result of birth: 'His daughter was born in New York'. As an adjective, it means having natural ability: 'He grew up in the Netherlands, but was widely acknowledged to be a born skier'.

borne /bɔːn/ *past participle*, is also related to the verb 'bear', and refers to the act of having given birth: 'She has borne four sons'. It also means having endured something, as in: 'I have borne the pain as long as I can'. See **BEAR**.

BOTH, THE TWO, EACH

both /bəʊθ/ *determiner & pronoun*, means the two things referred to or duality. It always takes a plural verb. In a context such as 'Both projects will cost $12 million', 'both' is ambiguous, since it is not clear whether the amount referred to is the total cost or the cost of each project. In cases like this, 'both' could be replaced by 'each'. When making comparisons, balance the structure and use either: 'both in Russia and in China' or 'in both Russia and China'. 'Both' is often unnecessary with words like 'equal' and 'equally', which already convey the idea of two parts: 'The football teams were equal at half time' (not 'both equal'). Similar words are 'the sexes' (not 'both the sexes') and 'the twins' (not 'both the twins'). See **TAUTOLOGY**.

the two /ðə 'tuː/ can also be used instead of 'both' in order to avoid ambiguity. 'Both project teams met' might mean either separately or together. However, 'the two project teams met' must mean that they met each other. Remember to use a plural verb with 'the two'.

each /iːtʃ/ *determiner & pronoun*, means every one of the two or more people or things considered separately: 'Each project costs $12 million'. When 'each' is followed by a noun, a singular verb is used: 'Each of the projects was finished'. When 'each' follows a plural noun, a plural verb is used: 'The politicians each have their own opinion'.

BOTTOM LINE, BOTTOM OUT, ROCK BOTTOM

bottom line /bɒtəm 'laɪn/ *noun*, means the final total on a balance sheet or financial document that shows the profit or loss for the year: 'The bottom line is the annual surplus'. In more general use, the 'bottom line' means the final price that can be offered or the most important thing: 'The bottom line is this: will the market pay extra for this safety feature?' The expressions 'fundamental issue' or 'crux of the matter' are alternatives to 'bottom line' used in this sense.

bottom out /ˈbɒtəm ˈaʊt/ *phrasal verb*, means that the price of goods or a difficult situation starts to level off or not get any worse: 'The price of oil bottomed out after the news of the conflict'. Note that prices are likely to rise, but they are unlikely to fall further after they 'bottom out'.

rock bottom /ˈrɒk ˈbɒtəm/ *adjective*, refers to the lowest point or level possible. The reference is to someone digging who hits bedrock and cannot dig any further: 'The price of oil has reached rock bottom'. Note that when the price of goods or a relationship between people hits 'rock bottom' this is the lowest level that they can reach.

> *An American businessperson in China was trying to get a better deal and said: 'The bottom line is the bottom line'. This was translated as: 'The line is on the bottom, never on the top'.*

BOYISH, GIRLISH

boyish /ˈbɔɪɪʃ/ *adjective*, means characteristic of a young man. This is positive and flattering: 'His tanned body and boyish charm were a combination many girls fell for'.

girlish /ˈɡɜːlɪʃ/ *adjective*, means characteristic of a young woman. This is often negative: 'Her giggles and general girlish behaviour irritated her teachers'. See **WOMANLY ⇨ FEMALE**.

BRACKETS, PARENTHESES

brackets /ˈbrækɪts/ *noun*, means a pair of marks used to enclose words or figures. They have various shapes and names.

parentheses /pəˈrenθɪsiːz/ *noun*, is an alternative term for 'round brackets', especially in AE. Note that the last syllable rhymes with 'seas'. The singular form is 'parenthesis' /pəˈrenθɪsɪs/, which is sometimes used in a wider sense to indicate an afterthought or a digression: 'The last president's short term in office was a political parenthesis'.

brackets: some transatlantic differences

BE	Symbol	AE
round brackets/brackets	(...)	parentheses
square brackets	[...]	square brackets/brackets
braces/curly brackets	{...}	braces
angle brackets	<...>	angle brackets

BRAKE[S], BREAK[S]

brake /breɪk/ *noun & verb*, as a noun, means the device to stop a vehicle: 'The boy managed to release the brake and the car started to roll towards the main road'. As a verb, 'brake' means to stop something: 'The skidmarks on the road showed that he had been braking hard for twenty metres'.

break /breɪk/ *noun & verb*, has a number of meanings. As a noun, this means a pause or interval: 'We will have a break in an hour'. As a verb, 'break' means to disobey something such as a law: 'Do not break the speed limit'. It also means to destroy something: 'If you drop the cup it will break', or force illegal entry: 'He was breaking into the car'. Note that the past participle 'broken' can describe the way a language is used by a non native speaker who is not very fluent: 'I asked the way to the station in broken French'.

 'Broken English spoken perfectly.' (Shop sign)

BREAKDOWN[S], BREAK DOWN[S]

breakdown /ˈbreɪkdaʊn/ *noun*, means both a collapse: 'We are witnessing a breakdown in moral standards', and also a classification, especially relating to statistics. Note that when 'breakdown' means classification or analysis, it is followed by 'of': 'A breakdown of family income according to education level'. Compare this with 'a family breakdown', which suggests the failure of relationships within a family.

break down /breɪk ˈdaʊn/ *verb*, written as two words, is the verbal equivalent of the noun 'breakdown'. However, although the verb 'break down' means to analyse, it has other meanings such as to stop functioning: 'My car has broken down again'; and to lose self-control due to emotional distress: 'She broke down when she heard the bad news'.

BREAKFAST, LUNCH, DINNER, TEA, SUPPER

breakfast /'brekfəst/ *noun*, means the first meal of the day: 'In hotels, an English breakfast is an extremely substantial meal'. Note that the first syllable rhymes with 'neck'. A derived word is 'brunch' /brʌntʃ/, a blend of 'breakfast' and 'lunch' which is a meal for late risers at about 11 a.m. See **BLEND WORDS**.

lunch /lʌntʃ/ *noun*, is the midday meal which is normally lighter than the main evening meal. The expression, 'There is no such thing as a free lunch', means that everything has a price.

dinner /'dɪnər/ *noun*, is the main meal of the day, which can be eaten either around midday or in the evening. BE middle class and most AE speakers tend to use 'dinner' to mean only the evening meal. Note that 'Christmas dinner' is often eaten in the afternoon on both sides of the Atlantic. 'Dinner' is usually a formal event in a restaurant if it is used with either the indefinite or definite article: 'We have been invited to a dinner at the Hilton'.

tea /tiː/ *noun*, as a meal, can mean several things in Britain: a cup of tea, perhaps with a biscuit at any time of the day; tea and cakes at about 4 p.m.; a cooked meal at about 5 or 6 p.m. (sometimes called 'supper', or more traditionally, 'high tea'). It is, of course, also the name for the drink, usually taken hot with milk in the UK, but often cold with lemon in the USA.

supper /'sʌpər/ *noun*, means a light meal eaten in the evening. Sometimes this is at about 5 or 6 p.m. or it may be a late evening snack, just before bedtime.

> *'Lunch is a restaurateur's term for the working man's dinner.'*

BREAST, BUST, BOSOM, CHEST

breast /brest/ *noun*, means a milk-producing organ in mammals. 'Breast' is also the word used to describe the cut of meat taken from the front of a lamb or bird between its forelegs or wings.

bust /bʌst/ *noun*, means the measurement of a woman's chest. This is used in the sizes of clothes. It is also the term used for a head-and-shoulders sculpture of either sex.

bosom /'bʊzəm/ *noun*, means a woman's breasts. This is a poetic word that is always used in the singular: 'She held the baby close to her bosom'.

chest /tʃest/ *noun*, is the anatomical and medical term for both males and females, and is the measurement for men's clothes: 'His chest size was out of stock'. The expression 'get something off your chest' can be both literal and, as in this example, a confession: 'She had to tell her family the truth and get the matter off her chest'.

BREATH, BREATHE

breath /breθ/ *noun*, means the air coming into or out of the lungs: 'His breath smelt strongly of garlic'. It also means fresh air: 'They went to the seaside and had a good breath of spring air'. Note that 'breath' rhymes with 'death'.

breathe /briːð/ *verb*, means to inhale and exhale: 'It was so stuffy he felt that he could not breathe'. When the -ing form is used, drop the final 'e': 'His breathing was irregular'. Note that 'breathe' rhymes with 'teethe'.

BRING, ACCOMPANY, TAKE

bring /brɪŋ/ *verb*, means move something or someone towards the speaker: 'Please bring the report to me'. 'Bring' can also mean cause something: 'The cold weather will bring icy roads with it'. The past tense and past participle is 'brought'. See **BROUGHT**. See **COME** ⇨ **FOLLOW**.

accompany /ə'kʌmpəni/ *verb*, means to go with someone to a particular place. This is a formal word. Compare: 'He accompanied her part of the way home', with the less formal: 'He went part of the way home with her'.

take /teɪk/ *verb*, implies movement away from the speaker either on foot or using some means of transport: 'Please take this confidential report back to your office'. 'Take' is also used when someone accompanies the speaker: 'I can take you home at 7'.

BRING UP, TOUCH UPON, BROACH

bring up /brɪŋ 'ʌp/ *verb*, means to raise children: 'They managed to bring up three children in a small flat'. It also means to raise a subject for discussion in a meeting: 'The club's secretary asked if she could bring up the subject of a regular meeting place'. In a third sense, 'bring up' means to vomit, and for this reason it is a phrase that needs to be treated with care.

touch (up)on /'tʌtʃ (əp)ɒn/ *verb*, means to discuss something briefly, and without going into detail: 'In his analysis of the sales figures, he also touched on the difficulties of finding researchers willing to do the field work'.

broach /brəʊtʃ/ *verb*, means to start talking about a matter for discussion. It is often used before a delicate topic: 'He disliked broaching the subject of money'. This is a formal word and 'bring up' or 'touch on' are alternatives.

'If you want breakfast, lift the telephone and our waitress will arrive. This will be enough to bring up your food.'
(Hotel notice)

BRITAIN/GREAT BRITAIN, ENGLAND, UNITED KINGDOM/UK, BRITISH ISLES

Britain/Great Britain /(greit) 'britn/ is the island which includes England, Scotland, and Wales. These are official geographical terms but are often used to mean the United Kingdom.

England /'ɪŋglənd/ is the largest of the four countries which make up the UK. Note that 'England' may mean the English, or the English sports team, but never the entire British people.

(The) United Kingdom /ðə juːˈnaɪtɪd ˈkɪŋdəm/ or '(the) UK' means Britain and Northern Ireland. This is a political unit, with the full name 'the United Kingdom of Great Britain and Northern Ireland'. As with other countries whose names refer to plural entities, use the definite article in running text: 'France, Germany and the UK.' See **DEFINITE ARTICLE**.

British Isles /'britɪʃ 'aɪlz/ is a geographical term for Great Britain, the whole of Ireland, and smaller offshore islands from Shetland to the Channel Islands: 'Snow closed all main airports in the British Isles from Glasgow to Shannon and Gatwick'.

'On the outline map of England and Wales, indicate where the Highlands of Scotland are.'
(School examination paper, UK)

BRITISH, BRITON, BRITISHER, BRIT, ENGLISH

British /'britɪʃ/ means people from the United Kingdom. The word 'British' is always capitalized.

Briton /'britn/ means a single British person, but it is rare for Britons to use it about themselves. It occurs in newspapers to save space: '12 Britons missing', and is correct for the 'ancient Britons'.

Britisher /'britɪʃər/ is an AE term for a British subject. It is a rare word in BE.

Brit /brit/ is a short form for 'British', 'Britisher' and 'Briton' and is an informal term used in AE and BE.

English /'ɪŋglɪʃ/ is the main language of most British people but it also means only the people who come from England. Remember that many British people are Scottish, Welsh or Northern Irish, not just English. The word English is always capitalized.

British English (BE), American English (AE)

BE and AE are the two main varieties of English. They are classified as different in dictionaries and are defined with different spellcheckers in computer software and should always be kept apart. It is best to be consistent and use only one variety.

This book has listed some of the differences between BE and AE usage under the respective headwords. Though BE and AE are about 80 – 90% the same, the main differences can be summarized as follows:

• **pronunciation**

There are wide regional differences of pronunciation even within both BE and AE. The way BE and AE speakers pronounce the vowels of words like: *new, Tuesday, clerk, data* and *dance/grass* (in southern BE), reveals some of the main differences between BE and AE. Also, the pronunciations of *fertile* and *missile* are a good indication of BE/AE differences (/'fɜːtaɪl, 'mɪsaɪl/ in BE and /'fɜrtl, 'mɪsl/ in AE). For those with a particular interest in pronunciation differences, see **Bibliography**.

• **stress**

Many words are stressed differently in BE and AE. Some typical differences are BE *ad'vertisement* and AE *adver'tisement*; BE *alu'minium* and AE *a'luminum* (note also the difference in spelling); and BE *la'boratory* and AE *'laboratory*.

• **grammar**

The AE past participle of get is gotten when it means acquired; in BE it is got. AE: *I've gotten a new automobile*; BE: *I've got a new car*. There are some other irregular verb differences.

Many differences occur in the use of prepositions. Examples:

BE	AE
a quarter past three	*a quarter after three*
a quarter to four	*a quarter of four*
at school	*in school*
check something	*check something out*
fill in a form	*fill out a form*
Friday to Sunday	*Friday through Sunday*
meet somebody	*meet with somebody*
stay at home	*stay home*
visit somebody	*visit with somebody*

• **spelling**

Some of the most common differences, by type:

BE		AE	
-ce	*defence**	*-se*	*defense**
-eable	*saleable*	*-able*	*salable*
-ll-	*travelling*	*-l-*	*traveling*
-mme	*programme***	*-m*	*program*
non-	*non-profit*		*nonprofit*
-oe-	*diarrhoea*	*-e-*	*diarrhea*
-ogue	*catalogue*	*-og*	*catalog*
-oul-	*mould*	*-ol-*	*mold*
-our	*colour*	*-or*	*color*
	neighbour		*neighbor*
-re	*centre*	*-er*	*center*
	metre		*meter*
-yse	*analyse*	*-yze*	*analyze*

*Ministry of Defence (BE) and *Defense Department* (AE) should always be spelt in these ways, as they are proper names.

**Program in BE refers to software.

Note that both *-ize* and *-ise* are used at the end of verbs in BE and AE. See **-IZE, -ISE**.

Spelling differences in some common words:

BE	AE
aluminium	*aluminum*
cheque	*check*
draught	*draft*
grey	*gray*
kerb (pavement)	*curb* (sidewalk)
manoeuvre	*maneuver*
pyjamas	*pajamas*
skilful	*skillful*
speciality	*specialty*

storey	*story*
sulphur	*sulfur*
tyre	*tire*

Note that some words that are hyphenated in BE are written as one word in AE. Example: *non-linear* (BE) and *nonlinear* (AE).

See **HYPHENATION IN INDIVIDUAL WORDS**.

• **vocabulary**

Some of the most common differences:

BE	AE
aeroplane	*airplane*
anywhere	*anyplace*
autumn	*fall*
banknote (note)	*bill*
barrister, solicitor	*attorney*
bill (in a restaurant)	*check*
bonnet (of a car)	*hood*
boot (of a car)	*trunk*
bumper (of a car)	*fender*
biscuit	*cookie*
car	*automobile*
carriage (railway)	*car* (railroad)
chemist	*drugstore*
cupboard	*closet*
draughts	*checkers*
drawing-pin	*thumbtack*
dustbin, rubbish bin	*garbage can, trash can*
estate (car)	*station wagon*
estate agent	*realtor*
flat	*apartment*
gear lever	*gear shift*
ground floor	*first floor*
handbag	*purse*
hoarding	*billboard*
lift (for people)	*elevator*
maize	*corn*
maths	*math*
motorway	*expressway, freeway*
nappy	*diaper*
off-licence	*liquor store*
pants	*underwear, shorts*
paraffin	*kerosene*
pavement	*sidewalk*
petrol	*gas/gasoline*
postal worker	*mail carrier*
purse	*pocketbook*
railway(s)	*railroad*
return ticket	*round-trip ticket*
road surface	*pavement*
roundabout	*traffic circle*
saloon (car)	*sedan*

single ticket	one-way ticket
spanner	wrench
sweets	candy
tap	faucet
toll road	turnpike, toll road
trousers	pants
turn-ups (on trousers)	cuffs
vest	undershirt
waistcoat	vest
wallet	pocketbook

Note the difference in weights and measures:

British/metric scale:	American scale:
tonne (1000 kg) also called metric ton	short ton (907 kg)
fluid ounce (28.4 ml)	fluid ounce (29.6 ml)
pint (0.57 l)	pint (0.47 l)
gallon (4.55 l)	US gallon (3.78 l)

British place names

Place names can tell us a lot about the history and geography of Britain, but there are considerable pronunciation problems.

It is important, both out of courtesy, and in order to be understood, to pronounce place names correctly. Two famous difficulties are *Thames* /temz/ - the h is silent, and has no basis in history, and *London* /'lʌndən/ - the u sound goes back to Anglo-Saxon times at least. A particular problem is the ending -wich: in *Ipswich* the w is pronounced: /'ɪpswɪtʃ/, but in *Norwich* and *Greenwich* it is silent: /'nɒrɪtʃ/, /'grɪnɪdʒ/. Wherever possible, check the pronunciation of British place names in a pronouncing dictionary – or ask a long-time resident. See **FOREIGN PLACE NAMES**. See **NATIONALITY WORDS**.

BROTHER, BROTHERHOOD, BRETHREN

brother /'brʌðər/ *noun*, is either a male with the same mother or father as another, or a male member of certain groups, like religious orders and trade unions. In AE, black males use this as a form of address for other black males.

brotherhood /'brʌðəhʊd/ *noun*, means either the feeling of friendship and understanding among people: 'They worked towards global peace and the brotherhood of Man'; or the feeling of closeness among people with common interests. This is usually restricted to religious or trade union contexts.

brethren /'breðrən/ *noun*, is the old plural of 'brother'. It is now only used for members of religious groups: 'He spoke to the brethren in his monastic order', or for the names of sects, such as the Plymouth Brethren. 'Brethren' may include women. It is sometimes used humorously as an alternative to comrades: 'Our brethren in the Labour Party'.
See **PLURAL NOUNS**.

BROUGHT, BOUGHT

brought /brɔːt/ *verb*, is the past tense and past participle of 'bring': 'He brought the children to see us'. See **BRING**.

bought /bɔːt/ *verb*, is the past tense and past participle of 'buy': 'He bought the expensive car second hand'. The phrase 'cannot be bought' means that someone cannot be bribed: 'The gang concluded that the official could not be bought'. See **BUY**.

BUFFET (NOUN & VERB)

buffet /'bʌfeɪ, 'buːfeɪ/ *noun*, means a meal where you can serve yourself or a place where food is served on a train: 'Meals are in the buffet car' (called 'diner' in AE). Note that the last vowel is pronounced the same as in the word 'day', and that the 't' is silent.
See **DINER**. See **RESTAURANT**.

buffet /'bʌfɪt/ *verb*, means to hit something and cause it to move unsteadily. 'Buffet' usually refers to the action of natural phenomena, such as air or sea currents. It is commonly used in the passive: 'The plane was buffeted by the strong winds'. Note that the final 't' is pronounced.

BURIAL, FUNERAL, INTERMENT, INTERNMENT

burial /'berɪəl/ *noun* means the practice of burying the dead: 'Burial is a fairly general custom in Western society'.

funeral /'fjuːnərəl/ *noun*, means the ceremony at which a dead person is buried or cremated: 'The funeral service was held at the crematorium'. 'Funeral' is also used informally in a wider sense to advise someone that they are responsible for any negative outcome: 'If you get involved in illegal activities, that's your funeral'.

interment /ɪn'tɜːmənt/ *noun*, means the act of burying a corpse: 'The coroner ordered the interment of the unidentified body that had been washed up on the beach'. This is a clinical and legal term and is not suitable in general contexts. Note that the stress is on the second syllable.

internment /ɪn'tɜːnmənt/ *noun*, means imprisonment without trial, usually of enemy nationals during wartime. Do not confuse this with 'interment'.

BUS, COACH

bus /bʌs/ *noun & verb*, as a noun, is a vehicle for public transport on a fixed route: 'The red double-decker buses in London are a tourist attraction'. In BE, a 'bus' is normally reserved for the local public transport of people and is not the same as a 'coach'. In AE, 'bus' covers both the BE sense of the term and the term 'coach': 'The Greyhound bus only takes 5 hours to Boston'. The plural of 'bus' is 'buses' in BE but may also be 'busses' in AE. As a verb, it means to transport by 'bus': 'In parts of the US, busing students has political significance'. The verb forms are best spelt with single 's': 'bused' and 'busing', although the alternative with double 'ss' also exists.

coach /kəʊtʃ/ *noun*, is a single-decker bus, used for more luxurious transport for medium-distance and long journeys. This is a BE term: 'A coach tour of the Riviera sounds like my idea of a good spring holiday'. 'Coach' in BE is associated with luxury: 'Express coach service to Heathrow'. Note that in AE, 'coach' means economy class: 'We enjoyed the trip even though we only paid coach-class fares'.

BUSINESS, FIRM, ENTERPRISE, COMPANY, CONCERN

business /'bɪznɪs/ *noun*, and **firm** /fɜːm/ *noun*, mean commercial organizations of various sizes. 'Business' is used with the indefinite article to mean a specific shop or a 'company': 'She has a small hair salon business'. This has the plural 'businesses'. 'Business' without the indefinite article means commerce and trade: 'Business is thriving at the moment'. In this sense, 'business' is an uncountable noun, and therefore has a singular verb.

enterprise /'entəpraɪz/ *noun*, also means a commercial organization. A synonym is an 'undertaking' ['ʌndəteɪkɪŋ]. A 'small or medium-sized enterprise (SME)' may differ considerably in size or in the number of staff from one country to another.

company /'kʌmpəni/ *noun*, is the term used for registered enterprises with shareholders: 'Limited company (Ltd)', or 'Public Limited Company (PLC)'. See **PLC**.

concern /kən'sɜːn/ *noun*, means any type of commercial organization such as a business, enterprise or firm. Note that this term can refer to small as well as large enterprises. A 'going concern' is a business that is making a profit: 'The owners are trying to sell their shop as a going concern'. See **GROUP**.

BUY, PURCHASE

buy /baɪ/ *verb & noun*, as a verb, means to obtain something in exchange for money: 'They saved up and decided to buy some new furniture'. The phrase 'the best that money can buy' means that something is excellent value: 'This Rolls Royce is said to be the best that money can buy'. As a noun, 'buy' means something that is worth the money: 'That car was a really good buy'.

purchase /'pɜːtʃɪs/ *verb & noun*, as a verb, means to obtain something in exchange for money, but is a more formal word than 'buy': 'Alaska was purchased from Russia in 1867'. As a noun, 'purchase' means the process of buying something: 'The purchase of land close to urban areas has always been a good investment'.

BY, WITHIN, UNTIL, DURING, FOR (*PREPOSITIONS OF TIME*)

by /baɪ/ *preposition*, refers to something that will happen at or before a certain time: 'I'll get the lottery ticket by 5 p.m.' See **WITH**. See **PREPOSITIONS**.

within /wɪ'ðɪn/ *preposition*, means that something has to be done or completed before the end of a period of time: 'I'll get the lottery ticket within the next 24 hours'.

until /ʌn'tɪl/ *preposition*, refers to a situation that will continue up to a certain time: 'We didn't know that we really had won the lottery until Monday'. 'Till' is an informal version of 'until'.

during /'djʊərɪŋ/ *preposition*, means all through a period of time or when an event occurred: 'The window was broken some time during the weekend'.

for /fər, fɔːr/ *preposition*, refers either to the duration of an event: 'We are going away for the weekend', or to something arranged at a specific time: 'He rang the doctor and made an appointment for 25 March'. The strong form /fɔːr/ is only used when this is the final word of a sentence.

BY-^s, BYE^s

by- /baɪ-/ is a prefix used in combination with nouns to mean secondary or local. It is sometimes hyphenated in BE, for example: 'by-election' and 'by-product'. Some of the 'by-' words are written in one word in BE, for example : 'byname' and 'byline', which is usual in AE. There are other words with a 'by-' prefix, where the adverb 'by' is placed first: A 'bygone age' (a time long ago) or 'bystander' (someone who is a passive witness to an event). 'Bye-' is an alternative BE spelling in 'bye-election' and 'bye-law'.

bye /baɪ/ *exclamation*, is an informal way of saying goodbye, and may be repeated as 'bye-bye'. See **GOODBYE**.

Cc

c^s, ca^s, circa^s

c and **ca** are both abbreviations for 'circa', and are read as 'circa'.

circa /'sɜːkə/ *preposition*, means approximately. 'Circa' and its abbreviations are restricted to certain specific contexts, such as job advertisements: 'circa £35k plus car' (meaning GBP 35 000 approx. plus car), and dates given on captions to museum exhibits: 'Norman, c 1100'. In running text, it is recommended to use 'about', 'roughly', 'approximately', or 'approx.', not 'circa' or its abbreviations. See **APPROXIMATION**.

CABIN, CHALET, LODGE, COTTAGE

cabin /'kæbɪn/ *noun*, means a small shelter or house made of wood. Cabins are located in remote areas: 'Our log cabin in the mountains is the place to get away from it all'.

chalet /'ʃæleɪ/ *noun*, means either a Swiss-style house for skiers to stay in, or, in the UK, a small cabin designed for holidaymakers as part of a leisure or holiday complex.

lodge /lɒdʒ/ *noun*, means many types of building. In the open-air context, there is both 'mountain lodge' and 'hunting lodge': 'We will stay the night in a mountain lodge in the Pyrenees'. A 'lodge' by itself also means a building for a porter or gardener on an estate.

cottage /'kɒtɪdʒ/ *noun*, means a simple small house, typically in the countryside: 'Her cottage in Wales had roses growing around the front door'. See **SUMMER HOUSE** ⟹ **HUT**.

CALM, TRANQUIL, TRANQUILLITY

calm /kɑːm/ *adjective & noun*, as an adjective, means not excited, worried or angry: 'People in a dangerous situation can often survive if they keep calm and do not panic'. 'Calm' is also used to describe the sea when it does not have large waves, or weather that is not stormy: 'After the storms it was good to have a week of calm seas'. As a noun, 'calm' means a peaceful situation: 'The riots had destroyed part of the city, but now there was an uneasy calm'. The phrase 'the calm before the storm' describes a situation where everyone is waiting for something dramatic to happen: 'After the company director resigned, share prices remained unchanged. Perhaps it was just the calm before the storm'.

tranquil /'træŋkwɪl/ *adjective*, describes a place or a situation that is quiet and peaceful: 'They were impressed by the view and by how tranquil everything looked'. This is a typical word to use in written English.

tranquillity /træŋ'kwɪlɪti/ *noun*, means a state of being tranquil: 'Walking in the mountains gave them a feeling of tranquillity'. An alternative AE spelling is 'tranquility'.

CAMPUS, GROUNDS (OF UNIVERSITIES)

campus /'kæmpəs/ *noun*, means the land and buildings of a university, which may be in different locations: 'The main campus can be reached by motorway'. In BE, a 'campus university' is one which is outside a town or city, with all teaching facilities, student accommodation and some shops on one site. The plural is 'campuses'. In AE, 'campus' is commonly used to refer to the land and buildings of a range of institutions, including schools and hospitals.

grounds /graʊndz/ *plural noun*, means the enclosed land or gardens around a large building, usually a large house: 'The grounds of Buckingham Palace have been opened to the public for the first time'. 'Grounds' also means an area of land or sea used for a specific purpose such as fishing or hunting: 'We would like to expand our fishing grounds'.
See **GROUNDS ⇨ CAUSE**.

CAN, COULD, MAY, MIGHT

can /kən, kæn/ *verb*, indicates ability: 'After six months of lessons, she can ride a horse'. It is also used for asking and giving permission in non-formal contexts: 'Can I use your phone, please?' 'Yes, of course you can'. In another sense, 'can' refers to something or someone whose behaviour is predictable: 'The train can get very full at rush hour'. It is also used with verbs expressing the five senses, i.e. hear, see, touch, taste, and smell: 'I can touch my toes easily'. 'Cannot' /'kænɒt, kə'nɒt/ is the usual negative form in writing and formal English. Note that it is normally written as one word. It is only written as two words, can not /'kæn 'nɒt/ when there is equal stress on both parts, as in: 'I can not agree, I can refuse to do it'. 'Can't' /kɑːnt/ is a contraction of 'cannot'. This

is an oral expression which should be avoided in formal English and in general written English for business or academic contexts.
See **CONTRACTIONS**.

could /kʊd/ *verb*, is the past of 'can', but also has other uses, including making a request: 'Could I use your phone, please?' This is more polite and formal than 'can', but note that unlike 'can' and 'may', 'could' is not used for giving permission. Use 'may' instead. 'Could' is also used either to make a suggestion: 'If you don't want to cook, we could go out for a meal'; or to show annoyance: 'How could you be so rude?' The negative form is 'could not', or informally, 'couldn't'.

may /meɪ/ *verb*, is used to ask for and to give permission in more formal contexts than 'can', and therefore 'may' sounds more polite: 'May I speak to the Ambassador, please?' 'May' is also used to express a possibility: 'The train may be late this morning because of engineering work on the line'. However, it is more common and less formal to use 'might' in this sense. The phrase 'may have' is used to indicate the possibility of a past action: 'I don't know where John is. He may have gone home'. Note that the only negative form is 'may not'.

might /maɪt/ *verb*, normally expresses possibility. 'Are you coming to the party?' 'Yes, I might'. The phrase 'might have' is used in a similar way to 'may have'. However, 'might have' also refers to different possible results from an action in the past: 'If I had not cleaned the kitchen, I might have managed to do the re-painting'. Note that the negative forms are 'might not' and, less formally, 'mightn't'.

CAN, TIN (*NOUN*)

can /kæn/ *noun*, is a sealed metal container holding drink, or in AE, drink or food: 'Three cans of cola'. Other types of can may be made of non-metallic materials: 'Both the watering can and the petrol can were made of plastic'.

tin /tɪn/ *noun*, is uncountable when referring to the metal itself (chemical symbol Sn): 'The box was not very strong as it was made out of tin'. However, it is countable when used to mean a sealed metal container for food: 'There was only a tin of beans in the cupboard'. 'Tin' is also a food container used for roasting or baking food, such as a 'cake tin'.

CANAL, CHANNEL

canal /kə'næl/ noun, means an artificial waterway for the passage of ships or the transport of irrigation water: 'The Suez Canal was nationalized by Egypt'. The word is also used medically for the 'alimentary canal' and the 'birth canal'.

channel /'tʃænəl/ noun, means a natural length of water that typically joins seas and oceans: 'The English Channel links the North Sea to the Atlantic Ocean'. 'Channel' is often used in the context of communications: 'You will need to find out through official channels. Note that the verb forms 'channelled' and 'channelling' in BE are spelt 'channeled' and 'channeling' in AE.

CANCEL, ANNUL, INVALIDATE

cancel /'kænsl/ verb, means to decide or announce that a planned event will not take place: 'After their defeat in the elections, the planned party celebrations were cancelled'. See ADJOURN.

annul /ə'nʌl/ verb, is a legal term meaning to officially declare that something is no longer legally valid: 'The president declared that the elections had been unfair and had to be annulled'.

invalidate /ɪn'vælɪdeɪt/ verb, means to make a thing officially unacceptable. 'Because of his criminal record, the candidate's selection was invalidated'. The stress is on the second syllable. See INVALID.

CAPITAL^S, CAPITOL^S

capital /'kæpɪtl/ noun, means the principal city in a country that is usually the seat of government. As an uncountable noun, it can refer to money that is invested: 'Security for your capital is our first priority'. 'Capital' is also used in the expression 'capital punishment', meaning execution by order of law.

capitol /'kæpɪtl/ noun, is a building where the legislature of each state in the US meets: 'There was a fire in the state capitol last month'. More famous, however, is The Capitol, which refers to the building in Washington DC where the US Congress meets.

capital letters

always capitalize:

- **proper nouns or adjectives**

Always use initial capital letters for proper nouns and adjectives derived from proper nouns (a proper noun is the name and title of a specific person, a company, institution, place, location, country, month, day, or a holiday). For example: '... he is Professor Henrik from Imperial College' '... Central and Eastern Europe' '... French Canadian' '... in late December on the Friday after Boxing Day'. See NORTH. See SOUTH. See EAST. See WEST.

- **acronyms and abbreviations**

Use capitals for all the letters in abbreviations and many acronyms: a VIP ticket

But note that the plural of an abbreviation or acronym has a lower case 's': All the ISDNs in the file.

- **in reports**

Words like appendix, chapter, equation, figure, section, and table are capitalized when followed by a number or letter: Equation 3-2; Section 4.2.

never capitalize:

- Names of elements in mid position: This is a mixture of iron, aluminium and copper.
- Names of methods, unit symbols (except for the proper name part): pattern recognition, kilometre, degree Celsius.

capitalization: the king or the King?

- Both are possible. When referring to a specific person, capitalize King, Queen, Prince, Bishop, Ambassador, Professor and similar titles. References to the institution such as the Crown and the Monarchy are capitalized. However, if a general group is being referred to, use lower case: all the kings of Spain; all the professors in the Department. A capitalized reference to the Prime Minister means a specific person, but just like a typical prime minister means like many of them, and is not capitalized.
- This is also the general pattern to follow with parts of recognized political units. Thus, Northern Territory, in Australia, is capitalized but northern Queensland is not, as the latter refers to a general area, not a defined political unit. Capitalization is correct for the West as a force in American History, the West Bank, the West

Country in the UK and *the West* when it refers to North America and Europe. Otherwise, *west* is lower case when the direction towards the setting sun is being referred to: *they moved west*. Referring simply to *the South* may mean different things to different people: the SE part of the USA to many Americans, the developing countries to some and the southern hemisphere to others.

- Words that are derived from a geographical name where there is a distant connection with the original place are written in lower case. Examples: *bohemian* (meaning a lifestyle), *italics* (print font), and *morocco* (fine leather). Note that these words are used alone. When such words are used in fixed phrases like *Danish pastry*, *French window*, *Arabic numerals*, and *Roman numerals*, many modern BE dictionaries recommend upper case for the nationality word. See **NATIONALITY WORDS**.

capitalization in report and publication titles

- **titles of books and reports**

The general standard in scientific and academic work is to use upper case for the first letter of the main words in the titles of books and reports. Use lower case for *a, an, the, and, or, for, nor* and prepositions, unless they are the first or last word in a title. Examples: *The New Oxford Dictionary of English*; *The History of the New West*.

- **chapters and sections**

In scientific and academic papers, reports and doctoral theses, there are few general standards about when to use capitals in chapter or section headings. Follow the Guidelines for Authors of the specific journal, or the house style of the organization.

- **brochures, press material, web**

Many people feel that capital letters shout at the reader, and that when capitals are optional, titles without capitals are softer and easier to read. Thus sales brochures, press material and text on the web show a clear movement away from capitals in titles.

- **hyphenation and capitalization in report and publication titles**

The general rule is to capitalize only the first element in the hyphenated phrase: *Low-pressurized Aircraft Design* and *Near-critical Values*. This also applies when the second

element in a hyphenated phrase modifies the first word or both elements are parts of the same word: *Moscow's English-speaking Community* and *Measuring X-ray Radiation*.

See **HYPHENATION IN INDIVIDUAL WORDS**.
See **HYPHENATION IN COMPOUNDS**.

CARE ABOUT, CARE FOR

care about /ˈkeər əbaʊt/ *verb*, means to be interested in or concerned about somebody or something: 'He did not care about other people'.

care for /ˈkeə fər/ *verb*, means to look after: 'He is caring for three orphans in India'. In the negative, it can also be a formal way of expressing disapproval: 'I do not care for your sense of humour'. Note that the question 'Would you care for a/some ...?' is a polite way of offering something to someone: 'Would you care for something to drink?'
See **WANT ⇨ WISH**.

CAREFUL, CAUTIOUS

careful /ˈkeəfʊl/ *adjective*, means paying attention or thought to an activity in order to avoid damage or injury: 'We passed some overgrown roses and were careful not to let the thorns rip our clothes'. In another sense, 'careful' means paying considerable attention: 'Henry is a very careful driver and has never had any problems in heavy traffic'.

cautious /ˈkɔːʃəs/ *adjective*, means being 'careful' about things that are said or done to avoid mistakes: 'When the reporter asked about the financial situation, the company spokesperson was deliberately cautious'. A person who is cautious does not take risks: 'John is such an extremely cautious driver that he is a menace on the road'.

CARELESS, CASUAL

careless /ˈkeələs/ *adjective*, relates to physical activity where a lack of attention causes errors or mistakes: 'We were careless and the roses ripped Anne's silk dress'. 'Careless' is often followed by 'with' when referring to objects that someone owns: 'He is extremely careless with his credit card'.

casual /ˈkæʒʊəl/ *adjective*, relates to attitudes such as showing a lack of care or thought, or seeming to be unworried: 'She appeared so casual when she told us that she had lost her job'. 'Casual' is often combined with 'about': 'She was furious that he was so casual about her silk dress being ruined'. 'Casual' is also used before a noun in phrases like 'casual dress' (informal clothes) and 'casual worker' (temporary worker).

CASH MACHINE, HOLE IN THE WALL, AUTOMATED TELLER MACHINE

cash machine /'kæʃ mə,ʃiːn/ means an automatic machine that enables users to withdraw cash or carry out other banking services using a bank card: 'At last, a cash machine that works'. Other terms for the same thing are 'cash dispenser' and 'cash point'. See **CASH CARD ⇨ BANK CARD**.

hole in the wall /'həʊl ɪn ðə 'wɔːl/ is an informal BE term for a 'cash machine'. It refers to the fact that the machine is located in a wall, usually of a bank.

automated teller machine /'ɔːtəmeɪtɪd 'telə məʃiːn/ means a 'cash machine'. This is a formal term in BE and is commonly used in AE. It is abbreviated as ATM.

CAST[s], CASTE[s]

cast /kɑːst/ *noun & verb*, as a noun means the actors in a play. 'Cast' can take either a singular or plural verb: 'After two seasons on Broadway, the cast was/were very tired'. As with other collective nouns, the singular verb focuses on the group as a unit, and the plural verb focuses on the individual members. As a verb, 'cast' can mean to recruit suitable actors for a specific play or film: 'They are going to start casting in the autumn'. It also means to form something in a mould: 'The statue was cast in bronze'. The simple past and past participle forms are the same as the infinitive.

caste /kɑːst/ *noun*, is a hereditary social system in Hinduism. In a wider context it means any system where one social group has exclusive advantages: 'The training of the diplomatic corps often helps to breed a special caste'.

CAUSE, REASON, GROUNDS

cause /kɔːz/ *noun*, is the person or thing that makes something happen. This is expressed by 'the cause (of)'. 'Contaminated drinking water is a common cause of disease'. 'Cause' also means a principle or movement to which there is great commitment: 'Many students volunteered to fight for the environmental cause'.

reason /'riːzn/ *noun*, is the explanation of why something happened. 'Reason' is used here in phrases like 'the reason for' (+ noun phrase or verb), or 'the reason why' (+ verb): 'The principal reason for the disease is the contaminated water'. See **PRETEXT ⇨ EXCUSE**.

grounds /graʊndz/ *noun*, are the reason for an action or thought : 'The Minister of Health resigned on the grounds of inadequate support for her policies'. 'Grounds' is usually used with a plural verb. See **GROUNDS ⇨ CAMPUS**.

-cede, -ceed, -sede

- Words with these suffixes are often misspelt, but the pronunciation is /-siːd/ in them all.

  -cede is the normal spelling in almost all words ending with this syllable: *precede, recede*.

  -ceed is used in a few words such as: *exceed, proceed* and *succeed*.

  -sede is used in only one word: *supersede*.

CELLAR, BASEMENT

cellar /'selər/ *noun*, means a room below ground level that is typically used for storing things. A cellar is not used for accommodation: 'He has an excellent cellar for his woodworking tools'. In modern usage, a 'wine cellar' need not be underground.

basement /'beɪsmənt/ *noun*, means a whole storey of a house that is partly or entirely below ground level, and which can be used for accommodation: 'The basement flat is often the cheapest one in a house'.

CELSIUS, CENTIGRADE

Celsius /'selsɪəs/ and **centigrade** /'sentɪgreɪd/ are both names for the temperature scale in which water boils at 100 degrees and freezes at 0 degrees at normal atmospheric pressure. The abbreviation 'C' is used for both. 'Celsius' is the normal term in technical and scientific contexts for giving temperatures. It is also the standard term elsewhere when stating the temperature. 'Celsius' is capitalized, as it is derived from the inventor of the scale, Anders Celsius, an 18th century Swedish astronomer.

centigrade is a French 19th century term for the 'Celsius' scale of temperature. Modern BE dictionaries often recommend that people use 'Celsius' not 'centigrade' when giving the temperature.

CELT, CELTIC

Celt /kelt/ *noun*, in the British context refers to the earliest known inhabitants of the British Isles, whose culture now survives mainly on the western fringes of Great Britain and in Ireland. 'Celt' was formerly often spelt 'Kelt', which is reflected in the pronunciation.

Celtic /'keltɪk/ *adjective*, is derived from 'Celt'. There are two exceptions to the pronunciation with initial /k/: these are the names of the Glasgow and Belfast football clubs originally founded by Catholic organizations, which are both pronounced /'seltɪk/.

CEMENT, CONCRETE, PLASTER

cement /sɪ'ment/ *noun & verb*, as a noun, is a grey lime-based powder that can be mixed with sand and water to make bricks stick together, or to make durable floors: 'Don't walk there, we have just laid a cement floor in the garage'. Both as a noun and a verb, 'cement' can also refer to things that join people, organizations, countries etc. together: 'The meeting was called to try to cement the relations between the two groups in the party'.

concrete /'kɒŋkriːt/ *noun & adjective*, as a noun, means a building material made from mixing cement and sand or small stones. 'Concrete' can be used to make numerous building elements and can also be reinforced with steel or iron rods: 'Many of the concrete tower blocks built in the 1960s are being demolished'. As an adjective, it can refer either to things that are built of concrete such as a concrete bridge, or in a wider sense, to things that are based on real, tangible facts, not ideas: 'The police finally had enough concrete evidence to charge the suspect'.

plaster /'plɑːstər/ *noun & verb*, as a noun, is a substance used for coating walls and ceilings to give a smooth surface: 'The cottage has plaster on all the interior walls and ceilings'. As a verb, this means either to cover a wall with 'plaster' or to cover any surface with objects. Note that this latter meaning has hostile overtones: 'She has plastered the wall with all her posters'.

CENSOR^S, SENSOR^S, CENSER^S, CENSURE

censor /'sensər/ *noun & verb*, as a noun, means a moral judge, or a person who removes objectionable words or scenes from a book, play or film: 'The censor cut so much out of the film that it was difficult to follow'. As a verb, 'censor' means to remove items from a play, film, book, letter or other document which is regarded as unacceptable for any reason: 'Letters sent by prisoners from prison are always censored'.

sensor /'sensər/ *noun*, usually means a device that senses movement or light: 'The fire alarm goes off every time a guest has a shower in that room. We must adjust the sensor'.

censer /'sensər/ *noun*, means a holder for incense, which is often swung on a chain in church.

censure /'senʃər/ *noun & verb*, are both used in parliamentary life to refer to negative criticism: 'The House passed a vote of censure and stopped the government's plans to change taxation law'.

CENSUS, CONSENSUS

census /'sensəs/ *noun*, is an official count, usually of a population: 'The next British census will be in 2011'.

consensus /kən'sensəs/ *noun*, means agreement that is reached in a group. Avoid the term 'general consensus', as a 'consensus' has to be general. Note the spelling.

CENTENARY, CENTENNIAL

centenary /sen'tiːnəri/ *noun & adjective*, means a 100th anniversary of a significant event. This is the BE form: 'The company celebrated its centenary in 2002'. Note that the second syllable is pronounced 'teen'. See **BICENTENARY**. See **CENTURY** ⇨ **MILLENNIUM**.

centennial /sen'tenɪəl/ *noun & adjective*, is the AE equivalent of 'centenary'. Note the correct spelling of 'centennial', and that the second syllable is pronounced 'ten'.

CENTRE, MIDDLE

centre /'sentər/ *noun & verb*, means a precise midpoint: 'The town was in the centre of Spain'. In an urban context, going into the centre means moving towards the main part of a town or city (AE downtown). As a verb, 'centre' means to place something at the centre. The AE spelling of both noun and verb is 'center'.

middle /'mɪdl̩/ *noun*, means somewhere in the central area, and is slightly less precise than 'centre': 'She was somewhere in the middle of the forest'. Note that 'middle' can also be used figuratively to mean in the process of doing something: 'I can't answer the door because I'm in the middle of washing my hair'.

CENTRE IN — CHAIR

CENTRE IN, CENTRE ON, REVOLVE AROUND

centre in /'sentər ɪn/ *verb*, is used in the passive to refer to the place where an activity or event is concentrated: 'The computer industry is still centred in Silicon Valley'.

centre on /'sentər ɒn/ *verb*, means to focus attention on an event, situation or concern and is often used in the passive: 'Every fourth year global attention is centred on the Olympic Games'. Careful writers avoid 'centre around', as a central point cannot go around something else.

revolve around /rɪ'vɒlv əraʊnd/ *verb*, means to move in a circular orbit, like a planet around a star. In a figurative sense it means to treat a person or thing as the most important element: 'His entire life revolved around one thing – Manchester United'.

CEREAL⁵, SERIAL⁵

cereal /'sɪərɪəl/ *noun*, is a general term for grain. In this context, it is often used in the plural: 'The price of cereals is going up'. It also means a type of breakfast food, and in this context it is singular: 'This cereal is an old favourite'.

serial /'sɪərɪəl/ *noun & adjective*, as a noun is a radio or TV programme that is broadcast in instalments: '*Lord of the Rings* was broadcast as a 26-part radio serial'. As an adjective, 'serial' describes a phenomenon that happens repeatedly and in the same way, such as a 'serial killer'.

CERTAIN, SURE

certain /'sɜːtn̩/ *adjective*, refers to something that you can rely on happening and being true: 'I am certain that the weather will be good tomorrow'. This means that there is little doubt that the weather will be good. See **SATISFIED**.

sure /ʃʊər/ *adjective*, is used to express a degree of confidence that something will happen: 'I am sure that there will be good weather for the beach tomorrow'. As this is a belief, not a conviction, many people use phrases like 'completely sure' to convey that something is certain.

CERTIFIED, CHARTERED, CHARTED

certified /'sɜːtɪfaɪd/ *adjective*, means that someone's qualifications are officially recognized: 'He was a certified accountant with twenty years of experience'. Ships, planes and films are also 'certified' by authorized bodies. In another sense, 'certified' means someone who has been officially declared insane. See **MAD**.

chartered /'tʃɑːtəd/ *adjective*, describes a member of a professional organization appointed by a Royal Charter: 'She was the youngest chartered engineer in the company'. Note that a 'chartered accountant' in the UK is the equivalent of a 'certified accountant' in the US. In another sense, a ship or plane that is hired is described as 'chartered': 'Chartered yachts available on a monthly basis'.

charted /'tʃɑːtɪd/ *verb*, is the past tense and past participle of 'chart', meaning to plan a course at sea: 'They charted a course which would avoid the most dangerous waters'. See **CHART ⇨ MAP**.

> '*The ship was certified as seaworthy by Lloyds. Unfortunately, the captain was also certified by a medical specialist.*'

CF., REF.

cf. /siː 'ef/ *abbreviation*, means compare with. It is used in writing to refer a reader to another book or part of the same present book or report : 'Cf. pages 12 to 24'. This is read as 'see eff'.

ref. /'refərəns, ref/ *abbreviation*, means reference. It is used in business English to refer to something in a document: 'We refer to our order, ref. 12345, and your invoice dated 2004-08-12'. This is read as 'reference'. Note that 'ref' (without a stop) is an informal abbreviation for 'referee': 'The ref must be blind not to have seen that blatant foul right in front of the goal'. This is read as 'ref'. See **RE**. See **REFEREE**.

CHAIR, CHAIRPERSON, CHAIRMAN, CHAIRWOMAN (MEETINGS)

chair /tʃeər/, **chairperson** /'tʃeəpɜːsn̩/ *noun*, means either someone who is in charge of a meeting, or the position of being in charge: 'The delegates were all welcomed to the

41

meeting by the chair'. 'Chair' is a neutral term that avoids the sexist language that is found in the term 'chairman'. 'Chairperson' is another neutral alternative. See **SEXIST LANGUAGE**.

chairman /ˈtʃeəmən/ *noun*, means the person in charge of a meeting, and can be either a man or a woman: 'Madam Chairman' is not impossible but 'chair' or 'chairperson' is a neat way of avoiding this strange phrase.

chairwoman /ˈtʃeəwʊmən/ *noun*, must be a female who is chairing a meeting.

CHANGE, ALTER, MODIFY

change /tʃeɪndʒ/ *verb*, means either to become different: 'She has changed so much since I last saw her'; or to make things different: 'We need to change a lot of things to make this town into a safer place'. It also has a number of other meanings including to replace things, such as a tyre or clothes, or to exchange money: 'He changed some dollars into euro'. 'Change' also means to move from one train or bus to a connecting train or bus: 'Change at Lille for Brussels'.

alter /ˈɔːltər/ *verb*, means to change the appearance or character of something, rather than to replace it completely: 'At night, the town centre is completely altered'. It also means to make changes to clothes: 'His clothes will need to be altered now that he's lost weight'.

modify /ˈmɒdɪfaɪ/ *verb*, also means become different in the sense of making something more suitable or efficient: 'This car engine has been radically modified to suit the new pollution regulations'.

'We have a room where you can change your baby.' (Cafe notice)

CHAPTER, SECTION (REPORTS)

chapter /ˈtʃæptər/ *noun*, is the basic structural unit in long reports and theses. 'Chapter' is capitalized when it is followed by a number: 'This is discussed in Chapter 4', but not otherwise: 'The present chapter contains the conclusions'.

section /ˈsekʃn̩/ *noun*. In short reports, a section is the basic structural unit: 'See Section 1 and Section 4'. Note that this is capitalized when it is followed by a number, but not otherwise. In long reports use 'section' for all levels below 'chapter': 'See Sections 1.2, 1.3.2, and 3.2.1.4'.

CHEAP, INEXPENSIVE

cheap /tʃiːp/ *adjective*, always means low in cost, but it can also suggest poor quality as well: 'She was wearing a cheap dress'. As price is the cost expressed as a number, careful writers will avoid a combination such as 'cheap price'. Objects, such as vegetables, hats and cars may be 'cheap', but their price is described as 'low' or 'reasonable'.

inexpensive /ˌɪneks'pensɪv/ *adjective*, also means low in cost. An inexpensive item may cost the same as a cheap one, but it is often a better choice of word as it avoids the poor quality connotation: 'She was wearing an inexpensive dress'.

CHEQUE^S, CHECK^S, CONTROL

cheque /tʃek/ *noun*, is only used in BE and means a bank order: 'He felt his pockets to see whether he still had his cheque book'. This is spelt 'check' in AE. See **BANKNOTE**.

check /tʃek/ *verb & noun*, as a verb, means to examine and make sure either that something is accurate or that its quality and condition are satisfactory: 'We will check if the car has started to rust'. In BE 'check' can mean to inspect something. In AE it also means to deposit something. Thus, 'to check your bag' may cause some transatlantic confusion. As a noun, 'check' means the examination of something. A 'check-up' means an examination or inspection: 'His doctor gave him a thorough check-up'.

control /kənˈtrəʊl/ *verb*, means to have power over other people or things, often in order to influence behaviour or action: 'She controlled the committee by threatening to reveal their corruption'. It can also mean to stop oneself from doing something: 'She controlled her anger with difficulty'.

CHILDLIKE, CHILDISH

childlike /ˈtʃaɪldlaɪk/ *adjective*, means having the qualities of a child, or describes something that is typical of a child: 'He talked about his fast new car with childlike enthusiasm'. This is nearly always a positive word.

childish /ˈtʃaɪldɪʃ/ *adjective*, means having the qualities of a child or something that is typical of a child: 'I knew from the childish handwriting that the note was from my young nephew'. This is a neutral term in this context. However, when it is applied to adults, 'childish' means 'immature', and is always disapproving: 'My boss often plays childish jokes on his staff'.

CHINESE, CHINAMAN

Chinese /tʃaɪˈniːz/ *noun & adjective*, is the correct term to mean the people of China: 'We met ten Chinese doctoral students'. It can also refer to the language and culture of China. In informal BE, 'a Chinese' may be either a meal of Chinese food, or a Chinese restaurant. See **NATIONALITY WORDS**.

Chinaman /ˈtʃaɪnəmən/ *noun*, as a reference to a native of China is old-fashioned and offensive.

CHIPS, CRISPS

chips /tʃɪps/ *noun*, is the BE term for potatoes that are sliced into narrow strips and fried: 'Fish and chips is one of the national dishes in Britain'. In AE, chips are called 'French fries'.

crisps /krɪsps/ *noun*, is the BE term for wafer-thin potatoes fried and served as a snack: 'They enjoyed a pint and a packet of crisps in the pub'. In AE, 'crisps' are called 'potato chips'.

CHOOSE, SELECT, PICK

choose /tʃuːz/ *verb*, means to decide a preference, often between only two items: 'Choose the strong cheese as the mild looks rather expensive'. The past tense is spelt 'chose' /tʃəʊz/ (rhymes with 'shows') and the past participle is 'chosen' /ˈtʃəʊzn/ (rhymes with 'frozen').

select /sɪˈlekt/ *verb*, means to decide something carefully: 'The company took three weeks working out whom to select as sales manager'. 'Select' is used with more than two possibilities.

pick /pɪk/ *verb*, means to decide a preference among more than two things. It is less formal than 'choose' or 'select', and suggests a more random procedure than 'choose' or 'select': 'Pick any number between 1 and 36'. In another sense, 'pick' means to gather fruit, vegetables etc., that grow above the ground: 'He picked the berries and she picked the peas'.

CHRISTMAS⁵, XMAS⁵, NOEL, YULETIDE, BOXING DAY

Christmas /ˈkrɪsməs/ *noun*, is the Christian festival in late December. Note that the preposition 'on' is used for specific days: 'on Christmas Eve', but 'at' with the festival name: 'at Christmas'.

Xmas /ˈkrɪsməs/ *noun*, means and is read as 'Christmas'. This is an informal expression that is only used in commercial or casual writing.

Noel /nəʊˈel/ *noun*, is the French word for Christmas, used in English particularly in Christmas carols: *The First Noel*, and on Christmas greetings cards. The French spelling, Noël, is not used in English.

Yuletide /ˈjuːltaɪd/ *noun*, means the Christmas festival. This is classified as an archaic term for Christmas.

Boxing Day /ˈbɒksɪŋ deɪ/ is the day after Christmas Day. The term has nothing to do with the sport of boxing, but comes from 'Christmas Box', the tradition of giving a small gift to people such as those who deliver newspapers or provide other services during the year. This is specifically a BE term.

CITE⁵, SITE⁵, SIGHT⁵

cite /saɪt/ *verb*, means to refer to or quote: 'He cited a famous passage from *Hamlet*'. When citing a word or phrase in running text, distinguish it by means of inverted commas or the use of italics – but not both. 'Cite' is frequently used in legal contexts.

site /saɪt/ *noun & verb*, as a noun, means the area of ground where a building or town will be located: 'This is the site for the new laboratory'. As a verb, this means to locate: 'This is where they have planned to site the new office'.

sight /saɪt/ *noun*, refers to vision or the capacity to see something: 'The boat was just in sight near the harbour wall'. 'Sight' is often used figuratively, and expressions like 'the end of the course was in sight' are frequently used. A 'sight for sore eyes' refers to a very surprising but welcome sight.

'A site for sore eyes.'
(Student essay)

CITY, TOWN

city /'sɪti/ *noun*, usually means more than just a large town. It may have 'civic status' which is granted by the monarch, as in Britain, or by the state, as in the US. Most cities have a cathedral and/or a university. Size is usually, but not always, important. London's financial centre, the City of London, has over a million people working there, but has an area of only one square mile and a population of about 6000. When 'city' is used to mean the City of London, 'city' is capitalized and requires the definite article: 'He is something in the City'. There are also quite small cities in the American West. In other parts of the English-speaking world, many large towns are called 'city' without any legal rights or royal charter.

town /taʊn/ *noun*, is often used for places that are larger than villages but smaller than cities. Sometimes part of a city is called a 'town', as in 'the old town'. The expression 'going into town' means going into the centre, where the shops and other businesses are concentrated. 'Town' is also used in compound adjectives. For example, 'small-town' could refer to small towns in general or to narrow-minded values. See **VILLAGE**.

CIVIC, CIVICS, CIVIL

civic /'sɪvɪk/ *adjective*, relates to a town or city, particularly its administration: 'The tourist office is in the civic centre'. In another sense, 'civic' relates to the activities and duties of those living in a town or local area: 'The mayor was the natural centre of civic life'.

civics /'sɪvɪks/ *noun*, means the study of the rights and duties of citizens: 'Civics is taught well at that college'. Note that this takes a singular verb and follows the pattern of other nouns with '-ics' endings. See **-ICS**.

civil /'sɪvɪl/ *adjective*, means matters concerning ordinary citizens as opposed to religious or military groups. 'Civil' also means behaving correctly and politely. It is a fairly formal word: 'I will speak to you when you have learned to be more civil'. Typical terms which include 'civil' are 'civil war', which refers to war between citizens of a country; 'civil aviation' in contrast to military activities; and 'civil rights', the political and social rights of a citizen.

CLASSIC, CLASSICAL

classic /'klæsɪk/ *adjective*, refers either to lasting high quality: 'He was wearing a suit with a classic cut'; or to something that is typical: 'A classic example of the Oedipus complex'.

classical /'klæsɪkl/ *adjective*, refers to certain historical genres or periods as in 'classical music' or 'classical literature' (Latin and Greek). Many films like *Casablanca* can be described as 'classic', but only a film about life in ancient Rome or Greece will be 'classical'.

CLEAN, CLEANSE

clean /kliːn/ *verb & adjective*, as a verb, means the act of removing dirt and dust by washing or rubbing: 'He cleaned the windows and the floor before lunch'. As an adjective, this refers to the state of not being dirty: 'The house was extremely clean and tidy'. Things that are not harmful or offensive are also 'clean': 'We all want clean air'; 'The show was just good clean fun'.

cleanse /klenz/ *verb*, means removing all impurities. Thus, when a wound is cleansed this is a more thorough process than 'clean': 'The wound was cleansed with disinfectant'. 'Cleanse' is used figuratively to mean free from guilt: 'Cleanse us of our sins'. Advertisers often use 'cleanse' to help sell cleaning liquids and skin treatment products.

cliché

• A cliché is a phrase or idea that has been used so much that it has lost all or much of its value. Typical examples are parts of, or entire proverbs or sayings. Examples: *Many hands make light work, Dead as a doornail, For love or money, A stitch in time saves nine, Don't count your chickens before they're hatched*. Many modern style guides point out that using a cliché or two is not the end of the world. They can scarcely be avoided and are known ways of reinforcing an idea. Many modern phrases like *bottom line, rain check* are used widely, and a few are included in this book. For some, these phrases are new, for others they are clichés. It is best not to overdo the use of the cliché as too many of them make what is said appear trite and unexciting. Consider the example of a sports broadcast that contained twelve clichés in just five minutes, including: *The home team may pull this off...It's a real pressure cooker down there...It's a nail biter...It's a see-saw game...At least the fans are getting their money's worth.*

- In business English it is best to avoid clichés if you can. It does not sound very impressive to end all correspondence with clichés like: 'Thanking you in advance' (perhaps you should thank people afterwards); 'Yours in anticipation of an early reply' (an alternative here is *Looking forward to your comments by the end of ...*). See **VERBIAGE**.

CLIMATIC, CLIMACTIC

climatic /klaɪˈmætɪk/ *adjective*, means something connected with the weather in a specific area: 'The climatic conditions in this part of Spain have changed over the last 100 years'.

climactic /klaɪˈmæktɪk/ *adjective*, refers to an event that is very exciting. This is nearly always restricted to written English: 'The climactic events in the murder scene in that play captivated the audience'.

CLOAKROOM, WARDROBE

cloakroom /ˈkləʊkruːm/ *noun*, means a room in a building where coats and luggage can be left: 'He asked the cloakroom attendant for his briefcase'. In AE, this is also called the checkroom. 'Cloakroom' may also be used as a polite term for toilet. In BE, a room in a public building with toilets is often called 'cloakroom': 'Gentlemen's cloakroom'. See **TOILET**.

wardrobe /ˈwɔːdrəʊb/ *noun*, means a large tall cupboard where a person's clothes are stored: 'They bought a beautiful fitted wardrobe for their new bedroom'. 'Wardrobe' also means a collection of clothes: 'Her spring wardrobe was bought in Paris'.

CLOCK, WATCH

clock /klɒk/ *noun*, means an instrument for showing the time that is larger than a wristwatch. The clock also means a measurement of time: 'They are running against the clock'. Informally and in a more general sense, 'clock' can refer to other measuring devices, such as a speedometer or mileometer: 'The car only had 25 000 km on the clock'.

watch /wɒtʃ/ *noun*, means a small instrument for showing the time that is worn on the wrist: 'She kept glancing at her expensive watch'. A 'watch' may gain or lose time: 'This hopeless watch loses two minutes a week'. 'Watch' is a short form for 'wristwatch'.

CLOTHES, CLOTHING, GARMENT, CLOTH

clothes /kləʊðz/ *noun*, means items that are worn to cover the body: 'Summer clothes are now in the shops'. 'Clothes' is always used in the plural, and a way to refer to the singular is an 'item of clothing'.

clothing /ˈkləʊðɪŋ/ *noun*, means either clothes collectively: 'In BE the clothing industry is often informally called the rag trade', or specific types of clothes: 'Sportswear and outdoor clothing'. A single item of 'clothes' is referred to as a piece/article/item of clothing: 'My beach clothes were stolen and now I only have one item of clothing left'.

garment /'gɑːmənt/ *noun*, means an item of clothing that is considered high quality or special: 'The garment was made of genuine silk'. This is a formal word. See **SUIT**.

cloth /klɒθ/ *noun*, means fabric made by weaving or similar processes: 'This cotton cloth will last for ever'. In this case it is uncountable and has no plural. When it refers to a piece of cloth for specific use, 'cloth' is often used in a compound: 'This is a beautiful tablecloth'. Here there is a plural form: cloths /klɒθs/.

'Ladies, leave your clothes here and spend the afternoon having a good time'. (Notice outside dry cleaners shop)

CO, CO-

Words beginning with *co-* fall into three groups:

- Without a hyphen, which is the usual spelling, as in: *cohabit*, *coincide*, *cooperate* and *coordinate*. Note that the latter two can be spelt with a hyphen in BE.
- With a hyphen in BE, often no hyphen in AE. These are words that are new or may be confusing. Here the sense is joint and mutual. Examples include: *co-driver*, *co-editor*, *co-pilot* and *co-worker*.
- With a hyphen in both BE and AE. This is found in some words when *co-* is followed by *o*. Examples: *co-opt*, *co-own*.

Note that hyphenation is to be used where two words can be confused. See **CO-RESPONDENT**. See **HYPHENATION IN INDIVIDUAL WORDS**

COAST, SHORE

coast /kəʊst/ *noun*, means a long stretch of land beside or near the sea or an ocean: 'The coast is so low that it is often flooded'. A related noun is 'coastline', which means the shape of the land along the edge of the sea. The informal phrase 'the coast is clear' usually has nothing to do with beaches in modern English and means that no one can see you: 'Run now: the coast is clear'. See **BEACH**.

shore /ʃɔːr/ *noun*, means the land on the edge of the sea, ocean or a lake: 'The shores of Lake Geneva are steeped in history'. A related noun is 'shoreline', which means the shape of the land along the edge of the sea or the lake. Note that when a ship is anchored 'off shore', this is

two words; but when activities such as banking or oil are referred to, 'offshore' is one word: 'The offshore oil industry is moving exploration into deeper waters'.

COLLECT, PICK UP

collect /kə'lekt/ *verb*, means to go to fetch a thing or a person: 'I will collect you at the airport'. This is a typical formal equivalent to the informal 'pick up'.

pick up /pɪk 'ʌp/ *verb*, means to collect, but this is an informal equivalent with a number of other meanings, one of which is to speak to a stranger in order to invite them to start a relationship. See **FORMAL ENGLISH**.

'The Ambassador was horrified at the letter from a student organization which offered to pick up his wife at the airport.'

collective nouns

- Collective nouns are those which have a singular form, but refer to things which by their nature contain more than one item, such as *bank*, *company*, *department*, *family*, *government*, *group*, and *team*. People have argued for many years about the rights and wrongs of using a singular or plural verb after a collective noun. For instance, should the newspaper headline read *England loses again* or *England lose again*? Most dictionaries suggest that both solutions are possible in BE, with slightly different meanings. When a singular verb is used, the emphasis is on the collective noun as a single unit, so that in the case of *England is winning*, the team of footballers is considered as one single entity. When a plural verb is used, the emphasis is on the individual players: *England are spread all over the pitch*. When a singular verb is used make sure that further references are also singular. Likewise with a plural verb: *The Conservative government was first elected in 1979. It then won four elections in a row*, or: *The Conservative government were first elected in 1979. They then won ...*. Note that collective nouns are always treated as singular in AE.

colon (:)

- Use a *colon* to make a break within a sentence in order to add a clause or phrase that gives more information about what has already been stated: *Take care when handling this liquid: it can burn your skin.* Note that the clause following the colon has a lower-case letter, not a capital. However, when the part of the sentence after the colon represents speech or a quotation, the first word after the colon is capitalized: *I've said it once and I'll say it again: This is just like home.*

- A colon is also used to show that something is to follow. This may be a summary, a complete sentence, a question or a list of items: *Three factors will play a major role in our development strategy: time, money, and skilled staff.* See **LISTS**. See **SEMI-COLON**.

colour words

- Words to describe colours are often used by advertisers to make products attractive. Thus, a car that is the colour of *bronzed sand with a metallic finish* sounds more attractive than one described as *brown*. Some manufacturers also have a colour associated with their products, like Ferrari (*red*), Levis (*faded blue*) and IBM (*dark blue*). Nevertheless, most colour words are free from commercial ownership. *Biscuit, marmalade* and *oyster* are examples of colour words that also describe objects. There may be problems using colour words in English to describe the colour of hair. See **BLOND**. See **GREY**.

- Colour words for *skin colour* are not easy to use without becoming guilty of linguistic racism. Collections of synonyms must be used with care in this tricky area. See **BLACK**. See **NATIVE AMERICAN**.

COMIC, COMICAL

comic /'kɒmɪk/ *adjective & noun*, as an adjective, means funny and amusing: 'He is a comic actor who has been very successful on TV'. It is also used in the phrase 'comic opera'. As a noun, a 'comic' is an alternative term for comedian: 'He is a stand-up comic'; and also a children's magazine, often containing cartoons, such as *Donald Duck*. See **FUNNY**.

comical /'kɒmɪkəl/ *adjective*, means unintentionally amusing: 'He is such a strange little man, and really quite comical'.

comma (,)

A comma is a punctuation sign that signals an interruption in a sentence. There are numerous rules, but the basic one is that commas should make a text easy to read. A rule of thumb which is often helpful is to place a comma at a point where someone reading the text aloud should pause, change intonation, or take a breath. So, if in doubt, read the text aloud and remember that readers have to breathe. If you want to express two ideas, sometimes a full stop is preferable to a comma.

 'Closing down, thanks to all our customers.' (Notice on a shop door.)

using commas with adverbs/adverb phrases

- Sentences sometimes start with a single adverb, a link word, or a phrase that states the manner, place, reason, or time in relation to the main statement that follows: *Suddenly, ...; In London, ...; In order to find the solution, ...; In 2005, ...* When speaking, the end of such units is signalled by intonation and a pause. In writing, readers are given the same signals by a comma at the end of these preliminary units. With no comma in this position, readers may be confused:

Compare:
Suddenly, rising prices are in the news (rising prices are now news), and:
Suddenly rising prices are in the news (prices that are rising suddenly are in the news).

Otherwise, adverbs in mid-sentence have a comma on both sides if this is a natural place to change the intonation or to breathe when reading aloud.

Compare:
The temperature was steady when, suddenly, there was an explosion and:
The temperature was probably too high.

using commas with adjectives in a series

- Use commas to separate two or more adjectives in a series, when each modifies the noun separately: *a fast, new laptop computer.* As *and* can be inserted between fast and new, both modify laptop computer. Thus a comma is required. If *and* is inserted between new and laptop, this does not make sense, so do not put a comma here.

using commas in lists before 'and'

- One rule in BE is to use commas in a list of items and insert *and* without a comma before the final item: *Our office equipment consists of a photocopier, a fax, three PCs, a printer and six filing cabinets.*

- As this form of punctuation can lead to confusion if the final item in the list contains *and*, some publishing houses follow the practice of Oxford University Press, inserting a comma (the *Oxford comma*) between all items in such lists. This makes the meaning absolutely clear: *The fax has the following function messages: Error, Out of paper, Repeat and Send, and Receive.* In AE, a comma is normal before 'and' in this type of list.

only use commas in non-defining clauses

- A defining clause, which is essential to the meaning of a sentence, is not separated by commas: *The new secretary who speaks excellent German works in the office upstairs* (there are several new secretaries, but only one who speaks excellent German).

- A non-defining clause gives additional information about a noun and is always placed within commas: *The new secretary, who speaks excellent German, works in the office upstairs* (there is only one new secretary). See **THAT**.

using commas with numbers

- According to some standardization bodies, the comma is not used as a divider in large numbers. For numbers above 9999, insert a space between each thousand. Examples: 3000   30 000   30 000 000

- By using a space and not a comma to divide thousands in English there is no risk of confusing those who use the comma as a decimal marker in their language. Example: *The weight is 11 856 kg.* This has only one meaning, whereas: *The weight is 11,856 kg* might be confusing.

'The new lightweight bike only weighs 11,856 kg.' (Advert)

COMMENT, COMMENTARY, COMMENTATE

comment /'kɒment/ *noun & verb*, as a noun, means an opinion or an explanation: 'We would like to hear your comments on the last election'. As a verb, 'comment' is followed by on or upon: 'Would you care to comment on the latest development?'

commentary /'kɒməntri/ *noun*, can mean either a written expression of opinion: 'This commentary on the recent bomb attacks tried to put the conflict into perspective'; or a spoken description of an event as it is happening. In this sense, it is very common in sport: 'The race commentary was virtually inaudible above the sound of the crowd'.

commentate /'kɒmənteɪt/ *verb*, means to provide a spoken commentary, generally on a sporting event: 'You need to think quickly when you are commentating on a football match, since everything happens so fast'.

COMMISSION, COMMITTEE

commission /kə'mɪʃn̩/ *noun*, means a percentage of a sale that is paid to an agent: 'He made a good living from commission sales'. It is also a task assigned to a person or company: 'The commission to build the palace came from the Royal Family'.

Commission /kə'mɪʃn̩/ *noun*, usually capitalized, means an officially appointed body with the authority to do something: 'The Securities and Exchange Commission'. In the

EU, the 'Commission' or 'European Commission' is the body responsible for initiating Union action and safeguarding the interests of the EU.

committee /kə'mɪti/ *noun*, means a group of people chosen by a larger group to discuss and make decisions on a specific subject: 'The committee decided to offer the title fight to Madrid'.

COMMIT, PERPETRATE, PERPETUATE

commit /kə'mɪt/ *verb*, means to carry out a crime, make a mistake, and also to send someone to prison or mental hospital: 'He was committed to a long term in prison'. 'Commit' can also mean to get involved in things, promise, or just remember something: 'Here is your PIN code: commit it to memory'. More formally, to 'commit oneself to' means to promise to follow a course of action or keep to an agreement: 'I am not going to sign this form because I do not want to commit myself to anything'.

perpetrate /'pɜːpɪtreɪt/ *verb*, means to carry out an illegal action or crime: 'Crimes are usually perpetrated against people'. This is a formal term.

perpetuate /pə'petjʊeɪt/ *verb*, means to cause something, such as a belief, to continue for a long time: 'Disputes over land rights have often been perpetuated for centuries'.

> *'Many children's cartoons perpetrate the myth that "boys don't cry".' (Student essay)*

COMMUNICATION, COMMUNICATIONS

communication /kəmjuːnɪ'keɪʃn/ *noun*, means the exchange of information by speech or in a letter or message. It can also be a formal term used in diplomacy and military contexts, or it can mean social contact, as in: 'Communication between the sexes is not always easy'.

communications /kəmjuːnɪ'keɪʃnz/ *noun*, is a means of connection (road, rail, or electronic) between people or places: 'The communications in this part of the country are poor'. Note that 'communications' has a plural verb when it means ways of transmission or transmitting ideas: 'There is so much static, communications are poor'. However, as a subject for study, it normally has a singular verb: 'Radio communications is a fascinating subject'.

COMPARE TO, COMPARE WITH, INCOMPARABLE

compare to /kəm'peə tə/ *verb*, is used to point out a resemblance between two people, things or situations: 'With his small eyes and thin face, he was often compared to a rat'. 'Compare to' is often used figuratively, as in Shakespeare's famous line: 'Shall I compare thee to a summer's day?'

compare with /kəm'peə wɪð/ *verb*, is used to show the similarity or dissimilarity between things that are usually in the same category: 'If you compare the sound of a woodpigeon with that of a cuckoo, you can hear the difference immediately'. One way to remember the difference between the two forms of 'compare' is to think of the symmetry in the letter 'w' in 'with', since 'compare with' often refers to things in the same category.

incomparable /ɪn'kɒmpərəbl/ *adjective*, means that something is without an equal in terms of quality or extent. Things that are 'incomparable' cannot be matched: 'Scoring that winning goal was an incomparable climax to his footballing career'.

COMPEL, COMPELLING, IMPEL, IMPULSIVE

compel /kəm'pel/ *verb*, means to force someone else to do something: 'The police had guns, and compelled him to surrender'.

compelling /kəm'pelɪŋ/ *adjective*, refers either to something that is very interesting that holds someone's attention: 'That book is a real page-turner, an utterly compelling read'; or to something that is completely convincing: 'The police presented some very compelling evidence'. See **COMPULSIVE**.

impel /ɪm'pel/ *verb*, refers to feeling forced to do something due to internal motivation: 'He claimed that it was the voices in his head that impelled him to steal'.

impulsive /ɪm'pʌlsɪv/ *adjective*, refers to sudden action or behaviour without careful consideration of the consequences: 'That flat was a very impulsive buy that has cost us too much'.

COMPETENCE, COMPETENCY, SKILL, PROFICIENCY, EXPERTISE

competence /'kɒmpɪtəns/ *noun*, means having the ability to do a task adequately but not necessarily outstandingly. As 'competence' does not indicate the quality involved, it may mean that a person has merely appropriate or sufficient skill: 'He was without enthusiasm, but showed adequate competence as an office worker'. On the other hand, a researcher with great competence demonstrates both the quality and skill of their work. 'Competence' is generally uncountable, although it can also be used as a countable noun to mean a skill that is required in order to perform a specific professional task. In this sense, 'competency' is the more common form.

competency /'kɒmpɪtənsi/ noun, is an alternative form for 'competence' in the sense of a specific skill required of an employee in order to do their job: 'The employee will acquire competency in a range of key skills'. 'Competency' is a countable noun; the plural form is 'competencies'.

skill /skɪl/ noun, means the ability to do something well. It is often combined with terms which underline the quality being referred to: 'Great skill and accuracy are required to do this job'.

proficiency /prə'fɪʃn̩si/ noun, means a more advanced level of ability than 'competence' or 'skill' in doing something in a particular field: 'Aircrew must demonstrate their proficiency in handling this type of navigation equipment before being permitted to land in fog'.

expertise /ekspə'tiːz/ noun, means expert skill or knowledge. It combines an understanding of both theory and practice: 'His expertise in programming is eagerly sought by several companies'.

COMPETITION, CONTEST, MATCH, CHAMPIONSHIP, TOURNAMENT

competition /kɒmpɪ'tɪʃn̩/ noun, means an event in which people compete against each other, often for prizes: 'They won the ballroom dancing competition'. The related verb is 'compete' /kəm'piːt/.

contest /'kɒntest/ noun, /kən'test/ verb, as a noun, has a similar meaning to 'competition'. However, 'contest' also refers to a competition for a title or role: 'There will be a strongly fought contest for the leadership'. As a verb, 'contest' means to be engaged in a competitive situation: 'He contested the leadership on several occasions'. Note the change of stress in this word from noun to verb.

match /mætʃ/ noun, means a number of things, including something that looks the same or very similar to something else: 'The couple were a good match for each other'. This idea is extended to the matching of skills in sporting events, such as a tennis match or a football match. Hence if one team is clearly inferior to its opponent, the verb 'outmatch' can be used.

championship /'tʃæmpɪənʃɪp/ noun, means a series of contests over a season. The purpose is to find a champion: 'The UEFA Championship qualifiers start in July'.

tournament /'tɔːnəmənt/ noun, is also a championship but is often of limited duration. The purpose of a tournament is to compete for an overall prize: 'This tennis tournament is going to make a lot of money'.

COMPETITOR, CONCURRENT

competitor /kəm'petɪtər/ noun, means someone or something that is involved in rivalry with another: 'Our nearest competitors are based on the US West Coast'.

concurrent /kən'kʌrənt/ adjective, means something that exists or is done at the same time: 'As these Olympic events were concurrent, only the TV viewers could watch them all'.

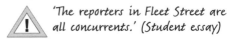

'The reporters in Fleet Street are all concurrents.' (Student essay)

COMPLEMENT^S, COMPLIMENT^S

complement /'kɒmplɪmənt/ noun, /'kɒmplɪment/ verb, as a noun, refers to something which, when added to something else, improves its quality or makes it complete. 'Complement' also means the required total or quota, particularly relating to the number of staff in a company. It is often used in the phrase 'the full complement': 'There is no need to continue recruiting, as we have the full complement of staff'. Note that the last syllable has a neutral vowel. As a verb, 'complement' means to add an element to make something complete or perfect: 'The fine port wine complemented a perfect meal'. As this word is often confused with its soundalike 'compliment', remember that the 'e' in the middle means 'something extra'. Note that there is a full vowel in the last syllable of the verb.

compliment /'kɒplɪmənt/ *noun*, /'kɒplɪment/ *verb*, as a noun, is a remark or action that expresses praise for something: 'Receiving the Oscar was a great compliment'. This word is often used in the phrase 'pay a compliment'. As a verb, it means to pay respect, praise, or say something admiringly: 'We complimented the conductor after the outstanding performance'. Note the difference in pronunciation between the noun and verb.

COMPLETE, FINISH, READY

complete /kəm'pliːt/ *verb & adjective*, as a verb, means either to finish something: 'He completed his doctoral work by defending his thesis'; or to make perfect: 'The paintings completed the harmony of the room'. 'Complete' also means to provide information on a form: 'Please complete your name and address and send the coupon to the following address'. As an adjective, 'complete' means having no part missing: 'He had been collecting the novels of Ian Fleming for years, and when he found a copy of *Moonraker*, his set was complete'. Careful writers should avoid the comparatives: 'more complete' or 'most complete'. See **ABSOLUTES & FUZZY ABSOLUTES**. See **TOTAL**.

finish /'fɪnɪʃ/ *verb*, means either to end something, as in: 'He finished his meal quickly', or to come to an end: 'The film finishes quite late'. 'Finish' lacks the idea of completing by rounding off or perfecting something. 'Finish' or 'finish off' mean to destroy, either physically or figuratively: 'Three hours of jogging almost finished him (off)'.

ready /'redi/ *adjective*, means either that a person has completed the process of preparing themselves for something: 'We were ready at 7', or that a thing is prepared for use: 'Lunch is ready'. 'Ready' also means easy to find and use, as in the phrase 'ready cash', which refers to coins and notes, rather than a cheque. 'The readies' is BE slang for cash.

COMPOSE, COMPILE (ARTISTIC, LITERARY WORK)

compose /kəm'pəʊz/ *verb*, means to combine elements together to form a whole such as a poem or symphony: 'He composed a beautiful poem while walking on the beach and looking at the seagulls'. The related noun is 'composition'.

compile /kəm'paɪl/ *verb*, means to use existing material from elsewhere in a new composition such as a CD, book, report or anthology of poetry: 'On the album they have compiled the best of their live recordings'. The related noun is 'compilation'.

COMPOSE OF, COMPRISE, CONSIST OF, INCLUDE

compose of /kəm'pəʊz əv/ *phrasal verb*, refers to a whole unit rather than to its individual components. It is usually found in the passive 'be composed of': 'The minority government is composed of three non-Socialist parties'.

comprise /kəm'praɪz/ *verb*, refers to a whole unit rather than to its components. Note that 'comprise' does not take 'of': 'Three parties comprise the minority government'. However, it is possible to use the passive phrase 'be comprised of': 'The minority government is comprised of three parties'.

consist of /kən'sɪst əv/ *verb*, refers to a whole unit: 'The computer package consists of a PC, a 17" screen, a keyboard, software, and user support'.

include /ɪŋ'kluːd/ *verb*, refers to a whole unit when the verb is used in the active form: 'The computer package includes user support and a free repair service'. When used in the passive, 'be included', the individual components are the subject not the entire unit: 'User support and a free repair service are included with this computer package'.

COMPULSIVE, COMPULSORY

compulsive /kəm'pʌlsɪv/ *adjective*, refers to behaviour caused by a strong impulse that is difficult to control: 'The TV series had its weak points, but the strong characterization made it compulsive viewing'.
See **COMPELLING ⇨ COMPEL**.

compulsory /kəm'pʌlsəri/ *adjective*, refers to behaviour and actions that have to be followed, according to a law or other official decision: 'In Britain, full-time education is compulsory between the ages of 5 and 16'.

CONFORM, CORRESPOND, COINCIDE

conform /kən'fɔːm/ *verb*, means to agree to an established pattern or idea: 'After a phase of rebellion, he eventually conformed to the rules'.

correspond /kɒrɪs'pɒnd/ verb, means to make an analogy: 'The spelling of aluminium in BE corresponds to the AE spelling aluminum'. In a formal sense, 'correspond with' means to write to someone.

coincide /kəʊ.ɪn'saɪd/ verb, means that two or more events match exactly in time or position: 'Thanks to careful planning, the venue of the conference and the trade fair coincided'.

CONGRESS, CONFERENCE, SYMPOSIUM, SEMINAR, WORKSHOP

congress /'kɒŋgres/ noun, is a large formal meeting where delegates discuss ideas. 'Congress' is capitalized in the USA, and other countries when referring to the law-making assembly of representatives: 'The US Congress is the name given to the House of Representatives and the Senate'.

conference /'kɒnfərəns/ noun, means a large formal meeting or gathering and is an alternative term for a 'congress': 'The last International UFO Conference produced little news'. The phrase 'to be in conference' means to be in a meeting where people are not expected to be disturbed: 'The directors are in conference with the lawyers' (note there is no definite article in this sense).

symposium /sɪm'pəʊzɪəm/ noun, means a small conference or meeting of experts on a particular issue. The plural is either 'symposia' or 'symposiums'. This is a formal word.

seminar /'semɪnɑːr/ noun, means a small meeting for teaching or training where the participants are expected to be active in discussions.

workshop /'wɜːkʃɒp/ noun, means a meeting on a specific theme involving practical work.

connotations

The meaning of a word is often more than its dictionary definition. These added values are termed its connotations. For example, if you are thinking about a male person who is above-average weight, it is possible to divide the connotations into three classes:

favourable: beefy, burly, chubby, stocky, well built

neutral: heavy, thickset

unfavourable: fat, paunchy, obese, gross, blubbery, elephantine

CONNOTE, DENOTE

connote /kə'nəʊt/ verb, means to suggest something implied or associated with the literal meaning of a term: 'A dog connotes a faithful friend and a lively pet'.

denote /dɪ'nəʊt/ verb, means to give the explicit meaning of something: 'The term dog denotes a member of the species canis familiaris'.

CONSERVATORY, CONSERVATOIRE

conservatory /kən'sɜːvətri/ noun, is a room attached to a house, but with glass walls and roof, used as a sun lounge. In AE it is also used as an alternative to 'conservatoire'.
See **SUMMER HOUSE ➪ HUT**.

conservatoire /kən'sɜːvətwɑːr/ noun, is a college for the teaching and study of the arts, principally classical music.

CONSERVE, PRESERVE

conserve /kən'sɜːv/ verb, means to protect. This is used especially for environmentally or culturally important things or places: 'After three years of drought, the country had to conserve its groundwater resources'.

preserve /prɪ'zɜːv/ verb, means to maintain something in its original or existing state: 'The remains of the mammoth had been preserved in the ice'. When referring to food, 'preserve' means to prevent decay: 'Fish used to be preserved in salt and then stored in barrels'.

CONSISTENT, CONSEQUENT, SUBSEQUENT

consistent /kən'sɪstənt/ adjective, refers to something which has unchanging standards: 'The quality of our paint is always consistent'. The phrasal verb 'be consistent with' means that something conforms to the same pattern or line of thinking as something else: 'This new evidence is consistent with what we already know about the criminal'.

consequent /'kɒnsɪkwənt/ adjective, means following as a result of something: 'The earthquake and its consequent destruction of the infrastructure will always be remembered'. A less formal alternative is 'resulting'.

subsequent /'sʌbsɪkwənt/ adjective, means happening after something else, but not as a result of it: 'Newspaper reports suggested he was unreliable, and subsequent events, when he was shown to have lied in court, proved it'.

CONTAGIOUS, INFECTIOUS

contagious /kən'teɪdʒəs/ *adjective*, refers to diseases that are transmitted by direct physical contact with a diseased person. 'Contagious' focuses on the person or animal that is diseased. When used figuratively, 'contagious' can describe both pleasant and unpleasant things, such as laughter and panic.

infectious /ɪn'fekʃəs/ *adjective*, refers to diseases that are spread by germs or viruses in the air or water: 'SARS is highly infectious'. 'Infectious' focuses on the agent that carries the disease: 'The drinking water was infectious'. When used figuratively, 'infectious' only describes pleasant things, such as laughter.

CONTAMINATION, POLLUTION

contamination /kəntæmɪ'neɪʃn/ *noun*, stresses the process of making something impure: 'The contamination in the drinking water was caused by sewage leaking into the reservoir'.

pollution /pə'ljuːʃn/ *noun*, is the state where the process of contamination is complete: 'There was pollution in the drinking water supply and it was declared non-drinkable'.

CONTENT, CONTENTS

content /kən'tent/ *adjective*, means in a state of satisfaction, happiness and peacefulness: 'She is very content with her new way of life in Greece'. Note that the stress is on the second syllable.

content /'kɒntent/ *noun*, means the amount of a particular component in a material or substance: 'What is the lead content of this petrol?' 'Content' also means the subject matter in a book, film or a talk: 'The content of the book was very poor despite its catchy title'. Note that the stress is on the first syllable.

contents /'kɒntents/ *noun*, is the material or substance inside a bottle or other type of container: 'She dropped her bag and the contents fell on the floor'. Note that a plural verb is used in this sense. 'Contents' takes a singular verb when it refers to the list of sections in a report, sometimes called the 'List of Contents': 'The contents is too long'.

CONTINUOUS, CONTINUAL

continuous /kən'tɪnjʊəs/ *adjective*, refers to an unbroken and uninterrupted sequence: 'This continuous noise from the factory is keeping me awake'.

continual /kən'tɪnjʊəl/ *adjective*, refers to something that either never stops or reoccurs frequently. Thus, 'continual noise' may be 'continuous', or it may be a noise which pauses from time to time. 'Continual' is often used to express annoyance: 'Every time I fall asleep, the continual noise from aircraft landing wakes me up'.

contractions

- Scientific and academic writing is in a style called formal English. This type of English does not allow contractions, except in written dialogue. Informal letters to friends and even informal emails often use contractions to stress the lack of formality. Examples of contractions including ***not*** are: *aren't, can't, couldn't, doesn't, don't, hasn't, haven't, isn't, wasn't, weren't, won't,* and *wouldn't.*
- Forms of the verb ***to be*** are contracted: *I'm, you're, he's, she's, it's, we're, they're* and *who's.*
- ***shall*** is not generally contracted, since it is mostly used as an emphatic first-person form.
- ***will*** is contracted in speech and written dialogue to *'ll: I'll, you'll, he'll, she'll, it'll, we'll,* and *they'll.*
- ***has*** is often contracted to *'s: 'John's got a new car'.* (See below for *is* and *has.*)

confusing contractions and their soundalikes

- ***it's*** (it is or it has) is often confused with the possessive ***its***. Compare: *It's time to land* (contraction), *the plane lost its rudder* (possessive).
- ***they're*** (they are) may be confused with the possessive ***their*** or even the adverb ***there*** (all of which may be soundalikes).
- ***you're*** (you are) may be confused with the possessive ***your*** (*You're late; has your watch stopped again?*)
- ***who's*** (who is or who has) may be confused with the possessive ***whose***. Compare: *Who's driving to town?* (contraction), *whose car is that?* (possessive).
- It is also necessary to be careful with ***is*** and ***has*** when used as auxiliary verbs, since their contracted forms are the same. Compare: *He's finished* (he is finished) and *He's finished* (he has finished). The context should make it clear which verb is being used, but if there is any potential ambiguity, it is safer to use the full form of the verb.
- Remember that the apostrophe in the contraction indicates that letters have been left out. See **APOSTROPHE**. See **FORMAL ENGLISH**.

CONTRARY, CONTRAST, DISTINCT

contrary /ˈkɒntrəri/ *adjective*, means different from something or against something. It is always followed by 'to': 'Contrary to expectations, the stock market fell all year'. Remember that there are two 'r's in the word, both of which should be pronounced.

contrast /ˈkɒntrɑːst/ *noun*, means a comparison between two things that are usually related but very different: 'There was a sharp contrast between the night frost and the burning sun at midday'. The corresponding verb 'contrast' /kənˈtrɑːst/ is stressed on the second syllable, with a neutral vowel in the first.

distinct /dɪsˈtɪŋkt/ *adjective*, refers to a recognizable difference between things that are similar: 'There was a distinct difference between how Italy and Great Britain prepared for the winter Olympics'.

CONVERSATION, CHAT

conversation /kɒnvəˈseɪʃn̩/ *noun*, means a talk that is usually social and friendly, often for the exchange of ideas and information: 'Television has killed the art of conversation'. Note that 'to make conversation' means to talk about neutral topics without any real purpose.
See **TALKS**.

chat /tʃæt/ *noun*, means friendly talk that is usually to exchange personal news: 'We had a long chat about our days at school'. This is an informal word. In computer use, 'chat' means discussion with others on the Internet, usually on a specific theme. Terms such as 'chat group' and 'chat room' have developed from this meaning.

CONVINCE, PERSUADE

convince /kənˈvɪns/ *verb*, means to make someone believe that something is true: 'The man convinced me that he was a prince'. In recent years 'convince' has started to mean to persuade: 'I don't like shopping, but my friends always convince me to go with them'.

persuade /pəˈsweɪd/ *verb*, means to make someone do something by giving good reasons or a convincing argument: 'The international pressure successfully persuaded the army to release the prisoners'.

COOPERATE, COLLUSION, COLLABORATE

cooperate /kəʊˌɒpəˈreɪt/ *verb*, means to act jointly or work towards the same end. It is a positive word that often indicates a willingness to work together: 'If we cooperate we will clean the house more quickly'. 'Cooperate' is the term to use for inviting someone to work on a joint venture: 'We are seeking a partner to cooperate in a new venture in Asia'. 'Cooperate' is not hyphenated in modern BE or in AE.

collusion /kəˈljuːʒn̩/ *noun*, means illegal or secret cooperation in order to cheat or deceive others. Terrorists may work 'in collusion' but scientists and students 'cooperate'. Use 'collusion' with care as it has strong negative associations: '"Scholastic dishonesty" includes, but is not limited to, cheating, plagiarism, collusion, falsifying academic records' (Institutional Rules on Academic Integrity, The University of Texas at Austin). The related verb is 'collude' /kəˈljuːd/, which is a formal word.

collaborate /kəˈlæbəreɪt/ *verb*, means to cooperate towards the production or creation of something that often involves joint scientific or literary activity: 'This play is the result of two distinguished Shakespearean producers collaborating'. Note that 'cooperate' and 'collaborate' can often be used interchangeably, but that 'collaborate' can also mean to help an enemy, and so may be a disapproving term. A person who collaborates in both senses of the word is a 'collaborator'. A related noun, 'collaboration', is uncountable and therefore always takes a singular verb.

COOPERATION, CORPORATION, CORPORATE

cooperation /kəʊˌɒpəˈreɪʃn̩/ *noun*, is the act of two or more people or organizations working together to achieve the same end: 'The Chunnel was built as a result of Anglo-French cooperation'. Note that there is no hyphenation in modern English, and that it is uncountable, thus always takes a singular verb.

corporation /kɔːpəˈreɪʃn̩/, *noun*, is a large commercial company in AE. In BE the term is normally used only in the names of semi-public organizations such as the BBC (British Broadcasting Corporation). In another sense, 'corporation' is used to describe the governing body of a town or city in BE, also known as the Town Council. See **BUSINESS**.

corporate /'kɔːpərət/ *adjective*, is used to refer to the characteristic features of a large company: 'Many companies invest heavily in a corporate identity that distinguishes them from other companies'. Sometimes 'corporate' is used in terms like 'corporate management' to identify an activity in large corporations.

COORDINATE, HARMONIZE

coordinate /kəʊ.'ɔːdɪneɪt/ *verb*, means to organize the parts of an operation so that they work well together: 'The Red Cross successfully coordinated the work of several NGOs in the relief operation'. 'Coordinate' (without a hyphen) is the usual spelling in modern BE and in AE.

harmonize /'hɑːmənaɪz/ *verb*, means either to add musical notes to produce chords, or to form and design visually pleasing combinations. In a figurative sense, it means more than 'coordinate', as 'harmonize' involves a move to bring about consistency: 'The introduction of the euro may help to harmonize taxation in the member states of the European Union'.

CO-RESPONDENT, CORRESPONDENT

co-respondent /ˌkəʊrɪs'pɒndənt/ *noun*, means the alleged lover of the person accused of adultery in a divorce action: 'The Hollywood actor was involved once more as the co-respondent in a divorce case'. 'Co-respondent' is the preferred spelling, but 'corespondent' is sometimes used in AE. Note that the stress is on the third syllable, and that the first syllable rhymes with 'so'.

correspondent /kɒrɪs'pɒndənt/ *noun*, means a person who writes and receives letters, or is a contributor to a newspaper or radio programme: 'The reporter from CNN was the only foreign correspondent allowed into the country'.

CORN, MAIZE

corn /kɔːn/ *noun*, in BE means cereals such as wheat, oats, or barley: 'The golden corn swayed in the summer breeze'. In AE, 'corn' means 'maize', hence the name of the breakfast cereal, 'cornflakes', which is made from maize, as well as other foods such as sweet corn and corn on the cob.

maize /meɪz/ *noun*, is the BE term for the plant called 'corn' in AE: 'We lost €100 000 when the price of maize dropped on world markets'.

CORPSE, CORPS

corpse /kɔːps/ *noun*, means a dead body. The plural, 'corpses', is pronounced /'kɔːpsɪz/.

corps /kɔːr/ *noun*, is an organized group of people, such as: 'The Army Corps of Engineers'. Corps is also used in phrases such as 'press corps'; 'diplomatic corps'. Note that the singular and plural are spelt the same, but that the plural is pronounced /kɔːz/.

 'He planned to join the diplomatic corpse.' (Student essay)

COUNCIL, COUNSEL

council /'kaʊnsl/ *noun*, means an organized body of people having a specific purpose: 'The city council are now discussing the budget'.

counsel /'kaʊnsl/ *noun & verb*, as a noun, is a formal word that means advice. In legal contexts, 'counsel' means a lawyer. It is not used with 'a'. As a verb, it means to give advice: 'He was counselled by the Pentagon that civil war was likely in that region'. See **LAWYER**.

COUNCILLOR, COUNSELLOR

councillor /'kaʊnsələr/ *noun*, means a member of a council. The AE spelling is 'councilor'.

counsellor /'kaʊnsələr/ *noun*, means an adviser or lawyer. The AE spelling is 'counselor'.

CRACKER, BISCUIT

cracker /'krækər/ *noun*, in BE is the coloured paper tube that makes a bang at parties. Also in BE, the 'cream cracker' is one of the few types of biscuit that is called a 'cracker'. In AE, most people will think of a savoury crispy biscuit when the word 'cracker' is used.

biscuit /'bɪskɪt/ *noun*, is the most common word in BE for a 'cracker' in the AE sense of the word: 'We have both sweet and savoury biscuits'.

CRAWL, CREEP

crawl /krɔːl/ *verb*, means to move on all four limbs: 'The baby crawled into the room'.

creep /kriːp/ *verb*, means to move slowly and without making any noise in a bent position: 'They were creeping along by the wall'.

CREDIBLE, CREDULOUS, CREDITABLE

credible /'kredɪbl̩/ *adjective*, means able to be believed, or convincing: 'A credible account of the war has been difficult to obtain because of all the military propaganda'. The opposite is 'incredible'. See **INCREDIBLE**.

credulous /'kredjʊləs/ *adjective*, is usually applied to people who are gullible and easily believe things: 'He was so credulous that he believed the story about haggis-hunting in November'. The opposite is 'incredulous'. See **INCREDULOUS ⇨ INCREDIBLE**.

creditable /'kredɪtəbl̩/ *adjective*, refers to something of satisfactory standard and deserving praise: 'The actors in that play gave a highly creditable performance'. This is a formal word. The opposite is 'discreditable', which means harmful to a person's reputation.

CREVASSE, CREVICE

crevasse /krɪ'væs/ *noun*, is a large fissure in ice, usually in a glacier: 'They roped themselves together because of the crevasses'. In AE, the term means a breach in the embankment of a river or canal.

crevice /'krevɪs/ *noun*, means a narrow cleft, crack or fissure, usually in rock: 'There were enough crevices to allow the mountaineers to climb the rockface'.

CRITERION, CRITERIA

criterion /kraɪ'tɪərɪən/ *noun*, means a standard of judgement: 'This is a criterion that has to be studied carefully'. Note that this is the singular form, and always takes a singular verb.

criteria /kraɪ'tɪərɪə/ *noun*, is the plural of 'criterion': 'These criteria need to be studied carefully'. Note that this is a plural noun and always takes a plural verb.

CRITIC, CRITICISM, CRITIQUE

critic /'krɪtɪk/ *noun*, is someone who assesses an artistic performance or exhibition. It is often used for people who have this as their job: 'He is literary critic for *The Washington Post*'. However, it can be used more generally to mean a person who speaks badly of others in public, and in this context is a negative term.

criticism /'krɪtɪsɪzm̩/ *noun*, means the expression of disapproval: 'He resigned from his job because he could not stand the unjust criticism'. It also means the positive assessment of literature and the like: 'Literary criticism should stimulate our appreciation of works of literature'.

critique /krɪ'tiːk/ *noun*, means a detailed review of a book, film or play. Note that the stress is on the second syllable.

CRY, WEEP, SOB, WAIL

cry /kraɪ/ *verb*, means either to produce tears: 'He cried uncontrollably' or to shout loudly: '"Stop thief", she cried desperately'. In the first sense, this is the most general term for tears following pain, sadness, or even happiness.

weep /wiːp/ *verb*, means to cry quietly, usually for a long time: 'Many of the audience started to weep during the film'. Although weeping is nearly always the result of unhappiness or sadness, 'weep' is also associated with extreme happiness: 'The parents wept for joy when their missing child was found'.

sob /sɒb/ *verb*, means to cry noisily in bursts: 'The child was sobbing hysterically'. The expression to 'sob something out' means to say something at the same time as crying: 'The person who was arrested suddenly sobbed out his story'. Note that the AE abbreviation SOB means 'son of a bitch' and is pronounced as three letters: /'es əʊ 'biː/.

wail /weɪl/ *verb*, means long loud crying by someone who is in pain or is sad: 'The women started to wail with despair when they heard the news of the shooting'. Note that 'wail' means 'cry' in the sense of making a noise, not with tears. The expression 'weeping and wailing' means both wailing and tears.

currency units

- Although many still use the national symbols for currency units like £, and $, the three-digit currency codes listed in ISO 4217 are preferred in business and technical contents because they are easier to write and they also give greater precision. In business life, the ISO currency codes such as *EUR* (euro) and *USD* (US dollar) are recommended, especially as using USD should avoid confusion with various types of $ around the world. Consult the latest ISO listings of currency codes on web site www.iso.ch

- Note that the currency code is always written before the amount, but read after the amount in English.

Written as:	Read as:
EUR 55.50	Fifty-five euro fifty (cent)
USD 25.50	Twenty-five US dollars fifty (cents)
GBP 3.20	Three pounds sterling twenty (pence)

When there are decimals, the currency unit is read where the decimal point is.

- The use of K for *kilo*, T for *thousand* and M for *million* before an ISO currency code may cause confusion. It is safer to write *EUR 25 million*, rather than 'KEUR 25 000'; also it is recommended to write *USD 25 million*, rather than 'MUSD 25'.

CURRANT, RAISIN

currant /'kʌrənt/ *noun*, is the dried fruit of a small variety of seedless grape: 'She is mad about currant buns'. It is also a small berry that is found in compounds such as 'blackcurrant'.

raisin /'reɪzɪn/ *noun*, is the normal word for a dried grape: 'Many people sprinkle raisins on their breakfast cereal'.

CURRICULUM, SYLLABUS

curriculum /kʊ'rɪkjʊləm/ *noun*, means the subjects included in a course of study at school, college or university: 'The National Curriculum stipulates the core subjects and foundation subjects to be taught in state schools in England and Wales'. 'Curriculum' is the singular and 'curricula' /kʊ'rɪkjʊlə/ or 'curriculums' /kʊ'rɪkjʊləmz/ are the plural forms. The adjective is 'curricular' /kʊ'rɪkjʊlər/.

syllabus /'sɪləbəs/ *noun*, means the list of topics that a student will be required to study in a particular subject at school, college or university: 'The French literature option has a very extensive syllabus'. Note that 'syllabus' means the content of one subject and 'curriculum' means the content of a complete course of study. 'Syllabuses' /'sɪləbəsɪz/ and the rarer 'syllabi' /'sɪləbaɪ/ are the recommended plural forms.

CURRICULUM VITAE, RESUMÉ, RESUME

curriculum vitae /kʊ'rɪkjʊləm 'vaɪtiː, 'viːtaɪ/ *noun*, is a brief written record of a person's life, education, and career that is commonly required with job applications or as career

documentation. 'CV' is a normal abbreviation of 'curriculum vitae'. The plural form is 'curricula vitae /kʊ'rɪkjʊlə 'vaɪtiː, 'viːtaɪ/, although the abbreviated form is more common: 'We enclose the CVs from the research team'. Note that CV and CVs are read as /'siː 'viː(z)/.

resumé /'rezjʊmeɪ/ *noun*, means a summary: 'I will now give a quick resumé of the results from the initial meeting'. In AE, 'resumé' is an alternative to 'curriculum vitae' : 'Applicants are invited to submit their resumés'. Remember to write the accent above the final 'e' or there may be confusion with 'resume'.

resume /rɪ'zjuːm/ *verb*, means to start to do something again after a pause: 'After the strike it took two days before production resumed'. The related noun is 'resumption' /rɪ'zʌmpʃn̩/.

CV writing

A curriculum vitae is an important part of any job application. It is often demanded in other contexts as well, such as documenting the qualifications of a research team (research profile) as part of an application for research funding. Given the importance of this document it is surprising that many still confine themselves to the traditional CV. There are other alternatives:

traditional CV

- This is a listing of basic information with name, address, contact details, then a series of headings, such as:
  Education Career Publications Appointments Interests Referees
- Most people place the most recent activities first. Sometimes the names and contact details of two referees are added (one about you as a person and the other a professional reference). The *traditional CV* is criticized because it does little to 'sell' your superb qualities to a potential employer or funding body. It is often too factual, and usually not tailored to the recipient's needs.

chronological CV

- The focus of the chronological CV is on what you have done in your studies or working life. It is based on headings, such as:
  Personal Experience Qualifications and training Interests Referees
- The main feature is the *Experience* section that comes after *Personal*. Instead of just listing your positions and your employers, a chronological CV lists what you have done in your career

starting with the most recent activities. A successful *Experience* section is written in complete sentences using active constructions such as *responsible for...*, *in charge of...*, *managing...*, *conducted research in...*. This means that you can tailor the *Experience* section to each job you apply for or the research profile required. The drawback is that as the chronological order has to be followed, any empty periods in your track record will be very evident. The rest of the CV is similar to the traditional one.

functional CV

• The functional CV is organized by skills and qualities, so if an advertised job or research profile requires certain skills such as IT competence and international experience, you can present yourself accordingly. This means you can focus on your strengths and the skills the employer is looking for. A functional CV uses headings, such as:
Personal Career Profile Skills Experience Education and training Interests Referees

• The sections that come after *Personal* are characteristic of this type of CV: *Career Profile, Skills* and *Experience*. The *Career Profile* is written in complete sentences and uses active constructions, such as: *Responsible chemical engineer with good organizational skills* (give examples). *The ability to work independently* (give examples), *and successful experience of working in a project team* (give examples). *Strong background in IT* (see Skills), *matched by three years of international experience in* (country) *working for* (name) – *a leading software company*.

• The *Skills* section lists your skills: *Biotechnology, specializing in...; IT skills, desktop publishing; Languages, French – native language, English – proficient, Japanese – working knowledge*.

• The *Experience* section is similar to the chronological CV but lists the most relevant periods of your career first.

• The other sections list what you have done factually as in the traditional CV. A rule of thumb is that a CV should be as concise as possible, and limited to one page.

The European CV is now available in all languages of the Member States, and is largely based on the structure of the functional CV.

CUSHION, PILLOW

cushion /ˈkʊʃn̩/ *noun & verb*, as a noun, means a soft object to put on a chair or sofa for support: 'Three woven cushions were damaged'. It can also suggest a more figurative kind of support: 'The team is unlikely to be relegated to a lower league now that they have the ten-point cushion'. 'Cushion' as a verb means to protect someone or something: 'The snow cushioned his fall'.

pillow /ˈpɪləʊ/ *noun*, means the soft object on a bed that the head rests on.

CUSTOMER, CLIENT, CLIENTELE

customer /ˈkʌstəmər/ *noun*, means a person or organization that buys things from a shop or business, but who does not pay to use that service: 'The regular customers at the local supermarket were mostly women'. It is a term used by business instead of 'shoppers' and 'passengers' to underline the customer's power of choice.

client /ˈklaɪənt/ *noun*, is a person who pays to obtain professional advice, for example from a lawyer, accountant, architect, engineer. (Note that doctors and dentists have patients.) 'Client' is therefore a word that carries more prestige than 'customer'. An exception is the term 'social client', which is used by social workers instead of the negative 'social case'.

clientele /kliː.ɒnˈtel/ *noun*, is a body of customers of an establishment: 'The clientele of the beach club is superior to those who hang around the bar down the road'. This word should be used with care as 'clientele' is associated with the people using clubs, pubs, shops etc. not with professional people's clients. Note the pronunciation.

Dd

DAMAGE, DAMAGES

damage /'dæmɪdʒ/ *noun & verb*, as a noun, means physical harm caused to things: 'The damage to both houses was considerable'; 'Any damage must be paid for'. In BE, the question 'What is the damage?' in a pub or cafe is an informal way of asking how much the drinks or food cost. This is an uncountable noun. As a verb, 'damage' means to cause harm to something : 'The fire damaged the refinery'. Physically, people are 'injured', although their reputations may be damaged. Machinery is damaged if the cause is external; otherwise it is said to malfunction or break down.
See **INJURE ➪ WOUND**.
See **MALFUNCTION ➪ MISTAKE**.

damages /'dæmɪdʒɪz/ *noun*, is a legal term for an amount of money claimed or received for injury or harm to a company's or person's reputation. It is not the plural of 'damage': 'Following adverse press comments in a newspaper, the company is filing a claim for damages'. Note that in AE, 'damages' can be used informally about the cost of something: 'What are the damages for the repair job?'

> ⚠ *'Dear guests, In order to prevent possible fire damages we kindly ask you to consider the following rules.' (Hotel notice)*

dash, en dash, em dash

dash /dæʃ/ noun, occurs in two main forms: *en dash* and *em dash*. A way of distinguishing between the dash and the hyphen is to say that a dash separates words, whereas a hyphen connects parts of a word. See **HYPHENATION**.

en dash /'en dæʃ/ is a short dash, the length of the letter *n*. This is used in many ways such as creating a break, giving a range or period: *1985–1995*, or when there are two units: *The Chelsea–Man. U. match*.

em dash /'em dæʃ/ is a longer dash, the length of the letter *m*. This is used to indicate pauses in speech: 'Two types of fuel — diesel and petrol — are going to be taxed more heavily'.

DATA, DATUM

data /'deɪtə/ *noun*, means facts and statistics collected for analysis or reference. 'Data' is the plural form of 'datum'. However, 'data' is often used as an uncountable noun, especially in computer science and in data processing: 'The correct data was vital'. 'Data' is used as a plural noun in scientific and formal writing or when referring to different types of data: 'Oceanographic, meteorological, and environmental data were gathered'. In AE, an alternative pronunciation is /'dɑːtə/.

datum /'deɪtəm/ *noun*, means one piece of information. Its most common use is as a standard of comparison or reference point in surveying: 'This is our datum line'. 'Datum' is rarely used, except in this context.

dates (digital and non-digital)

digital dates

Many companies have their standard letter/fax/report title page set up so that they automatically generate dates in digital form according to the ISO 8601 standard (ccyy-mm-dd or 2006-05-11) in the date space on the first page and on following pages. Unfortunately, many report-writers do not follow this standard and use 11/05/06 elsewhere in letters and reports. This can lead to expensive misunderstandings. As Americans place the month before the day, 11/05/06 means either 11 May 2006 or November 5, 2006 according to which side of the Atlantic the readers are on.

One solution is to follow the ISO 8601 standard and systematically use the model ccyy mm dd or 2006-04-12 (i.e. 12 April 2006). It is stipulated in this standard that four digits should be used for years (i.e. 2006-04-12) and that hyphens, not dots or slashes, should be used to separate the units. If you have to give a time interval, an em dash can be used (i.e. 2002-06-01 — 2004-05-31). ISO 8601 only specifies digital notations and does not cover dates where words are used in the representation.

non-digital dates

Another way of avoiding confusions with digital dates is always to write the month in words. The two main customs in English are *12 April 2006*, which is common in BE and *April 12, 2006*, which is common in AE (do not forget the comma in AE). Note that there are no stops after the day and that the first letter of the month is always capitalized in English. The ordinal form of *1st, 2nd, 3rd, 4th* etc. is now considered old-fashioned for written dates in business English. However, when reading dates aloud, use the model: *the twelfth of April 2006* in BE and *April twelfth 2006* in AE.

weeks and months

The widespread use of week numbers in some countries to identify a date is unusual in many parts of the world. Instead of suggesting a meeting in week 38 or 39, it is better to say *the week commencing …* or to use the date. Abbreviations for the longer months are often used: *Jan., Feb., Aug., Sept., Oct., Nov., Dec.,* (March—July are written in full).
See **LETTERS AND EMAILS**.

DAY, DAYTIME, 24 HOURS, 24-7, ROUND-THE-CLOCK

day /deɪ/ *noun,* means both a 24-hour period, starting at midnight, and the period of office hours. Compare 'work on this for a day' (24 hours) with 'work on this during the day' (during office hours). The first of these is unusual in English, and if this sense is intended, then it is better to spell out the number of hours rather than use the vaguer term 'day'. Most office staff now work a five-day week, meaning Monday to Friday, or are given one of these days off 'in lieu' (meaning 'instead of'), if they have to work on Saturday or Sunday.

daytime /'deɪtaɪm/ *noun & adjective,* as a noun, means the hours of daylight, as opposed to night-time: 'Owls generally sleep in the daytime'. As an adjective, 'daytime' is used to describe activities that take place during daylight hours. Specifically, it is used in the expression 'daytime TV', to refer to the entertainment programmes (game shows, chat shows, etc.) broadcast by television stations during office hours for people who are at home at that time.

24 hours /'twentɪfɔːr 'aʊəz/ *noun,* means 'day' in the sense of a 24-hour period or refers to a facility that is never closed: 'The security office is manned 24 hours a day'. Note that before a noun the adjectival form '24-hour' is hyphenated and has no final 's': '24-hour service is available'.

24-7 /'twenti fɔː 'sevn̩/ *adverb,* means something that is open 24 hours a day and 7 days a week: 'That petrol station is open 24-7'. It is originally an AE term, and is now becoming more familiar in BE.

round-the-clock /'raʊnd ðə 'klɒk/ *adjective,* refers to something that operates permanently, both day and night: 'As emergency plumbers, we offer a round-the-clock service'.

DECEPTIVE, DECEITFUL

deceptive /dɪ'septɪv/ *adjective,* means giving an impression that is different from the true one: 'The footballer trained at scoring penalties for an hour a day and when his penalty won the match, he did it with deceptive ease'.

deceitful /dɪ'siːtfʊl/ *adjective,* means misleading others on purpose, usually on a regular basis: 'He was thoroughly deceitful and never told his wife about his mistress'.

DECIDE, DETERMINE, DETERMINED, RESOLVE

decide /dɪ'saɪd/ *verb,* means to make a decision, either quickly or based on careful consideration: 'They found a cheap flight and decided to go away for the weekend'.

determine /dɪ'tɜːmɪn/ *verb,* means to establish the facts about something: 'After much research, they were able to determine the cause of the explosion'.

determined /dɪ'tɜːmɪnd/ *adjective,* describes someone whose personality is very decisive, even if a course of action is difficult to achieve: 'My sister is very determined, and if she said she would give up smoking, then she will'. 'Determined' also forms part of the phrasal verb 'be determined to', meaning that a person has made a decision about a course of action, and will not be deterred. This is not necessarily a part of their personality: 'He was determined to give up smoking this time, even though he had failed before'.

resolve /rɪ'zɒlv/ *verb,* is a formal word meaning to make a firm decision: 'After three months in hospital, he resolved never to smoke in bed again'. It also means to find a solution to an issue or problem: 'This situation must be resolved as soon as possible, before our reputation is damaged'. Related words are the noun 'resolution' /rezə'ljuːʃn̩/, and the adjective 'resolute' /'rezəljuːt/.

DEFECT, DEFECTION

defect /'diːfekt/ *noun,* means a fault either in a piece of equipment: 'This defect has cost the company hundreds of thousands of dollars'; or in the means of producing something: 'Everyone in the family had the same speech defect'. It is best to stress this on the first syllable. See **MALFUNCTION ⇨ MISTAKE**.

defection /dɪ'fekʃn/ *noun,* means the act of leaving a country or a political organization in order to join an opposing country or body: 'Civil war broke out after the defection of the President'. A related verb is 'defect' /dɪ'fekt/ (stressed on the second syllable). Careful speakers distinguish between the pronunciation of the noun and verb, which have the same spelling.

DEFECTIVE, DEFICIENT

defective /dɪ'fektɪv/ *adjective,* means malfunctioning, such as 'defective software'. It is old fashioned and offensive to use 'defective' for someone with a mental illness.
See **MENTAL HANDICAP ⇨ LEARNING DIFFICULTY**.

deficient /dɪ'fɪʃnt/ *adjective,* means insufficient. 'Deficient software' means software that is not good enough for a task.

'We apologize for the error in last week's paper in which we stated that Mr Arnold Dogbody was a defective in the police force.' (Correction notice, English newspaper)

DEFINITE, DEFINITIVE

definite /'defɪnɪt/ *adjective,* means clearly stated or decided, precisely and unambiguously: 'The minister issued a very definite statement in an attempt to distance himself from the situation'. Careful writers should avoid using 'definite' to give emphasis to something. Instead of writing 'definite answer', just use 'answer'. Always remember the word 'finite' to avoid the common misspelling of this word.

definitive /dɪ'fɪnɪtɪv/ *adjective,* refers to conclusions that are reached decisively and with authority. Books are also 'definitive' when they are authoritative works. 'The extensive research conducted by the author makes this the definitive biography of Bernard Shaw'.

definite article

- A problem area for non-native speakers of English is the difference between a noun being used in its general and specific senses. Take the word *industry* as an example. When it is written without the definite article: *Industry must survive,* this means industry in general. When it has the definite article: *The industry must survive,* this means a specific industrial sector. This distinction applies to many words. Here are some other examples:

general sense	specific sense
staff (all employees)	the staff (those in a specific organization)
life is good (in general)	the life of Brian (a specific one in a film)
modern society (in general)	the geological society (specific group)
music calms (all types)	the music of Brahms (his specific music)

names of countries

- Some island groups retain the definite article in their official name: *The Philippines, The Maldives, The Channel Islands,* but note that *Seychelles,* although an island nation, does not retain the article. Country names which refer to 'plural' entities also have the definite article as a part of their official name, but are indexed under the following word. Examples are *the United Kingdom, the United States of America,* and *the United Arab Emirates* (note the lower case 'the'). Some country names that used to include the definite article no longer do so. Examples are *Lebanon, Ukraine, Gambia,* and *Netherlands.* As for the *Netherlands,* the definite article is no longer part of its official name in English, but in running text it is still normal to write, and say, the Netherlands.

reference lists and indexing

- Many reference lists are in the order: author, date, title. If the title of a book or paper starts with *The,* this should appear in the reference list. (*Gowers, E. 1973. The Complete Plain Words. Penguin Books*)
- However, if an index of books, journals, and papers lists the titles and some of these start with *The,* the normal rule is to ignore the definite article and use the first main word in the title. For example, *The Complete Plain Words* is listed under *C,* even though *The* is really the first word in the title: *Complete Plain Words, The.*

• The same is true for proper names in English. Although the Dutch town is called *The Hague*, the general rule is to list it according to the principal element: *Hague*. This will be written *The Hague* but should be listed under *H* in the index or reference list: *Hague, The*.

• This also applies to institutions, such as *The United Nations*, which is listed under *U*.

pronunciation

• **the** is pronounced /ðə/ before words beginning with a consonant sound, unless you are stressing a particular object or person. Compare *this is the* /ðə/ *report* with *this is the* /ði:/ *report – the one that caused all the trouble*.

• **the** is usually pronounced /ði/ before words beginning with a vowel sound, *the examples*. See **INDEFINITE ARTICLE**.

DEFLATION, DEVALUATION

deflation /dɪˈfleɪʃn/ *noun*, means the reduction of money available in an economy in order to lower prices and wages or to keep them at the same level. When an economy is 'deflated', people are unable to buy as much as they could before.

devaluation /di:væljʊˈeɪʃn/ *noun*, means the lowering of the value of one currency in relation to others, with the aim of slowing inflation or increasing exports, or both. When a currency is 'devalued', the price of goods made abroad goes up, and so people can afford to buy fewer of them, while still being able to afford products made in their own country.

> President George W. Bush's comments about Japanese devaluation, when he meant deflation, caused the yen to fall heavily on currency markets in February 2002.

DEFUSE, DIFFUSE

defuse /ˈdiːˈfjuːz/ *verb*, means to remove a fuse: 'The Army successfully defused the car bomb, and shoppers were allowed back into the area'. Figuratively it means to remove tension: 'The religious leader spoke to the crowd and defused the situation'. For clarity, the word should be stressed on each syllable.

diffuse /dɪˈfjuːz/ *verb* & /dɪˈfjuːs/ *adjective*, as a verb, means to disperse or scatter: 'The light was diffused around the laboratory'. As an adjective, 'diffuse' can only come before a noun, and means either scattered, less concentrated: 'The diffuse support meant that it was a political party without ideology'; or difficult to understand: 'His diffuse arguments left the audience no wiser when he sat down'.

> 'The report is a time bomb stealthy politicians are trying to diffuse.' (Newspaper story)

DEGREE, DIPLOMA, CERTIFICATE

degree /dɪˈgriː/ *noun*, is the academic qualification given by a college or university after examinations and successful completion of a course of study: 'She was awarded a bachelor's degree in 2002'. In BE, it also refers to the course that is in progress: 'He is taking a degree at Oxford'.

diploma /dɪˈpləʊmə/ *noun*, is an official document awarded by an educational body to show that someone has successfully completed a course of study: 'He brought his High School diploma to the job interview'. A 'diploma' is generally limited in meaning to a certificate issued by schools, colleges and universities. 'Diploma' also means a course at college or university. This is a BE term in this sense: 'The Diploma in Education is a one-year full-time course for graduates'.

certificate /səˈtɪfɪkət/ *noun*, means an official document awarded by a body to show that someone has successfully completed a course, not necessarily an academic one: 'They were awarded certificates after completing the first aid course'. A 'certificate' can be used to document other things such as birth ('birth certificate'), marriage or death. 'Certificate' is also the name of a qualification after a course of study. This is a BE term in this sense: 'The Cambridge Certificate of Proficiency in English is very popular'.

DELIBERATE, CONSIDER

deliberate /dɪˈlɪbərət/ *adjective* & /dɪˈlɪbəreɪt/ *verb*, as an adjective, refers to something done on purpose, not accidentally: 'The shooting down of the jet was found to be a deliberate plan to raise tension'. 'Deliberate' may also mean careful and slow. Note that the final syllable contains a neutral vowel. As a verb, 'deliberate' means to think about something carefully and discuss it at length: 'The military council deliberated for 24 hours on their response to this incident'. Note that the final syllable is pronounced 'rate'. The related noun is 'deliberation'.

consider /kən'sɪdər/ verb, means either to think about something carefully, particularly when a decision has to made: 'We are seriously considering buying a house in France'; or to say how something or somebody is regarded: 'The professor is considered to be one of the leading experts in phonetics'. The related noun is 'consideration'.

DELIVERY, DELIVERABLES

delivery /dɪ'lɪvəri/ noun, means the act or date of delivering something: 'Delivery of the interim report is to be by 6 p.m. on 1 October 2006 to the European Commission'. 'Delivery' can also refer to the way in which a person speaks, such as: 'The presentation was marred by his poor delivery'. The phrase 'take delivery of' means to receive something: 'They take delivery of the new oil tanker next year'.

deliverables /dɪ'lɪvrəblz/ noun, means something provided, such as a product at the end of a development process: 'The project deliverables include plans for the financial programme and tailored software'. Note that this noun usually occurs in the plural.

DELUSION, ALLUSION, ILLUSION

delusion /dɪ'lju:ʒn/ noun, means a false belief, not based on reality: 'The art teacher suffers from the delusion that he is the new Leonardo da Vinci'.

allusion /ə'lju:ʒn/ noun, means an indirect reference to another person or thing: 'The boy's scathing comments about modern painting were an allusion to his art teacher's lack of talent'. See **ELUDE ⇨ ALLUDE**.

illusion /ɪ'lju:ʒn/ noun, means either a false impression: 'The illusion of prosperity in the USA was shaken in 1929 by the Great Crash'; or a deceptive appearance: 'The conjurer gave the illusion of walking through a massive wall'. A common phrase is 'be under the illusion that', meaning to falsely believe something.

DEMAND, DEMANDS, CLAIM, REQUIRE

demand /dɪ'mɑ:nd/ noun & verb, as a noun, means a firm request for something: 'The company has said it will not consider a demand for higher wages'. In another sense, 'demand' means the pressure from customers for a product : 'TV stations are always looking for new ways to meet the demand for entertaining programmes'. As a verb, 'demand' means to ask authoritatively in order to insist on getting something: 'She demanded to speak to the doctor'.

demands /dɪ'mɑ:ndz/ plural noun, means the pressures imposed on someone: 'Motorway driving places considerable demands on the over 70s'. The related adjective is 'demanding'. This refers to a person or thing that requires a lot of time and attention: 'I am often tired because my job is so demanding'.

claim /kleɪm/ noun & verb, as a noun, means a request for something as a legal right: 'The accident was not my fault, and therefore my claim for compensation is justified'. As a verb, 'claim' means to present a request for compensation or to state confidently that something is true, often without any proof: 'He claims that he has been abducted by aliens'.

require /rɪ'kwaɪər/ verb, means to insist on someone doing something: 'The wearing of crash helmets for motorcyclists is required by law'. This is a formal word. In another sense, 'require' means to need: 'We require more recruits for the armed forces'. 'Require' can also be used in a polite question: 'What do you require?' The related noun is 'requirement'. See **REQUEST ⇨ ASK**.

DEMONSTRATION, DISPLAY, EXHIBITION, TRADE FAIR

demonstration /demən'streɪʃn/ noun, is a performance to show how something works, or to try out something new: 'The demonstration of the new 4WD Ford'. A 'demonstration' does not require a specific or permanent site, and may refer to virtual presentations on the Internet. A test product that is connected with software or music is often termed a 'demo' /'deməu/.

display /dɪs'pleɪ/ noun & verb, as a noun, means an exhibition or performance often for public entertainment: 'The fireworks display lasted for thirty minutes'. A 'display' may be semi-permanent, such as a shop window display, or a one-off event. As a verb, 'display' means either to exhibit: 'The museum displayed a magnificent collection of antique silver'; or to show information: 'The screen is displaying the wrong train times'.

exhibition /eksɪ'bɪʃn̩/ *noun*, means a public display of works of art. An 'exhibition' needs a site that may be in a hall, gallery or centre: 'The Louvre is planning an exciting exhibition next spring'. Note that an 'exhibition' is normally of limited duration in this context. The items that are on permanent display are called 'exhibits' and form part of a collection.

trade fair /'treɪd feər/ *noun*, means a type of exhibition for commercial or industrial goods: 'All the companies in the agricultural equipment sector are represented at the trade fair'. Note that this is also called a 'trade show' or just 'fair'.

DEPARTMENT, DIVISION

department /dɪ'pɑːtmənt/ *noun*, means a division in a large organization such as a university or business that deals with one subject, commodity, or area of activity: 'the Department of History'; 'the personnel department'. In national administrations, both the UK and the USA often use 'department' as the main term for the structure of government: Department of Health (UK), State Department (USA). (The term ministry is also used in the UK for some of the governmental units.)

division /dɪ'vɪʒn̩/ *noun*, means a major unit in an organization, typically one that is in charge of a particular function: 'The financial division will check with the wage office'. The terms 'division' and 'department' overlap, and many organizations in the UK use the structure 'department-division-section', with 'department' as the largest unit. Elsewhere, 'division' is often the largest unit, particularly in business organizations.

DEPENDANTˢ, DEPENDENTˢ, INDEPENDENT

dependant /dɪ'pendənt/ *noun*, means a person who is financially reliant on another: 'Her parents are hard up as they have six dependants'. An alternative spelling for 'dependant' is 'dependent'.

dependent /dɪ'pendənt/ *adjective*, means reliant on or determined by: 'This island is dependent on tourism'. 'Dependent' takes the preposition 'on' or 'upon'.

independent /ɪndɪ'pendənt/ *adjective*, means free of outside control, particularly with the preposition 'from': 'America has been independent from Britain for over two hundred

years'. The expression 'independent of' means separate, either generally or financially: 'In many countries, you are legally independent of your parents at 18'.

DEPRECIATE, DEPRECATE

depreciate /dɪ'priːʃieɪt/ *verb*, usually means to fall in value: 'The value of this car has depreciated by 50% during the past three years'. A second and more formal meaning is to dismiss or reduce in importance: 'He depreciated his role in solving the murder mystery'.

deprecate /'deprɪkeɪt/ *verb*, is a formal word meaning to disapprove of strongly: 'He deprecated the government's plans to build on polluted land'. 'Deprecate' also means to dismiss or reduce the importance of something. Note that the adjective 'self-deprecating' refers to playing down one's own achievements: 'He began his talk with several self-deprecating comments which made the audience feel at ease'.

DESCENDENTˢ, DESCENDANTˢ, HEIR

descendent /dɪ'sendənt/ *adjective*, means moving downwards or falling: 'A descendent scale'. An alternative term here is 'descending'.

descendant /dɪ'sendənt/ *noun*, means a plant, animal or person that is descended from another, such as offspring: 'Many families in Boston, Mass. are descendants of the Pilgrim Fathers'.

heir /eər/ *noun*, means a person who is legally entitled to the estate of another upon the latter's death: 'Although he was heir to a vast fortune, he was not a descendant of the founder of the company'. An heir does not have to be related by blood. Note that the 'h' is silent, and that the word is pronounced the same as 'air'.

DESERTˢ, DESERTS, DESSERTˢ

desert /'dezət/ *noun*, is a dry, barren region: 'The surface of the moon is a desert'. It is also used figuratively to refer to a situation that is lacking in a given quality, such as a 'cultural desert'. 'Deserts', pronounced /'dezəts/, is the plural of 'desert'.

desert /dɪ'zɜːt/ *verb*, means to abandon and leave without support: 'He deserted his family and fled the country'. Someone who runs away from the army is a 'deserter' /dɪ'zɜːtər/. Note that this verb is pronounced the same as the noun 'dessert'.

deserts /dɪ'zɜːts/ *plural noun*, is used as part of the idiom to 'get one's just deserts'. This means to receive what one deserves, often because of having done something bad: 'The convicted killer got his just deserts: life imprisonment'. Note that this is stressed on the second syllable.

dessert /dɪ'zɜːt/ *noun*, is the sweet course at the end of a meal. Note that this is one of the very few words in English spelt with '-ss-' but which is pronounced /z/. It is stressed on the second syllable.

DETACHED HOUSE, SEMI-DETACHED HOUSE, DUPLEX, TERRACED HOUSE, VILLA

detached house /dɪ'tætʃt 'haʊs/ *noun*, means a house in its own grounds not joined to any other: 'They had a four-bedroom, detached house just outside Oxford'. See **HOUSE**.

semi-detached house /'semɪdɪtætʃt 'haʊs/ *noun*, is the BE term for a house sharing a common wall with another house. This is also known informally as a 'semi'.

duplex /'djuːpleks/ *noun*, is the AE term for a semi-detached house, as well as for a residential building divided into two flats. In AE and BE, a 'duplex' apartment/flat means a unit with two floors.

terraced house /'terɪst 'haʊs/ *noun*, means one house in a row of attached houses, usually in the same style.

villa /'vɪlə/ *noun*, means a large, luxurious house in the country in its own grounds, often in southern Europe: 'Our villa is in Saint Tropez'. Occasionally, in BE, the term can be used for Victorian houses in residential districts.

DEVELOP, EXPLOIT

develop /dɪ'veləp/ *verb*, means to become, or cause something to become, more mature or advanced: 'Mobile phones have developed new possibilities for communication'. 'Develop' can also mean to expand the potential of something, especially in the context of resources: 'We have decided to develop the gas resources in this region'. Note that there is no 'e' after the 'p' in 'develop'. The related noun is 'development'. See **UTILIZE ⇨ USE**.

exploit /ɪks'plɔɪt/ *verb*, means to make full use of a possibility, often at the expense of others: 'The manufacturers of mobile phones have exploited new possibilities for earning money'. Although 'exploit' usually has a negative association, it is the correct word to use for

deriving benefit from a resource. 'They are going to begin exploiting another mine in the area'. However, because of this potential ambiguity, 'develop' is often preferred. The related noun is 'exploitation' /eksplɔɪ'teɪʃn/.

DEVICE, DEVISE

device /dɪ'vaɪs/ *noun*, means a piece of equipment designed for a specific task: 'The wheel clamp is a device to deter illegal parking in cities'.

devise /dɪ'vaɪz/ *verb*, means to plan or invent something: 'Whoever devised the wheel clamp must be making a lot of money'. Note that despite the pronunciation, the spelling is '-ise' in both BE and AE.

DIAGNOSE, DIAGNOSIS, PROGNOSIS

diagnose /daɪəg'nəʊz/ *verb*, means to identify a mechanical problem or a disease: 'They developed a new test that could diagnose a disease in ten minutes'. It is not possible to diagnose a patient, only his or her disease. Note that the third person singular form 'diagnoses' is pronounced /daɪəg'nəʊzɪz/, the last two syllables rhyming with 'roses'.

diagnosis /daɪəg'nəʊsɪs/ *noun*, is the identification of a medical problem: 'The doctor said that exact diagnosis would require numerous tests'. Note that the plural form 'diagnoses' /daɪəg'nəʊsiːz/ has the final syllable pronounced 'seas'.

prognosis /prɒg'nəʊsɪs/ *noun*, is an opinion about how a problem is likely to develop: 'International medical experience with this disease is so limited that we cannot make a reliable prognosis'. 'Prognosis' is used in numerous contexts to refer to a judgement about how something is likely to develop: 'Our prognosis for the consequences of global warming in this area will be presented next year'. This is a formal word. Note that the plural 'prognoses' /prɒg'nəʊsiːz/ has the final syllable pronounced 'seas'.

DIARY, DAYBOOK, JOURNAL, LOG

diary /'daɪəri/ *noun*, means a personal record of events and experiences that is often kept on a daily basis: 'Most people remember the diary that was kept by Anne Frank'. See **SCHEDULE**.

daybook /'deɪbʊk/ *noun,* is a record of accounts in business used to keep track of money received or expenditure. In AE, this term also means a diary.

journal /'dʒɜːnəl/ *noun,* means a written record of things that are done usually in the context of an expedition or journey: 'They kept a journal of their voyage around the world'. 'Journal' also means a newspaper or periodical (especially scientific), and many of these have the word in their titles: *Wall Street Journal* and *British Medical Journal.*

log /lɒg/ *noun,* means an official record of events particularly during voyages by sea or air: 'The captain's log explained the causes of the shipwreck'. 'Logbook' is an old-fashioned alternative, although in BE it is the correct term for a vehicle's registration document.

DIFFERENT, VARIOUS

different /'dɪfərənt/ *adjective,* means unlike in nature, shape, form, and quality: 'This country is different from anywhere else in Europe'. 'Different' should be used where there is a clear distinction: 'That is a different language'. 'Different from' is the most common construction in BE and AE. 'Different than' is used in AE as an alternative. 'Different to' is used informally in BE, but is best avoided in careful writing. The related noun is 'difference'.

various /'veərɪəs/ *adjective,* means several different things or types. When discussing a range of things, use 'various' rather than 'different': 'There are various languages that have evolved from Latin'. 'Various' is only used with plural nouns. The related noun is 'variety' /və'raɪəti/. See **FEW**.

DINNER JACKET, TUXEDO

dinner jacket /'dɪnə dʒækɪt/ *noun,* is a type of suit for men with a short jacket without tails that is worn at a formal dinner. This is usually black, and a bow tie (often black as well) is normal. The expression 'Dress: black tie' on an invitation means a dinner jacket for men and an evening dress for women. The abbreviation is DJ. In some languages, the English word 'smoking' has been borrowed for 'dinner jacket', but this is never correct in English.

tuxedo /tʌk'siːdəʊ/ is an AE word for a white or cream dinner jacket. It can also mean a formal evening suit.

DISBURSE, DISPERSE

disburse /dɪs'bɜːs/ *verb,* means to pay money from a fund: 'Money was disbursed by the director without the authorization of the board'. This is a formal word.

disperse /dɪs'pɜːs/ *verb,* means to distribute or scatter over a wide area: 'We now have to find where the company funds have been dispersed'.

DISC[s], DISK[s]

disc /dɪsk/ *noun,* means a flat round plate: 'The dog's name was on a disc hanging from its collar'. This spelling is generally preferred in BE, and is found in terms such as: 'compact disc' and 'disc jockey'.

disk /dɪsk/ *noun,* is the usual spelling of the word in most contexts in AE, such as: 'compact disk' and 'disk jockey'. The 'disk' spelling is also used in BE in connection with computer equipment such as 'floppy disk' and 'disk drive'.

DISCIPLINE, SUBJECT, FIELD, AREA (EDUCATION)

discipline /'dɪsɪplɪn/ *noun,* means a branch of knowledge, but its use is restricted to higher education: 'She is an authority in her discipline'. Apart from its academic sense, 'discipline' also means order and punishment: 'The discipline in the primary school made his life a misery'.

subject /'sʌbdʒɪkt/ *noun,* means a branch of knowledge, and as it applies to all educational levels, it is more widely used than 'discipline': 'College students study a broad range of subjects'.

field /fiːld/ *noun,* is used for a restricted branch of specialized knowledge: 'As professor of commercial law, he had a pretty good grasp of developments in his field'.

area /'eərɪə/ *noun,* in education can be an alternative word for 'field'. but is often used in a wider context: 'Film music was an area of study he had never considered before'.

DISCOUNT, REDUCTION, REBATE

discount /'dɪskaʊnt/ *noun,* means a deduction from the price of something: 'There is a 30% discount on these goods during the sale'. 'Discount' is often connected to a percentage.

reduction /rɪ'dʌkʃn̩/ *noun*, means an arrangement that makes the prices of goods lower: 'Special reduction on ice cream, all week'. In shops, this is often termed 'a special offer' or just 'a special'.

rebate /'riːbeɪt/ *noun*, means a reduction or a refund, often from the tax authorities: 'After several letters to the tax office, his claim for a tax rebate was accepted'.

DISCREET[S], DISCRETE[S]

discreet /dɪs'kriːt/ *adjective*, means tactful and taking care about what is said and done: 'A discreet waiter tries to be as invisible as possible'. A related noun is 'discretion' /dɪs'kreʃn̩/: 'All benefits are at the discretion of the company'.

discrete /dɪs'kriːt/ *adjective*, means separate and individually distinct: 'The enhanced processing of the tape revealed the discrete units of sound'. This is a technical term.

DISCREPANCY, DISPARITY

discrepancy /dɪs'krepənsi/ *noun*, means a difference that should not be there: 'The police pointed out the discrepancies in the alibis given by the suspects'.

disparity /dɪs'pærɪti/ *noun*, means a wide difference that is due to inequality: 'There is a huge disparity in income levels in this part of the world'. This is a formal word, and a less formal alternative is 'difference'.

DISCRIMINATE, DISCRIMINATION, DISCRIMINATING

discriminate /dɪs'krɪmɪneɪt/ *verb*, means to block or make an unfavourable distinction between people based on factors such as social background, race or sex: 'Apartheid formed a legal basis on which to discriminate between the races in South Africa'.

discrimination /dɪskrɪmɪ'neɪʃn̩/ *noun*, may have either positive or negative associations. On its own, 'discrimination' means the unfair treatment of people because of their race or sex, for instance. The term 'positive discrimination' refers to a means of favouring a group that had previously been excluded, through a special measure or quota: 'The university is using positive discrimination to attract girls to computer science studies'.

discriminating /dɪs'krɪmɪneɪtɪŋ/ *adjective*, refers to a person of fine taste and refinement: 'He was a discriminating art critic who worked for *The Times* for 36 years'.

DISGUISE, GUISE

disguise /dɪz'gaɪz/ *noun & verb*, as a noun, means a false appearance: 'No-one recognized him in his Father Christmas disguise'. As a verb, 'disguise' means to present a false appearance, in order to deceive, and can be used in phrases such as 'disguise oneself' or 'be disguised as': 'He disguised himself as Father Christmas'.

guise /gaɪz/ *noun*, means having a different appearance or presentation from normal, but not necessarily with the aim of deceiving someone: 'The myth that the end of the world is close appears in numerous guises around the world'.

DISMISS, FIRE, SACK, NOTICE

dismiss /dɪs'mɪs/ *verb*, means to officially terminate someone's employment, typically due to unsatisfactory performance or dishonourable conduct by the employee: 'You will be dismissed at the end of next month'. 'Dismiss' can also mean to overlook as unimportant: 'The company dismissed rumours that it was in trouble'. The related noun is 'dismissal'.

fire /faɪər/ *verb*, is an informal equivalent of 'dismiss': 'You are fired as of now'. The related noun is 'firing', as in the common expression 'hiring and firing'.

sack /sæk/ *verb & noun*, is another informal equivalent of 'dismiss'. When used as a verb, it is possible to say 'to sack' someone. As a noun, 'sack' is combined with 'the' in this sense, and is often used in fixed phrases such as 'give someone the sack': 'He was caught stealing and given the sack'. The person being dismissed can also be said to 'get the sack'.

notice /'nəʊtɪs/ *noun*, means the formal announcement of termination of employment and can be from either the employer or the employee: 'She was worried that she was required to give three months' notice'. The period of time between the announcement and the last day of employment is known as 'working one's notice'.

See **REDUNDANT**. See **RESIGN**.

 Under list of main achievements on a CV: 'December 1998: Fired as general director of...'

DISPROVE, DISAPPROVE

disprove /dɪsˈpruːv/ *verb*, means to prove something to be untrue or false: 'They disproved his theory on innate intelligence'.

disapprove /dɪsəˈpruːv/ *verb*, means to consider something or someone unsuitable, or to dislike, often for moral reasons: 'My parents disapprove of my new boyfriend because he hasn't got a job'.

doctor, Dr, Dr.

doctor /ˈdɒktər/ noun, is a professional title, abbreviated *Dr* in BE and *Dr.* in AE. The abbreviated form is read *doctor*. In Britain, medical practitioners have a degree in medicine and surgery. Specialized surgeons, including dentists, usually call themselves *Mr* or a female equivalent. In AE, physicians, surgeons, dentists and vets are called *doctor*. Those who hold doctorates in any field are to be formally addressed as *Dr*, not 'Mr' in letters etc. This may sometimes cause confusion with medical doctors.

doctoral degree, PhD

A doctoral /ˈdɒktərəl/ degree or doctorate /ˈdɒktərət/ is the highest degree awarded by a university. The most common type awarded by universities in or based on the UK/US higher education systems is the *Doctor of Philosophy* (abbreviated *PhD* in BE and *Ph.D.* in AE, read as /ˈpiː ˈeɪtʃ ˈdiː/). Do not translate a degree from any other country's system into the UK/US one. On the English language version of a CV or business card, it is always best to write a degree in its original language. If necessary, this can then be followed by an approximate translation, in brackets. As such degrees are placed after personal names in English, a model to use is: *John Smith, PhD*. Do not use both *Dr* and *PhD* at the same time.

'He took a doctorate in unclear physics.' (An obituary)

DOWNWARD, DOWNWARDS

downward /ˈdaʊnwəd/ *adjective*, means moving or leading to a lower level: 'A downward trend in the Gallup polls'.

downwards /ˈdaʊnwədz/ *adverb*, means moving or leading to a lower level: 'Share prices moved downwards, month after month'. This is the BE spelling. 'Downward' is an alternative spelling, especially in AE.

DRAFT[S], DRAUGHT[S]

draft /drɑːft/ *noun & verb*, as a noun means a preliminary version: 'Draft report'. In banking it means a payment order: 'Pay by bank draft'. In AE, 'draft' can mean a current of cold air, a type of beer served from the barrel rather than sold in bottles, and the water depth required under a boat (all spelt 'draught' in BE), or compulsory military service: 'He was a draft dodger'. A BE alternative to 'draft' in the latter sense is 'conscription'. As a verb, 'draft' means to make a preliminary version of something: 'After months of thought, he slowly drafted his letter of resignation'. It can also mean calling someone into service in the armed forces: 'They were drafted into the army'; or selecting and transferring a group of people to carry out a specific task: 'Extra firefighters were drafted into service'.

draught /drɑːft/ *noun*, means a current of air: 'He got a stiff neck from the draught'. 'Draught' is also the water depth required under a boat. In a pub, it may also mean beer served from the barrel, rather than sold in bottles: 'What beers have you got on draught?' (all spelt 'draft' in AE).

A report with 'draught' as a header on every page was sent to a foreign ministry of the environment.

DRYER[S], DRIER[S]

dryer /ˈdraɪər/ *noun*, means a drying device: 'The hotel had a hair dryer in the room'.

drier /ˈdraɪər/ *noun & comparative adjective*, as a noun, is an alternative spelling of 'dryer'. As an adjective, 'drier' compares something that is less moist: 'This towel is drier than that one'.

DUAL[S], DUEL[S]

dual /ˈdjuːəl/ *adjective*, means either duplication: 'dual nationality', or having two parts: 'dual carriageway'. See **BI-**.
See **DUAL CARRIAGEWAY ⇨ MOTORWAY**.

duel /'dju:əl/ *noun*, is historically a pre-arranged contest with weapons to settle a dispute between two people: 'The duel was to be fought at dawn'. It is used figuratively nowadays to refer to an intellectual contest between two people or groups: 'The verbal duel between the two politicians was fascinating'.

DYE⁵, DIE⁵, DICE

dye /daɪ/ *noun & verb*, as a noun, means a substance to change the colour of cloth, etc. As a verb, this means to change the colour of something. Note that 'dyed', 'dyes', and 'dyeing' are pronounced the same as 'died', 'dies', and 'dying', which are formed from the verb 'die'.

die /daɪ/ *verb*, means come to the end of life. The related noun is 'death'.

die /daɪ/ *noun*, means the form used in the shaping of metal. Originally, a die was also the small cube used in games such as 'poker dice', but now 'die' is replaced by the plural 'dice'. Note that the expression: 'The die is cast' means a serious move has been made that is difficult to reverse.

dice /daɪs/ *noun*, is now the usual word for the cubes used in games such as 'poker dice'. 'Dice' is both the singular and the plural: 'That dice was lucky'.

Ee

EARTH, GROUND, SOIL

earth /ɜ:θ/ *noun*, means a number of things. As the name of our planet it is usually capitalized in a comparative context referring to other planets: 'Mars and Earth'. It also means 'soil': 'We have to use more earth to cover all these stones'. In electricity, 'connecting to earth' means inserting a wire in the electrical connection with no current. In AE, the term for this electrical connection is 'ground'.

ground /graʊnd/ *noun*, means the solid surface of the earth. It occurs in the idiomatic phrase: 'His feet never touched the ground', meaning that someone caused, or was the target of, an action that happened very quickly. In the plural, 'grounds' may mean an enclosed area of land or sea, or a good reason for doing something. See **CAMPUS**. See **GROUNDS ⇨ CAMPUS**. See **GROUNDS ⇨ CAUSE**.

soil /sɔɪl/ *noun*, is the upper layer of earth where plants grow and occurs more figuratively to mean land as a whole: 'He was the first American pilot to land on French soil after the war'.

EAST, EASTERN, EASTERLY

east /i:st/ *noun, adjective & adverb*, is the direction of the sunrise. When it refers to a direction, 'east' is not usually capitalized: 'The wind was blowing from the east'. It is capitalized when it is a regional name: 'East Anglia'; a defined region: 'He returned East' (eastern region of the USA); a country: East Timor; or part of a continent: 'East Africa', (note that these are not hyphenated in English, and remain separate words).
See **CAPITAL LETTERS**.

eastern /'i:stən/ *adjective*, is used for the region of a country to the east: 'There will be rain across eastern England'. 'Eastern' is capitalized when it refers to a proper noun such as: 'Central and Eastern Europe (CEE)', or 'Eastern languages' (languages of Asia).
See **WESTERN ⇨ WEST**.

easterly /'iːstəli/ *adjective*, means either in a direction towards the east: 'The animals were moving over the plains in an easterly direction'; or a wind that is blowing from the east: 'The ship started to roll when it was exposed to the easterly gale'. Note that 'easterly' is normally immediately followed by a noun.

EASY, EASILY, FACILE

easy /'iːzi/ *adjective & adverb*, means not difficult, or done without great effort. It is usually an adjective: 'The easy part of the exam was reading the questions'. There are only a few expressions that use 'easy' as an adverb: 'Stand easy', 'take it easy', 'easy come, easy go'.

easily /'iːzɪli/ *adverb*, means without effort and is more common than 'easy' as an adverb: 'She easily learned how to ski'.

facile /'fæsaɪl/ *adjective*, is a formal word that refers to something with little value as it is obtained too easily: 'This was a facile examination: the level was too low'. It is often used disapprovingly about things that are not carefully thought over: 'We asked for an investigation into the accident, but the politicians just gave a string of facile comments'.

EATABLE, EDIBLE

eatable /'iːtəbl̩/ *adjective*, means can be eaten, but without any great enjoyment: 'The fish had so many bones that it was scarcely eatable'. The plural noun form 'eatables', which means any food, is only used informally. See **UNEATABLE**.

edible /'edɪbl̩/ *adjective*, also means can be eaten, but this is in contrast to poisonous: 'Edible mushrooms are easily confused with poisonous toadstools'. See **INEDIBLE** ⇨ **UNEATABLE**.

ECONOMIC, ECONOMICS, ECONOMICAL, ECONOMICALLY, FINANCIAL

economic /iːkə'nɒmɪk/ *adjective*, refers to the practical distribution of goods and services: 'The new government's economic policy'. It is also connected with the profitability of a business or other concern: 'Natural gas is an economic resource'.

economics /iːkə'nɒmɪks/ *noun*, means the study of the production and distribution of wealth. Note that as an academic subject 'economics' always takes a singular verb: 'Economics is a sound choice at this university'. In other uses, 'economics' can take both singular and plural verbs. See **-ICS**.

economical /iːkə'nɒmɪkl̩/ *adjective*, refers to saving money, resources and time. Compare: 'Britain's economic performance' (the state of its economy) with 'a vehicle's economical performance' (cost saving because of its low fuel consumption). When describing a person, it is more common to use either a positive adjective such as thrifty or a negative one such as mean. The exception to this is the idiom 'economical with the truth', which means that a person is lying. See **LIE (2)**.

economically /iːkə'nɒmɪkəli/ *adverb*, has two uses. The first is related to the adjective 'economic': 'The gasfield is economically viable', meaning that it is profitable to develop. The second is related to 'economical': 'The factory was built as economically as possible', meaning that it was built as cheaply as possible.

financial /faɪ'nænʃl̩/ *adjective*, means associated with money or with the organization of monetary matters: 'The company's financial position was poor'. People and companies that are having 'financial' problems are described as being 'in financial difficulties' or experiencing 'financial setbacks'. A person who is responsible for the financial division or department of a company is the 'financial manager' or 'financial director'.

 'Let me introduce Mr Schmidt, our economical director.'

-ee, -er/or nouns

- The **-ee** form is added to a verb to refer to the person who receives something. Examples are: *addressee, employee, trainee*. Some -ee forms have general equivalents for those on the other side of an interaction, where *-er* (or *-or*) is added to equivalent verbs. Examples are: *addresser, employer, trainer*. (But note exceptions such as *escapee* and *escaper*, which are both people who have escaped.) However, not all these -er words correspond to an -ee form, for instance *lover, teacher, worker*.

- The **-er** form can also be applied to objects, such as *silencer* or *lawnmower*. Sometimes only the *-or* form is used for people: *author, elector, generator, perpetrator*. In other cases, the -er form and the *-or* form exist side by side, as alternatives with no difference in meaning: *adviser* (BE) / *advisor* (AE).

EFFECT^s, AFFECT^s

effect /ɪ'fekt/ *verb & noun*, as a verb, means to do or achieve something: 'The plane was grounded until repairs to the engine could be effected'. This is a formal word, and either 'done' or 'carried out' are alternatives. As a noun, 'effect' means a result or consequence: 'Rising prices are having an effect on the government's popularity'.

affect /ə'fekt/ *verb & /'æfekt/ noun*, as a verb, means to make a difference to or influence something: 'Computers are affecting our lives'; 'Her illness affected the whole family'. As a noun, 'affect' is only used in psychology, to mean an emotion which may influence behaviour. As both 'effect' and 'affect' are frequently misused, a useful rule of thumb is to consider 'effect' only as a noun ('the effects of pollution'), and 'affect' only as a verb ('pollution affects us all').

EFFECTIVE, EFFICIENT

effective /ɪ'fektɪv/ *adjective*, refers to something that solves a problem or creates a real result: 'The measures to halt inflation proved to be effective and prices stabilized'. 'Effective' can also be used about the date when a measure is to be implemented: 'These changes are effective as of 15 June'. 'Cost-effective' means something that is effective or productive in relation to its cost: 'The widespread use of email has proved to be highly cost-effective in most businesses'. Another term for this is 'cost-efficient'.

efficient /ɪ'fɪʃnt/ *adjective*, is used to describe people, machines, organizations or measures that produce results without wasting time or energy: 'I've bought a more efficient car which doesn't consume so much petrol'.

E.G., FOR EXAMPLE, FOR INSTANCE

e.g. /i: 'dʒi:/ is an abbreviation of 'for example' formed from the Latin *exempli gratia*, which is never written or read. Avoid home-made abbreviations such as 'f. ex.' Most style guides suggest that 'e.g.' should not be used in running text, but should only be written before examples in footnotes, brackets, and notes. Never use 'etc.' at the end of a phrase beginning with 'e.g.' See **I.E.**

for example /fər ɪg'zɑːmpl/, **for instance** /fər 'ɪnstəns/ are used to stress exemplification. They are synonymous and are recommended in running text. Normally they are placed after

the example: '... in London and Paris, for example'. When giving an example, do not combine 'such as' with 'for example'/'for instance' in the same phrase.

---

either ... or, neither ... nor

either ... or /'aɪðər...ɔːr/ and **neither ... nor** /'naɪðər ... nɔːr/ are used to show a choice between two objects and must only refer to two things: 'Neither the green nor the white labels are any good'. 'Either...or' can also be used to emphasize 'or': 'Either the blue or the black labels can be used'. Their position in the sentence depends on which aspect is being highlighted: 'She wants either a dog or a cat for her birthday', but: 'Either he apologizes or I will complain'. Note the following points about subject – verb agreement with 'either ... or' and 'neither ... nor':

- When 'either ... or', 'neither ... nor' link two singular subjects, the verb is singular: 'Either John or Mary is at the door'. When there are plural subjects, the verb is plural: 'Either the boys or the girls are here'.
- When 'either ... or', 'neither ... nor' link a singular subject and a plural subject, the verb agrees with the last subject: 'Either storms or flooding is likely'; 'Either flooding or storms are likely'.
- When 'either' or 'neither' is the subject of a verb, the verb is singular: 'We have contacted Renault and Fiat: neither is interested'.

The words 'either' and 'neither' have well established alternative pronunciations: both /'(n)aɪðər/ and /'(n)iːðər/ are generally acceptable in all forms of English.

ELAPSE, LAPSE

elapse /ɪ'læps/ *verb*, refers to the slow passing of time: 'Six months elapsed before he even started looking for a job'.

lapse /læps/ *verb*, means to be terminated: 'The insurance premium was not paid and the policy finally lapsed'. 'Lapse' can also be used about people who slowly drift into a negative manner of behaviour: 'He lapsed into a way of life that cost him his job'.

ELDER/ELDEST, OLDER/OLDEST

elder/eldest /'eldər, 'eldɪst/ *adjective*, refer to the age difference between two people, especially within a family: 'My elder brother is 25' or 'My eldest brother is 25, and my other brother is 23'. These words are also used without a noun: 'He is the elder/eldest'. It is not possible to use 'elder' with 'than'.
See **ELDERLY ⇨ AGE**.

older/oldest /'əʊldər, 'əʊldɪst/ *adjective*, are also used for comparing age, but are used in a broader range of contexts than 'elder/eldest': 'This is the oldest church in the country'. It has now become common for 'older' and 'oldest' to be used instead of 'elder' and 'eldest': 'She is the oldest of the four sisters'.

ELECTRIC, ELECTRICAL

electric /ɪ'lektrɪk/ *adjective*, refers to the direct production or use of electricity. Examples include: 'electric energy' and 'electric iron'.

electrical /ɪ'lektrɪkl̩/ *adjective*, refers to things connected less directly with electricity, such as 'electrical appliance' and 'electrical fault'. However, some expressions, such as 'electric/electrical shock' can use either combination. Note that graduates in 'electrical engineering' are called 'electrical engineers', and that 'electric engineers' would mean engineers powered by electricity.

 'Male 25, electric engineer, speak English well.' (From a CV)

ELK, MOOSE^S, MOUSSE^S

elk /elk/ *noun*, is the largest species of the deer family (*Alces alces*): 'Look. That elk is moving this way'. When considered as a target for hunters, the plural is 'elk', but in other contexts, 'elks' may be used as the plural form.

moose /muːs/ *noun*, is the AE term for *Alces alces*. The plural form is also 'moose'.

mousse /muːs/ *noun*, is a culinary term for a sweet or savoury dish made with whipped cream and eggs. This is pronounced the same as 'moose'.

 'Mousse hunting is one of our specialities.' (Tourist brochure)

EMAIL, E-COMMERCE

email /'iːmeɪl/ *noun*, is a system for sending electronic messages between registered computer users. The spelling 'email' is now more commonly used than 'e-mail'.
See **LETTERS AND EMAILS**. See **MAIL**.

e-commerce /'iːkɒmɜːs/ *noun*, means electronic commerce and has generated a number of similar terms. While 'e-business' is generally accepted, 'e-conomy' is not.

email addresses

There are two things to remember about email addresses in English:

- The @ sign is called *at* in English. This comes from bookkeeping/invoicing (*4 tyres @ GBP 45 each*). It is interesting how other languages have found different names for this sign. The French call it *arobas*, Spaniards *arroba*, Italians use *chiocciola* (snail). The German name is *Klammeraffe* (spider monkey), Dutch has *apestaart* (monkey tail), and in Russian it is called *sobachka* (dog). In Norwegian, it is *krøllalfa* (curly *a*), Swedish uses *snabel-a* (elephant's trunk), and *snabel* is used in Danish.
- Use the term *dot* to indicate a full stop on the line to divide the letters or words in the address. See **LETTERS AND EMAILS**. See **WEB ADRESSES**.

EMIGRANT, IMMIGRANT, MIGRANT

emigrant /'emɪgrənt/ *noun & adjective*, refers to movement from a country on a permanent basis (think of the 'e' for exit): '*The Titanic* carried many emigrants who departed from Liverpool'. A related noun is 'emigration'.

immigrant /'ɪmɪgrənt/ *noun & adjective*, refers to movement into a country on a permanent basis (think of the 'i' for into): 'Most early 20th century American immigrants from Europe were processed at Ellis Island'. A related noun is 'immigration'.

migrant /'maɪgrənt/ *noun & adjective*, refers to the process whereby people (or birds and other animals) move between countries on a temporary basis: 'The Turkish migrant workers in Germany have made an important contribution to the economy'. A related noun is 'migration'. Birds and some other animals tend to migrate seasonally.

EMPLOY, TAKE ON

employ /ɪmˈplɔɪ/ *verb*, means either to give someone a job that they will be paid for: 'We have just employed six more members of staff in the computer section'; or to have someone working for a company for a time: 'We employ 30 members of staff in the computer section'.

take on /teɪk ˈɒn/ *verb*, means to give someone a job: 'We have just taken on two temporary members of staff in the computer section'. 'Take on' is more informal than 'employ'. In AE, this would be 'hire'.
See **HIRE ⇨ RENT**.

EMPLOYER, EMPLOYEE, STAFF

employer /ɪmˈplɔɪər/ *noun*, means the person, company, or organization that employs workers and staff.

employee /ɪmˈplɔɪ.iː/ *noun*, means a paid worker: 'An employee of the Ford Motor Corporation'. Use 'employee(s)' when focusing on individuals as paid workers and the more general group word 'staff' otherwise.
See **-EE, -ER/OR NOUNS**.

staff /stɑːf/ *noun*, means workers who are employed in a company or organization considered as a group. There may be full-time, part-time, professional, skilled or technical staff. Note that in BE the verb is usually plural: 'The teaching staff are angry about the volume of administration'. In AE, however, the verb is always singular: 'The staff in our company is well-paid'. See **COLLECTIVE NOUNS**.
See **PERSONNEL ⇨ PERSONAL**. See **STAFF**.

ENDORSE, ENDORSEMENT

endorse /ɪnˈdɔːs/ *verb*, literally means write on the back of something, as in: "Will you sign the back of the cheque to endorse it?' It can also mean to give public support: '60% of the party endorse the policy of the new leader'.

endorsement /ɪnˈdɔːsmənt/ *noun*, is the act of giving public support to someone or something: 'They gave the candidate their full endorsement'. In BE, this term also refers to driving offences, which are recorded on someone's driving licence. After receiving a certain number of these, the licence is withdrawn: 'He received three endorsements for speeding in two years'.

ENOUGH, ADEQUATE, SUFFICIENT

enough /ɪˈnʌf/ *determiner, adverb & pronoun*, means as much or as many as required. It is less formal than 'adequate' and 'sufficient', and is consequently used more often. As a determiner, 'enough' is used before the noun in expressions like 'enough money', 'enough problems'. As an adverb, 'enough' follows the adjective: 'It is not good enough: he is old enough to know better'. Examples of 'enough' used as a pronoun are: 'I have got enough'; and in the idiomatic expression 'enough is enough'.

adequate /ˈædɪkwət/ *adjective*, usually means satisfactory in quantity or quality. Like satisfactory, 'adequate' can mean only just good enough: 'His results at school were adequate, but not especially good'.

sufficient /səˈfɪʃnt/ *adjective*, means as much as is needed for a specific purpose: 'When we have sufficient funds from industry, we will announce the new scholarship scheme'.

ENQUIRE/ENQUIRY⁵, INQUIRE/INQUIRY⁵

enquire /ɪnˈkwaɪər/ *verb*, means to ask about something or require information: 'She enquired about his children'. A more informal choice would be 'ask'. The related noun is 'enquiry' /ɪnˈkwaɪəri/. These are the usual spellings in BE.

inquire /ɪnˈkwaɪər/ *verb*, is the AE spelling of 'enquire'. The related noun 'inquiry' is usually pronounced /ˈɪnkwəri/ in AE. Note that in BE, 'inquiry' is normally used for a formal investigation: 'A government inquiry into violence in the home.'

ENTRY, ENTRANCE, ADMISSION, ADMITTANCE

entry /ˈentri/ *noun*, means the act of getting into a building or enclosed space and is often seen in the negative sign 'No Entry'. 'Entry' also means a person's application to join an organization or take part in a competition: 'Entry forms are available from the Secretary'. In another sense, 'entry' means a contribution to a competition: 'His entry for the essay competition was so good that no one could believe he had written it himself'. See **ACCESS**.

entrance /ˈentrəns/ *noun*, is the place where a person can get into a building or enclosed space: 'The tradesmen's entrance is at the back'. 'Entrance' also means the act of entering a room, especially in a conspicuous way: 'She made a grand entrance down the central staircase'. Like 'entry', it can mean an application to join an institution or group, and is often used in the term: 'entrance exam'.

admission /əd'mɪʃn/ *noun*, means the act of entering a place or being accepted as a member of an institution: 'Admission charges to cinemas are still reasonable'; 'It was difficult to gain admission to the golf club'. 'Admission' also means a confession: 'His admission of guilt shocked the court'. See **ACCESS**.
See **ADMIT ⇨ ACKNOWLEDGE**.

admittance /əd'mɪtəns/ *noun*, means permission to enter a place. It is often used in phrases forbidding access: 'No admittance' or 'Admittance is prohibited'.

ENVELOP, ENVELOPE

envelop /ɪn'veləp/ *verb*, means to enclose or encase: 'She enveloped herself in her towel'. Note that the stress is on the second syllable, and that there is no final 'e' in the spelling.

envelope /'envələʊp/ *noun*, is what letters are placed inside: 'We bought 10 A4 self-adhesive envelopes at the supermarket'. The stress is on the first syllable.

ENVIOUS, ENVIABLE

envious /'envɪəs/ *adjective*, describes the feeling of wanting something that belongs to or is enjoyed by another person: 'He was envious of the TV star's popularity'. The related noun is 'envy'.

enviable /'envɪəbl/ *adjective*, means being in a position worthy of envy: 'His position as bank manager made him an enviable member of the local community'.

ENVIRONMENT, MILIEU, SURROUNDINGS, SETTING

environment /ɪn'vaɪərənmənt/ *noun*, means the physical and natural world as well as the social conditions: 'People's lack of involvement in the threats to their environment is a matter of widespread concern'.

milieu /miː'ljɜː/ *noun*, refers only to the social environment: 'The artistic milieu around the London theatres'. 'Milieus' or 'milieux' /miː'ljɜːz/ are the plurals of 'milieu'.

surroundings /sə'raʊndɪŋz/ *noun*, refers to the land or conditions around a person or animal: 'They grew up in delightful surroundings in the countryside of Wales'.

setting /'setɪŋ/ *noun*, means physical surroundings, and is often restricted to literature and films: 'They really captured the setting of Victorian England in that West End show'.

EQUAL, MORE EQUAL

equal /'iːkwəl/ *adjective*, means of the same quantity, size or degree as something else: 'They have always fought for equal pay and equal rights'.

more equal /'mɔːr iːkwəl/ and 'very equal' /'veri iːkwəl/ *adverbial phrases* are not recommended in formal English. If something is 'equal' to another thing, it cannot logically be compared with it, and termed as 'more equal', because there are no degrees in equality. However, things can be 'almost equal' and 'exactly equal', or even 'less than equal'. As all rules are made to be broken, there is the famous quotation from George Orwell who wrote ironically: 'Some animals are more equal than others' (*Animal Farm*, 1945).
See **ABSOLUTES AND FUZZY ABSOLUTES**.

-es, -s after nouns ending in o

- A rule of thumb about how to form plurals with nouns ending in *o* is the following: *-es* is added to form the plural of nouns such as *potato*, *cargo* and *hero*. *-s* is added to form the plural of nouns ending in *io* or *eo* such as: *radio*, *cameo*; to musical terms like *soprano*, *banjo*; to truncations such as *kilo*, *photo*; and to newer nouns such as *commando*.
- There are a few exceptions, so always use a spellchecker or dictionary. See **PLURAL NOUNS**.

Former US Vice-President Dan Quayle will always be remembered for trying to correct a pupil's spelling by adding an 'e' to 'potato'.

ESPECIAL/ESPECIALLY, SPECIAL/SPECIALLY, PARTICULAR/PARTICULARLY

especial/especially /ɪ'speʃl/ɪ'speʃəli/ *adjective/adverb*, mean exceptional, particular and more outstanding than others: 'Pelé was an especially skilled footballer'. When used as an adjective, it is formal, and a matter of 'especial importance' is more informally termed 'special importance' or 'particular importance'.

special/specially /'speʃl/'speʃəli/ *adjective/adverb*, mean specific, made for a specific purpose or a designated reason: 'The hotel was specially designed for wheelchair users'. See **SPECIALITY**.

particular/particularly /pə'tɪkjolər/ pə'tɪkjoləli/ *adjective/adverb*, mean 'especially', and the adverb form 'particularly' always has a comma before it when it is used to introduce extra information. 'She likes seafood, particularly lobsters'. Remember that 'particularly' has two 'l's, and that both should be pronounced.

ESTATE AGENT, REALTOR

estate agent /ɪ'steɪt ˌeɪdʒənt/ is a BE term for someone who sells houses and property: 'The estate agent sold twenty houses last year, but could still not afford to buy one himself'. The term comes from 'real estate', meaning property.

realtor /'rɪəltɔːr/ *noun*, is an AE term for an estate agent.

ESTIMATE, BALLPARK FIGURE

estimate /'estɪmət/ *noun &* /'estɪmeɪt/ *verb*, as a noun, means an approximate calculation. Note that the final syllable contains a neutral vowel. As a verb, 'estimate' means to make an approximate calculation of the number, quantity or price of something: 'I estimate that this order will cost about $12,000'. Note that the final syllable is pronounced 'mate'.

ballpark figure /'bɔːlpɑːk 'fɪgər/ *noun*, is an informal AE expression that suggests arriving at an estimated figure or price range which is within certain limits, as exemplified by the boundary of a sports field ('ballpark'): 'Our best ballpark figure is from $10 000 to $14 000' See **PARAMETER**.

ET AL., CO-WORKERS

et al. /et 'æl/ is generally used when referring to three co-authors or more in a text or in reference lists. Remember always to use plural verbs and pronouns when 'et al.' is part of the subject: 'Franks et al. develop a new approach to syntactic analysis'. Also never use a stop after 'et', which means and. 'Et al.' is an abbreviation of *et alii* (or possibly *et aliae*, if all the authors are female) although the full forms are never used.

co-workers /'kəʊ.wɜːkəz/ *noun*, is a common AE alternative to 'et al.': 'Jones and co-workers (1995) claim that an alternative method is possible'. It is recommended to use a hyphen after 'co' to avoid any confusion with 'cow'.

I WOULD LIKE TO THANK MY COW-WORKERS

etc.[s], et cetera[s]

etc. /et 'setərə/ is the abbreviation for *et cetera*, and is hardly ever used in its full form. Some tips about how to use *etc.*:

* In formal writing, it is recommended to use *etc.* only in footnotes, brackets, and references.
* *And so on* or *and so forth* are recommended alternatives for *etc.* in reports and other types of formal writing.
* Never pronounce *etc.* as /ek'setərə/ or /iː'tiːsiː/.
* Use *etc.* for things, not people: *Popular models are Ford, Opel, Toyota, etc.*, rather than: 'Her boyfriends were Tom, Dick, Harry, etc.'
* Always write *etc.*, not the ampersand and c, as in '&c'.
* Avoid writing 'and etc.', since *et* means *and*.
* Never place *etc.* at the end of a list beginning with words such as: *include, such as* or *for example*, or other words that already convey the idea of representative examples.

Et cetera is occasionally written out in full instead of *etc.* particularly when quoting spoken English. This shows that a list is too uninteresting and extensive to complete: *The trainer gave the usual talk about lazy players, lack of effort, tiredness, et cetera, et cetera.*

EURO[s], EUR[s]

euro /'jʊərəʊ/ *noun*, means the single European currency and the EU's official currency, which replaced the national currencies in most EU member states on 2002-01-01. The indefinite article which is used with 'euro' is 'a', not 'an'. Officially, this is both the singular and plural form of the currency in English: 'one euro', 'ten euro'. Do not combine the euro sign € with the term 'euro'. The cent, formally known as the eurocent, is also invariable, as in 'ten cent'. Note that 'euro' is not capitalized.

EUR is the ISO currency code for the 'euro'. Although EUR is written before an amount 'EUR 52 000', this is read as '52 000 euro'. See **CURRENCY UNITS**.

EVENT, INCIDENT, HAPPENING, EPISODE, OCCURRENCE

event /ɪ'vent/ *noun*, indicates something of significance: 'The recent political discussions in Geneva were a historic event'. This is usually the strongest of the words in this group.

incident /'ɪnsɪdənt/ *noun*, means an event of minor importance: 'There were many such incidents that eventually made the police suspicious'. In diplomatic terms, an 'incident' can be a serious conflict or disagreement that is often violent: 'The attack caused an international incident'.

happening /'hæpənɪŋ/ *noun*, refers to a strange event: 'They say that the house is haunted, after a strange happening there once'. In this sense, it is often used in the plural. A 'happening' can also be an artistic event, such as a rock concert: 'U2's show was a real happening'.

episode /'epɪsəʊd/ *noun*, means something that happened or a period of time in a person's life that was memorable for good or bad reasons: 'That was a nasty episode in her life'. It can also mean a part of a TV series: 'Tonight's episode is on at 8 p.m.'

occurrence /'əkʌrəns/ *noun*, means an event, but does not indicate any quality or type of event: 'Hearing English spoken on Swedish TV news is an everyday occurrence'. This is the most neutral of these words. Note the spelling, which has double 'c' and double 'r'.

EVENTUALLY, EVENTUAL, EVENTUALITY

eventually /ɪ'ventjʊəli/ *adverb*, refers to something that will happen after a period of time. This usually involves a considerable delay or a series of problems: 'Passengers at the new international airport may eventually get better service'. See **PRESENTLY ▷ NOW**.

eventual /ɪ'ventjʊəl/ *adjective*, means happening at the end of a process: 'We do not know what the eventual profit will be this early in the project'. This means that it is known that there will be a profit, but not how much it may be.

eventuality /ɪventjʊ'ælɪti/ *noun*, means something unfortunate that may possibly happen: 'Our contingency planning is based on being prepared for any eventuality or emergency'.

Many passengers were alarmed when a pilot announced: 'Ladies and gentlemen, we will eventually be landing at London Heathrow'.

EVERYDAY^S, EVERY DAY^S, DAILY

everyday /'evrɪdeɪ/ *adjective*, means commonplace and usual: 'He treated the news of his huge win on the lottery like an everyday occurrence'. There is no stress on 'day'.

every day /'evri 'deɪ/ *adverb*, means each day considered separately: 'She wakes up at 6 a.m. every day'. Note that this is written as two words and that there is stress on both.

daily /'deɪli/ *adjective & adverb*, means done or produced 'every day' or on every weekday: 'The daily paper is here' (as opposed to the Sunday paper).

EVERYONE/EVERYBODY^S, EVERY ONE, EVERY BODY^S

everyone/everybody /'evrɪwʌn, 'evrɪbɒdi/ *noun*, means all the people suggested by the context: 'Everyone in Europe knows what Brussels represents'. 'Everyone' and 'everybody' are synonyms, but 'everybody' is more formal than 'everyone'. One of the apparently illogical things about English is that although the subject may be many tens of millions of people, 'everyone/everybody' always has a singular verb, because it refers to 'every single one/body', and 'one/body' is the subject. See **ANYONE**. See **NO ONE**. See **SOMEONE**.

every one /'evri 'wʌn/ *adverb*, means each person or object considered separately, and may be used for people or things: 'Not just some, but every one of the cars had been broken into during the night'. 'Every one' is written as two words and both words are stressed. Note that 'every one' always takes a singular verb, because it refers to 'every single one', and 'one' is the subject.

every body /'evri 'bɒdi/ *noun*, means all the dead bodies: 'Every body was dug up for medical examination after the press report about a massacre'. 'Every body' is written as two words and both words are stressed. Note that 'every body' always takes a singular verb, because it refers to 'every single body', and 'body' is the subject.

EVERYTHING[S], EVERY THING[S]

everything /'evrɪθɪŋ/ *noun*, means the entire situation, as a whole: 'Everything in the house was destroyed'. Note that 'everything' always takes a singular verb.

every thing /'evri 'θɪŋ/ *noun*, means each item in a given situation: 'Every single thing in her wardrobe was destroyed'. This is written as two words and both words are stressed. As in the example given here, the two words may be separated by an adjective. Note that 'every thing' always takes a singular verb.

EVERYWHERE, EVERYPLACE

everywhere /'evrɪhweər/ *adverb*, means in all places: 'They looked for the cat everywhere'.

everyplace /'evrɪpleɪs/ *adverb*, means the same as 'everywhere', but this word is only used in AE.

EVIDENCE, TESTIMONY

evidence /'evɪdəns/ *noun*, means a fact or object that reveals the truth of a matter. 'There's no evidence to suggest that he's the best student in the class'. 'Evidence' also means the information presented to the court during a legal investigation: 'Since he was not considered a reliable witness, his evidence was disregarded by the jury'.

testimony /'testɪməni/ *noun*, is a written or spoken statement by a witness in a court of law: 'The expert testimony produced proved to be contradictory and thus worthless'.

EXCELLENT, EXCELLENCE, EXCELLENCY

excellent /'eksələnt/ *adjective*, means outstanding and extremely good. There should be no qualifying adverb of degree if something is 'excellent'. Things can be 'almost excellent', 'nearly excellent' or 'quite excellent'. But 'more excellent' and 'very excellent' are not recommended in formal English.
See **ABSOLUTES AND FUZZY ABSOLUTES**.

excellence /'eksələns/ *noun*, is the quality of being outstanding and extremely good: 'This restaurant is renowned for its excellence and warm hospitality'.

Excellency /'eksələnsi/ *noun*, is a title given to high officials of a state, particularly ambassadors. 'Your Excellency' is the formally correct salutation in letters to such a person.

EXCEPTIONAL, EXTRAORDINARY

exceptional /ɪk'sepʃuəl/ *adjective*, means outstanding or extremely good: 'The standard of the dancing at the school play was quite exceptional'. It also means 'special' when referring to a situation in which certain conditions apply: 'These regulations can only be waived in exceptional circumstances'.

extraordinary /ɪk'strɔːdn̩ri/ *adjective*, means out of the ordinary or unexpectedly extreme: 'Thunderstorms one day and sun the next: what extraordinary weather for July in Madrid'. See **SELDOM ⟹ RARE**.

exclamation mark, exclamation point (!)

There is a tendency by some writers to overuse the *exclamation mark* (*exclamation point* in AE) in English. When correctly used, an exclamation mark is there to stress a forceful utterance that gives a warning or indicates astonishment and surprise. *Note that cyanide gas can cause severe poisoning. Always avoid inhaling the gas!*

All English style guides agree that exclamation marks should be used sparingly. Emails starting with *Hi!* are likely to cause irritation in business life. See **LETTERS AND EMAILS**.

EXCLUDE, PREVENT, INHIBIT

exclude /ɪksˈkluːd/ *verb*, means to deliberately leave out or not consider something: 'An oil price of USD 20 a barrel is completely excluded in this forecast'. 'Exclude' can also mean deny access: 'When he was convicted, he was excluded from the guest list at the Embassy'. See **EXCEPT ⟹ ACCEPT**.

prevent /prɪˈvent/ *verb*, means to hinder or avoid something happening. If 'prevent' refers to hindering an action by someone, this means that physical or legal force may be involved: 'He was prevented from seeing his children on weekdays by a court order'.

inhibit /ɪnˈhɪbɪt/ *verb*, means to hinder, restrain or prevent. If 'inhibit' refers to restraining someone's action, this means that moral or social pressure is being applied: 'He was inhibited from telling his usual crude jokes because there were young children present'.

EXCUSE, PRETEXT

excuse /ɪksˈkjuːs/ *noun*, is a true or invented reason for doing something: 'She had a very convenient excuse for opening a bottle of champagne'.

pretext /ˈpriːtekst/ *noun*, is a false reason that is given for doing something else: 'That business trip provided a pretext for him to attend a job interview in Rome'. See **REASON ⟹ CAUSE**.

EXECUTIVE, EXECUTIONER, EXECUTOR

executive /ɪgˈzekjʊtɪv/ *noun & adjective*, as a noun, means a person with an important position in an organization: 'Many top executives also have a high-powered lifestyle'. 'Executive' can also refer to a group of people who run an organization: 'The national executive of the football association is going to a meeting in Geneva tomorrow'. 'The executive' means the part of an Anglo-European type government that puts laws into effect: 'The executive often has problems agreeing with the Senate'. As an adjective, 'executive' is only used together with a noun: 'executive suite' at a hotel and 'executive lounge' in an airport (a lounge reserved for special classes of passengers). Always remember to put the stress on the second syllable 'zeck', to avoid any confusion with 'executioner'.
See **MANAGING DIRECTOR**.
See **SALES REPRESENTATIVE ⟹ SALESPERSON**.

executioner /eksɪˈkjuːʃənər/ *noun*, means a public official whose job is to put convicted criminals to death: 'The executioner met the prisoners on death row'. Always remember to put the stress on the third syllable 'kew'.

executor /ɪgˈzekjʊtər/ *noun*, is a legal term that means the person or bank that is selected by someone making a will. When death occurs, the 'executor' has the task of carrying out the instructions in the will. Always remember to put the stress on the second syllable 'zeck', to avoid any confusion with 'executioner'.

 'He described his job as financial executioner.'

EXPENSE, EXPENDITURE

expense /ɪksˈpens/ *noun*, means the cost or the money required for something: 'Look at the view over the sea: this house is well worth the expense'. 'Expenses' (only plural) means money spent on hotel and travel costs in the course of work, that is refunded by an employer: 'The manager refused to accept the expenses the agent had claimed for travel'.

expenditure /ɪksˈpendɪtʃər/ *noun*, means the act of spending official funds: 'Public expenditure on the Health Service is out of hand'. This is a formal word that is almost always used in connection with governments, the national economy, and in business.

EXPERIENCE, EXPERIMENT

experience /ɪksˈpɪərɪəns/ *noun*, means knowledge, skill or practice: 'She gained extensive experience in biology after ten years of teaching'. 'Experience' is uncountable when used in this collective sense. However, when it refers to isolated events that form part of a person's life, it is countable: 'She had had a tough life and published her story in a novel called *My experiences in Hollywood*'. See **CV WRITING**.

experiment /ɪksˈperɪmənt/ *noun*, is a scientific procedure to test a theory. If a scientific experiment is reliable it can be repeated and, by using the same method, will produce the same results. In a more general use, an 'experiment' tests what happens when a new idea is tried out: 'I've never tried to make Christmas pudding before: this is an experiment'.

 'Extensive experiences in Biology.' (From a CV)

Ff

-f, -fe endings in nouns and plurals -fes, -fs, -ves

- There are no rules about how to form the plural of words ending with -f or -fe. Here is a list of some of the most common words that have these endings:

  belief-beliefs calf-calves dwarf-dwarfs/dwarves elf-elves grief-griefs half-halves himself/herself/itself-themselves knife-knives leaf-leaves[1] life-lives[2] loaf-loaves myself-ourselves oaf-oafs proof-proofs relief-reliefs roof-roofs scarf-scarfs/scarves self-selves sheaf-sheaves shelf-shelves staff-staffs thief-thieves wharf-wharfs/wharves wife-wives yourself-yourselves

- [1]The Canadian ice hockey team is the *Toronto Maple Leafs*, not 'Leaves'.

  [2]The plural of the type of painting known as a still life is *still lifes*, not 'lives'.

  See **PLURAL NOUNS**.

FACILITY, FACULTY

facility /fə'sɪlɪti/ *noun*, means an ability to do something easily: 'He had a considerable facility for speaking in public'. In this sense it is a fairly formal word. Another, more general meaning is that of buildings or equipment provided for a specific purpose: 'The college has very good sports facilities'. 'Facility' can also refer to an additional feature of a machine, etc.: 'The cash machine has a facility for paying out different currencies'.

faculty /'fækəlti/ *noun*, means any of the human senses: 'He lost the faculty of speech at an early age'. It also refers to the abilities and talents that someone is born with: 'The Prince has the faculty for saying the right thing, although often not in the right place'. In another sense, 'faculty' is a group of related university departments: 'The languages faculty is now in a separate building from the law faculty'. Note that 'faculty' is capitalized when it is part of a title: 'Faculty of Arts'. 'Faculty' in AE means a member of the teaching staff and administration in a university, college or school.

FACT, IN FACT, AS A MATTER OF FACT

fact /fækt/ *noun*, means a situation that undisputedly exists: 'The fact that he was at home means that he could not have committed the crime'. In another sense, 'fact' means something that can be proved to be true: 'It is a fact that water boils at 100°C'. Therefore the word 'true' in the phrase 'true fact' /'truː 'fækt/ is redundant, and is best avoided. Recommended alternatives are 'this is true' or 'it is true that... '.

in fact /ɪn 'fækt/ and **as a matter of fact** /əz ə 'mætər əv 'fækt/ are used to develop or correct what has already been said: 'The morning was chilly. In fact, it was close to freezing'; 'It was a beautiful city. As a matter of fact, we stayed there last summer'. Avoid using 'in fact' and 'as a matter of fact' in general or introductory statements: 'The expansion of the IT industry has created a demand for new skills', (not: '... has in fact created a demand...'. See **VERBIAGE**.

FAIL, FAILURE

fail /feɪl/ *verb*, means to be unsuccessful: 'He wanted the job but unfortunately failed the interview'. 'Fail' also implies negligence about something that was not done: 'The government failed to inform us of the radioactive fallout'. Avoid using 'fail' when something that was not done was unplanned. Machine parts and human organs that stop working are said to have 'failed': 'The engines failed, and the crash was inevitable'.

failure /'feɪljər/ *noun*, means lack of success: 'She found it difficult to accept failure'. It also means not following procedure: 'Failure to follow these installation instructions will invalidate your guarantee'; or refers to something that does not work as it is expected to: 'She suffered liver failure at a young age'. Note that 'business failure' means the collapse of a business, and 'crop failure' means that crops have not grown sufficiently to produce food.

FAIRLY, PRETTY, RATHER

fairly /'feəli/ *adverb*, means in a just and reasonable manner: 'His lawyer told him that he had been judged fairly'. When used before an adjective, 'fairly' means 'to some extent, but no more than average': 'She's a fairly good tennis player'. See **FAIR ⇨ JUST**. See **QUITE**.

pretty /'prɪti/ *adverb*, means 'to some extent': 'I haven't got my watch on, but I'm pretty sure it's about three o'clock'. The British love of understatement has led to 'pretty' also being used to mean 'very': 'He was pretty angry when I stood on his toe'. This is an informal word, and mostly used in spoken English. See **QUITE**.

rather /'rɑːðər/ *adverb*, means 'to a certain extent', but is a more forceful expression than 'fairly': 'It's rather warm today, isn't it?' 'Rather' is often used to modify adjectives which express criticism: 'She's a rather silly girl'. However, when used before a verb, 'rather' makes a sentence sound less forceful: 'I rather think you are wrong'. In another sense, 'rather' is used to mean 'more precisely': 'We need more teachers. Rather, we need qualified science teachers'; and it can also mean 'on the contrary': 'There is nothing wrong with the workforce. Rather, it is the management holding them back'. See **QUITE**.

false friends

Whenever we learn a new language, we have to beware of false friends, or words which look or sound the same, or almost the same, as words in our native language. For instance, the English word *actual* has an apparent equivalent in most European languages: *actuel* (French), *actual* (Spanish), *atual* (Portuguese), *attuale* (Italian), *aktuell* (German), *actueel* (Dutch), *aktuelan* (Croatian) etc. Unfortunately, the English word rarely, if ever, means the same as the false friend in any of these languages. The English translation of any one of these is 'current', or 'topical', and the meaning of the English word *actual* is 'real' or 'true'. This example is a problem to many learners of English, but there are many more which may be specific to one language or to only a small group of languages. The English word *raisin* means a dried grape, but the French for any grape is *raisin*, while *grappe* is French for a bunch of grapes. The Italian *grappa* meanwhile is a distilled spirit, and the Finnish *greippi* means grapefruit. This book includes examples of false friends, but the best advice is: when tempted to use an unfamiliar English word which looks or sounds almost the same as the one you would use in your native language — look it up in a good English dictionary, and make certain that you are not falling into a trap.

FAMILIAR, FAMILIAL

familiar /fə'mɪljər/ *adjective*, refers to a person or place that is well-known: 'She was on TV every week and soon became a familiar face in her home town'.

familial /fə'mɪliəl/ *adjective*, means related to or typical of a family: 'He was delighted to see that his baby had red hair, which was a familial characteristic'. This is a formal word. It is more common to use the adjective 'family', as in a 'family occasion' or a 'family custom'.

FAMOUS, INFAMOUS, NOTORIOUS

famous /'feɪməs/ *adjective*, refers to a person, thing or place that receives widespread attention. It is a neutral word: 'Tom is famous in his home town for being the unluckiest man on earth'.

infamous /'ɪnfəməs/ *adjective*, means being famous for being bad: 'Several of the prison officers were infamous for the way they treated prisoners'. Note that this word is stressed on the first syllable, not the second.

notorious /nəʊ'tɔːriəs/ *adjective*, also means being famous for being bad. It is generally interchangeable with 'infamous', but as an adverb, 'notoriously' is more common than 'infamously'.

FANATIC, FANATICAL, FANATICISM

fanatic /fə'nætɪk/ *noun*, means either a person who is extremely enthusiastic about something, such as a 'football fanatic'; or someone with extreme opinions about something: 'He's a fanatic about healthy food'. See **-IC, -ICAL**.

fanatical /fə'nætɪkl̩/ *adjective*, means extremely enthusiastic: 'My brother is fanatical about going to the gym, even if he isn't feeling well'. It also refers to a person or ideology that is considered to hold or promote extreme views: 'The leader of the sect was fanatical about obedience from the members'.

fanaticism /fə'nætɪsɪzm̩/ *noun*, refers to extreme views or behaviour: 'The police prevented football fanaticism from exploding into violence'.

FAR AWAY[S], FARAWAY[S]

far away /'fɑːr ə'weɪ/ *adverb*, refers to distance and is spelt as two words: 'The mountains are not far away'. Both words are stressed.

faraway /'fɑːrəweɪ/ *adjective*, also refers to distance but is spelt as one word: 'A glimpse of the faraway mountains'. There is only one stress, which is on the first syllable.

FARTHER/FARTHEST, FURTHER/FURTHEST

farther /'fɑːðər/ *comparative adjective & adverb*, is the comparative form of far, and means at or to a greater physical distance: 'The restaurant is farther from the town centre than I thought'. 'Farthest' /'fɑːðɪst/ is the superlative form, and is more common in AE than 'furthest'.

further /'fɜːðər/ *comparative adjective*, is an alternative to 'farther' in the sense of physical distance: 'Is the beach much further?' However, 'further' can also mean more: 'Do you have any further questions?' As an adverb, 'further', but not 'farther', is used to mean to a greater extent: 'The police are going to question the man further'. As a verb, 'further one's chances/ambitions' means to improve the chances of achieving an ambition: 'He furthered his ambitions of finding a good job by moving to London'. 'Furthest' /'fɜːðɪst/ is the superlative form.

FEEDBACK, RESPONSE

feedback /'fiːdbæk/ *noun*, means information or advice about the quality of something: 'In advertising, systematic feedback from consumers is always recorded'. 'Feedback' is also used in a technical sense to mean the distortion of sound caused by the return of power to a system such as an amplifier. This is an uncountable noun.

response /rɪs'pɒns/ *noun*, means either an individual answer: 'He gave a negative response'; or a collective reaction. In this sense, it is a general term for 'feedback': 'There has been very little response to the advert that we put in the paper'. See REPLY, ANSWER.

FEMALE, FEMININE, WOMANLY, EFFEMINATE

female /'fiːmeɪl/ *adjective & noun*, refers to the sex of a human or animal which is capable of producing offspring, or of a plant that can produce fruit: 'Many female birds have plain-coloured feathers'. It also means related to a woman: 'In pantomimes, it is common for a man to play a female role'. See MALE. See SEXIST LANGUAGE.

feminine /'femɪnɪn/ *adjective*, means the qualities traditionally associated with women, such as gracefulness and lack of aggression: 'She is a very feminine woman'. 'Feminine' is also a grammatical term referring to the gender of a part of speech. See GENDER ⟹ SEX. See MASCULINE ⟹ MALE.

womanly /'wʊmənli/ *adjective*, refers to the behaviour or appearance associated with a woman rather than a girl: 'Her womanly figure meant that she was perfect for the role of the mother in the play'. Note that the adjective 'girlish' suggests a less mature appearance or manner. See GIRLISH ⟹ BOYISH.

effeminate /ɪ'femɪnɪt/ *adjective*, is used of men who have feminine characteristics: 'He was really effeminate and even used make-up and false eyelashes'. It may be considered insulting to use this word.

FERMENT, BREW, DISTIL

ferment /fə'ment/ *verb*, means to produce alcohol from yeast and sugar. Figuratively it means to develop ideas, often through anger, over a long period of time: 'His plan for revenge had been fermenting in his brain for months'. Never confuse 'ferment' with its soundalike 'foment', which means encourage someone to stir up trouble.

brew /bruː/ *verb*, means to make a drink like tea by soaking and boiling the dry ingredients. Beer is first brewed, then fermented with hops for flavouring. Figuratively, 'brew' can also be used to mean develop: 'A storm is brewing'. This may mean stormy weather, or a political argument.

distil /dɪs'tɪl/ *verb*, means to produce a concentrated substance by boiling and condensation. Alcoholic spirits are produced by fermenting and then distilling the substance. 'Scotch whisky is distilled from malted barley'. The AE spelling is 'distill'.

FEW, A FEW, SEVERAL, MANY

few /fjuː/ *adjective*, means not many: 'There were few people at the exhibition'. 'Few' emphasizes the absence of something, particularly when combined with very. It is used with plural nouns and a plural verb.

a few /ə 'fjuː/ means some or a small number: 'There were a few people at the exhibition'. 'A few' suggests a small number, but gives a more positive impression than 'few'. 'Quite a few' means a fairly large number: 'Quite a few of his colleagues could not afford to retire'.

several /'sevərəl/ adjective, means an unspecified small quantity that is more than two: 'There are several people on my course who come from the same town as me'.

many /'meni/ adjective, means a large number and is always greater than 'several': 'During her life she had many boyfriends'. In spoken English, 'a lot (of)' is a more common alternative.

FEWER, LESS

fewer /'fjuːər/ adjective, is the comparative form of 'few', and is used with plural nouns: 'Due to the high cost of petrol, there were fewer cars on the road'.

less /les/ adjective, is the comparative form of 'little', and is used with uncountable nouns, like information and damage: 'There was less information about that person's health than the doctors would have liked'.

FIANCÉ[S], FIANCÉE[S]

fiancé /fi'āseɪ/ or /fi'ɒnseɪ/ noun, means the man that a woman is engaged to be married to: 'Marie met her fiancé in Paris'. Note the use of the acute accent.

fiancée /fi'āseɪ/ or /fi'ɒnseɪ/ noun, means the woman that a man is engaged to be married to: 'John met his fiancée in Spain'. Note the use of the acute accent.

FILE, FOLDER, BINDER

file /faɪl/ noun, means the documentation about a case (legal, medical, etc.) or one unit in a filing system. 'File' may also refer to the physical container of the data, such as a 'lever-arch file', which is a large holder for documents. A 'file' in computing terms means a collection of information on a disk: 'We have tried to access that file but the diskette was accidentally damaged'.

folder /'fəʊldər/ noun, means a lightweight cardboard holder for documents. Files on PCs are collected in folders, as a way of organizing and storing them: 'I have just created three new folders so that I can sort out these files'.

binder /'baɪndər/ noun, means a stiff cardboard holder for documents. 'Loose-leaf binders' and 'ring binders' are common features in most offices.

FILL IN, FILL OUT

fill in /fɪl 'ɪn/ verb, means to complete something: 'He filled in the passport renewal form'. To 'fill someone in' is an informal way of saying to give them more details: 'When he returned to work, he asked to be filled in on developments'.

fill out /fɪl 'aʊt/ verb, in BE means to put on weight: 'She filled out after a long summer of cream teas'. In AE, 'fill out' means to complete something: 'He filled out his passport renewal form'. This is the equivalent of the BE 'fill in', and is becoming common in BE.

FINANCE, FUND, FUNDING

finance /'faɪnæns, faɪ'næns/ verb & noun, as a verb, means to provide money for a specific purpose, or to give financial support: 'This development in Africa was financed by the Red Cross'. As a noun, 'finance' means the money used in order to run a business or other activity, or the management of large amounts of money, by a government or a large enterprise: 'I am studying economics, but would like to specialize in banking and finance'. 'Finance' is uncountable in the above senses. The plural form 'finances' is also used in this sense, but in addition can refer to a person's monetary resources: 'My finances are in a poor state at the moment'.

fund /fʌnd/ verb & noun, as a verb, means to provide money for a specific purpose: 'The European Commission has funded this research programme'. As a noun, a 'fund' is a sum of money set aside for a specific purpose: 'The Worldwide Fund for Nature'. Figuratively it may be used for a large amount of anything: 'A fund of useless information'. The plural form 'funds' means money that is available for a particular purpose, or financial resources in general: 'Public funds are available to those wishing to start a small business'.

funding /'fʌndɪŋ/ noun, means the same as funds, but is used with a singular verb: 'The funding for this project is inadequate'.

FIND OUT, ASCERTAIN

find out /faɪnd 'aʊt/ verb, means to discover something either on purpose or by accident: 'I need to find out what time the next train leaves'. Note that to 'find someone out' means to discover that a person has not been telling the truth, or has been attempting to deceive in some other way: 'He had been stealing from the company for a long time before he was eventually found out'.

ascertain /æsə'teɪn/ verb, means to discover beyond doubt the truth of a situation. It is a stronger and more formal word than 'find out': 'The police are going to talk to her at length to try to ascertain how much she knows about this'. Although the adjective 'certain' /'sɜ:tn̩/ is very similar in spelling and meaning to 'ascertain', note the pronunciation differences between these two words. See CERTAIN.

FIRST NAME, FORENAME, CHRISTIAN NAME, GIVEN NAME

first name /'fɜ:st neɪm/ noun, is the name or names given at birth. This term is often used on registration cards and other forms requiring personal information: 'Write your first name(s) in capital letters'. See SURNAME.

forename /'fɔ:neɪm/ noun, is an alternative term to 'first name'.

Christian name /'krɪstjən neɪm/ noun, is the old term used for 'first name'. This is no longer in official use since many English-speaking groups are not Christians.

given name /'gɪvn̩ neɪm/ noun, is in many ways preferable to any of the above, as in many places, for instance China, Korea, Japan, and Hungary, it is customary to use the family name first, and the given names last: 'Mao Zedong'. In the West, it is usual to address people by their given name(s) followed by their family name: 'Stewart Clark'. In lists, it is normal to put the family name first, followed by a comma: 'Pointon, Graham'. See SURNAME.

FISH, FISHES

fish /fɪʃ/ noun, means the individual animal or its flesh. Thus, 'fish' meaning food is an uncountable noun which takes a singular verb: 'The fish is delicious in that restaurant'. A plural verb is used only for more than one living fish: 'The fish are biting tonight; they must be after the flies'.

fishes /'fɪʃɪz/ plural noun, is used only when referring to more than one species: 'The whitemeat fishes such as haddock and cod are becoming more expensive'.

FLAIR⁵, FLARE⁵

flair /fleər/ noun, is a natural ability or skill: 'He survived in politics for a long time, because of his flair for telling the public what it wanted to hear'. It is also used in the expression 'to have a flair for': 'She had a flair for languages'. Note that 'flair' should not be confused with preference or liking, both of which express a choice.

flare /fleər/ verb & noun, as a verb combined with 'up', means a sudden flaming of a fire: 'The log flared up'. It can also refer to a person's quick temper: 'She flared up at the slightest provocation'. As a noun, 'flare' means a blaze of light: 'The flares on the runway were visible from a long way away'. In the plural, this also means trousers which become wider from the knee downwards, also known as flared trousers: 'Flares are not very practical for riding a bike'.

FLAMMABLE, INFLAMMABLE, NON-FLAMMABLE

flammable /'flæməbl̩/ adjective, means easily set on fire. The British Standards Institution has ruled that 'flammable' and its opposite, 'non-flammable' are to be used for substances and materials, rather than 'inflammable' and its opposite, 'non-inflammable'.

inflammable /ɪn'flæməbl̩/ adjective, means almost the same as 'flammable', not the opposite as some people think because of the prefix 'in'. Consequently, these words both mean easily set on fire and have caused confusion and injury, as goods can be labelled 'flammable' or 'inflammable' according to the place of origin. 'Inflammable' can be used figuratively to mean aggressively emotional: 'The two governments now find themselves locked in a highly inflammable situation'.

non-flammable /'nɒn'flæməbl̩/ adjective, means the opposite of 'flammable'.

FLEA⁵, FLEE⁵

flea /fli:/ noun, is a small jumping insect which bites humans and/or animals: 'The dog was infested with fleas'.

flee /fli:/ verb, means to run away: 'The volcano erupted and the villagers had to flee'.

FLOAT, FLOW, FLUENT, FLUID

float /fləʊt/ *verb*, means to be on or close to the surface of a liquid. It is often used for ships and other buoyant objects: 'There was a fly floating in his soup'.

flow /fləʊ/ *verb*, implies movement, and is often used for water and traffic: 'After the new bridge opened the traffic flowed better'.

fluent /'fluːənt/ *adjective*, means having a thorough command of a language, or speaking and writing smoothly: 'A fluent command of English'.

fluid /'fluːɪd/ *adjective*, is often used for gases and liquids that are capable of flowing. In figurative use, such as 'our plans are fluid', this means that they are still open to change.

I SPEAK ENGLISH FLOATINGLY

FLOOR, STOREY, STORY

floor /flɔːr/ *noun*, is the part of a building where all the rooms are on the same level. The term 'floor' stresses the activity or its use: 'Our offices are on the third floor'. Note that the preposition must be 'on the third floor'; 'in the third floor' would be under the floorboards.

storey /'stɔːri/ *noun*, is also the part of a building where all the rooms are on the same level but 'storey' is used in more structural contexts than 'floor': 'A six-storey building'. 'Storey' and 'floor' are traditionally counted in BE starting with a ground floor and continuing with the first, second, third etc, above it. In the American system of numbering, the ground level of a building is the first floor, and those above it the second, third, etc. There are signs

that the more logical American system is starting to be used in high buildings all over the world. 'Storey' is the BE spelling and the plural is 'storeys'.

story is the AE spelling of 'storey'. The AE plural form is 'stories'.

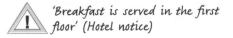

⚠️ *'Breakfast is served in the first floor' (Hotel notice)*

FLOUNDER, FOUNDER

flounder /'flaʊndər/ *verb*, means to struggle to move in water, etc.: 'The lifeguard rescued the boy when he started floundering in the deep water'. It can also be used more figuratively to mean struggling in a state of confusion: 'The company spokesperson floundered in front of the TV cameras'.

founder /'faʊndər/ *verb*, means to sink. If a boat runs aground, it is said to have 'foundered'. In a figurative context, a company is said to 'founder' if it fails: 'The company foundered as a result of the accounts being falsified'.

FOG, MIST, SMOG

fog /fɒg/ *noun*, means a thick cloud of water droplets in the air that reduces visibility. 'Fog' is sometimes defined as visibility that is less than 1 km. If someone says that they are 'in a fog', this may be a physical fog or it can mean that they are feeling confused.

mist /mɪst/ *noun*, means a thin cloud of water droplets that reduces visibility slightly: 'There is usually a lot of mist in these hills in October'.

smog /smɒg/ *noun*, is a blend of smoke and fog. This is a pollution problem that occurs in some industrialized areas. See **BLEND WORDS**.

'Mist is thin fog; fog is thick mist.' (Dictionary definitions)

FOLK, FOLKS

folk /fəʊk/ *noun*, means people in general. In BE, it is linked to the generic terms 'menfolk' and 'womenfolk'. It is also found in expressions such as 'folk dance', 'folk music', 'folk song', 'folklore', and 'folk story', in which 'folk' refers to traditional dancing, music, myths or stories. In AE, 'folk' is used alone as a common term for people. In this context it sounds archaic to British speakers who use 'people' instead. See **PEOPLE**.

FOLLOW — FOREIGN PLACE NAMES

folks /fəʊks/ *noun plural*, means a closely related group, and conveys mutual friendship. The expression: 'How are your folks?' is usually a friendly enquiry about the health of someone's parents. In AE, it also refers to people in general. 'Folks' is an informal term.

FOLLOW, COME

follow /'fɒləʊ/ *verb*, means to walk or drive behind someone. 'Follow' also means to go immediately after something in a sequence of numbers or events: 'The storm was followed by a period of calm'; or in a logical sequence: 'It doesn't necessarily follow that everyone living in Spain considers Spanish to be their first language'. The phrase 'to follow in someone's footsteps' means to be inspired by someone, often a parent, in one's choice of work or lifestyle: 'She followed in her mother's footsteps and became a doctor'.

come /kʌm/ *verb*, means movement towards the person speaking: 'Come here, please'. In another sense, 'come' also means movement towards a place that is near or familiar: 'He came back to his birthplace'. If someone has come a long way, this may refer to the distance travelled or figuratively the amount of progress made: 'He has come a long way as a teacher'. See **BRING**.

FOOT, INCH

foot /fʊt/ *noun*, is a unit of length equivalent to about 0.3 metres that is widely used in the English-speaking world. It has the plural 'feet' /fiːt/. When it is combined with a number to form an adjective, written '-foot' (hyphenated), it has no plural: 'A 6-foot goalkeeper'. On the other hand, when a distance is measured, the number and 'feet' (always in the plural) are not hyphenated: 'The river was 60 feet wide'. The word 'foot' here is a noun, which is why it appears in the plural. It is abbreviated 'ft' and the symbol ' is also used, as in 6' 4" (six feet, four inches).

inch /ɪntʃ/ *noun*, is a unit of measurement equivalent to 2.54 cm. When 'inch' is used adjectivally in compounds such as a 'four inch nail', it behaves like all other adjectives, and has no plural form. The abbreviation is 'in.' and the symbol " is used to denote inches, as in 'a 6" nail'. 'Inches' is the plural of 'inch': 'I measured that nail: it is four inches long'. With height or other measurements over a foot, 'inches' is often omitted, as in: 'He is six foot six'. Note

that singular verbs are used with these units of measurement: 'Seven feet tall is quite impressive'; 'Twelve inches equals one foot'. See **MEASUREMENTS**.

FORECAST, PREDICTION

forecast /'fɔːkɑːst/ *noun & verb*, as a noun, is a prediction or estimate about a future incident or trend. A 'forecast' is based on factual records and is used for the weather: 'The Meteorological Office has a good record for their 5-day forecasts'. As a verb form, 'forecast' is preferred as the past tense and past participle to the alternative 'forecasted'.

prediction /prɪ'dɪkʃn/ *noun*, means a statement or estimate that something will happen in the future: 'This prediction about oil prices next year is based on educated guesswork'. Note that a 'forecast' is based on factual information while a 'prediction' is often based on assumptions.

foreign place names

- Country names, capital and other major cities, and some sea and river names, are often spelt and pronounced in English differently from how they appear in their homelands. In some cases, the differences are small, but the correct English versions should be used whenever possible, to avoid misunderstandings. Here is a selection, English on the left, original on the right:

Athens	*Athínai*
Baltic Sea	*Ostsee* (German)
Brussels	*Bruxelles* (French), *Brussel* (Dutch)
Bucharest	*Bucuresti*
Florence	*Firenze*
Hanover	*Hannover*
Nicosia	*Lefkosia* (Greek)
Paris /'pærɪs/	*Paris* /pari/
Prague	*Praha*
Rangoon	*Yangon*
Rhine	*Rhein* (German), *Rhin* (French), *Rijn* (Dutch)
Saragossa	*Zaragoza*

- From time to time, a change may be made, so that a place name acquires an English spelling and pronunciation that are closer to the original: *Peking* has become *Beijing*, *Byelorussia* has become *Belarus*.

• Some geographical features keep their original name to the extent that the word for 'mountain' or 'river' is retained: *Rio Grande*, not 'River Grande'; *Mont Blanc*, not 'Mount White'. Where the name is from a language that is less well-known to English speakers than Spanish or French, tautology sometimes occurs: *Sahara* is Arabic for 'desert', but both *The Sahara* and *Sahara Desert* are found in English dictionaries.
See **BRITISH PLACE NAMES**.
See **NATIONALITY WORDS**.

FOREST, WOOD

forest /'fɒrɪst/ *noun*, means an extensive area of trees: 'There is over-exploitation of this pine forest'. Figuratively, it can refer to a large number of tall narrow objects: 'We could not see the procession through the forest of waving arms and flags'.

wood /wʊd/ *noun*, means a small area of trees. This is also known as 'the woods': 'I was walking in the woods yesterday'. Figuratively the BE expression: 'Cannot see the wood for the trees' means that too much detail or confusing information is making it difficult to understand a situation clearly. The AE equivalent is: 'Cannot see the forest for the trees'. See **TIMBER**.

FOREWORD, PREFACE

foreword /'fɔːwɜːd/ *noun*, refers to the preliminary pages in a technical or academic report. It is written by a distinguished person who is not the author of the work.

preface /'prefɪs/ *noun*, also refers to the preliminary pages in a technical or academic report or book. It is written by the author. If a book has both a 'Foreword' and a 'Preface', the Foreword is always placed first.

formal English

The formal, written English that is expected in reports, business correspondence and documents is different from spoken everyday English. Here are three features of formal English.

use suitable vocabulary:

• Formal vocabulary is mainly from classical words. These are usually only found in written English. Informal vocabulary consists mainly of short Anglo-Saxon words. These are typical in spoken English or used in informal notes.

formal	informal
arrange (dinner)	lay on (dinner)
by coincidence	by chance
collect (someone)	pick up (someone)
commence	begin, start
conceal	hide
consider	weigh up
construct	build
donation	gift
endeavour	try
enquire	ask
inspect	look over
reserve	book
position	job
purchase	buy
review (problems)	look at (problems)
settle (matters)	sort out (matters)

avoid slang expressions or jargon:

• Slang and jargon are typical characteristics of oral English. They are verbal shortcuts when speakers and their audience share common assumptions and knowledge. Using slang can cause irritation and make what is written appear very casual. Compare *do this ASAP* with the formal, *please do this as soon as possible*; or *we will fix things after the hard disk foul up* with the formal *we will rectify matters after the malfunction in the computer system*. Slangy expressions like *belt and braces* (meaning taking extra care to make sure something is successful) and the use of text messaging abbreviations from mobile phones can also cause misunderstanding. Thus a formal report, a letter or even an email written as a representative of a company or organization is no place for smiley symbols such as :-) or :-(or cryptic SMS (Short Message Service) abbreviations like *Which one r u?*

avoid contractions (*I'm ... won't ...* etc.):

• Contractions or short forms are to be avoided in official letters, reports and other types of formal English. These should only be used in informal, conversational writing and when reporting speech. Compare the formal English with corresponding contractions:

We are looking forward to this	*We're looking forward to this*
The contract does not commence until ...	*The contract doesn't start until ...*

• Using short forms in the wrong context looks sloppy and may also lead to mistakes such as confusing *it's* with the soundalike possessive pronoun *its*.
See **CONTRACTIONS**. See **ITS**.

FORMER, LATTER

former /ˈfɔːmər/ *adjective*, when combined with 'the', refers to the first of two, but never more: 'Mr Smith and Ms Taylor both taught geography at this school. The former has now returned to take up the post of headteacher'. (More informally, 'the former' could have been replaced here by 'he'.) If there are more than two use 'the first (of these)' or 'the first-named'. When preceded by the indefinite article, 'a former' means one of any number of predecessors: 'She is a former CEO'.

latter /ˈlætər/ *adjective*, refers to the second of two. If there are more than two use 'the last (of these)' or 'the last-named'. 'Latter' can also mean towards the end: 'In the latter part of his acting career he was awarded an Oscar'.

FORMULA, FORMULAE, FORMULAS

formula /ˈfɔːmjʊlə/ *noun*, is the singular form and refers to the letters and symbols that represent a chemical compound, or which indicate a mathematical relationship: 'It is necessary to use the correct formula in order to complete this calculation'. It also means a method for achieving something: 'This new branch of operations may well be a formula for success'. In AE, 'formula' may also mean liquid baby food. Here it is an uncountable noun.

formulae /ˈfɔːmjʊliː/ *noun*, is, according to most style guides the plural form of 'formula' when it refers to mathematical rules and chemical compounds: 'Chemical formulae contain abbreviations of the names of the elements'. See **AE**.

formulas /ˈfɔːmjʊləz/ *noun*, is the alternative plural of 'formula' in non-scientific contexts: 'Two alternative formulas for greater European integration were proposed by NATO'.

FORTH[S], FOURTH[S], QUARTER

forth /fɔːθ/ *adverb*, refers to movement onwards or out of something. The term is almost archaic: 'Livingstone pressed forth into Africa'. However, it is used in a number of fixed expressions, including 'so on and so forth'.

fourth /fɔːθ/ *adjective*, is the ordinal number: 'The fourth person in the room was unknown'. Note that AE speakers tend to use 'fourth' as a noun when describing 25% of something: 'A fourth of the votes'. BE speakers tend to use 'quarter' here. See **NUMBERS**.

quarter /ˈkwɔːtər/ *noun*, is the usual BE word to describe 25% of something. When followed by of and a noun, it is the noun which decides whether a singular or plural verb should be used: 'A quarter of the flock was killed'; 'A quarter of the goats were killed'. See **BLOC**. See **MEASUREMENTS**.

FORTNIGHT, TWO WEEKS

fortnight /ˈfɔːtnaɪt/ *noun*, means a period of approximately two weeks: 'I will be here in a fortnight'. This is a BE expression.

two weeks /ˈtuː ˈwiːks/ is the standard AE expression for 'fortnight', although 'two weeks' is also used in BE: 'Our department meetings are held every two weeks'.

FORWARD, FORWARDS

forward /ˈfɔːwəd/ *adverb, adjective & verb*, describes movement either towards the front, or towards something positive: 'I am pleased that we are at last moving forward on this project'. This second meaning is often expressed by the phrase 'to look forward to something': 'I am looking forward to meeting you'. As an adjective, 'forward' either means advanced: 'The boys were forward for their age; or refers to movement ahead: 'The police managed to stop the forward push of the demonstrators'. As a verb, 'forward' means to send letters or other information to another person: 'After I've moved out could you forward any post to my new address?'

forwards /ˈfɔːwədz/ *adverb*, is an alternative spelling to 'forward' that is only used in BE meaning physical movement straight ahead: 'We moved forwards in the fog, and slowly but surely, found the car'.

four-letter word

four-letter word means one of many short words, of Anglo-Saxon origin, but not all containing four letters, that refer to sexual or excretory functions and are considered offensive and crude. They include *arse, balls, cunt, fuck, piss, prick, shit, tit*. In many older dictionaries these words were written as the first letter followed by asterisks, or by using only the first and last letters, separated by a dash: *f**** or *f—k*. Although these words are used fairly frequently in some contexts, they may cause offence and are best avoided.

FRAGRANT, FLAGRANT

fragrant /ˈfreɪɡrənt/ *adjective*, means having a sweet or pleasant smell: 'The fragrant smell of roses came into the room'. See **ODOUR**. See **SMELL**.

flagrant /ˈfleɪɡrənt/ *adjective*, means conspicuous or obvious: 'He showed a flagrant disregard for his children's safety'. This is a negative word. See **BLATANT** ⟳ **OBVIOUS**.

FRAIL, FRAGILE, DELICATE

frail /freɪl/ *adjective*, when referring to people, means weak and in poor physical health: 'The 90-year-old patient was mentally alert but too frail to walk'. When referring to things, 'frail' means easily broken, or not complete: 'A frail hope of peace became apparent'.

fragile /ˈfrædʒaɪl/ *adjective*, when referring to people, means not strong, and vulnerable: 'Her fragile beauty attracted so much attention that she took up modelling'. When referring to things, 'fragile' means that they are easily broken: 'The fragile porcelain had to be handled with great care'.

delicate /ˈdelɪkət/ *adjective*, when referring to people, means someone who is prone to illness: 'The child always had delicate health'. When referring to things, 'delicate' means something that is fine in texture and colour, fragile and beautiful: 'The painted china was a delicate piece of artwork'.

FRAME, FRAMEWORK

frame /freɪm/ *noun & verb*, as a noun, means a structure to mount paintings on. It is also used for doors and windows: 'The car door could not be locked because the frame was buckled'. As a verb, 'frame' can mean to put a frame around, or to produce false evidence in order to incriminate a person: 'The police released the suspect after they discovered he had been framed'.

framework /ˈfreɪmwɜːk/ *noun*, means the essential supporting structure of a building, vehicle or object. In research, it means the scope of a project, proposal or agreement. 'This framework agreement covers cooperation between our organizations'.

FREIGHT, GOODS, CARGO

freight /freɪt/ *noun*, means goods transported in bulk by ship, aircraft, or train: 'We can send it by air freight'. 'Freight' also means the cost of this transport: 'What is the freight charge?' In AE, a 'freight train' carries freight. Also in AE, a passenger train may have some 'freight cars'. As a verb, 'freight' means to transport goods by sea, rail, road, or air: 'We guarantee to freight goods anywhere in Europe within three days'. In this sense, 'freight' is an alternative to 'ship'. See **SHIP** ⟳ **BOAT**.

goods /ɡʊdz/ *noun*, is a BE term for objects that are transported. 'Goods' is only used in the plural in this sense: 'Goods are carried on all our services'. A 'goods train' carries goods. A passenger train may have some 'goods wagons'.

cargo /ˈkɑːɡəʊ/ *noun*, means goods carried by ship, aircraft, or lorry: 'The majority of the fleet carries cargo, not passengers'. When the indefinite article is used, this refers to a particular load that is being transported: 'A cargo of oil'. The plural is 'cargoes', but note that 'cargos' is an alternative spelling in use in AE.

FRENCH, GALLIC⁵, GAELIC⁵

French /frentʃ/ *adjective & noun*, is a general word referring to the customs, language and nationality of France. It is used in general contexts such as 'French wine' or 'French law'. The noun form 'the French' means French people as a whole. See **NICKNAMES**.

Gallic /ˈɡælɪk/ *adjective*, refers to something that is considered characteristic of France or the French, such as Gallic humour or Gallic behaviour.

Gaelic /ˈɡælɪk/ (referring to Scotland) /ˈɡeɪlɪk/ (referring to Ireland), *adjective & noun*, today refers to the Celtic languages: 'Road signs are written in Gaelic in parts of Ireland'.

FRIEND, ACQUAINTANCE

friend /frend/ *noun*, is used for a person with whom mutual affection has developed. The terms a 'close friend' or a 'special friend' suggest a stronger friendship: 'We are inviting only close friends and family to the wedding'. See **MATE** ⟳ **GUY**. See **PARTNER**.

acquaintance /əˈkweɪntəns/ *noun*, is a person that you know, but not very well: 'It will be nice to meet all my old friends and acquaintances at the school reunion'.

FRINGE BENEFITS, PERK

fringe benefits /ˈfrɪndʒ ˈbenɪfɪts/ *noun*, means the extras given or paid to a worker by the employer: 'Our fringe benefits include a company car and travel allowance'. Sometimes these are just called 'benefits'.

perk /pɜːk/ *noun*, is an informal term for 'fringe benefits'. This is an abbreviation of the more formal 'perquisite' /'pɜːkwɪzɪt/ which is rarely used in this context.

FRUITFUL, FERTILE

fruitful /'fruːtfʊl/ *adjective*, describes a tree or plant that produces a large crop. This word is most often used in a figurative sense, when it means a situation that produces a lot of useful results: 'These were very fruitful discussions'. Note that the adjective 'fruitless' refers to a situation that did not bring any useful results: 'The search for information proved fruitless'.

fertile /'fɜːtaɪl/ *adjective*, is used of land or soil that produces a lot of crops or vegetation. A person or animal that is 'fertile' is capable of producing offspring. Plants produce fruit if they are fertile. In a figurative sense, 'fertile' also refers to the capacity to generate ideas: 'The management will have to have fertile minds to stay ahead of the competition'. Note that the AE pronunciation rhymes with 'turtle'. The negative form is 'infertile'.

full stop, period (punctuation)

- Use a *full stop* (*period* in AF) to mark the end of a sentence. Use full stops to mark abbreviated words: *Jan., a.m., no.* In BE, it is normal to omit the full stop when the last letter in a word ends the abbreviation: *Mr, Mrs, Ms, Dr*, and in the abbreviations of degrees: *BA, MSc, PhD, etc.* This is not the case in AE, and *Mr., Dr., M.A.* are typical of AE style.

- Abbreviations and acronyms are not punctuated with full stops: *BBC, NATO* and *UNESCO*. See **ACRONYMS**.

- With quotations, a normal rule is to use three dots to mark an omission (called ellipsis) and a fourth dot at the end of a sentence.

- Use a full stop to mark a decimal in English and between units of money involving decimals: €55.50. This is called the decimal point: *25.67%.* See **CURRENCY UNITS**.

- When expressing time, BE uses a stop between hours and minutes: *7.30 a.m.* and AE often uses a colon: *7:30 a.m.* An alternative in AE is A.M.

- In lists, there are stops at the end of items in a list if they are full sentences. Otherwise, there are no stops after keywords or at the end of a bulleted list. See **LISTS**.

- In email and Internet addresses the full stop is used between elements, but this is read as 'dot' throughout the English-speaking world. See **EMAIL ADDRESSES**.

FUNNY, ODD

funny /'fʌni/ *adjective*, means amusing or comical: 'I heard a funny joke on the radio'. It can also mean 'strange': 'I cannot understand why he gave me such a funny look'. However, this sense is informal and can be replaced by 'odd', 'strange', or 'peculiar'. The expression 'it is funny that …' refers to something that is strange, rather than humorous. See **COMIC**.

odd /ɒd/ *adjective*, usually means strange or peculiar: 'She was feeling odd; it must have been the heat'. Another use of the word is the hyphenated form, as in: 'Twenty-odd students' (meaning just over 20 of them) in contrast to 'Twenty odd students' (meaning 20 strange ones). See **APPROXIMATION**.

Gg

GASP, YAWN

gasp /gɑːsp/ *verb*, means to catch one's breath as a sign of pain or astonishment: 'He gasped when he saw the size of the tooth'.

yawn /jɔːn/ *verb*, means to open your mouth and breathe out deeply, due to tiredness or boredom: 'They started to yawn after the third hour in the meeting'.

GAY, HOMOSEXUAL, LESBIAN

gay /geɪ/ *adjective & noun*, is the preferred word used by homosexuals for themselves, and has become the standard term in general usage. The noun form tends to be used more in the plural: 'This is an area popular with gays'. As an adjective, 'gay' used to mean bright, carefree and happy, but this sense is now considered old-fashioned.

homosexual /hɒməʊˈsekʃʊəl, həʊməʊ-/ *adjective & noun*, refers to both male and female homosexuals. See **HOMO- ⇨ HOMO**.

lesbian /ˈlezbɪən/ *adjective & noun*, refers to a female homosexual.

> The Christmas song: 'Have yourself a merry little Christmas, make the Yuletide gay', has also been recorded with an alternative second line: 'It's a special day'.

GENIAL, CONGENIAL, GENIUS, GENUS

genial /ˈdʒiːnɪəl/ *adjective*, means good-tempered or friendly: 'It was easy to feel welcome in Henry's home: he was so genial'. This is a formal word.

congenial /kənˈdʒiːnɪəl/ *adjective*, means pleasant, and is used by someone of a person or environment that complements their interests, character and outlook on life: 'The members of the tennis club were congenial company'. Less formal alternatives to 'congenial' are 'pleasant' and 'friendly'.

genius /ˈdʒiːnɪəs/ *noun*, means a person who has exceptional talent or who is highly intelligent: 'Einstein was a genius'. 'Geniuses' is the plural of 'genius'. See **INGENIOUS**.

genius /ˈdʒiːnɪəs/ *noun*, also means a spirit from folklore, and has given rise to the more commonly used word *genie* /ˈdʒiːni/ found in the Arabian folk stories: 'The genie of the lamp'. The plurals of 'genius' in this sense are both 'genii' /ˈdʒiːnɪaɪ/ and 'genies' /ˈdʒiːnɪz/.

genus /ˈdʒiːnəs, ˈdʒenəs/ *noun*, is a class of living things that is used in biology for groups of species which share certain characteristics: 'The rose genus consists of many popular flowering shrubs'. The plural is 'genera' /ˈdʒenərə/.

genitive forms: 's'-genitive and 'of'-genitive

The genitive is the form of a noun that indicates possession or close connection between two things. This can be written as either *John's hat* (the hat belonging to John), which is called the *'s'-genitive*; or *the people of Paris* (the people who come from Paris), which is called the *'of'-genitive*.

The **'s'-genitive** is used to form the possessive of people and animals, as well as things people are fond of. Two general rules are:

- Place *-s* after singular nouns that end in *-s*, or after a noun (singular or plural) that does not end in *-s*. (Examples: *Charles's, the class's teacher, dog's dinner, the children's toys, the boat's performance*.) An exception is names of people ending in *-s* that sometimes only have an apostrophe and no extra *'s'*: *King James' Bible*.
- Place an apostrophe after plural nouns that end in *-s*. (Example: *the classes' teacher*.)

These rules make it clear whether a class has one teacher (*class's*) or shares a teacher (*classes'*).

The **'of'-genitive** is used to form the possessive of objects and things. (Examples: *the Tower of London, the people of Paris, toy of the year, a performance of Hamlet*.)

GENTLEMAN, MAN

gentleman /ˈdʒentl̩mən/ *noun*, was formerly a mark of social rank. Today it is only found in expressions like: 'Ladies and Gentlemen' (used to open a speech or a formal business letter in AE), or when there is some extra politeness involved: 'He sends me flowers every day: a perfect gentleman'. Members of the House of Commons use it when referring to male MPs:

'The Honourable Gentleman for East Sussex'. Staff in hotels and restaurants often use the term 'gentleman' to refer to their male guests: 'Show the gentleman to his table'.

man /mæn/ *noun,* is the term that is used in most other senses. There may be confusion between 'man', short for 'mankind': 'Every man for himself' (which means every person), and 'man' when it means just males: 'Every man in the village was questioned by the police'. In slang, 'man' is used more in AE than in BE, for example in the colloquial form of address to another male: 'Hey man'. See **SEXIST LANGUAGE**.

'Gentlemen's throats cut with very sharp razors with great care and skill. No irritating feeling afterwards' (Barber's shop notice)

GESTICULATE, GESTURE

gesticulate /dʒes'tɪkjʊleɪt/ *verb,* means to make signals with the arms: 'They gesticulated to catch the police officer's attention'. The related noun is 'gesticulation'.

gesture /'dʒestʃər/ *noun & verb,* as a noun, means a movement of the hand or head made in order to express meaning: 'The bully raised a finger in an obscene gesture'. It is also an action performed in order to express a feeling: 'His offer to buy lunch was a very kind gesture'. As a verb, 'gesture' means to move the hands or head as a signal: 'The waiter gestured with his head that the table was ready'.

GET, GOT, GOTTEN

get /get/ *verb,* in a basic sense means to receive. However, it has a broad range of meanings, including become, come, experience, go, obtain, receive, succeed, suffer, and understand. 'Get' is among the top five most-frequently used verbs in English, and is part of many phrasal verbs. 'Get' is often avoided in formal English. Compare the informal: 'I get your message' with the formal: 'I understand what you mean'.

got /gɒt/ *verb,* is the past participle in BE, and the past form in BE and AE of 'get'. 'Got' has the same range of meanings as 'get'. 'He got enough food for all the family', and should also be avoided in formal English. Note that in addition, 'got' is often used with the simple present form of have, in BE. The sentence 'I have got three cars' simply refers to possessing, rather than receiving, the cars.

gotten /'gɒtn̩/ *verb,* is the past participle of 'get' in spoken AE, and has the same range of meanings: 'He's just gotten a new pick-up'. Standard written AE uses 'got' in this sense.

GOLDEN HANDSHAKE, GOLDEN HANDCUFFS, GOLDEN HELLO, GOLDEN PARACHUTE

golden handshake /'gəʊldən 'hændʃeɪk/ *noun,* is a large sum of money, shares, or other benefits given to an employee leaving the company in recognition of their contribution to its success. It is sometimes given as an inducement to unwanted employees to force their resignation.

golden handcuffs /'gəʊldən 'hændkʌfs/ *noun,* is a large sum of money or other benefits given to employees to induce them to remain with the company.

golden hello /'gəʊldən he'ləʊ/ *noun,* is a large sum of money or other benefits given by a company to persuade a potential employee to join that company.

golden parachute /'gəʊldən 'pærəʃuːt/ *noun,* is a long-term arrangement guaranteeing the financial security of senior employees that are forced to resign, or are dismissed as a result of a company reorganization or merger.

GOODBYE, CHEERS

goodbye /gʊd'baɪ/ is used to express good wishes when parting. This is the BE spelling, and the plural is 'goodbyes', as in: 'I'm going to have a party so that I can say all my goodbyes before I go to live in Canada'. 'Bye' is a friendly short version of 'goodbye'. The AE spelling is 'goodby', plural 'goodbys'. See **BYE ⇨ BY-**.

cheers /tʃɪəz/ is the word used when toasting someone's health with a drink. However, in informal BE it can also mean 'thank you for helping'. In addition, 'cheers' is an informal parting remark meaning 'goodbye'.

GOOD MORNING, GOOD AFTERNOON, GOOD DAY, GOOD EVENING, GOOD NIGHT

good morning /gʊd ˈmɔːnɪŋ/ is a normal greeting and is used up to noon.

good afternoon /gʊd ɑːftəˈnuːn/ is also a normal greeting that is used from noon to about 6 p.m.

good day /gʊd ˈdeɪ/ is a formal way in BE to express good wishes to another when meeting or leaving during the day. In AE, and in parts of the English-speaking world, it is a normal greeting, especially on radio and TV.

good evening /gʊd ˈiːvnɪŋ/ is a greeting used after 6 p.m.

goodnight /gʊdˈnaɪt/ is used to say goodbye at night.

GORILLA^S, GUERRILLA^S

gorilla /gəˈrɪlə/ *noun*, is a large African ape. In slang, this means a bodyguard.

guerrilla /gəˈrɪlə/ *noun*, is a member of an independent force who fights against an officially recognized army.

GOURMET, GOURMAND, GLUTTON

gourmet /ˈgʊəmeɪ/ *noun*, is a knowledgeable lover of good food and drink. This is a complimentary word: 'His reputation as a gourmet grew after he retired to Provence'.

gourmand /ˈgʊəmɑ̃ː, ˈgʊəmənd/ *noun*, means someone who enjoys eating large amounts: 'Anyone who eats a five-course meal every lunchtime can be classed as a true gourmand'. In this sense it is usually a disapproving word, although 'gourmand' can also means someone who appreciates good food and drink.

glutton /ˈglʌtn̩/ *noun*, is someone who eats too much out of greed, and is the least complimentary of the three words. Figuratively, this word is used in a neutral sense in the phrase 'a glutton for punishment', meaning someone who takes on difficult tasks and enjoys doing them.

GOVERNMENT, ADMINISTRATION

Government /ˈgʌvənmənt/ *noun*, has very different meanings in the UK and the USA. In Britain, the 'Government' consists of the elected Prime Minister and his/her ministers. It may also include MPs of the governing party who hold no office, but does not include the Civil Service, which serves successive governments. In the USA, the 'Government' includes the whole range of structures from President of the Republic down to the town mayor and his council, including salaried staff. This word is capitalized when it refers to specific parts of a national political system.

Administration /ədmɪnɪsˈtreɪʃn̩/ *noun*, is the American equivalent of the British term 'Government'. The Administration changes with every Presidential election, as in 'the first and second Clinton Administrations'. Although 'administration' exists as a common noun in BE, meaning the process of running a business, there is no political equivalent in Britain to the American 'Administration'. This word is capitalized when it refers to specific parts of a national political system.

GOVERNOR, GOVERNESS

governor /ˈgʌvənər/ *noun*, means a person who is responsible for the executive control of a geographical territory, such as a state in the USA: 'Many presidents were previously state governors'. When used as a title with a name, this is capitalized: 'Governor Bush of Florida'. In BE, 'governor' refers to a person in charge of an institution such as a prison or the Bank of England, or one of a member of a team responsible for running an organization, such as a school. A 'governor' may be either male or female: 'My sister was a governor of the village school for five years'. In very informal BE, 'governor' means the person in charge, usually an employer. This is only used in spoken BE, but in reported dialogue it is often spelt 'guv'nor' /ˈgʌvnər/: 'Wait a minute, I'll get the guv'nor for you'. This is sometimes shortened to 'guv'. A more standard, but still informal, term for employer is boss.

governess /ˈgʌvənɪs/ *noun*, means a woman employed privately to teach the children of a family, living in their home. This is now mainly a historical term. See **SEXIST LANGUAGE**.

GRACIOUS, GRACEFUL

gracious /ˈgreɪʃəs/ *adjective*, often describes polite behaviour by the rich and influential and implies kindness and courtesy. 'Gracious living' means an elegant and comfortable lifestyle.

graceful /ˈgreɪsfʊl/ *adjective*, is used to describe elegant physical movement: 'The swan moved gracefully on the lake'.

GRAFFITI, THE WRITING ON THE WALL

graffiti /grə'fiːti/ *noun*, means the slogans and sprayed pictures on walls, trains etc. In western cities. Originally it referred to the messages scratched on the walls of what are now classical ruins, such as in Pompeii. Although it is the plural form of the original Italian word, 'graffiti' takes a singular verb: 'Graffiti is a serious problem in some parts of the town'.

the writing on the wall /ðə 'raɪtɪŋ ɒn the 'wɔːl/ *noun phrase*, describes a situation when something is likely to fail or be problematical, but is not connected with 'graffiti': 'The director knew that when his board saw the company accounts, the writing would be on the wall'.

GRAVE, SERIOUS

grave /greɪv/ *noun & adjective*, as a noun means a place of burial. As an adjective, 'grave' means something that is very worrying: 'Things look very grave for the missing climbers, now that the weather has worsened'. 'Grave' can also refer to a solemn reaction: 'He had a very grave look on his face'.

serious /'sɪərɪəs/ *adjective*, means important, as well as sincere, not joking, and significant. 'Serious' is also used informally to mean a large quantity: 'He earns a serious amount of money'.

In China, the advert 'Come alive with the Pepsi Generation' was translated as 'Pepsi brings your ancestors back from the grave'.

GREAT–GRANDFATHER, GREAT GRANDFATHER

great-grandfather /greɪt'grændfɑːðər/ *noun*, is what a grandfather becomes when his grandchild has a child. The word 'great' used in this way indicates the distance in generations between members of a family. Thus, a 'great-grandfather' would become a great-great-grandfather when his grandchild has grandchildren. 'Great' cannot be used for closer family relationships, such as mother, son, sister. Note that the stress is on 'grand'.

great grandfather /'greɪt 'grændfɑːðər/ *noun phrase*, means a grandfather who is adored by his grandchildren (they think he is 'great'). Here there is no hyphen and stress on 'great' as well as 'grand'. The distinction between these terms applies to other such words, including: 'great grandmother' and 'great grandson'.

GREEK, GRECIAN

Greek /griːk/ *adjective & noun*, means the people of Greece and its language or culture: 'The history of Greek politics stretches back 2500 years'. The expression 'it's all Greek to me' means that something is incomprehensible.

Grecian /'griːʃn/ *adjective*, refers to ancient Greece, its architecture and some objects of beauty: '*Ode to a Grecian Urn* is read by advanced students of English throughout the world'.

GREY, SILVER (HAIR)

grey /greɪ/ *adjective*, is a smoky, silvery colour. As well as being used to describe features such as hair or eye colour, 'grey' may be associated with being uninteresting or lacking in variety: 'He was one of those grey men who had spent their whole life working for the company without seeking promotion'. This is the BE spelling. The AE spelling is 'gray'.

silver /'sɪlvər/ *adjective*, is a greyish colour, and is a more complimentary alternative to grey when describing someone's hair colour. See **BLOND(E)**.

GRILL⁵, GRILLE⁵

grill /grɪl/ *noun & verb*, as a noun, is an item of cooking equipment: 'The barbecue grill on the patio was covered in steaks'. As a verb, it means to cook by placing the food on a grill. It can also mean to question someone in detail and at great length: 'She was grilled by the police regarding her relationship with the accused man'.

grille /grɪl/ *noun*, is a cover or screen made of metal bars, used for protection: 'The car smashed into a lorry and damaged both headlights and the radiator grille'. This may also be spelt 'grill'.

GRIZZLY⁵, GRISLY⁵

grizzly /'grɪzli/ *adjective*, means grey, and is also a short form for 'grizzly bear', a large American bear.

grisly /'grɪzli/ *adjective*, means terrible and frightening: 'That murder was the most grisly on record'.

GROUP, PARENT COMPANY, SUBSIDIARY COMPANY

group /gruːp/ *noun*, in a business context means a large industrial enterprise usually consisting of a parent company, and several subsidiary companies. See **COMPANY ⇨ BUSINESS**.

parent company /'peərənt kʌmpəni/ *noun phrase*, means the main core company in a group. The term 'mother company' is not used in English.

subsidiary company /səb'sɪdɪəri kʌmpəni/ *noun phrase*, means one or more companies that are owned or acquired by a group. The term 'daughter company' is not used in English.

 'Both the mother company and the daughter company have performed well this year.'

group names

The names for people, animals or things in a group have developed in various ways and the following list is just a selection of some common ones:

actors: *a company*
aeroplanes: *a flight*
angels: *a host*
bees: *a swarm*
birds: *a flock*
cards: *a pack* or (mainly AE) *deck*
cars: *a fleet*
cubs: *a litter*
deer: *a herd*
dogs: *a pack*
elephants: *a herd*
flies: *a cloud*
flowers: *a bunch* or *bouquet*
fish: *a shoal*
goats: *a flock* or *herd*
grapes: *a bunch* or *cluster*
insects: *a swarm*
keys: *a bunch*
lions: *a pride*
pigs: *a herd*
pups: *a litter*
sheep: *a flock*
ships: *a fleet*
stars: *a constellation*
steps: *a flight*
thieves: *a gang*
wolves: *a pack*

GUARANTEE, GUARANTOR, WARRANTY

guarantee /gærən'tiː/ *noun & verb*, as a noun, means a formal, usually written, promise that certain conditions will be met: 'The fridge stopped working and we could not find the guarantee'. As a verb, 'guarantee' means to promise that something will occur: 'She guaranteed that she would be home by twelve'.

guarantor /gærən'tɔːr/ *noun*, means someone who is responsible for paying another person's debts: 'The bank requires a guarantor before it will process the application'.

warranty /'wɒrənti/ *noun*, means a legal written binding guarantee from a company that an object they have supplied will be repaired or that parts will be replaced: 'This car has a six-year warranty'. The phrase 'under warranty' refers to the duration of this period: 'My car is still under warranty'.

GUY, MATE

guy /gaɪ/ *noun*, can be an informal word for a man, where it usually occurs in phrases such as 'wise guy' (clever), 'tough guy' (brutal) and 'bad guy' (criminal). In AE especially, the plural form can be used informally to refer to a group of people of either sex: 'What are you guys doing tonight?' In BE, it also means Guy Fawkes, a man who was involved in a plot to blow up the Houses of Parliament in 1605. Today, effigies of him are burnt on Guy Fawkes' Night, 5 November, and children beg for money to buy fireworks. This practice is known as 'a penny for the guy'.

mate /meɪt/ *noun*, means a good friend in informal BE, especially between males: 'John is my mate'. This may cause confusion, as 'mate' can also mean the sexual partner of a person, bird or other animal. 'Mate' is also used together with another noun to show the social relationship between two people: 'flatmate', 'room-mate', 'classmate'. There are no sexual connotations in such terms. See **FRIEND**. See **PARTNER**.

Hh

HABITABLE, INHABITABLE, UNINHABITABLE

habitable /'hæbɪtəbl̩/ *adjective*, means suitable for living in. This is often applied to buildings: 'The new bathroom finally made the flat habitable'. See **INHABITANT**.

inhabitable /ɪn'hæbɪtəbl̩/ *adjective*, despite the negative prefix, refers to a place or geographical area that can be lived in: 'Even Antarctica is inhabitable because the energy supply is so efficient'.

uninhabitable /ʌnɪn'hæbɪtəbl̩/ *adjective*, refers to either housing or a place that cannot be lived in: 'As the floorboards were all rotten, the house was completely uninhabitable'.

> *'Busy beach bar on small uninhabited island requires full-time manager.'* (Advert in catering magazine)

HALF, HALVE

half /hɑːf/ *noun*, means either one of two equal parts, or part of something that has been divided into two. When telling the time, 'half past' means thirty minutes after the hour. Informally, this may be shortened to 'half two', etc. In AE, the equivalent is 'half after two', etc. Note that one thing that is divided is cut in half, whereas several things that are divided are cut into halves. See **-F, -FE ENDINGS IN NOUNS**. See **TIME OF DAY**.

halve /hɑːv/ *verb*, means either to divide into two equal parts, or to reduce by half: 'The price of oil was halved in a year'.

HANGED, HUNG

hanged /hæŋd/ *verb*, is the past tense and past participle of the verb 'hang' when it means to kill someone by suspending them from a rope around their neck: 'The person to be hanged was pushed roughly through the crowd'.

hung /hʌŋ/ *verb*, is the past tense and past participle of the verb 'hang' in all senses of the verb apart from hanging a person. Washing, wallpaper, a door or a painting can all be 'hung'; or it can refer to something that droops: 'The dog looked at the puddle and hung its head'. 'Hung' also refers to something that remains motionless in the air: 'The smoke from the fire hung over the city for a week'.

HAPPEN, OCCUR, TAKE PLACE

happen /'hæpən/ *verb*, means to take place, and can refer to an unplanned event: 'You never know what will happen next'. It can also mean the result of an action: 'I don't know what will happen when she finds out'. 'Happen to' means that something takes place by chance: 'I happened to look out of the window and saw someone running away'. The related noun is 'happening'. See **HAPPENING ⇨ EVENT**.

occur /ə'kɜːr/ *verb*, also means to take place and is a more formal equivalent of 'happen'. 'Occur' refers to the existence of a phenomenon or substance: 'Allergies seem to occur less frequently in families who own pets'. 'Occur to' means to come into someone's mind: 'It occurs to me that they might want something to eat when they get here'. Note the double 'r' in 'occurred' and 'occurring', and the noun form 'occurrence' /ə'kʌrəns/. The stress is on the second syllable in all these words.

take place /teɪk 'pleɪs/ *verb*, means to happen, and refers particularly to an event that is planned: 'The formal handover of the new hospital will take place on 12 December'.

HAPPINESS, GOOD FORTUNE

happiness /'hæpɪnəs/ *noun*, means a state of pleasure and contentment: 'It was like a golden age with happiness all around'.

good fortune /'gʊd 'fɔːtʃuːn/ *noun*, means a happy chance or piece of good luck: 'Despite his good fortune, he was miserable and unhappy'. This is a fixed phrase. 'A fortune' refers to a large amount of money. Note that 'fortunes' is not only the plural of 'fortune' in the money sense, but also means circumstances, both good and bad: 'This new treatment may potentially reverse the fortunes of millions of sufferers'.

HARBOUR, PORT

harbour /'hɑːbər/ *noun*, means a place where ships can moor, either to get shelter or as a part of a port. A harbour may be natural or can be protected from the sea by man-made jetties. This is the BE spelling: the AE spelling is 'harbor'.

port /pɔːt/ *noun*, means a place where ships travel to for loading or unloading cargo. Ports have harbours as well as quays and docks. See **BERTH**. See **QUAY** ⇨ **KEY**.

HARD, HARDLY, SCARCELY

hard /hɑːd/ *adverb*, means a lot, heavily and deeply: 'Many export businesses in Argentina were hard hit by the sudden economic crisis'. See **HARD** ⇨ **STRICT**.

hardly /'hɑːdli/ *adverb*, means only just, or almost not at all: 'We had hardly any money left'. 'Hardly' can never replace 'hard'. Note the difference in meaning between: 'She hardly worked' and 'She worked hard'.

scarcely /'skeəsli/ *adverb*, also means only just, or almost not at all. 'Scarcely' and 'hardly' are often used interchangeably: 'You could scarcely/hardly see the sea because of the mist'. Both words are negatives, and should not be used with other negative words such as 'not' or 'never'.

 'The company found it difficult to recover after being hardly hit by the recession.' (Student essay)

HARMONIOUS, HARMONIC

harmonious /hɑːˈməʊnɪəs/ *adjective*, means tuneful, and also forming a pleasant whole: 'They led a harmonious life in the country'.

harmonic /hɑːˈmɒnɪk/ *adjective*, means relating to musical harmony. The term is also widely used in physics and mathematics.

he, she, they

- The personal pronouns are the only words in English that change according to their position and use in the sentence. Here is the complete set of the third person pronouns and adjectives, in the masculine, feminine and plural forms respectively, together with examples:

*He looked up; John spoke to **him**; That is **his** book; No, it is **his**; Peter looked at **himself** in the mirror.*

*She looked up; John spoke to **her**; That is **her** book; No, it is **hers**; Jane looked at **herself**.*

*They looked up; John spoke to **them**; That is **their** book; No it is **theirs**; They looked at **themselves**.*

- In these non-sexist times, the fact that we have no 'neutral' – not neuter – term causes a problem if one person is being referred to, and that person's sex is either unknown or irrelevant. Several solutions have been suggested, none of them are totally satisfactory:
- **He or she** is good enough if it is only needed once, but becomes heavy if used again and again.
- **S/he** has been proposed, but while this works in a job advert: *We are looking for an accountant. S/he will report to the Managing Director*, it is unsuitable for everyday use, and causes problems in speech: how should it be pronounced?
- **They** is preferred by most people in informal contexts. *Someone phoned you earlier, but they said that they would call back* It is often argued that this must be wrong as 'they' is plural. Nevertheless, examples of 'they' in this usage have been found as early as the 16th century, so there is a long history behind it, and it is recommended by modern BE dictionaries. See **SEXIST LANGUAGE**.

HEIGHT, ALTITUDE

height /haɪt/ *noun*, is used when referring to how tall someone or something is: 'His lack of height made it difficult for him to reach the lever'. 'Height' can be used figuratively to refer to extremes: 'I considered it the height of rudeness not to be invited in'.

altitude /'æltɪtjuːd/ *noun*, means the height of an object in relation to sea level: 'We have now reached our cruising altitude of 9000 metres'. In the context of sport, an activity performed 'at altitude' is one that is carried out at a great height above sea level. Note that 'altitude' is not used figuratively.

HELLO, HOW DO YOU DO?

hello /həˈləʊ/ *exclamation*, is a typical informal greeting to someone you meet or speak to on the phone: 'Hello, this is George speaking'. The word can also be spelt 'hallo' and 'hullo'. In BE, 'hello' also indicates surprise: 'Hello, what's this?'

how do you do? /'haʊ də ju ˈduː/ *exclamation*, is a formal greeting. It is usually said as you shake hands, just after being introduced. The expected answer, irrespective of how you feel, is something positive like

'Fine, thank you', or 'Very well, thank you. And you?' 'How do you do?' is being replaced by less formal alternatives, such as 'Pleased to meet you'.

HESITANCY, HESITATION

hesitancy /'hezɪtənsi/ *noun*, is a slowness or uncertainty in thought or action. It reveals evidence of unwillingness or doubt: 'His hesitancy during the interview was one of the reasons why he was not offered the job'.

hesitation /hezɪ'teɪʃn/ *noun*, is the fact or action of hesitating: 'I accepted the job offer without any hesitation'.

HIGH, HIGHLY, TALL

high /haɪ/ *adjective & adverb*, can mean at a great distance above ground or sea level: 'The rooms in the flat all had high ceilings'. It is also used to express the exact height of something: 'The door is two metres high and one metre wide'. 'High' also means 'to a great extent', in terms of quality or quantity: 'The standards at that school are very high'. As an adverb, it means 'at a great distance above the ground': 'The plane flew high above the clouds'. 'High' also means 'to a great extent', in a limited number of expressions such as 'aim high', 'jump high' or, when referring to strong emotions, to 'run high'.

highly /'haɪli/ *adverb*, means 'to a great degree': 'They were highly intelligent and highly talented students'. It is also used in expressions such as 'speak/think highly of', to indicate a favourable attitude towards a person: 'He must enjoy teaching, because he always speaks highly of his pupils'.

tall /tɔːl/ *adjective*, is used to refer to the height of people, animals, and narrow objects such as plants: 'That tall tree is blocking our TV signal'. See **MEASUREMENTS**.

HIGH SCHOOL, JUNIOR HIGH SCHOOL, JUNIOR COLLEGE, SIXTH—FORM COLLEGE

High School /'haɪ skuːl/ is a secondary school in the USA, for pupils aged 14 to 18. In the UK, 'High School' is sometimes used in the titles of independent schools, such as Wycombe High School. See **SCHOOL**.

Junior High School /'dʒuːnɪə 'haɪ skuːl/ *noun*, is part of the compulsory education system in the USA and Canada, for pupils aged 12 to 14.

Junior College /'dʒuːnɪə 'kɒlɪdʒ/ *noun*, is part of the higher education system in the USA. Education at junior college starts after high school and offers either a complete 2-year course or preparation for full degree education.

Sixth-Form College /'sɪksθ fɔːm 'kɒlɪdʒ/ is part of the education system at secondary level in England and Wales and is for pupils aged 16 to 19.

HINDI, HINDU

Hindi /'hɪndi/ *noun*, is one of the official languages of India.

Hindu /'hɪnduː/ *noun*, is a believer in Hinduism, who is usually of Indian nationality or descent.

HISTORIC, HISTORICAL

historic /hɪs'tɒrɪk/ *adjective*, means important or famous, and likely to be remembered: 'President Lincoln's historic Gettysburg Address is a short but famous speech'.

historical /hɪs'tɒrɪkl/ *adjective*, refers to people or things that existed in the past: 'Many of Shakespeare's plays were based on historical characters'. Note that 'historical time' is often contrasted with 'prehistoric time', and that 'historical' has nothing to do with the importance of the event. Contrast 'Lenin's historic theories' (those of great significance) with 'Lenin's historical theories' (those about history). Modern English style guides recommend that the indefinite article 'a' (not 'an') should be used before 'historic' and 'historical'. See **INDEFINITE ARTICLE**. See **-IC**.

HOARD^S, HORDE^S

hoard /hɔːd/ *noun & verb*, as a noun, means an accumulation or hidden store of something: 'The squirrel's hoard of nuts'. As a verb, it means to accumulate a store of something, often food: 'When prices rose, everyone started hoarding coffee'.

horde /hɔːd/ *noun*, refers to a swarm or a multitude of people or animals: 'A threatening horde of football supporters approached the railway station'. Originally 'horde' referred to nomadic tribes, such as the hordes of Genghis Khan, and this negative association still remains. Remember that things are 'hoarded', but only people and animals come in 'hordes'.

HOLD, KEEP

hold /həʊld/ *verb*, means to carry or support a person or thing: 'She held the ladder while her father climbed up'. In a figurative sense, it means to maintain a person's interest: 'It was going to be difficult to hold the audience's attention for a whole hour'. 'Hold' can be combined with numerous adverbs and prepositions.

keep /ki:p/ *verb*, means to continue to have, save or store something: 'If you keep milk in a fridge it will stay fresh for several days'. 'Keep (on)' means to continue doing something: 'We need to keep (on) walking or we will get cold'. 'Keep' also has a range of meanings when it is used with different adverbs and prepositions.

HOLIDAY, LEAVE, VACATION, RECESS

holiday /'hɒlɪdeɪ/ *noun*, is the standard BE term for a period of time spent away from work or school: 'We are going on holiday next week'. See **PUBLIC HOLIDAY**.

leave /li:v/ *noun*, means time spent away from work for an approved reason, for example, a holiday or illness. It is usual to differentiate between types of leave, such as 'compassionate leave' and 'sick leave'; otherwise, 'leave' is understood to mean a holiday: 'She's on leave until next week'. Note that 'leave' is uncountable.

vacation /və'keɪʃn̩/ *noun*, is a standard AE term for 'holiday': 'We took our vacation in Europe'. It is also used in BE for the interval between terms at university.

recess /rɪ'ses/ *noun*, is used in BE and AE for the time when Parliament or Congress is not officially working: 'Parliament will discuss several new bills when it convenes after the summer recess'. 'Recess' is also used in AE to mean a break during the school day. The equivalent BE term is 'breaktime'. Note that the stress is on the second syllable.

HOMO, HOMO-

homo /'həʊməʊ, 'hɒməʊ/ *noun*, is a Latin word for man. It is used in English as the name of the genus to which Man belongs, and for our species, *homo sapiens*.

homo- /hɒməʊ-, hə'mɒ-/ *prefix*, is taken from the Greek word meaning 'same'. The stress and pronunciation depend on what follows in the word. 'Homonym' /'hɒmənɪm/ (stressed on the first syllable) means a word spelt the same as another, but with a different meaning; 'homogenized' /hə'mɒdʒənaɪzd/ (stressed on the second syllable) is used for milk and means that it is treated so that the cream does not separate; 'homosexual' /hɒməʊ-, həʊməʊ'sekʃʊəl/ (stressed on the third syllable) means attracted to the same sex. See **GAY**.

HOMOGENEOUS, HOMOGENOUS

homogeneous /hɒməʊ'dʒi:nɪəs/ *adjective*, is a formal word used to describe a group of people or things which are of the same type: 'A culturally homogeneous society like Iceland'. Note that the third syllable is stressed.

homogenous /hə'mɒdʒɪnəs/ *adjective*, is a specialized technical term that means sharing the same structure or evolutionary origin. Note that the second syllable is stressed.

HORRID, HORRIBLE, HORRIFYING

horrid /'hɒrɪd/ *adjective*, means nasty and unkind: 'That was a horrid trick to play on me'. This is an informal word.

horrible /'hɒrɪbl̩/ *adjective*, means causing horror and shock. It is stronger than 'horrid': 'There was a horrible accident on the motorway last night'. This is typically used in spoken English.

horrifying /'hɒrɪfaɪɪŋ/ *adjective*, means to fill with horror and be a great shock. It is stronger than 'horrible': 'There were horrifying reports of murder in central Africa'. Note that this is the only one of this group of words that should be used in formal written English.

HOST, HOSTESS

host /həʊst/ *noun & verb*, as a noun, means a person who invites others to an event such as a private party at home: 'He was a very good host, and invitations to his dinner parties were always welcomed'. 'Host' can also be the presenter of a public event such as a television programme: 'Your host for this evening is George'. In this second sense, a 'host' may be female. A 'host' may also be an organization presenting a special event: 'Oxfam was the host of the reception, whose purpose was to draw attention to poverty around the world'. As a verb, 'host' means to present a television programme, or give a reception or other special event: 'Oxfam hosted the reception for all the African delegations'.

hostess /ˈhəʊstɪs/, *noun*, is the female equivalent of 'host' in the first sense above. It is also correct to use 'hostess' to refer to the wife or partner of the host in this sense. In another sense, 'hostess' means a woman employed to entertain men in a nightclub. The term 'air hostess', which was once used to describe female cabin staff on an aircraft, has generally been replaced by 'flight attendant'. See **SEXIST LANGUAGE**.

HOUSE, HOME, BUILDING

house /haʊs/ *noun*, is a dwelling or a structure in which people live. A house can be detached, semi-detached in BE (duplex in AE), or terraced: 'We have just bought a new house'. 'House' is more widely used in BE than in AE, where 'home' is common. See **DETACHED HOUSE**.

home /həʊm/ *noun*, can be any kind of dwelling: a flat, a tent or even a hotel, since the word 'home' is associated with warmth and security: 'Welcome to our home'.

building /ˈbɪldɪŋ/ *noun*, is the normal word for any sort of construction containing a roof and walls. The name of some buildings may contain the word 'house', as in 'The White House', but nevertheless, it should be referred to as a 'building', not as a 'house'.

> 'Come and stay here and you will feel like being at home.' (Hotel advert)

HOUSEWIFE, HOMEMAKER

housewife /ˈhaʊswaɪf/ *noun*, means a woman who runs a house, and does not go out to work. The male equivalent 'househusband' is becoming more common, reflecting the fact that families' domestic arrangements are more flexible than they used to be.

homemaker /ˈhəʊm.meɪkər/ *noun*, is the neutral equivalent of 'housewife' and is used for both men and women. This is mainly an AE term.

HOWEVER, HOW EVER

however /haʊˈevər/ *adverb*, means nevertheless, or in contrast to a statement or idea said previously: 'There is great wealth in that country. However, a substantial number of people are living in poverty'. Note that in this sense, 'however' is followed by a comma, especially when it is the first word in a

sentence. In another sense, 'however' means in whatever way: 'However they earn their daily bread, they survive'. (Note that there is no comma after 'however' in this sense.) It is best to place 'however' as the first word in the sentence. See **THOUGH ⇨ ALTHOUGH**.

how ever /ˌhaʊ ˈevər/ *adverb*, means in whatever way. It is spelt as two separate words when the speaker wishes to stress how: 'How ever did you manage to survive three weeks in the desert?'

HUMAN, HUMANE, HUMANITARIAN

human /ˈhjuːmən/ *noun & adjective* means a person as opposed to an animal when used in the noun form. An alternative is 'human being'. It is possible to use the plural form 'humans' in order to avoid sexist terms like 'man' and 'mankind', although humankind or people are other options. When used as an adjective, 'human' means connected with people, or more specifically having qualities such as kindness and generosity: 'I saw a more human side to my boss when everyone in the office went out for a meal together'. It is more common to use 'human' as an adjective than as a noun: 'human error', 'human race'. See **SEXIST LANGUAGE**.

humane /hjuːˈmeɪn/ *adjective*, indicates the quality of compassion: a 'humane killer' is a device for killing animals painlessly.

humanitarian /hjʊmænɪˈteəriən/ *adjective*, means concerned with improving the quality of life for people and easing suffering. 'Humanitarian' is often used to describe the efforts of charities to promote better health and welfare: 'Following the earthquake, humanitarian aid flowed into the country'.

HUMILITY, HUMILIATION

humility /hjuːˈmɪlɪti/ *noun*, means the state of being humble: 'The world would be a better place if politicians showed greater humility'.

humiliation /hjuːmɪlɪˈeɪʃn/ *noun*, is the state of being humbled: 'The humiliation of losing to such a poor team was unbearable'.

HUMOUR, HUMOROUS

humour /ˈhjuːmər/ *noun*, means the quality of being amusing or comic. This is the spelling in BE. The AE spelling is 'humor'.

humorous /'hju:mərəs/ *adjective*, is something that causes laughter and amusement. The word is spelt the same way in BE and AE, and there is no 'u' in the second syllable.
See **-OR, -OUR SPELLINGS**.

HUNDRED, HUNDREDS

hundred /'hʌndrəd/ *adjective*, can be either an exact number: 'three hundred people'; or an approximate amount, when it follows the words 'a few' or 'several': 'A few hundred soldiers'. In both cases, it takes a plural verb. 'Hundred' only takes a singular verb when it is included as a unit of time, distance, money, temperature, etc.: 'Five hundred dollars is required'. 'Hundred' is also used in speech to express whole hours in the twenty-four hour clock system: 'Thirteen hundred hours'.
See **TIME OF DAY**.

hundreds /'hʌndrədz/ *noun*, refers to an unspecified large number ranging from a few 'hundred' to many 'hundred': 'If you need any spare paper clips, I've got hundreds'. 'Hundreds' is followed by 'of' when used before a noun, and always takes a plural verb: 'Hundreds of litres were spilled'.

HURRICANE, TYPHOON, CYCLONE

hurricane /'hʌrɪkən/ (BE) /'hʌrɪkeɪn/ (AE) *noun*, is an extreme weather phenomenon that occurs east of the International Date Line: 'The Gulf of Mexico is where most hurricanes originate'.

typhoon /taɪ'fu:n/ *noun*, is the same weather phenomenon as a 'hurricane' but it occurs west of the International Date Line in the area of the Philippines, the China Sea, or India. They are atmospheric disturbances of about equal intensity. The difference between 'typhoon' and 'hurricane' is only a matter of where they occur.

cyclone /'saɪkləʊn/ *noun*, is both a meteorological depression and a tropical storm. This means that 'cyclone' is an alternative to both 'hurricane' and 'typhoon'. See **STORM**.

HUT, SHED, SUMMER HOUSE

hut /hʌt/ *noun*, means a primitive single-storey building used for temporary accommodation or shelter, such as a 'beach hut'.

shed /ʃed/ *noun*, is a small, usually wooden, building erected in a garden, and typically used to store tools and garden furniture.

summer house /'sʌmə haʊs/ *noun*, is also a small, often wooden, building in the garden of a house that is larger than a shed, and used for sitting in during fine weather.
See **CONSERVATORY**. See **COTTAGE** ⇨ **CABIN**.

HYDROFOIL, HOVERCRAFT

hydrofoil /'haɪdrəfɔɪl/ *noun*, is a vessel that travels partly over water, as the hull of a hydrofoil is almost out of the water at high speed.

hovercraft /'hɒvəkrɑːft/ *noun*, is a vessel that is supported on a cushion of air, and can travel over flat land and water.

HYPER-, HYPO-

hyper- /haɪpər-/ *prefix*, means above, beyond normal, so that 'hyperthermia' is a very high body temperature, and 'hypertension' is above average blood pressure.

hypo- /haɪpəʊ-/ *prefix*, means under and is often the opposite of words starting with 'hyper-'. As 'hypo-' indicates below normal or deficient, 'hypothermia' indicates a very low body temperature, and 'hypotension' is very low blood pressure.

HYPERCRITICAL, HYPOCRITICAL

hypercritical /haɪpə'krɪtɪkl̩/ *adjective*, means being very critical: 'It's very difficult to do anything right for him, as he's so hypercritical'.

hypocritical /hɪpə'krɪtɪkl̩/ adjective, refers to a person who claims to have higher moral standards than he or she actually has: 'Those well-paid managers who block pay rises for their workers are extremely hypocritical'. Note that the first syllable is pronounced /hɪp-/. A person who is 'hypocritical' is a 'hypocrite'.

hyphenation in individual words

- A hyphen shows that parts of a word, or two or more words, belong together. Hyphenation has an important function, as a hyphen in the right place will prevent misunderstandings. Consider a *light-blue compound* meaning a pale blue compound, not one that is lightweight and blue. Similarly, a *high-voltage cable* means a cable that has a high voltage, not one that is high up.

- In AE, words which are hyphenated in BE are often written as a single word, but modern BE is changing accordingly. For example, the spellings *co-operate* and *co-ordinate* in BE have been replaced by *cooperate* and *coordinate* (although not all BE spell checkers are updated here). Not all *co-* words follow this pattern and both BE and AE have a hyphen in *co-opt* (elect) as in *they co-opted a woman to the committee*. In BE, most words with *non-* and *semi-* prefixes have hyphens, hence AE *nonlinear* and BE *non-linear*. Nevertheless, the *uni-* prefixes are usually written in one word in BE. See **CO, CO-**.

- In general, as words become more familiar, hyphens tend to be dropped. A typical example is *offshore*, as in offshore drilling, offshore racing or offshore banking, which used to be spelt *off-shore* (hyphenated) in BE a few years ago. Otherwise, it is difficult to determine any consistency between *off-licence* (wine and spirits shops in the UK) and *off-peak* which are hyphenated in BE, and *offside* and *offload* which are not. It is advisable to consult the most recent edition of a good dictionary for advice on the current spelling of such words.

- One general rule relates to prefixes like *anti-* and *quasi-*, which are hyphenated when they are the first element in compound adjectives, such as *anti-American, quasi-scientific*, and not hyphenated when they form part of a compound noun: *antibody, antifreeze, quasicrystal, quasiparticle*.

- Hyphenation should be used if the second element is capitalized, as in: *non-European, pro-Irish*. Some prefixes such as: *all-* (*all-star, all-time*), *ex-* (*ex-marine, ex-works*), and *self-* (*self-suggestion*), are hyphenated in both BE and AE.

distinguishing between pairs of words

- A hyphen can also distinguish between pairs of words that are spelt the same, but have different meanings. When these words are read, the hyphen shows that there is stress on the prefix and on the word after the hyphen:

recover (get well)   *re-cover* (cover again)
reform (correction)   *re-form* (reshape)

As some soccer stars have found out, there is a considerable difference between:

resigning (leaving the club) and
re-signing (renewing a contract)

hyphenation in compounds

initial adjective phrases:

- A hyphen in the correct place can prevent ambiguity. Consider the difference between:

real time measurements (real ones)
real-time measurements (registered simultaneously)
more important people (more VIPs)
more-important people (people with higher status)
a third world war (all the world at war)
a third-world war (only the third world at war)
fifty odd students (50 strange ones)
fifty-odd students (just over 50 students)

- Otherwise, hyphens are needed:
state-of-the-art solutions
cost-effective methods

- Note that if compounds like *state of the art* are placed after the verb, they become noun phrases and have no hyphens:
these solutions are state of the art
these methods are cost effective

- If an *-ly* adverb is in this initial position, there is no hyphen:
environmentally friendly solutions
extremely fast driving

- However, with other adverbs, the hyphen is used:
close-cropped hair
well-dressed woman

numbers and colours:

- Use hyphens for number compounds such as: *thirty-three* and *one-third*. Note the hyphens in phrases like a *sixty-year-old plan*, and *a 70-kilometre-an-hour vessel*. Suspended hyphens are used to create compounds so that numbers are attached to the correct word: *Tests were at 60-, 75-, and 85-degrees Celsius* (three different sets of readings). See **MEASUREMENTS**.

- When the colour is a part of a compound, a hyphen is vital:
a blue-metallic vase (a special shade of blue) rather than *a blue metallic vase* (a blue vase made of metal).

single capitals:

- It is normal to put a hyphen after an initial single letter, particularly a capital: *T-shirt, U-turn, V-sign, X-ray*. See **EMAIL**.

misleading combinations:

- Use hyphens to create compounds in which an awkward combination of consonants would be formed by joining the words, particularly if there are two similar consonants:
animal-like bell-like pre-empt water-repellent

hyphenation at the end of lines

- Dividing a word at the end of a line can make it difficult to read or misleading (*mass-age, rest-less*). This shows that sometimes it is best not to hyphenate. Every once in a while our unthinking word processors fail to notice badly placed word divisions such as 'the leg-end of Robin Hood'. The main rule is to avoid dividing words across two lines if possible. However, if divisions must be made, here are some guidelines:

- Divide according to the origin and meaning of words: *trans-port* (not tran-sport), *tele-phone* (not te-lephone). Otherwise, follow the way a word is pronounced: *Euro-pean, chil-dren, de-scribe, de-pend-ent, thou-sand*. When a group of consonants forms one sound, do not split the group: *fea-ther* (not feat-her), *laugh-able* (not laug-hable), *wash-able* (not was-hable). As a rule of thumb, read the word aloud.

- Avoid divisions that create two confusing words: *re-adjust* (not read-just), *minis-ter* (not mini-ster). Some divisions such as wo-men and fe-male may confuse readers.

- If words already have a hyphen, only divide at the hyphen: *pseudo-intellectual* (not pseudo-intel-lectual), *anti-American* (not anti-Ameri-can).

- Words ending with *-ing* are usually divided at the end of the stem: *carry-ing, divid-ing, mov-ing*. But, if there is a double consonant before *-ing*, carry the last consonant over (*control-ling, puzz-ling*).

- Make sure that numbers followed by a unit of measurement, value or similar are kept together on the same line: *EUR 15 560* (not EUR 15-560), *166 kg* (not 166-kg), *55°C* (not 55-°C).

- Finally, many English dictionaries mark where words are to be divided by dots in mid-position in the headword, such as *tech · no · logy* and *tech · no · lo · gical*. As the pronunciation is generally the guiding rule in word division, make sure you are using the dictionary that suits the form of English you prefer. Webster's, which reflects American English, suggests *a · lu · mi · num* and *prog · ress*. However, Oxford dictionaries, which reflect British English, suggest *alu · mi · nium* and *pro · gress*.

Ii

IBID., OP.CIT.

ibid. /ˈɪbɪd/ *adverb*, means in the same book, chapter or passage as was quoted before. 'Ibid.' is an abbreviation for the Latin *ibidem*. It always refers to what immediately precedes it: 'ibid. Act II, Scene 4' (i.e. at a later place in the play already referred to). In modern style, 'ibid.' and an alternative abbreviation 'ib.' are replaced by the author's name, a date and page number: (Jones, 1992, pp. 11-14). In technical writing, either the name-and-year reference (Jones, 1992), or just a reference number is used.

op. cit. /ˌɒp ˈsɪt/ *adverb*, means the work already cited. 'Op. cit.' is the abbreviation of the Latin *opus citatum* or *opere citato* (which are not read or used in full). Only the abbreviation 'op. cit.' is used. It is written as: 'Jones, op. cit., pp. 11-14'.

–ic, –ical

There is no simple way to distinguish the words in English that end in *-ic* and *-ical*. There are three main categories:

- Those with no or a very slight difference in meaning between the two forms. Examples are: *arithmetic/arithmetical, cynic/cynical, dynamic/dynamical, fanatic/fanatical* (the origin of the modern word *fan*), *geographic/ geographical, geometric/geometrical, periodic/periodical, poetic/poetical*, and *strategic/strategical*.

- Those where there is a difference in meaning between the two. Examples of these are: *classic/classical, comic/comical, economic/economical, electric/electrical, historic/historical, lyric/lyrical*, and *politic/political*. See **HISTORIC**.

- The final category is the survivors, where either *-ic* or *-ical* survives, and the other is outdated, or even does not exist. Examples of *-ic* are: *academic, artistic, domestic, dramatic, linguistic, phonetic, scientific, systematic*, and *tragic*; and of *-ical*: *botanical, identical*, and *hypothetical*.

–ics

- Words that end in *-ics* that refer to academic disciplines, like *mathematics, acoustics, economics*, or similar words that describe a type of activity, for instance *athletics, gymnastics, hysterics* are all uncountable nouns. Note that they take a singular verb, despite the final -s: *Linguistics is the scientific study of language; Physics was never his strong point.* Certain of these words can also be treated as plural when they are used generally: *The acoustics in the concert hall were magnificent; The mathematics of space-time are very difficult for the layman to understand; Bill's politics have never changed despite everything he has seen.*

- Other words ending in -ics which are not disciplines, take a plural verb: *In handwriting, italics are indicated by underlining; The lyrics of this song are by Paul McCartney; The general's tactics were criticized by the press.*

I.E., NAMELY

i.e. /ˈaɪ ˈiː/ means 'that is to say', and is used to give an interpretation of something, or to repeat an idea in another way. It is an abbreviation for the Latin *id est*, which is never written out in full or pronounced; nor is it followed by a comma. Careful writers always avoid this term in running text and replace it with 'that is', which is followed by a comma: 'He demonstrated the wireless mouse, that is, one with no cable attaching it to the PC'. A typical place where 'i.e.' is used correctly is before an interpretation in notes, brackets and footnotes such as the following: 'Note: John Smith was told that his services were no longer required, i.e. he was fired'. When exemplifying or illustrating an idea, use 'e.g.' See **E.G.**

namely /ˈneɪmli/ *adverb*, means 'that is to say', and is used to identify or specify something mentioned immediately before: 'Leading environmentalists, namely Greenpeace and the Green Party, supported the measure'. In formal written English, especially BE, the Latin abbreviation 'viz' /vɪz/ is sometimes used instead of 'namely': 'Only the members of the board, viz. Dr Jones, Ms Maxwell, Mr Watson and Mr Winston, can vote on this issue'.

IF, WHETHER

if /ɪf/ *conjunction*, expresses a condition: 'If you are going into town, I'll meet you for lunch'. It can also be used to report a question, although 'if' in this sense is considered to be informal usage by some writers: 'He asked them if they would like anything to drink'. 'If' has a range of other meanings, including 'whenever': 'The cat always runs away if a motorbike goes past the house'. 'If' also expresses a concession: 'The dog is intelligent, if untrained'.

whether /ˈweðər/ *conjunction*, expresses an alternative, especially in written English: 'He never says whether he prefers tea or coffee'. Sometimes the alternative is emphasized by using the expression 'whether or not': 'We're going away for the weekend, whether or not the children come with us'. 'Whether', but not 'if', is typically used with verbs such as 'discuss', 'consider', or 'decide': 'We must discuss whether to expand our product range'. Note that 'whether' can never replace 'if' when referring to a condition.
See **WHETHER ⇨ WEATHER**.

IGNORE, IGNORANT

ignore /ɪgˈnɔːr/ *verb*, means to deliberately take no notice of someone or something: 'She tried to speak to him, but he ignored her completely'. It also means not to take something into account: 'The official's reply ignored her main complaint'.

ignorant /ˈɪgnərənt/ *adjective*, means lacking knowledge of: 'General managers are often ignorant of the way in which their staff work'. Somebody who 'ignores' activities is not 'ignorant' of them, since he or she knows what is happening, but chooses not to react.

ILL, SICK

ill /ɪl/ *adjective & adverb*, as an adjective in BE, means to be in poor health: 'He never really recovered from the infection and was ill for many years'. It is also commonly used to describe people who have been injured: 'He was still seriously ill three weeks after the crash'. As an adverb, 'ill' is most commonly used in compounds to mean badly, or not satisfactorily: 'The new bus service was an ill-considered plan'. 'Ill' is formal in this sense.

sick /sɪk/ *adjective*, usually means to vomit in BE: 'The child was sick twice during the car journey'. In AE, 'ill' and 'sick' are interchangeable, 'ill' being the more formal of the two and reserved for more serious illnesses. Some terms for general illness are used in both AE and BE, such as 'sick leave' and 'sick pay'. In more general contexts, 'sick' can mean in a bad state: 'The economy is sick'. 'Sick of' means tired of someone or something: 'She bought a car because she was sick of waiting for buses'. 'Sick' can also mean in bad taste or perverted, for example in the term 'sick humour'.
See **HEALTHY ⇨ WELL**.
See **PERVERT ⇨ PERVERSE**.

'Please do not feed the animals. They may get sick of being fed by the public.' (Notice in zoo)

ILLEGAL, UNLAWFUL, ILLEGITIMATE

illegal /ɪˈliːgḷ/ *adjective*, means something that is forbidden by law: 'The police arrested the illegal immigrants'. 'Illegal' is the term used in some expressions such as: 'illegal alien', and also refers to criminal activities such as 'illegal drugs and 'illegal exports'. See **LEGAL**.

unlawful /ʌnˈlɔːfʊl/ *adjective*, means something that is forbidden by law, or which does not conform to the law: 'The brutal behaviour of the police was unlawful'. 'Unlawful' is a formal word focusing on how the law is put into effect. See **LAWFUL ⇨ LEGAL**.

illegitimate /ɪlɪˈdʒɪtɪmət/ *adjective*, means a child who is born to unmarried parents: 'He was told that he could never inherit the family estate because he was illegitimate'. It also means something that is not allowed by law or by a set of accepted standards: 'The tax authorities ruled that the trip to Hawaii was pleasure, not business, and that the travel expenses were therefore illegitimate'. See **LEGITIMATE ⇨ LEGAL**.

ILLEGIBLE, UNREADABLE, ILLITERATE

illegible /ɪˈledʒɪbḷ/ *adjective*, means that a piece of writing cannot be read or deciphered, either because it is not expressed clearly enough or because the letter shapes are difficult to see: 'His illegible handwriting is like that of the typical mad professor'. The related noun is 'illegibility'. See **LEGIBLE ⇨ READABLE**. See **UNINTELLIGIBLE**.

unreadable /ʌnˈriːdəbḷ/ *adjective*, means that a piece of writing is too boring, unsuitable or difficult to read. Note that a handwritten text whose individual words can be clearly made out may still be unreadable: 'This unreadable trash is unworthy of the paper it is written on'. The related noun is 'unreadability'. See **READABLE**.

illiterate /ɪˈlɪtərət/ *adjective & noun*, as an adjective, means unable to read and write. It can also refer to a document that is poorly written in terms of grammar and spelling: 'Letters sent to newspapers are often so illiterate that much time has to be spent on making them readable'. 'Illiterate' is also used figuratively to mean ignorant of a subject: 'It is difficult for artists to establish themselves in a country that is culturally illiterate'. As a noun, this means a person who cannot read or write. The related noun is 'illiteracy', which means the state of being unable to read or write: 'Our education programme is successfully removing illiteracy from this part of the country'.

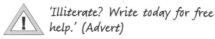

'Illiterate? Write today for free help.' (Advert)

ILLICIT[S], ELICIT[S]

illicit /ɪˈlɪsɪt/ *adjective*, means either not allowed by law, or refers to something that is forbidden by morality or custom: 'His wife divorced him when she discovered that he had had an illicit love affair for three years'.

elicit /ɪˈlɪsɪt/ *verb*, means to make someone reveal something or to obtain information with difficulty: 'The lawyer finally elicited the truth from his client'.

IMAGINARY, IMAGINATIVE

imaginary /ɪˈmædʒɪnəri/ *adjective*, means existing only in the imagination: 'The classic comedy film *Harvey* is about an imaginary 6-foot rabbit'.

imaginative /ɪˈmædʒɪnətɪv/ *adjective*, means being creative or stimulating the imagination of others: 'The characters in her stories are very imaginative'.

IMMATURE, PREMATURE

immature /ɪməˈtjʊər/ *adjective*, means undeveloped or not fully grown, when it refers to plants or animals. When referring to humans, 'immature' often implies restricted emotional or intellectual development: 'The fact that he shouts whenever there is a problem is an example of his immature attitude'.

premature /ˈpremətʃər/ *adjective*, refers to something that occurs before it is scheduled to, or before it is considered advisable: 'Her end-of-exam celebrations might be a little premature if she fails them all'. A 'premature baby' is one which arrives three or more weeks early.

IMMORAL, AMORAL, IMMORTAL

immoral /ɪˈmɒrəl/ *adjective*, refers to actions that are against accepted moral standards: 'Incest is universally termed immoral'. The related noun is 'immorality' /ɪməˈræləti/.

amoral /eɪ'mɒrəl/ *adjective*, means not having any moral standards or ethics: 'The way in which he exploited everyone that he met showed how amoral he was'.

immortal /ɪ'mɔːtl̩/ *adjective*, means living for ever, or deserving to be remembered: 'The continuing interest of film-makers ensures that Shakespeare's works will remain immortal'. The related noun is 'immortality' /ɪmɔː'tælɪti/.

'Her name will be remembered for immorality.'
(Funeral service, England)

IMMUNITY, IMPUNITY

immunity /ɪ'mjuːnɪti/ *noun*, means being exempted from an obligation or penalty: 'He was able to park wherever he wanted because of his diplomatic immunity'. 'Immunity' also refers to the body's capacity to protect itself from disease: 'His immunity to the virus astonished the doctors'.

impunity /ɪm'pjuːnɪti/ *noun*, means freedom from the negative consequences of an action. It is usually used in the phrase 'with impunity': 'The directors thought that they could manipulate the company accounts with impunity'.

IMPLEMENT, CARRY OUT, EXECUTE

implement /'ɪmplɪment/ *verb*, means to initiate an agreed decision, plan or course of action: 'The new sales agreement will be implemented in 2005'.

carry out /'kæri 'aʊt/ *verb*, means to perform and complete an action: 'The committee carried out the inspection of the building after the fire'.

execute /'eksɪkjuːt/ *verb*, means to complete an action, and is a word which may be used in military contexts: 'The orders from the commander in chief were executed with great precision'. 'Execute' also means to kill, officially, by the state, or unofficially, by a self-styled authority: 'The hostages were taken out and executed one by one'.

'Order your summer suit. Because of the rush we will execute customers in strict rotation.'

IMPLICIT, EXPLICIT

implicit /ɪm'plɪsɪt/ *adjective*, is used in two ways. First, it means that something is understood without being stated directly: 'It was implicit that everybody had to pay for his or her own drinks'. Second, 'implicit' means trusting in someone and not doubting their judgement: 'She had implicit trust in her children and never doubted the accuracy of what they said'.

explicit /ɪks'plɪsɪt/ *adjective*, means that something is understood after it has been stated clearly, exactly, and directly: 'We had some very explicit instructions about where to park'. 'Be explicit' means to say or do things in a very open and direct manner: 'She was very explicit about the problems in her marriage'. Television companies use the term 'explicit' to refer to programmes with bad language, violence or sex scenes: 'Parents are warned that the following programme contains explicit language'.

IMPOSSIBLE, IMPROBABLE

impossible /ɪm'pɒsɪbl̩/ *adjective*, means that something cannot be true, cannot exist or cannot happen: 'It is impossible for humans to fly like birds'. 'Impossible' also refers to a person or situation that is very difficult to deal with: 'They have put me in an impossible position: whatever I do I will lose my job'. See **ABSOLUTES AND FUZZY ABSOLUTES**.

improbable /ɪm'prɒbəbl̩/ *adjective*, can mean something that is unlikely to be true, to exist or to happen: 'It is highly improbable that there will be snow in England in July'.

'Improbable' also means something that is strange and unexpected: 'The whole town was an improbable mixture of baroque and modern architecture'.

IMPRACTICAL, IMPRACTICABLE

impractical /ɪm'præktɪkl̩/ *adjective*, means not practical, realistic or sensible: 'He may potentially be an excellent pilot, but as he is so short sighted, it is completely impractical for him to think of such a career'. 'Impractical' also refers to a person who is not very good at making or doing things with their hands: 'I'm so impractical that I can't even change a light bulb'. 'Impractical' is sometimes used to mean 'impracticable', especially in AE. If a clear distinction needs to be made, 'impractical' can be replaced by useless or not sensible.

impracticable /ɪm'præktɪkəbl̩/ *adjective*, means not feasible or impossible to carry out: 'Until 1960 it was considered impracticable to send someone to the moon'.

INAPT, INEPT, UNAPT

inapt /ɪn'æpt/ *adjective*, means not suitable: 'It is inapt to celebrate the life of a person who committed so many crimes against humanity'. The related noun is 'inaptitude'.

inept /ɪn'ept/ *adjective*, means foolish or unskilled: 'Our new ambassador is so clumsy and inept that he called the American an uneducated redskin'. The related noun is 'ineptitude'.

unapt /ʌn'æpt/ *adjective*, means not appropriate in the circumstances: 'It was unapt to mention bankruptcy in the disgraced director's presence'. The related noun is 'unaptness'.

INCREDIBLE, INCREDULOUS

incredible /ɪŋ'kredɪbl̩/ *adjective*, means unbelievable and wonderful, amazing: 'There was an incredible view over the city from the castle'. See **CREDIBLE**.

incredulous /ɪŋ'kredjʊləs/ *adjective*, means unwilling or unable to believe something: 'He was incredulous that anyone could utter such racist nonsense'. See **CREDULOUS ⇨ CREDIBLE**.

indefinite article

- **a** is used before words that begin with a *consonant sound*: 'a house', 'a unit'. **An** is used with words beginning with a *vowel sound*: *an apple, an hour*.

Always remember that it is the sound, not the spelling of the letter that follows **a** or **an**, which decides the form of the indefinite article.

e, o, h and u

- Most words starting with *e* take **an**, but use **a** before words starting with *eu*, if pronounced /jʊ-/ as in *a European, a euro*, or /juː-/ as in *a euphemism* and *a eulogy*.
- Most words starting with *o* take **an**, but use **a** before *one* and *once* as they are pronounced with an initial /w/, as in *a one-night stand, a once-in-a-lifetime opportunity*.
- In standard, modern English, use **a** before *h* when the *h* is pronounced: *a hotel, a historic date, a Hispanic*, and **an** before a silent *h*: *an hour, an heir, an honour*.
- Use **a** before *u* if it is pronounced /juː-/, which contains a consonant sound: *a union, a university*. If *u* is pronounced /ʌ/, as a vowel sound, it takes **an**: *an underwater vehicle, an umbrella*.

abbreviations/acronyms

- With abbreviations (which are read letter-by-letter), it is the sound of the initial letter that decides whether **a** or **an** is used. Thus it is *a Federal Bureau of Investigation report*, but when abbreviated, *an FBI report*. Similarly, it is correct to write *a Master of Science degree* and *a Massachussetts Institute of Technology student*, but when abbreviated, these are: *an MSc degree* and *an MIT student*. The following letters must have **an** in front when they are the first letter in an abbreviation: A, E, F, H, I, L, M, N, O, R, S, X.
- Note that **an** is used before most acronyms (read as one word) starting with A, E, I, O. *An ASCII ..., an EFTA ..., an ISO ..., an OPEC ....* See **FULL STOP**.

numbers

- Use **an** with all eight/eighteen/eighty combinations; *an 8, 18, 80, 800 ... degree variation*.

INDEX, INDEXES, INDICES

index /'ɪndeks/ *noun*, means both an alphabetic listing at the end of a report or textbook and a scale used for measuring changes in prices, etc.

indexes /'ɪndeksɪz/ is one of the plurals of 'index'. It refers to both alphabetical lists and the stock market indexes: 'The FT and Dow Jones indexes are both down again'.

indices /'ɪndɪsiːz/ is the other plural of 'index'. It is used in mathematics for the small superscript number in equations or elsewhere: 'Two common indices express a billion as 10^9 and a trillion as 10^{12}'. See **PLURAL NOUNS**.

INDOOR, INDOORS
indoor /'ɪndɔːr/ *adjective*, means inside or under cover. 'Indoor' is usually placed before a noun: 'The shop had a large reduction on indoor plants'.

indoors /ɪn'dɔːz/ *adverb*, refers to being inside a building, or to movement into a building: 'They moved indoors when it started to get cold outside'.

INDUSTRIAL, INDUSTRIOUS, INDUSTRY
industrial /ɪn'dʌstrɪəl/ *adjective*, means relating to industry: 'Finland has become an advanced industrial nation during the past fifty years'.

industrious /ɪn'dʌstrɪəs/ *adjective*, means diligent and hardworking: 'My class of students are all extremely industrious'.

industry /'ɪndəstri/ *noun*, means economic activity related to the processing of raw materials and goods in factories and plants, when used as an uncountable noun: 'Industry is doing well at the moment'. (Note that the definite article cannot be used before 'industry' in this sense.) 'Industry' as a countable noun refers to specific branches of commercial activity: 'Banking is the industry that is most attractive to business graduates'. See **BUSINESS**. See **UNCOUNTABLE NOUNS**.

INEQUALITY, INEQUITY, INIQUITY, INJUSTICE
inequality /ɪnɪ'kwɒlɪti/ *noun*, means difference in size, degree or circumstances between two categories of things. However, it is most commonly used to refer to an unfair difference between two groups of people or two sets of circumstances: 'Most democracies still have considerable social inequalities'.

inequity /ɪn'ɛkwɪti/ *noun*, is a formal word that means unfairness: 'This political party promises to correct the present inequities and shortcomings in the taxation system'.

iniquity /ɪn'ɪkwɪti/ *noun*, is a formal word that means wickedness or sinfulness: 'The director resigned when the press revealed that he was living in a den of iniquity'.

injustice /ɪn'dʒʌstɪs/ *noun*, is a more general word than the others in this group and means a lack of fairness or justice: 'Dickens' novels spoke out against social injustice'.

INFER, IMPLY
infer /ɪn'fɜːr/ *verb*, means that the listener draws a conclusion based on what is said: 'The spokesperson described the lively dinner the night before, which led us to infer that they had all had too much to eat and drink'.

imply /ɪm'plaɪ/ *verb*, means to suggest or hint about something, but without saying so directly: 'Although the spokesperson did not talk much about the previous evening's dinner, he implied that they had all had too much to eat and drink'. 'Imply' and 'infer' are often confused, but a useful distinction is that a speaker implies, while a listener infers.

INFLEXIBLE, UNBENDING
inflexible /ɪn'fleksɪbl/ *adjective*, means people or things that are unwilling or unable to change: 'It's difficult to reach an agreement when both sides are being so inflexible'. This word usually conveys a disapproving attitude, although it is neutral when referring to the rigid quality of a material or object. People or things with the opposite characteristic are 'flexible'.

unbending /ʌn'bendɪŋ/ *adjective*, means the same as 'inflexible': 'Unbending discipline'. This also conveys a disapproving attitude. However, the related verb 'unbend' means almost the opposite: to behave in a less reserved way than is expected. 'Unbend' is often qualified by phrases like a little or a bit: 'The bank's chief accountant has learned how to unbend a bit'.

INFLUENCE, IMPACT
influence /'ɪnfluəns/ *noun*, means the effect that someone or something has on another person or thing: 'The influence of the Vietnam War on American society is still evident'. It can also mean the capacity to have an effect: 'Television is considered by some to be a negative influence on society'.

impact /'ɪmpækt/ *noun*, means a great impression or strong effect. 'Impact' refers to events happening with a sudden force: 'The sharp drop in the stock market had an impact on global markets'.

INFORMATION, NEWS

information /ɪnfəˈmeɪʃn/ *noun*, means facts that are based on evidence or data. It is an uncountable noun that never has a plural form and always takes a singular verb: 'This information is important'. It is never possible to say 'an information'. Instead, use 'some', or 'a piece/bit of information'.

news /njuːz/ (BE) /nuːz/ (AE) *noun*, means recent information about current events: 'The director told his staff the latest news about the merger'. In another sense, 'news' can refer to media reports such as 'news of that plane crash is still coming in'. In some TV stations, the phrase 'breaking news' refers to events as they are happening. The regular scheduled broadcast of current events is called 'the news': 'Change the channel: the news is on'. Note that 'news' is an uncountable noun, thus is referred to by pronouns like 'it', and always takes a singular verb.

INGENIOUS, INGENUOUS

ingenious /ɪnˈdʒiːnɪəs/ *adjective*, means inventive, clever, original and resourceful: 'He discovered an ingenious way of opening beer cans and made a fortune'. Note that the second syllable rhymes with 'mean'.
See **GENIUS ⟹ GENIAL**.

ingenuous /ɪnˈdʒenjʊəs/ *adjective*, is used of someone who is unsophisticated, naive and unsuspecting: 'She was so ingenuous as to believe what the man said without questioning his motives'. Note that the second syllable rhymes with 'men'.

INHABITANT, CITIZEN, RESIDENT, SUBJECT

inhabitant /ɪnˈhæbɪtənt/ *noun*, means any person who lives in a town or country, and is not connected with citizenship or permanent settlement: 'London is a city of nearly seven million inhabitants'. 'Inhabitant' is a rather impersonal term, and is used in contexts where people might be considered misleading or too informal. The associated verb is 'inhabit'.
See **HABITABLE**. See **LOCAL**.

citizen /ˈsɪtɪzən/ *noun*, is a native or naturalized person of a particular state: 'The French were delighted when one of their citizens won the Tour de France'.

resident /ˈrezɪdənt/ *noun*, refers to someone who inhabits a place that is their permanent home: 'The residents of the village were very concerned about plans for a new road to be built across green fields'. 'Resident' can also refer to people who are staying in a hotel. The sign 'for residents only' indicates that only those staying can use a particular facility.
See **RESIDENCE**.

subject /ˈsʌbdʒɪkt/ *noun*, is used in some monarchies as an alternative to 'citizen': 'The TV news reported that thirty British subjects were in jail'.

INHERITANCE, HERITAGE, HEREDITY

inheritance /ɪnˈherɪtəns/ *noun*, means property or an estate received from a deceased person: 'His inheritance included his grandmother's large country house'. 'Inheritance' is also used in a limited number of expressions, such as 'cultural inheritance' and 'artistic inheritance', with a similar meaning to 'heritage'.

heritage /ˈherɪtɪdʒ/ *noun*, means a set of valued national or cultural traditions and qualities. This is a formal word: 'The rich heritage of English literature is studied around the world'.

heredity /hɪˈredɪti/ *noun*, means the characteristics, looks and diseases passed from generation to generation: 'The profile of the nose is part of his heredity'.

INHUMAN, INHUMANE

inhuman /ɪnˈhjuːmən/ *adjective*, means lacking the human qualities of kindness: 'She was cruel and inhuman to her children'. It also means not being human, either in character or form: 'An inhuman creature called King Kong was the main character of several films'.

inhumane /ɪnhjʊˈmeɪn/ *adjective*, means without compassion for suffering: 'The inhumane treatment of the dog was reported to the police'. Note that the last syllable is pronounced 'main'. See **HUMAN**.

IN-LAW, IN-LAWS

in-law /ˈ... ɪn ˌlɔː/ *suffix*, means relation by marriage to a husband's or wife's blood relations, or to a brother's wife or sister's husband: 'Meet George, he is my son-in-law'. Note the plurals: 'mothers-in-law', 'fathers-in-law', 'brothers-in-law' etc.

in-laws /'ɪn lɔːz/ *noun*, is the generic term for some, or all, of the relations-in-law: 'All our in-laws are in Spain at Christmas'. Do not confuse the noun 'in-laws' with the genitive form, as in: 'She was at her brother-in-law's', meaning at his house.

INNOVATION, INVENTION, DISCOVERY

innovation /ɪnə'veɪʃn/ *noun*, means a new product, system or idea: 'That type of ice cream was quite an innovation'. The term 'new innovation' is to be avoided, since all innovations are new by definition. Note that the stress is on the third syllable.
See **TAUTOLOGY**.

invention /ɪn'venʃn/ *noun*, means a creation or design that has not existed before: 'The invention of traffic lights reduced the risk of accidents at junctions'.

discovery /dɪs'kʌvəri/ *noun*, means the act of finding out something that already exists, such as a comet or a scientific law: 'Newton discovered some of the major laws of physics'.

INNOVATIVE, NEW

innovative /'ɪnəʊveɪtɪv/ *adjective*, refers to a product, method or idea that has new features that are advanced and original: 'Innovative research has improved medical treatment considerably'. Note that the stress is on the first syllable.

new /njuː/ *adjective*, means either not existing before or unused and unworn. Avoid using 'new' with 'innovative' or other words that convey newness, unless there is a contrast to an earlier innovation or record: 'A new world record has just been set.' If there is no such contrast, omit 'new'. In AE, the pronunciation is often /nuː/.

'Be sure to see the brand-new repeat of the old 'New Loretta Young Show'.'

INNUMERABLE, INNUMERATE

innumerable /ɪ'njuːmərəbl/ *adjective*, means too many to be counted. As this is rarely literally correct it usually means many: 'Inside the house, there were innumerable cats occupying every surface'.

innumerate /ɪ'njuːmərət/ *adjective*, refers to a person without basic mathematical or arithmetical skill: 'He was so innumerate that he could not even get the most basic office job'. The related noun is 'innumeracy'.

INSIGHT⁵, INCITE⁵

insight /'ɪnsaɪt/ *noun*, means a deep knowledge or understanding of something: 'She writes about the human condition with great insight'. Note that the stress is on the first syllable.

incite /ɪn'saɪt/ *verb*, means to try to persuade others to behave in a particular, often violent, way: 'He incited his followers to take to the streets and fight the government'. Note that the stress is on the second syllable.

INSTRUCTION, INSTRUCTIONS

instruction /ɪn'strʌkʃn/ *noun*, means the process of teaching a particular skill: 'The tennis instruction was excellent'; or the process of education: 'They received instruction in applying linguistic theory'. In these senses, 'instruction' is an uncountable noun. Note that as a countable noun, an instruction is either an order to do something, or a piece of information about how to do something.
See **TEACH**.

instructions /ɪn'strʌkʃnz/ *plural noun*, means detailed information about how to complete an operation: 'The flight attendant gave the passengers the standard safety instructions'.

INSULATE, ISOLATE

insulate /'ɪnsjʊleɪt/ *verb*, means to protect something by a material that prevents loss of heat or stops unwanted sound: 'They used polystyrene to insulate the machine room'. 'Insulate' also means to prevent direct contact with electricity: 'We had to use a lot of special tape to insulate the bare wires'. If a group is insulated from the real world, it is protected from it, but not completely cut off from it.

isolate /'aɪsəleɪt/ *verb*, means to keep someone or something apart or cut off from others. 'To be/feel isolated' means to experience a sense of being alone: 'When she first moved away from her friends and family to live in a different town, she felt quite isolated'.

INSURANCE, ASSURANCE

insurance /ɪnˈʃʊərəns/ *noun*, means protection against loss, and is used when referring to property, belongings, health and travel: 'The premium for the car insurance policy is overdue'. In AE, 'life insurance' is the term preferred over the BE 'life assurance'.

assurance /əˈʃʊərəns/ *noun*, means promise, and is used in the context of BE insurance terminology for insuring against certainties such as death: 'A life assurance policy was issued on her husband'. Nevertheless, most native English speakers use 'insurance' as a general term irrespective of whether a life is 'assured' or a car is 'insured'.

INTELLIGENT, INTELLECTUAL

intelligent /ɪnˈtelɪdʒənt/ *adjective*, refers to someone or something applying knowledge and understanding. Note that 'intelligent' does not necessarily imply academic ability: 'He was an intelligent boy, but for some reason never did very well in exams'.

intellectual /ɪntəˈlektʃʊəl/ *adjective & noun*. As an adjective, this refers to people who have or are developing a logical sense of reasoning: 'Teachers try to stimulate the intellectual development of their students'. As a noun, an 'intellectual' is a person who enjoys logical or academic activity: 'In some cultures, intellectuals are mistrusted by the government'.

INTENSE, INTENSIVE

intense /ɪnˈtens/ *adjective*, means extreme or very strong: 'They suffered because the heat in the room was so intense'.

intensive /ɪnˈtensɪv/ *adjective*, means requiring a high concentration of effort or resources: 'The course necessitated intensive reading'.

INTER-, INTRA-

inter- /ɪntər-/ *prefix*, means between or among, as in 'international' and 'Internet'. It also means mutual, as in 'interaction': 'The interaction between the two scientists resulted in an important medical breakthrough'.

intra- /ɪntrə-/ *prefix*, means within or inside: 'He had an intravenous drip'. An 'Intranet' is a local, restricted-access computer network based on World Wide Web technology.

INTEREST, INTERESTS

interest /ˈɪntrəst/ *verb & noun*, as a verb, means to engage someone's attention: 'English usage interests me'. As an uncountable noun, 'interest' means the money paid as a return to a depositor: 'The bank had a favourable rate of interest on deposits'. Note that here, the preposition 'on' is common. As a countable noun, 'interest' means the desire to know about or pay attention to something: 'She always had an interest in Italian art'. In this sense the only preposition that is used after 'interest' is 'in'. The related adjective is 'interested'. See **DISINTERESTED**.

interests /ˈɪntrəsts/ *noun*, means pastimes and hobbies: 'Her interests include reading and jogging'. It also means an organization, usually of a political character: 'Environmental interests are making themselves heard more and more today'.

INTERPRET, PERFORM, TRANSLATE

interpret /ɪnˈtɜːprɪt/ *verb*, means to explain the meaning of something in simpler terms: 'The students were asked to interpret the meaning of *Hamlet*'. 'Interpret' also means to simultaneously translate a speech or discussion from one language to another. The person doing this is the 'interpreter'. In an artistic sense, 'interpret' means to play either a piece of music or a theatrical role in a particular way. The related noun is 'interpretation'.

perform /pəˈfɔːm/ *verb*, is the word most commonly used for the playing of a piece of music or a theatrical work. The artist doing this is a 'performer'. The related noun is 'performance'.

translate /trænsˈleɪt/ *verb*, has a similar meaning to 'interpret', in the sense of conveying the meaning of a second language, but includes written as well as spoken language: 'The students took thirty minutes to translate that letter into French'. The person who translates is a 'translator'. The related noun is 'translation'.

INTERVAL, INTERMISSION

interval /ˈɪntəvəl/ *noun*, means the break at half time in sports: 'Liverpool was leading 2-1 at the interval'. It also means a gap: 'The CV revealed many intervals in his career'. In the sense of a break in a theatrical performance, 'interval' is an alternative to 'intermission' in BE, but not in AE.

intermission /ˌɪntəˈmɪʃn̩/ *noun,* means a break, particularly in a theatre performance or concert: 'We can stretch our legs in the intermission'.

INTO⁵, IN TO⁵, ON TO

into /ˈɪntə, tʊ, tuː/ *preposition,* means movement from the outside to the inside of something: 'They drove into the town'. In this sense, 'into' is written as one word.

in to /ˈɪn tə, tʊ, tuː/ *adverb & preposition,* is written as two words when forming part of a phrasal verb that is followed by the infinitive with 'to': 'She came in to water the plants while we were away'. This is also the case when 'in' is used as an adverb followed by 'to': 'He walked in to find that his flat had been burgled'.

on to /ˈɒn tə, tʊ, tuː/ *preposition,* means movement from one surface to another: 'The car went off the road on to the grass'. This is the standard BE spelling, in two words. 'Onto' is the standard AE spelling of 'on to' in this sense.

on to /ˈɒn tə, tʊ, tuː/ *adverb & preposition,* means further, and is written as two words when forming part of a phrasal verb: 'They drove on to the town'; 'They went on to win the election'. This is both the BE and AE spelling in this sense.

INTOLERABLE, INTOLERANT

intolerable /ɪnˈtɒlərəbl̩/ *adjective,* refers to someone or something that cannot be endured: 'The reason that we moved away from the airport was the intolerable noise of the aeroplanes'.

intolerant /ɪnˈtɒlərənt/ *adjective,* refers to someone who is not able to accept or agree with people whose ideas or behaviour are different from their own: 'They were intolerant of my liberal views and refused to listen'.

INTOXICATE, POISON

intoxicate /ɪnˈtɒksɪkeɪt/ *verb,* is usually used in the passive, and means to be drunk: 'After four glasses of wine he was too intoxicated to drive'. 'Intoxicate' can also be used in a figurative sense to mean feel very excited: 'After so many years in captivity, he was intoxicated by the thought of freedom'.

poison /ˈpɔɪzn̩/ *verb,* means to use a substance that will harm or kill a person, animal or plant: 'Almost all the fish in the lake had been poisoned by chemical waste'. In a figurative sense, 'poison' also means to have a negative effect on something: 'Relations between the two leaders had been poisoned since that row'.

INVALID, DISABILITY, DISABLED, INABILITY

invalid /ˈɪnvəlɪd/ *noun,* means someone who needs permanent care due to an illness: 'He was confined to a wheelchair and remained an invalid for the rest of his life'. Note that this word is stressed on the first syllable.

invalid /ɪnˈvælɪd/ *adjective,* refers to things such as documents or treaties that are no longer officially acceptable. In computing, 'invalid' refers to a command or operation that the software cannot execute: 'Here is that 'invalid access' message again'. Note that the stress is on the second syllable.
See **INVALIDATE** ⇨ **CANCEL**.

disability /ˌdɪsəˈbɪlɪti/ *noun,* means a physical or mental condition which may prevent a person from doing something: 'Poor eyesight is very common, but is a serious disability in some jobs'. See **MENTAL HANDICAP** ⇨ **LEARNING DIFFICULTY**.

disabled /dɪˈseɪbl̩d/ *adjective,* refers to someone who has a physical or mental condition that restricts their actions or affects their behaviour. Although 'disabled' has replaced old-fashioned terms like 'crippled' and 'handicapped', new terms have been introduced because of the negative associations of 'disabled'. Two of these are: 'differently abled' and 'physically challenged'. 'Disabled' may also be used to mean that a function has been switched off: 'The C-drive on the computer was disabled to prevent its misuse'.

inability /ˌɪnəˈbɪlɪti/ *noun,* means being unable to do something, even though there is no physical or mental disability that prevents this happening: 'Too many children in the slums suffer because of the city's inability to improve the standard of health'. Note that the only related adjective is 'unable' /ʌnˈeɪbl̩/ which means lacking the skill, means or opportunity to do something.

inverted commas, quotation marks

Inverted commas are a set of punctuation marks that are either single (' ') or double (" ") enclosing a quotation, a word, or an expression containing jargon. There are several typographical patterns such as the jagged version « ». An alternative term for inverted commas is quotation marks. See **QUOTATION**. See **SO-CALLED**.

INVITATION, INVITE

invitation /ɪnvɪˈteɪʃn̩/ *noun*, is a spoken or written request to attend an event somewhere, such as an invitation to dinner. In formal English, invitations are extended and are either accepted or declined: 'I must unfortunately decline your kind invitation due to a previous engagement'. Informally, an invitation is offered, and in the case of rejection can be turned down.

invite /ˈɪnvaɪt/ *noun*, is an informal shortening of the word 'invitation': 'Thanks for the invite. Carol and I look forward to seeing you at 8'. See **INVITE** ⇨ **ASK**.

INWARD, INWARDS

inward /ˈɪnwəd/ *adjective & adverb*, as an adjective, means directed towards the inside: 'inward peace' and 'inward mail'. In AE, 'inward' is also used as an adverb: 'Traffic driving inward must avoid City Bridge'.

inwards /ˈɪnwədz/ *adverb*, means towards the inside: 'This door opens inwards'. This is the BE spelling. 'Inward' is an alternative spelling, especially in AE.

IRON⁵, ION⁵

iron /ˈaɪən/ *noun*, has two meanings. First, it is the name of the metal with the chemical symbol Fe. Like all elements, 'iron' is an uncountable noun and always takes a singular verb: 'This ore is particularly rich in iron'. Second, 'iron' is an appliance for pressing clothes in order to eliminate creases in the fabric: 'The iron in the hotel room was faulty'. In this sense, 'iron' is a countable noun. Note that the 'r' is always silent in 'iron'.

ion /ˈaɪən/ *noun*, is a technical term in physics meaning a charged atom or molecule: 'A synthetic resin was used as the ion exchanger'.

 'For flattening of clothing, contact the housekeeper.' (Hotel notice)

IRRELIGIOUS, NON-RELIGIOUS, SACRILEGIOUS

irreligious /ɪrɪˈlɪdʒəs/ *adjective*, refers to a person or something that is hostile or against religion: 'It is widely believed that we are living in an ungodly, irreligious society'.

non-religious /nɒnrɪˈlɪdʒəs/ *adjective*, means secular, and is a more neutral term than 'irreligious'.

sacrilegious /sækrɪˈlɪdʒəs/ *adjective*, means treating something without respect: 'Cutting a piece out of the painting to make it fit the frame was a sacrilegious act'. Note that this word is not related to religious, and is spelt '-rileg-' in the middle.

IRREPARABLE, UNREPAIRABLE

irreparable /ɪˈrepərəbl̩/ *adjective*, refers to damage or loss that cannot be put right: 'After 45 years of smoking, his lungs had suffered irreparable damage'. The opposite adjective is 'reparable' /ˈrepərəbl̩/.

unrepairable /ʌnrɪˈpeərəbl̩/ *adjective*, refers to material objects that cannot be repaired: 'The tear in his diving suit was unrepairable'. The opposite adjective is 'repairable' /rɪˈpeərəbl̩/.

ISLE⁵, AISLE⁵

isle /aɪl/ *noun*, means an island. It is used in literary contexts or in proper names such as the Isle of Wight or the British Isles.

aisle /aɪl/ *noun*, means a passageway in buildings or in a plane or train: 'All luggage must be removed from the aisle for safety reasons'.

ISRAELI, ISRAELITE

Israeli /ɪzˈreɪli/ *noun & adjective*, as a noun, means a native of Israel. The plural is 'Israelis': 'There are several Israelis staying in the hotel'. As an adjective, it means of or relating to the modern state of Israel: 'There were noisy demonstrations outside the Israeli embassy'.

Israelite /ˈɪzreɪlaɪt/ *noun*, is a term for the ancient Hebrew nation and is only used in biblical and historical contexts. This is an offensive term if it is used for a Jew today. See **JEW**.

ISSUE, SUBJECT

issue /'ɪʃuː/ *noun & verb*, as a noun, means an important topic for discussion: 'The issue is not just whether to go on strike, but for how long'. It can also mean a problem: 'I cannot understand why the newspapers are making such an issue out of this story'. In another sense, an 'issue' is a particular edition of a periodical publication, such as a newspaper or magazine. As a verb, 'issue' means to publish, provide or hand out, especially in a formal or official context: 'The Prime Minister issued a statement to the country'.

subject /'sʌbdʒɪkt/ *noun*, can mean a topic: 'An important subject for us to discuss is quality control'. In academic use, 'subject' also means a branch of knowledge. See **DISCIPLINE**.

it is, there is/are

- **It is** (or **it's**) can be used to make a general statement, give an opinion or express a fact. *It's a lovely present. Thank you.* We use *it is* to refer to times, dates, distances and the weather. In short answers, only the full form *it is* can be used: *The sun is very hot/Yes, it is. It is* can refer to something already mentioned, or may mean an assumed subject: *It's raining for the third week in succession.* Note that the *it* in such sentences is not omitted in English.
- **There is/are** is used to state that something or someone exists: *There is a lot of rust on the car; There are a lot of people here.* Note that it is the subject (rust or people) that determines whether the verb is singular or plural.

ITS⁵, IT'S⁵

its /ɪts/ *pronoun*, means something belonging to a thing or animal: 'This is a book about Venezuela and its oil'. Note that none of the possessive pronouns take an apostrophe. See **APOSTROPHE**.

it's /ɪts/ is the short form for **it is**: 'It's ready to take away'; and 'it has': 'It's arrived'. **It's** is correct in spoken and informal written English. 'It is' and 'it has' are correct in formal writing. See **CONTRACTIONS**.

'*Use our full-text international translation – known for it's accuracy and readability.*' (Web advert)

–ization, –isation

- The rules for whether to use the spelling *–ization* or *–isation* follow the *–ize/–ise* pattern. Both *–ization* and *–isation* are used in British English (BE). Only the *–ization* spelling is used in American English (AE). As a result, all UN organizations, ISO – *the International Organization for Standardization*, and most of the international business community use the *–ization* spelling. However, much of British industry and some European institutions use the *–isation* spelling.

–ize, –ise

- It is incorrect to consider these spellings as the respective forms of AE and BE verb endings. Although AE has always used the *–ize* form with a few exceptions, the spelling in BE was *–ize* from the 16th century (from Greek or Latin stems) and it was the influence of French that brought *–ise* into more general use in BE.
- **–ise** is always the correct spelling in both BE and AE when the ending is pronounced /-aɪs/, /ɪs/ or /-iːz/ as in *precise, practise* and *expertise*, or when pronounced /-aɪz/ and the words are adjectives or nouns. There are also some verbs derived from nouns that have *–ise* in both BE and AE. The 'parent' nouns will usually have either an s or a c in the spelling, for example *advertise/advertisement; advise/advice; compromise* (noun & verb); *devise/device; disguise* (noun & verb); *televise/television*.
- In all cases where the verb is the base form, or where the ending has been added to a shorter word, the only spellings in AE with the ending pronounced /-aɪz/ are *–ize* and *–yze* (See **–YSE**). *organize, recognize, symbolize.* In BE, *–ize* is becoming established, as some recent BE dictionaries have acknowledged by using the *–ize* spelling throughout and noting *–ise* only as an alternative. This book is based on the house style of Oxford University Press which favours the *–ize* spelling wherever it reflects the root of the word.
- Adding **–ize** to create new verbs is standard and stresses an activity or change of state: *characterize, finalize, hospitalize, prioritize,* and *randomize*. All are accepted in BE. Some of these verbs are struggling to become accepted, and *tailored solutions* are better than *customized* ones in formal BE. It is best to use such new verbs with care, as *slim down* is preferred to *slenderize* and *burgle* is preferred

to *burglarize*. Some authors have produced home-made horrors such as *trialize* that have no place in formal English, scientific reports or any serious writing.

- Those who use British English and the *-ise/-isation* spellings (as is suggested by many BE spell checkers) may inadvertently make readers feel that the research paper, brochure, report or document is written exclusively for the British market. If your work is aimed at the international market, it is worth following the trend in the latest BE dictionaries and use the *-ize/-ization* alternatives in British English, which for once agrees with American spelling. A check of the spelling of policy statements on the Internet by senior executives of the major international oil companies revealed that all use the *-ize/-ization* forms (irrespective of whether the spelling was otherwise British or American). See **-IZATION**. See **-YSE**.

Jj

JAIL^S, GAOL^S

jail /dʒeɪl/ *noun*, means a prison. This is the normal BE spelling and the only AE spelling: 'A jailbird' is a person who is regularly imprisoned.

gaol /dʒeɪl/ *noun*, is an alternative BE spelling of 'jail'.

JEW, JEWISH, JUDAISM, HEBREW

Jew /dʒuː/ *noun*, is a member of the people and cultural community that claims descent from the Biblical children of Israel. The feminine form 'Jewess' /ˈdʒuːes/ is often offensive and can be replaced by 'Jewish woman/Jewish girl'. See **ISRAELI**.

Jewish /ˈdʒuːɪʃ/ *adjective*, means associated with 'Jews' or 'Judaism'. This is the correct adjective form. Example: 'My Jewish friend' (not 'my Jew friend'). There is no language called 'Jewish'; it is called 'Hebrew'.

Judaism /ˈdʒuːdeɪɪzm/ *noun*, is the religion of the Jews. Note that this word has three syllables and the second one is pronounced 'day'.

Hebrew /ˈhiːbruː/ *noun*, is the national language of Israel. In modern times, 'Hebrew' refers only to the language, although in Biblical usage, the 'Hebrews' were the children of Israel. Nowadays it may be offensive to refer to a person as a 'Hebrew'.

JOB, POSITION, SITUATION, POST

job /dʒɒb/ *noun*, means paid employment. This is an informal word that is used to convey an everyday tone: 'The lonely job of being Prime Minister'. 'Job' is used in many combinations such as: 'job description' and 'job satisfaction'. The phrase 'on the job' means at work: 'His first month was mainly on-the-job training'.

position /pəˈzɪʃn̩/ *noun*, also means 'job' but is often used in formal contexts as it conveys greater dignity: 'The candidate discussed the position with the head of the department'. A position will typically have a professional or academic status.

situation /sɪtjʊˈeɪʃn̩/ *noun*, means 'position' but is more formal. Advertisements for jobs are usually classified in newspapers under the heading 'situations vacant'.

post /pəʊst/ noun, also means 'position' but is the most formal of this group of terms and is usually reserved for professional, military or diplomatic work: 'His first post in the UN was in New York'.

JUDICIAL, JUDICIOUS

judicial /dʒuː'dɪʃl/ adjective, is the term to use when referring to legal matters and courts of law: 'The judicial system is being reviewed'. Note that the first syllable rhymes with 'new'.

judicious /dʒuː'dɪʃəs/ adjective, means something done with good judgement: 'She made the judicious decision not to speak to the press'. This word has nothing to do with 'judicial'.

JUNCTION, JUNCTURE

junction /'dʒʌŋkʃn/ noun, means a point where two or more things join: 'A road junction is always a place to take extra care'.

juncture /'dʒʌŋktʃər/ noun, means a particular point in time and is often used by politicians or business people in the phrase 'at this juncture' to refer to a delicate stage in a crisis or during negotiations.

JUROR, JURIST

juror /'dʒʊərər/ noun, means a member of a jury: 'All the jurors had to stay in a hotel throughout the trial'.

jurist /'dʒʊərɪst/ noun, means an expert on the law, particularly someone who writes on legal subjects: 'The professor was one of this country's leading jurists'. 'Jurist' may also mean a lawyer or judge in AE.

JUST, EQUITABLE, FAIR

just /dʒʌst/ adjective, means reasonable and fair: 'The sentence of imprisonment seemed harsh, but even the defendant admitted that it was just'. See UNJUST.

equitable /'ekwɪtəbl/ adjective, also means reasonable and fair, but is more formal than 'just': 'The government's policy was to redistribute wealth through equitable changes in taxation'.

fair /feər/ adjective, refers to equality of treatment: 'He is a very fair person, who always listens to both sides of an argument'. 'Fair' also means considerable, when referring to an amount: 'There is a fair bit of work to be done tonight'. In an assessment, 'fair' means at a satisfactory standard, but not especially good. See FAIRLY. See UNFAIR.

JUVENILE, PUERILE

juvenile /'dʒuːvənaɪl/ noun & adjective, as a noun, means someone who is young: 'It is worrying that juveniles are being allowed to buy alcohol in some shops'. As an adjective, 'juvenile' refers to young people: 'Juvenile crime rates have nearly doubled'. If it is used in a disapproving sense, 'juvenile' means childish: 'She was bored with his juvenile behaviour'. In this sense, it is very similar to 'puerile'.

puerile /'pjʊəraɪl/ adjective, means silly and childish: 'The class was well known among the teachers for its puerile humour'.

Kk

KERB^S, CURB^S

kerb /kɜːb/ *noun*, is the BE spelling for the edge of a pavement (BE) or sidewalk (AE). 'Curb' is the AE spelling in this sense.

curb /kɜːb/ *verb*, means to control or restrain something: 'He tried to curb his anger when the soccer referee showed him the red card'.

KEY^S, QUAY^S

key /kiː/ *noun*, means the device inserted in a lock to open or close it. In a figurative sense it can provide a solution: 'Education is the key to fighting poverty'. The keys on a PC are the buttons on the keyboard that are pressed to enter text. The black and white wooden blocks that are pressed down to create the sounds on a piano or organ are also called 'keys'. In a different musical sense, 'key' is the word given to the names of the scales: 'The singers made a terrible sound when they all started singing in the wrong key'. In addition, a reef or low island such as off the coast of Florida is known as a 'key' (also written 'cay'). See **TYPE IN**.

quay /kiː/ *noun*, is a platform alongside water or projecting into it so that ships can moor. 'They moored at the quay so that the passengers could embark'. 'Quay' has its root in 'key' and is pronounced the same. See **BERTH**. See **HARBOUR**.

> *'Please do not lock the door, as we have lost the key.' (Hotel notice)*

KICKBACK, KICK-OFF

kickback /ˈkɪkbæk/ *noun*, in business, is an informal term that means a payment to someone who enabled a transaction to take place. Otherwise, this word refers to the recoil from a gun: 'The kickback from the rifle hurt his shoulder'.

kick-off /ˈkɪk ɒf/ *noun*, in business, means the start of something: 'The project team all attended the kick-off meeting'. It is originally a football term meaning the point at which the game begins: 'Kick-off is at 3 p.m. on Saturday'.

KNOT, KILOMETRES PER HOUR

knot /nɒt/ *noun*, is a unit of speed that means one nautical mile per hour. As 'knot' is a speed, not a distance, 'knots per hour' is incorrect and is avoided by careful writers and speakers. The 'knot' is used by ships and aircraft: 'We are now travelling at 25 knots'. The phrase 'at a good rate of knots' means travelling fast.

kilometres per hour /ˈkɪləʊmiːtəz pər ˈaʊər/ is also a measure of speed. Here, 'per hour' must be included, as a kilometre is a distance, not a speed. Both 'kph' and 'km/h' are used as abbreviations.

Ll

LAMA⁵, LLAMA⁵

lama /'lɑːmə/ *noun*, is the name given to a priest in Tibetan Buddhism. The Dalai Lama is the leader of Tibetan Buddhism.

llama /'lɑːmə/ *noun*, is a South American mammal that is a member of the camel family.

 'His Holiness the Dalai Llama of Tibet' (Nobel Peace Prize nomination from the Congress of the United States)

LANE, CARRIAGEWAY

lane /leɪn/ *noun*, means both a narrow road, usually in the countryside, and a division of a road marked by painted lines which keeps the lines of traffic separate: 'He was stopped in the bus lane'. Three-lane motorways are divided into the slow lane, fast lane and overtaking lane.

carriageway /'kærɪdʒweɪ/ *noun*, refers to one of the two sides of a large road or motorway for traffic moving in the same direction. In BE, this is used particularly together with 'dual': 'The slow lane of the dual carriageway is being resurfaced'. Note that the 'carriageway' refers to the part of a road meant for vehicles, not pedestrians.
See **DUAL CARRIAGEWAY** ⇨ **MOTORWAY**.

LARGE, GREAT, BIG, SUBSTANTIAL, CONSIDERABLE, MAJOR, ENORMOUS

large /lɑːdʒ/ *adjective*, refers to size, quantity, and extent: 'a large house', 'a large salary', 'a large geographical area'. It is found in several expressions, including 'by and large', meaning 'generally'. It is similar to 'big' and 'great', but says nothing about importance.

great /greɪt/ *adjective*, means very large. It also refers to someone or something having exceptional ability or outstanding qualities: 'Napoleon was a great general'; 'We had a great holiday'.

big /bɪg/ *adjective*, means extensive in terms of size and importance: 'Tonight was going to be a big night for him'. Note that in the sentence 'He was a big man', 'big' could mean important or tall. In such cases, it is better to choose a less ambiguous adjective. 'Big' is found in a variety of informal expressions, including 'big-headed', which means having a high opinion of oneself. In formal contexts, big is often a poor choice and it is better to use 'large', 'great', 'substantial' or 'considerable'.

substantial /sʌb'stænʃl/ *adjective*, means extensive in size, amount, form or significance: 'The house was a substantial building'.

considerable /kən'sɪdərəbl/ *adjective*, is slightly more formal than 'substantial', and means extensive in size, amount or significance: 'The company is making a considerable profit'.

major /'meɪdʒər/ *adjective*, means either extensive in size: 'A major housing development is being planned for the dock area'; or very important: 'Major scientific breakthroughs have wiped out many serious diseases'. Take care not to overuse 'major'; some alternatives are 'important', 'principal', 'serious' or 'significant'. 'Major' also has special uses in the context of music and education, where 'major key' and 'major subjects' contrast with minor ones.

enormous /ɪ'nɔːməs/ *adjective*, means huge, or immense: 'The enormous wedding cake dwarfed the tiny bride'. Note that in business or scientific contexts this is regarded as an informal term.

Latin abbreviations in English

Academic papers, theses and formal documents written in English often contain Latin abbreviations. See entries for: **c.**, **ca**, **cf.**, **e.g.**, **etc.**, **et al.**, **ibid.**, **i.e.**, **op.cit.**, **viz.** for tips about how to use some of the most common ones.

 'I was recently on a tour of Latin America, and the only regret I have is that I didn't study my Latin harder in school so I could converse with those people.' (Former US Vice-President Dan Quayle)

LAWYER, ATTORNEY, BARRISTER, SOLICITOR

lawyer /'lɔːjər/ *noun*, is the general word for someone who practises law: 'The police arrested the man, and advised him to get a good lawyer'.

attorney /əˈtɜːnɪ/ *noun*, is the general AE term for a lawyer. In Britain, the word is used in 'power of attorney' and the title Attorney General, who is the legal adviser to the government.

barrister /ˈbærɪstər/ *noun*, is the BE term for a lawyer who appears in the higher courts.

solicitor /səˈlɪsɪtər/ *noun*, in BE means a lawyer who advises clients, draws up documents, and briefs barristers. In AE, a 'solicitor' means the law officer in a town or city.
See **COUNSEL** ⇨ **COUNCIL**.

LEAD, LED

lead (1) /led/ *noun*, is a soft metal, with the chemical symbol Pb: 'All the lead pipes had to be replaced'. Here 'lead' rhymes with 'fed'.

lead (2) /liːd/ *noun*, means the front of a group of moving people or animals: 'The gold medallist soon took the lead'. Note that 'lead' in this sense rhymes with 'feed'.

lead /liːd/ *verb*, means to show the way: 'I will lead those children across the road'. 'Lead' can also mean to cause: 'Smoking may lead to lung cancer'. In another sense, 'lead' means to be in charge of something or to be at the front.

led /led/ *verb*, is the past tense and past participle of the verb 'lead': 'The athlete who had led the race for most of the way actually came last'. Never confuse the spellings of 'lead' (metal) and 'led' (past tense), although they are pronounced the same.

LEAK⁵, LEEK⁵

leak /liːk/ *noun & verb*, refers to the accidental loss of gas or liquid from a pipe or container: 'The leak from the water pipe caused considerable damage to the road'. Figuratively, 'leak' refers to the disclosure of confidential information: 'The newspaper refused to tell the Prime Minister where the leak came from'; 'The leading politician leaked a number of issues to the press'.

leek /liːk/ *noun*, is a vegetable related to the onion. It is also the Welsh national emblem.

LEARNED, LEARNT

learned /ˈlɜːnɪd/ *adjective*, means scholarly, or refers to a person with much knowledge: 'A learned author'. It can also be applied to publications: 'This is a learned journal'. Note that this word is always pronounced in two syllables. See **LEARN** ⇨ **TEACH**.

learned /lɜːnd/ *verb*, in both BE and AE is the past tense of 'to learn' meaning to acquire knowledge through study or experience: 'He learned French easily'. In AE, 'learned' is also the only past participle form. When used as a past tense or past participle, 'learned' is pronounced in one syllable.

learnt /lɜːnt/ *verb*, is an alternative form of the past participle of 'to learn' but is only used in BE: 'He has learnt French very easily'.
See **LEARN** ⇨ **TEACH**.

LEARNING DIFFICULTY, MENTAL HANDICAP

learning difficulty /ˈlɜːnɪŋ ˌdɪfɪkʌlti/ *noun*, is a mental problem, often present from birth, which prevents someone from learning things effectively. This term, which is often used in the plural to cover a range of specific problems, has replaced the discriminatory 'mental handicap'. See **BACKWARD**. See **INSANE** ⇨ **MAD**.

mental handicap /ˈmentəl ˈhændɪkæp/ *noun*, is a term formerly used in Britain for someone with learning difficulties. It is now considered discriminatory, as it focuses on the cause, not the effect. The phrases 'mentally handicapped', 'mentally retarded' and 'mentally defective' should be avoided. See **DISABILITY** ⇨ **INVALID**.

LEFT, LEFT-HAND, LEFT-HANDED

left /left/ *noun, adjective, adverb & verb*, all refer to the side of a person or thing which is facing west when that object or person is looking north: 'Turn left, and you will see the bank on the left'. In a political context, 'left' also means connected with socialist groups or ideas: 'He used to be conservative but has now moved to the left'. 'Left' is also the past tense and past participle of the verb to leave: 'She had a row with her parents and left home for good'.

left-hand /ˈleft hænd/ *adjective*, only means on or towards the 'left'. Note that 'left-hand' as an adjective is hyphenated: 'This car has a left-hand drive'. Left-hand can only come before a noun.

left-handed /left ˈhændɪd/ *adjective*, refers to people who use their 'left' hand more naturally than their right: 'A left-handed boxer is often called a southpaw'.

LEFT BANK, RIGHT BANK

left bank /'left 'bæŋk/ *noun*, means either the left-hand side of a river looking downstream, or refers to the artistic and cultural people and their way of life on the south of the River Seine in Paris. In the latter sense it is capitalized: 'His philosophy was typical for a Left Bank Parisian'.

right bank /'raɪt 'bæŋk/ *noun*, means only the right-hand side of a river, looking downstream.

LEGAL, LAWFUL, LEGITIMATE

legal /'liːgl/ *adjective*, means related to the law, as in 'legal formalities' and 'the British legal system'. In this sense it must precede the noun. In another sense, 'legal' means permitted by law: 'It has recently become legal for shops to stay open all night'. See **ILLEGAL**.

lawful /'lɔːfʊl/ *adjective*, also means something that is permitted by law, but its use tends to be limited to technical or literary contexts, such as the wording in a wedding ceremony: 'Do you take this man to be your lawful wedded husband?' See **UNLAWFUL ⇨ ILLEGAL**.

legitimate /lɪ'dʒɪtɪmət/ *adjective*, means correct and acceptable according to law: 'He always paid his staff in cash, which led to suspicions that his business was not legitimate'. 'Legitimate' can also mean justifiable: 'She had a legitimate reason for being angry, when the airline lost her luggage yet again'. Children born to parents legally married to each other are also termed 'legitimate'. See **ILLEGITIMATE ⇨ ILLEGAL**.

LEGISLATION, LEGISLATURE

legislation /ledʒɪs'leɪʃn/ *noun*, means laws or a collective group of laws: 'Legislation about traffic safety is being prepared by the government'. This is an uncountable noun.

legislature /'ledʒɪslətʃər/ *noun*, is the law-making body in a country, such as Parliament in Britain. This is a formal word.

LEND, LOAN, BORROW

lend /lend/ *verb*, means to give someone else an object for a period of time so that they can use it: 'She lent him the car for the night'. One of the functions of banks and other financial institutions is to lend money, which they do at a rate of interest. The person or institution that does the lending is the owner and lender.

loan /ləʊn/ *noun & verb*, as a noun, means a quantity of money that a person or organization is given temporarily: 'This bank loan is costing a fortune in interest charges'. As a verb, 'loan' is used in AE as an alternative to 'lend': 'She loaned him the car for the night'. However, in BE, the verb 'to loan' is usually limited to the lending of money. Note that 'loans' are given <u>to</u> people.

borrow /'bɒrəʊ/ *verb*, means to request or to ask for the temporary use of an object that belongs to someone else: 'Can I borrow the car tonight, Mum?' It also means to be lent money by a financial institution, which must be paid back at a specified rate of interest: 'I will need to borrow another three thousand pounds from my bank in order to complete my degree course'. The person who borrows is the 'borrower'. Note that things are borrowed <u>from</u> people.

---

letters and emails

guidelines to writing letters, faxes and emails

Irrespective of whether you send a letter by post, fax or email, these guidelines still apply.

Remember:

- **keep to either the BE or AE standards.** There are differences between British English and American English customs in letter writing (see the boxes below).

- **use a salutation (greeting) in English.** In most cases this will be *Dear Mr Jones*, or *Dear John*. Occasionally in emails just use the first name: *John,*. The exception is letters of recommendation that start: *To whom it may concern.*

- **place the heading <u>under</u> the salutation.**

- **try to round off a letter with -ing forms when you expect a response.** This stresses that you have an on-going relationship and that there is unfinished business. Some examples are: *We are looking forward to receiving your comments on this report, by the end of April. We are considering your proposals and are looking forward to discussing matters with you on 12 April.*

- **use the ending that matches the salutation.** It is easy to make mistakes here, so follow the guidelines given in the boxes below.

• **write the month in letters or use the ISO standard for all-digit dates.** Write the month in letters, such as *2 May 2004* (BE); *May 2, 2004* (AE), or use the ISO standard for all-digit dates (ccyy-mm-dd) so that 2 May 2004 becomes *2004-05-02*.

Never:

• **write a date as 02.05.04 in English.** To Europeans, this probably means 2 May 2004; but most Americans will understand it as *February 5, 2004*.

• **use a place name in front of the letter date.** Do not write 'Birmingham, 2 May 2004' in English. Just write the date.

• **use exclamation marks (!) in formal business letters.** An exclamation mark in English is used to express astonishment or surprise.

• **use short forms like 'I'm' and 'don't' in business letters.** These should only be used in informal, conversational writing and when reporting another person's exact words. Sometimes they are used in personal emails to stress closeness and informality.

• **capitalize 'you' and 'your'** in mid-sentence in English. This is not being polite, it is just wrong.

• **treat a business email differently from a business letter.** Although many people try to avoid using the formal salutation (see 'Formal letters and emails', below), its use is recommended if the name of the recipient is not known. Though emails tend to be more friendly than letters, a salutation should always be used. A typical email starts with *Dear Mary*, or sometimes *Mary*, and ends *Regards,*. A recent survey of 2000 business people in the UK found that 60% objected to the lack of salutations in emails and were irritated by the use of a casual tone. Emails have been used as evidence in court cases, and a safe rule is to avoid salutations like *Hi!* and endings like *love and kisses* in business emails from your organization. See **ADDRESSES IN LETTERS**. See **DATES**. See **EMAIL ADDRESSES**.

how to start and end letters and emails in BE:

Formal letters and emails, where you are writing to an institution or an unnamed person:

• These start with the following salutations:

Dear Sirs,	(when you write to a company, organization, university)
Dear Sir,	(to an unnamed person, who you know is male)
Dear Madam,	(to an unnamed person, who you know is female)
Dear Sir or Madam,	(the safe option to an unnamed person, such as: Personnel Manager)
Dear Editor,	(of a newspaper)

• These always end:
Yours faithfully,

Normal business letters and emails, where you know the recipient's name:

• These start:

Dear Mr Jones,	(to a named man. Never use 'Mister')
Dear Ms Jones,	(to any named woman, without referring to her marital status. This is becoming more and more usual for any woman)
Dear Mrs Jones,	(to a named woman who is married. Some women write *(Mrs)* after their names in letters so that their correspondent knows that this is the expected salutation to use in their reply)
Dear Miss Jones,	(to a named woman who is unmarried)
Dear Professor Jones,	(used for all professors, including assistant- and associate professors. Avoid using the slangy Prof. and always capitalize *Professor*)
Dear Dr Jones,	(can be used for someone holding a PhD or other doctoral degree)

• These always end:
Yours sincerely,

• Note that in British English, you do not use a stop after abbreviations like *Mr, Ms* /mɪz/, *Mrs*, and *Dr*, as is the custom in American English.

Letters and emails to colleagues, associates and friends etc.:

• These start:

Dear Jim,	(if a person signs his letter with *Jim*, use this in your reply. If you use *Dear Mr Jones*, you signal coldness and distance to Jim)
Dear Mary,	(as for *Dear Jim*)

Dear colleagues,	(useful in group mailings, but you could be more personal)

- There are many endings. The ones below range from a business-like tone to close friendship:

Yours sincerely,	(Even though you start *Dear Jim,* you show that this is a business-like letter, fax or email)
Regards,	(although frequently used in emails and faxes, this is too informal for most business letters)
Kind regards, *Best wishes,*	(used to signal friendliness)
Warm regards,	(slightly 'hotter', frequently used for friends)
Love,	(only used for close friends)

how to start and end letters and emails in AE:

Formal letters and emails, where you are writing to an institution or an unnamed person:

- These start with the following salutations:

Dear Sirs:	(when you write to a company, organization, university)
Dear Sir:	(to an unnamed person, who you know is male)
Dear Madam:	(to an unnamed person, who you know is female)
Dear Madam or Sir:	(always the safe option for an unnamed person)

- These often end:
Sincerely, / Sincerely yours,

- Note the use of the colon after the salutation in AE. Some American letters and emails of this type also omit the *Dear* in these types of salutations, and just open *Madam or Sir:* Another such salutation is *Ladies and gentlemen:* (to a company etc.) Many feel that *Truly* has become overused as an ending and should be avoided. *Respectfully* is very formal and is rarely used today

Normal business letters and emails, where you know the recipient's name:

- These start:

Dear Mr. Jones:	(to a named male, never use 'Mister' in a letter)

Dear Mrs. Jones:	(to a named female, who is married)
Dear Miss Jones:	(to a named female, who is unmarried)
Dear Ms. Jones:	(to a named female, with unknown marital status)
Dear Professor Jones:	(use for all professors: also assistant and associate professors. Write Professor in full, do not use the slangy Prof.)
Dear Dr. Jones:	(can be used for someone holding a PhD, or other doctoral degree)

- These often end:
Sincerely, / Sincerely yours,

- Note that in American English, a stop is used after abbreviations like *Mr.*, *Ms.* (pronounced /mɪz/), *Mrs.*, and *Dr.*, and a colon placed after the name (as an alternative, a comma is sometimes used). Some Americans use just *Dear M. Jones:* to avoid the gender specific greeting. *Dear M./M. Jones:* is also sometimes used for the same reasons in place of *Mr.* and *Mrs.* in letters and emails.

Letters and emails to colleagues, associates and friends:

- These start:

Dear Jim,	(if a person signs his letter with *Jim,* use this in your reply. If you use *Dear Mr Jones,* you signal coldness and distance to Jim)
Dear Mary,	(same comments as for 'Dear Jim')
Dear colleagues,	(useful in group mailings, but you could be more personal)

- The endings vary on a scale that indicates a business tone to close friendship:

Sincerely,	(Even though you start *Dear Jim,* you show that this is a business-like letter, fax or email)
Regards,	(although frequently used in emails and faxes, this is too informal for most business letters)
Kind regards, *Best wishes,*	(used to signal friendliness)

Warm regards, (getting slightly 'hotter', frequently used for friends)

Love, (only used for close friends)

- Note that a comma is very frequent after such salutations and endings.

LIBEL, SLANDER

libel /'laɪbḷ/ *noun*, is a false statement which damages a person's reputation. 'Libel' can be written, broadcast, or published. The related adjective is 'libellous'.

slander /'slɑːndər/ *noun*, is a false spoken statement that damages a person's reputation, or even a gesture that is considered offensive. The related adjective is 'slanderous'.

LICENCE^S, LICENSE^S

licence /'laɪsṇs/ *noun*, means either a process to get official approval; or the giving of formal permission, as in: 'This product will be manufactured under licence'. In this sense, it is rare for the indefinite article to be used. However, when it refers to a specific 'licence' such as a 'driving licence', an indefinite article can be used. This spelling is used only in BE.

license /'laɪsṇs/ *verb & noun*, is the correct spelling of the verb form in both BE and AE: 'We are licensed to use this software'. 'License' is the correct spelling of the noun form in AE. The process of obtaining a 'licence' is called 'licensing'. Note that cars in the US have 'license plates'. These are called 'number plates' in the UK.

LIE (1), LIE (2), LAY, LAID

lie (1) /laɪ/ *verb*, means to be in a horizontal position: 'She fell asleep while lying on the grass'. In standard English it is incorrect to say that 'she is laying on the grass'. Note that 'lie' does not take an object and is followed by a preposition before a noun. The past tense of 'lie' is 'lay', and the past participle is 'lain'.

lie (2) /laɪ/ *verb*, means to write or say something that is untrue: 'She always lies about her age'. This verb, which has a different origin from both 'lay' and 'lie (1)', has the past tense and past participle form 'lied'.

lay /leɪ/ *verb*, means to put someone or something down or in place: 'Please lay the table for dinner'. It is always followed immediately by a noun or pronoun. An animal or insect is said to 'lay' eggs, when eggs are produced from its body and deposited. Note that 'lay' is also the past tense of the verb 'lie' (1).

laid /leɪd/ is the past tense and past participle of the verb 'lay': 'He laid the carpet in the bedroom'. Note that the phrase 'get laid' is a slang expression meaning have sex that originated in AE.

American readers of a geological textbook from Britain were amused at the title: 'How Strata Get Laid'.

LIFT, ELEVATOR

lift /lɪft/ *noun*, in BE means a device for transporting people up and down: 'The lift was stuck on the 12th floor'. In another context, skiers are transported by ski lifts.

elevator /'elɪveɪtər/ *noun*, is the AE term for the BE 'lift', used for transporting people inside a building. In BE, an elevator is a device for moving freight or goods: 'The grain elevator was very noisy'.

LIGHT, ILLUMINATE

light /laɪt/ *noun & verb*, as a noun, means the energy from the sun or another source that makes it possible to see things: 'It was getting light when we got back home from the party'. In this use, 'light' is an uncountable noun. In another sense, 'light' means an object such as a lamp: 'The car flashed its lights at us'. Here, 'light' is a countable noun. As a verb, 'light' means either to start to burn: 'She lit the candles because it was getting dark'; or make something brighter: 'The fireworks lit up the night sky'. In slang, 'to be lit up' means to be drunk.

illuminate /ɪ'ljuːmɪneɪt/ *verb*, means either to light something up: 'Only enter the lift when it is illuminated'; or, in formal use, to make a matter easier to understand: 'His clarity and presentation made this a most illuminating discussion'.

'Only enter the lift when lit up.'
(Lift notice)

LIGHTNING, LIGHTENING

lightning /'laɪtnɪŋ/ *noun*, means a high-intensity, natural discharge of electricity: 'Judging by the colour of the sky, we are in for thunder and lightning'. This word only has two syllables.

lightening /'laɪtənɪŋ/ *verb*, means either making lighter in weight: 'He looked forward to lightening his backpack'; or becoming less dark: 'The village became visible as the mist rose when the sky started lightening'. This word is the present participle of the verb 'lighten'. Note that 'lightening' has three syllables.

LIMIT, DELIMIT

limit /'lɪmɪt/ *verb*, means to restrict the movement of things, or the amount of something: 'Many people try to limit the number of cigarettes they smoke before finally giving up the habit'.

delimit /di'lɪmɪt/ *verb*, means to determine or fix boundaries or limits: 'An agreement was signed to delimit the economic zones on and around Antarctica'.

link words

a moderate use of link words improves the readability of documents

- A simple check of the readability of something you have written in English is counting how many sentences start with 'The'. '*The paper* presents...'. '*The* challenge was...'. '*The* work involved ...'. One way to liven up such 'machine-gun English' is to use link words or transitions that give signposts to your reader. However, do not throw the baby out with the bathwater. A text where every sentence starts with a link word is just as difficult to follow as a road where the signposting is overdone. Although the typical position of a link word in English is at the beginning of a sentence, this is not compulsory. The advantage of the preliminary link word is that the reader is not slowed down by a comma, link word and a second comma in mid sentence. Compare: '*Research in reducing emissions, as a rule, has provided ...*' with: '*As a rule, research in reducing emissions has provided ...*'. Here are some examples of link words and where to use them:

- When **comparing** things, useful link words include:
  By contrast, Conversely, However, In contrast, In spite of, Instead, Likewise, Nevertheless, Otherwise, On the contrary, On the one hand, On the other hand,

- When **generalizing**, use:
  As a rule, As usual, For the most part, Generally, In general, Ordinarily, Usually

- When **describing a sequence**, useful link words for a linear progression are:
  First, ... Second, ... Third, ... Next, ... Then, ... Finally, ...
  Note that most English style guides recommend: *First, ... Second, ... Third, ...* Rather than: *Firstly, ... Secondly, ... Thirdly, ...* When *First, ...* is used as a link word, your reader will expect *Second, ... Third, ...* and *Next, ...*

- Sequences can be signposted by link words that point backwards, like:
Having completed step one, the next step is …
After stage one, …   *Previously, …*
- Link words to describe simultaneous actions, include:
During this stage …   *While …*
At the same time …   *Simultaneously …*
- Finally, there are link words to end a sequence. Make sure that these are used at the very end:
Finally, …   *In the last stage, …*
The report finishes with, …   *In conclusion, …*

LIQUID, LIQUIDATE, LIQUIDIZE

liquid /'lɪkwɪd/ *noun & adjective*, as a noun, means a substance with a consistency like oil or water. It is also a state, so that temperature or pressure can convert a solid or gas into a liquid. As an adjective, in a financial sense, 'liquid' also means being easy to convert into cash: 'Our liquid assets are in the bank'.

liquidate /'lɪkwɪdeɪt/ *verb*, as a business term usually means to sell assets. 'Liquidate' also means to kill by using violence: 'In Hollywood movies, organized crime often liquidates the competition'. See **EXTERMINATE ⇨ MASSACRE**.

liquidize /'lɪkwɪdaɪz/ *verb*, means to make liquid: 'They bought a food processor to liquidize fruit and vegetables'. The machine that liquidizes substances is often called a 'liquidizer' or 'blender'.

LIQUOR, LIQUEUR, ALCOHOL

liquor /'lɪkər/ *noun*, means distilled spirits in a non-technical sense. Occasionally, 'liquor' may refer to any alcoholic drink. 'Liquor' is commonly used in AE to mean drinks such as vodka and whisky. The BE term for this is 'spirits'. 'Liquor' may also refer to the non-alcoholic liquid in which food is cooked.

liqueur /lɪ'kjʊər/ (BE) /lɪ'kɜːr/ (AE) *noun*, is a strong, sweet alcoholic drink, drunk in small quantities at the end of a meal: 'The restaurant has a good range of liqueurs'. Note that in BE the second syllable is pronounced 'cure'.

alcohol /'ælkəhɒl/ *noun*, means a liquid which is the intoxicating element in wine, spirits and beers. 'Low alcohol' drinks include wines and beers from which most of the alcohol has been removed. 'Non-alcoholic' drinks include soft drinks, which are not made with alcohol.

lists

- Use a colon to introduce a list. If the items in a list are in a sequence or hierarchy, use numbers after the colon:
1. time 2. money 3. skilled staff
or letters:
a) time b) money c) skilled staff
- Do not use commas, semi-colons, or stops after keywords in a list or at the end of the list. If the items in a list are separate and parallel, but in no significant order or hierarchy, use bullets, dashes, or some other symbol after the colon.
- Note that many modern style guides state that there are only stops at the end of the items in a list if they are full sentences. See **COLON**. See **FULL STOP**. See **LINK WORDS**.

LITERAL, LITERALLY

literal /'lɪtərəl/ *adjective*, means the usual, basic meaning of words, or refers to a translation which represents the exact words of the original text: 'This is a very literal translation which does not reflect the beauty of the original poem'.

literally /'lɪtərəli/ *adverb*, means in a literal sense, or exactly: 'I asked him to work on the project night and day, but unfortunately he took it literally'. It is considered substandard by some to use 'literally' in formal English as an intensifier. Use: 'Our staff are working themselves to death', not '… literally working themselves to death'.

LITTLE, SMALL

little /'lɪtḷ/ *adjective*, means not large in size, quantity or degree: 'I am feeling a little tired after the journey'. Note that when 'little' is used without an article it gives a hostile or unfavourable impression. Thus, the sentence: 'They have little money' means not enough money, whereas 'They have a little money' means an acceptable minimum. 'Little' is sometimes used to express dislike: 'Look at that silly little man', or even affection: 'I've got my own little place'.

small /smɔːl/ *adjective*, means not large in size, quantity or degree: 'Feeling tired is a small price to pay for having had such a good holiday'. 'Small' is used in comparatives and superlatives. In technical or official contexts, 'small' is a better choice than 'little': 'A small rise in temperature was registered'.

LIVE TOGETHER, COHABIT

live together /'lɪv təgeðər/ *verb*, means to share the same room, flat or house and it usually implies that there is a sexual relationship between the people concerned. If some people 'share a flat' this focuses on the flat and says nothing about the relationship between the people. A related adjective is 'live-in', which refers to a domestic helper who lives in their employer's home: 'Advert: Live-in housekeeper required'.

cohabit /kəʊ'hæbɪt/ *verb*, means to live together and have a sexual relationship without being married to each other. 'Cohabit' is more formal than 'live together'.

LIVING ROOM, LOUNGE

living room /'lɪvɪŋ ruːm/ is the room in a house which is used for relaxation: 'The family went into the living room to watch TV'. This is an alternative term to 'sitting room', which is only used in BE.

lounge /laʊndʒ/ *noun*, means a room for sitting in a public place: 'The airport lounge was crowded because of the delays'. Otherwise it means a living room in BE.

LOAF, BREAD

loaf /ləʊf/ *noun*, is a quantity of bread, and is the term to use for ordering bread: 'A brown loaf, please'. The plural of 'loaf' is 'loaves' /ləʊvz/. In rhyming slang, 'loaf' means 'head' and is short for 'loaf of bread'. See **–F, –FE ENDINGS IN NOUNS AND PLURALS**.

bread /bred/ *noun*, is the substance that rolls and loaves are made of. 'Bread' is an uncountable noun and cannot have 'a' in front. It always takes a singular verb: 'The bread on the table was freshly baked'. In slang, 'bread' means money.

 'Thieves stole 600 loaves of bread from an empty delivery van yesterday.' (English newspaper)

LOATH, LOATHE

loath /ləʊθ/ *adjective*, means reluctant and unwilling: 'Having built the house themselves, they were loath to leave their home'. This is a formal word.

loathe /ləʊð/ *verb*, means to dislike someone or something greatly: 'They loathed opera, despite having made an effort to understand it'.

LOCAL, LOCALITY, LOCALE, LOCATION

local /'ləʊkl/ *noun & adjective*, as a noun, means an inhabitant of an area: 'The locals were all at the meeting'. As an adjective, this describes someone or something which belongs to, or inhabits, an area: 'The local wildlife can be quite active at night'. In BE, 'the local' means a neighbourhood pub. 'The local' in AE means a branch of a union. It is often unnecessary to combine 'local' with terms like 'inhabitant' or 'resident'. See **INHABITANT**.

locality /ləʊ'kælɪti/ *noun*, means the area around the speaker, usually referred to as 'the locality': 'Is there a good restaurant in the locality?' It is also a term for any local area, or describes the position of something within that area: 'They lived in a good locality where house prices had doubled in the last five years'.

locale /ləʊ'kɑːl/ *noun*, is a place usually connected with specific events. It can also be a venue, the place where something happens: 'The producer of the film had problems deciding his locale'. Note that the stress is on the second syllable.

location /ləʊ'keɪʃn/ *noun*, is a particular position or site: 'The house was in a very exposed location'. The phrase 'on location' refers to a film made outside the studio.

LOOSE, LOOSEN, LOSE

loose /luːs/ *verb & adjective*, as a verb, is very formal when used by itself, and means to detach, set free or release: 'Can you loose those ropes and bring them here?' More common alternatives are phrases such as 'set loose', 'cut loose', or 'loosen'. As an adjective, 'loose' means not firmly in place: 'After the accident he only suffered a loose tooth'.

loosen /'luːsn/ *verb*, means make something less tight: 'His new shoes were killing him until he loosened the laces'.

lose /luːz/ *verb*, means either to be deprived of something, as in: 'He is losing his hair', or being unable to find something: 'He is always losing his car keys'. Note that 'lose' rhymes with 'news'.

'A poorly written CV can loose you that job. Ring the careers office for help and advice.'
(Notice on college noticeboard)

Mm

LOUD, ALOUD

loud /laʊd/ *adjective & adverb*, means making a lot of noise: 'We could hear extremely loud laughter and music coming from the house next door'. It can also be used for clashing or extreme colours: 'The colour scheme was too loud for my taste'. As an adverb, this is typically connected with verbs such as scream, shout, or cry: 'The pain became so bad that he cried out loud'.

aloud /əˈlaʊd/ *adverb*, means reading or saying something so that others can hear: 'The poet started to read aloud'; 'Politicians who think aloud may get themselves into trouble'.

LUXURIANT, LUXURIOUS

luxuriant /lʌgˈʒʊəriənt/ *adjective*, means rich and profuse in growth: 'The luxuriant green vegetation is typical of much of the island'.

luxurious /lʌgˈʒʊəriəs/ *adjective*, means characterized by luxury, and extravagance: 'The actors wore luxurious costumes which had to be looked after very carefully'.

LYRIC, LYRICS, LYRICAL

lyric /ˈlɪrɪk/ *adjective*, refers to a type of poetry with strong personal feelings. 'Lyric' also means the words of a song, but is less common in this sense than 'lyrics'.

lyrics /ˈlɪrɪks/ *plural noun*, is used to refer to the words of a song, particularly of popular songs: 'She wrote some very catchy lyrics'. See **-ICS**.

lyrical /ˈlɪrɪkl̩/ *adjective*, means enthusiastic about something. This usually has nothing to do with poetry: 'She became lyrical about the magnificent scenery'. It is often used in the expression 'to wax lyrical'.

MAD, INSANE

mad /mæd/ *adjective*, means foolish or ill-advised: 'She was mad to leave her car unlocked'. 'Mad' can also mean angry: 'He was mad at me because I kept him waiting for an hour', and to have a passionate interest in something: 'She is football mad'. As 'mad' is no longer used to mean 'insane' in psychiatry, it is always an informal word.

insane /ɪnˈseɪn/ *adjective*, means having a serious mental illness: 'He was certified as clinically insane'. 'Insane' can also be used to mean irrational: 'He had an insane desire to laugh during the funeral'. It comes close to 'mad' in the informal sense of being angry: 'That noise is driving me insane'.
See **LEARNING DIFFICULTY**.

MADAM, MA'AM, LADIES

Madam /ˈmædəm/ *noun*, is a polite way of addressing a woman at the start of a formal letter (Dear Madam) and is thus the female equivalent of 'Dear Sir'. In spoken English, it is used before a title to address a female: 'Madam President', 'Madam Mayor'. Otherwise it is only used to refer respectfully to a female customer in shops or restaurants: 'Would Madam like a seat by the window?'

Ma'am /mæm, mɑːm/ *noun*, in spoken AE, is used as a polite way to address any woman: 'Pleased to meet you, ma'am'. This word is archaic in BE except when addressing female royalty, and in this context, the pronunciation which rhymes with 'jam' is appropriate.

ladies /ˈleɪdɪz/ *noun*, is the normal plural of madam in English, as in 'Ladies and gentlemen'.

MAIL, POST

mail /meɪl/ *noun & verb*, means letters and packages sent through the postal service, or electronically. As 'mail' refers to two means of transferring correspondence, the slang expression 'snail mail' is often used to indicate that the postal service is being used. Note that both 'mail' and 'electronic mail' are uncountable and may only be used in the singular, but the abbreviated form 'email' can be plural: 'All these emails have to be answered today'. See **EMAIL**.

post /pəʊst/ *noun & verb*, as a noun, is a BE term to refer to a postal service. 'Post' is uncountable: 'Was there any post this morning?'. As a verb in BE, the phrases 'post a letter' or 'mail a letter' are both acceptable, but only 'mail' is used in AE. This difference is found in other related terms, such as 'postbox' (BE) / 'mailbox' (AE) and 'postal worker' (BE) / 'mail carrier' (AE).

MAJORITY, PLURALITY

majority /mə'dʒɒrɪti/ *noun*, means the number of votes by which a political party wins an election. In American politics, a 'majority' means more than half the total number of votes cast: 'The majority of Senators supported the ayes'. In BE this is called an 'absolute majority' or 'overall majority'. In British use, a candidate can have a majority without receiving more than half of the votes. 'Majority of' takes a plural verb: 'The majority of votes have been counted'. But 'majority' without 'of' may take either a singular or plural verb.

plurality /plʊ'rælɪti/ *noun*, in American politics means the largest number of votes cast, but less than half the total number: 'With 48% of the votes cast, the Democrat candidate won a plurality'. This term is equivalent to the BE use of 'majority'.

MAKE, DO

make /meɪk/ *verb*, means to create or build by combining parts of things: 'I am going to make some new clothes'. When referring to domestic tasks, it is used in the expressions 'make a meal' and 'make the beds'. 'Make' is used in many fixed expressions, such as 'make a decision' and 'make a suggestion'.

do /duː/ *verb*, is used for talking generally about an action: 'What are you going to do?' (Compare this with 'What are you going to make?', which asks about a specific creative activity.) Note that 'do' is used to talk about most domestic tasks, such as 'do the dishes'. It is often used informally as a substitute for other verbs, such as 'do a meal'. 'Do' is also found in a wide number of fixed phrases, as in: 'do some work'.

MAKE UP⁵, MAKE-UP⁵

make up /meɪk 'ʌp/ *verb*, means either to compose or constitute: 'Women make up only 10 per cent of top management', or to complete a group: 'He asked two junior players to make up the soccer team'. 'Make up' can also mean making friends again: 'After the row, he kissed her and asked to make up'. In another sense it can mean compensate for something: 'I will make up the lost time tomorrow'.

make-up /meɪk ʌp/ *noun*, refers to cosmetics such as lipstick: 'She had no time for make-up'. It also means the parts or composition of something: 'The make-up of the samples used in the experiment'. This is an uncountable noun.

MALE, MASCULINE, MACHO

male /meɪl/ *adjective*, refers to the biological sex of plants, animals or people: 'A male elephant'. When a contrast with female is implied, 'male' is used: 'The male domination of the legal system'.
See **FEMALE**. See **SEXIST LANGUAGE**.

masculine /'mæskjʊlɪn/ *adjective*, refers to characteristics that are generally accepted as being typical of men as opposed to women: 'His deep masculine voice made everyone stop talking'. 'Masculine' is not used to refer to the sex of animals or as a means of contrasting the male and female sexes in humans. In grammar, however, 'masculine' is one of the gender classifications for many languages: 'Learning the masculine genders in French is often a problem for English schoolchildren'.
See **FEMININE** ⊳ **FEMALE**.

macho /'mætʃəʊ/ *adjective*, refers to a male who takes pride in his masculinity in an aggressive manner: 'His macho appearance and tattoos put a lot of women off him'. Note that 'macho' is usually a disapproving term.

MANAGER, MANAGEMENT, SUPERVISOR

manager /'mænɪdʒər/ *noun*, means a person who is in charge of running a business. A manager can run a shop, an entire organization or just part of an organization. A typical small and medium-sized manufacturing company might have a 'production manager', a 'financial manager' and a 'personnel manager', all reporting to the managing director. In a large organization, the manager is typically in a middle management position. Thus a 'bank manager' runs one branch of a bank, and a 'hotel manager' runs one hotel, but a bank director is at the corporate level and the hotel director helps to run the chain of hotels. In sports such as soccer, the manager is the person who is in charge of the training, team selection and organization: 'That Italian team had three managers least season', meaning three in succession.

management /'mænɪdʒmənt/ *noun*, means the people who run and control a business. Large organizations distinguish between 'senior management' - those who make decisions that influence the whole organization; 'middle management' - those who are responsible for a section or department of the organization; and 'junior management' - those who have very limited responsibility or who are trainees in management. Only the members of the senior management are likely to have the individual titles of director.

supervisor /'sjuːpəvaɪzər/ *noun*, in the business world, means a person who is in charge of an operation or part of a work process at the operational level: 'Her main responsibility as supervisor was to ensure that the trucks were loaded correctly'. Students conducting postgraduate research at university have a supervisor, a member of the academic staff who provides support and guidance on their research project. At undergraduate level, students in the UK often have a personal tutor, who can offer more general support.

MANAGING DIRECTOR, CEO, PRESIDENT

managing director /'mænɪdʒɪŋ daɪ'rektər/ *noun*, means the person who is in charge of the day-to-day management of a business: 'The managing director seemed to be always away on business trips'. In some companies, the managing director is a member of the board. On business cards or conference programmes in English, it is normal to place titles such as managing director after a person's name and to capitalize them: 'John Jones, Managing Director'. In running text they are not usually capitalized and may be placed before the name: 'Our managing director, John H. Jones'. The abbreviation for 'managing director' is MD. This is a BE term.

CEO /'siː iː 'əʊ/ *noun*, is an abbreviation for Chief Executive Officer, and means the person with the highest rank in the day-to-day management of a business. In some companies, the 'CEO' is a member of the board. If the 'CEO' position is held by someone who is both a board member and in charge of daily management, the title 'Managing Director and CEO' is often used (In AE, this would be titled 'President and CEO').

president /'prezɪdənt/ *noun*, in the context of the words in this group, is the AE equivalent of the BE term 'managing director'. In a wider context, it is used in AE to refer to the person in charge of any commercial organization: 'The president of that airline is going to have to resign soon'. On business cards or conference programmes in English, it is normal to place such titles after a person's name and to capitalize them. In running text they are not usually capitalized: 'Our corporate president John H. Jones'. See **EXECUTIVE**.

MANIA, PHOBIA

mania /'meɪnɪə/ *noun*, is extreme enthusiasm or craze: 'Football mania stopped the entire country during the World Cup'.

phobia /'fəʊbɪə/ *noun*, is an extreme, unreasonable fear or dislike of something: 'Many people have a phobia about spiders'.

MANSLAUGHTER, MURDER, HOMICIDE

manslaughter /'mænslɔːtər/ *noun*, is the term used for a killing which is neither planned nor done with evil intent: 'Since he had killed the man in self-defence, he was charged with manslaughter rather than murder'.

murder /'mɜːdər/ *noun & verb*, is the term used for an unlawful, planned, killing: 'The shooting had been planned meticulously, and therefore was a clear case of murder'. 'Murder' is sometimes used figuratively to describe a difficult or unpleasant situation: 'The traffic in London is sheer murder'.

homicide /'hɒmɪsaɪd/ *noun*, is another term for 'murder'. In AE, 'Homicide' is the name of the police department that deals with such crimes.

MAP, CHART

map /mæp/ *noun*, is a representation in two or more dimensions of a geographical area, showing the relative positions of various features, such as towns, rivers, mountains. The phrase to 'put someone/something on the map' means to make them or it famous: 'The film really put my home town on the map'.

chart /tʃɑːt/ *noun*, means either a map, particularly of the sea, or stars: 'We do not have a chart for these waters', or a diagram showing information, lists of figures or a developing situation: 'A chart showing sales figures for the past year hung on the wall'.

MARITAL, MARTIAL

marital /'mærɪtl/ *adjective*, refers to marriage, or relations between husband and wife: 'Marital difficulties affect many couples at some point during their lives'.

martial /'mɑːʃl/ *adjective*, refers to war: 'Many people go to martial arts classes in order to learn self-defence'.

MARK, GRADE (EDUCATION)

mark /mɑːk/ *noun*, is a BE term for assessment in school or university on a numerical or letter scale: 'How many marks out of a hundred does the first section of this test carry?'

grade /ɡreɪd/ *noun*, means assessment, often according to an A, B, C, D scale, or other non-numerical types: 'More students obtained grade 'A' this year than ever before'. 'Grade' is the normal AE equivalent of BE 'mark'. The elementary level of education in AE is referred to as grade school. In AE, 'grade' also means the class level or form: 'My daughter is in the fifth grade'. The term 'grading system' is used in BE and AE for an assessment system that gives marks or grades.

MARKˢ, MARQUEˢ

mark /mɑːk/ *noun*, is used with a number to specify a particular model in a series of cars: 'They bought a Mark I Jaguar'.

marque /mɑːk/ *noun*, means a make of car, not a specific model: 'His sports car was an unusual and rather expensive marque'.

MASSACRE, DECIMATE, EXTERMINATE

massacre /'mæsəkər/ *noun*, means the killing of many people, particularly if cruelty is involved: 'It was clear from the terrible scene that there had been a massacre on a large scale'. Figuratively it is used when one sports team beats its opponent by a very large margin: 'Playing against Brazil would be a massacre for our team'. Note that massacre is spelt '-re' in both BE and AE.

decimate /'desɪmeɪt/ *verb*, means to kill a large proportion of a group: 'The population was decimated in the war'. Originally, 'decimate' meant killing one in ten. This use is generally classified as historical and most people now use 'decimate' in the sense of killing a large number.

exterminate /ɪks'tɜːmɪneɪt/ *verb*, means to kill everyone in a group by a planned process, or make a group of animals extinct: 'The seals off this coast were almost exterminated'.

MASTERLY, MASTERFUL

masterly /'mɑːstəli/ *adjective*, means performed very skilfully: 'He demonstrated masterly handling of a difficult horse'. Never use 'masterly' to describe someone who is domineering.

masterful /'mɑːstəfʊl/ *adjective*, has two meanings. First, to refer to something that is performed very skilfully: 'A masterful work of art'. Second, it means powerful and authoritative: 'A masterful ruler who kept the peace'.

master's degree, MA, MSc

A master's degree is a second or graduate degree from a university or equivalent institution. The most normal types in universities in or based on the UK/US higher education systems are *Master of Arts* (abbreviated *MA* in BE and *M.A.* in AE) and *Master of Science* (abbreviated *MSc* in BE and *M.Sc.* in AE). Note that in Scotland the first arts degree may be a master's: *MA*. On the English language version of a CV or business card, it is always best to write degrees in their original language. If necessary, this can then be followed by an approximate translation, in brackets, such as (*MA History*) or (*MSc Biology*).

MATHEMATICS, MATHS, MATH

mathematics /mæθ'mætɪks/ *noun*, is an academic subject dealing with number, quantity and space. Like other subjects ending with '-ics', mathematics takes a singular verb when it means the discipline: 'Mathematics is her best subject.' When it means operations involved in a problem, 'mathematics' is often treated as a plural: 'The mathematics involved in the calculation of voters' behaviour are very complex'. See **–ICS**.

maths /mæθs/ is the common BE abbreviation of 'mathematics'. It takes either a singular or a plural verb, in the same way as 'mathematics'.

math /mæθ/ is the AE abbreviation of
'mathematics': 'Math is his strong subject'. In
AE this is treated as an uncountable noun, and
always takes a singular verb.

MAXIMUM, MINIMUM, MAXIMAL, MINIMAL

maximum /ˈmæksɪməm/ adjective & noun, as
an adjective, means as great, as high or as
intense as possible: 'We sailed at maximum
speed'. Note that a 'maximum decrease'
reduces something to the smallest amount
possible, the 'minimum'. 'Maximum' as an
adjective is only used before a noun and is
often contrasted with 'minimum'. In its noun
form, the plural is 'maxima'.

minimum /ˈmɪnɪməm/ adjective & noun, as an
adjective, means as small as possible. Note that
a 'minimum decrease' means almost no change:
'Increasing sales taxes produced a minimum
decrease in demand'. 'Minimum' as an adjective
usually comes before a noun. In its noun form,
the plural is 'minima'.

maximal /ˈmæksɪməl/ adjective, means the
greatest possible: 'The engine was at maximal
revs'. 'Maximal' usually comes before a noun.
This word is often contrasted with 'minimal'.

minimal /ˈmɪnɪməl/ adjective, has a very similar
meaning to minimum. It also means negligible:
'The effect of the treatment was minimal'. Note
that minimal can be placed after the verb.

MEANS (SINGULAR AND PLURAL)

means /miːnz/ noun, is another word for
method or methods: 'He was determined to
win by fair means or foul'. It may be used as a
singular or plural: 'This means of travelling' or
'these means of travelling'. 'Means' is used in
numerous phrases, such as 'by all means' (of
course) and 'by means of' (with the help of).

means /miːnz/ plural noun, refers to income or
wealth: 'This luxury car is unfortunately
beyond my means'. If someone has insufficient
money this can be referred to as having
'limited means'.

MEANTIME, MEANWHILE

meantime /ˈmiːntaɪm/ noun & adverb, is used
in the phrase 'in the meantime', to describe the
interval between one event and another: 'It is
going to be an hour before we can start the
walk. In the meantime, we can relax'. As an
adverb, 'meantime' is used in the same way as
'meanwhile'. This is always written as one word.

meanwhile /miːnˈhwaɪl/ adverb, also refers to
the interval between one event and another. In
this sense, it means the same as 'in the
meantime'. 'Meanwhile' can also be used to
contrast two elements of a situation. In this
case, it is similar in meaning to 'whereas' or 'on
the other hand': 'Jogging can cause damage to
joints and muscles. Swimming, meanwhile, is an
excellent form of exercise, as the water supports
the body'. This is always written as one word.

measurements

- When referring to metric units like *kilo, metre*
and *tonne*, use decimals: *2.2 kg* (read as *two
point two kilos*). If the decimal is less than one,
e.g. *0.72*, this is read as *nought/oh/zero point
seven two*. Note that all digits following the
decimal point are read separately: never use a
number higher than 9.
- The imperial system of measurements is
common in some parts of the English-speaking
world and here it is normal to use fractions: *one
and a half miles, two and three-quarter gallons.*
Simple fractions like $^1/_3$, $^3/_4$ are read as *one
third* and *three quarters* (BE) or *three fourths*
(AE). Complex fractions such as $^{251}/_{625}$ use the
term *over: two hundred and fifty one over six
hundred and twenty five.*
- *Tall* can often be omitted when giving
measurements of height: *She is five feet four.*
When *the pool is six feet* or *the river is twenty
feet*, words like *deep, wide*, or *across* can be
added if there is a possibility of a
misunderstanding. When giving a series of
measurements, such as the dimensions of a
piece of furniture, these are written: *2 x 3 x 4
metres*, but read as *2 by 3 by 4 metres.*
- Units of measurement are hyphenated when
they are placed before the noun they refer to: *A
5000-kilometre journey, A ten-pound sack of
rice.* Here the hyphenated unit of measurement
is an adjective (thus there is no plural *s*). There
is no hyphenation if the noun comes first: *A
journey of 5000 kilometres.* Here the unit of
measurement is a noun and may be singular or
plural. See **FOOT**. See **HYPHENATION**. See **MILE**.
See **NUMBERS**. See **TONNE**.

MECHANICAL, AUTOMATIC, AUTOMATED

mechanical /mɪˈkænɪkl̩/ adjective, means
connected with machines, or capable of being
operated by engine power: 'I remember that I
was thrilled to receive a mechanical train set
for my tenth birthday'.

automatic /ɔ:təʊ'mætɪk/ *adjective*, refers to a device or unit that works by itself without human control: 'The automatic washing machine has saved the average household hundreds of hours a year'.

automated /'ɔ:təʊmeɪtɪd/ *adjective*, means converted to work automatically: 'This factory has an automated production line with robots and mechanical sorters'.

MEDIA, MEDIUM

media /'mi:dɪə/ *noun*, means mass communications. As with data and agenda, 'media' is often treated as a collective noun and takes a singular verb: 'The media is following drug issues again'. Careful writers still prefer a plural verb here. A useful distinction is to use the plural verb for different types of 'media': 'Traditionally, TV, radio and the press are the media', and a singular verb if the 'media' is treated as one group. Although it is now acceptable to write 'the media is', never write 'a media'. Also, as 'media' is the plural of 'medium', never write 'medias'.

medium /'mi:dɪəm/ *noun*, is the singular of 'media': 'Television, like the newspapers, is a medium of mass communication'. 'Medium' has two plural forms: 'media' and 'mediums'. A medium is a person who claims to communicate with the dead, by acting as an intermediary between the dead and the living. 'Medium' can also refer to the size of clothes: 'He looked at the T-shirts in the sale, but they were all medium.'

MEDIEVAL, MIDDLE AGE, MIDDLE AGES

medieval /medi'i:vl/ *adjective*, means of or related to the Middle Ages: 'The town has an impressive medieval castle'. In another sense, 'medieval' means primitive and old-fashioned usually in a negative way: 'He had a medieval attitude to women'. An alternative spelling is 'mediaeval'.

middle age /'mɪdl 'eɪdʒ/ *noun*, is the period of life from about 45 to 60, although this age range is rather subjective. Note that the adjective form 'middle-aged' is written with a hyphen: 'His middle-aged baldness didn't bother him'.

Middle Ages /mɪdl 'eɪdʒɪz/ *noun*, refers to a period of history. Note that this is capitalized and used in the plural. The Middle Ages is often narrowly defined as the period from about 1000 to 1450: 'It is thought that in Britain, surnames were used for the first time during the Middle Ages'.

'The Cathedral is one of our oldest middle-aged buildings.' (Tourist guide)

MEETING, RENDEZVOUS, APPOINTMENT

meeting /'mi:tɪŋ/ *noun*, is an arranged gathering, which can be on a personal level or an arrangement such as an athletics event. It stresses the activity and the place, not the time: 'He recalled that this was the third board meeting and the issue had still not been settled'.

rendezvous /'rɒndɪvu:/ *noun*, means a meeting place and time, but stresses the place where a meeting will be. The word is typically used for a meeting between two people: 'They had a rendezvous at the Red Lion'. It is also used in a military sense for a meeting place and time for troops, vehicles etc. The plural form is 'rendezvous' /'rɒndɪvu:z/. The derived verb form 'rendezvousing' is pronounced /'rɒndɪvu:ɪŋ/.

appointment /ə'pɔɪntmənt/ *noun*, means a meeting of a more personal nature: 'I have an 11.15 appointment with my bank manager'.

METHOD, METHODOLOGY, METHODIST

method /'meθəd/ *noun*, is a general word for a systematic procedure or particular way of achieving something: 'A new method for processing files made the company a lot of money'.

methodology /meθə'dɒlədʒi/ *noun*, is the system of methods used in a particular field or area of study. 'Methodology' is normally used in connection with academic work and research: 'There are many new theories emerging in the field of English language teaching methodology'.

Methodist /'meθədɪst/ *noun*, is a member of a Christian protestant church.

'Teeth extracted by the latest Methodists.' (Asian dentist's advert)

METRE^S, METER^S

metre /'mi:tər/ *noun*, is a unit of measurement in the metric scale. This is the spelling in BE of 'metre' and all combinations, such as 'centimetre'. Compounds of the word are stressed on the first syllable. The AE spelling is 'meter'.

meter /'miːtər/ *noun*, means a measuring instrument, such as 'speedometer'. Compounds of the word are stressed on the syllable before –meter, e.g. /spiːˈdɒmɪtər/.

MICROMETER, MICROMETRE

micrometer /maɪˈkrɒmɪtər/ *noun*, is an instrument for measuring very small distances.

micrometre /'maɪkrəʊmiːtər/ *noun*, is one millionth part of a metre. This is the BE spelling. In AE, it is spelt 'micrometer'. Note the difference in pronunciation between the two words.

MILE, LIGHT YEAR

mile /maɪl/ *noun*, is a unit of distance used in the UK and US. The term 'an English mile' is meaningless unless it is being distinguished from 'a nautical mile'. (A mile on land is 1760 yards, or approximately 1.6 km. A nautical mile is 2025.4 yards, or 1.852 km.) As with other units of distance, use the singular form when 'mile' is part of an adjective phrase, such as: 'A four-hundred-mile pipeline' (not 'miles'). The plural can be used if 'mile' is in a noun position: 'The pipeline is four hundred miles long'.

light year /'laɪt jɪər/ *noun*, is a unit of astronomical distance that represents the distance light travels in one year, which is about six trillion miles (6×10^{12}). As 'light year' is a distance, never use 'light year' with time, thus use 'six light years <u>away</u>' (not 'ago'). Informally, an idea that is way ahead of the competition can be described as being 'light years ahead'.

MIL.ˢ, MILL.ˢ, MILLI–, KILO–

mil. /mɪl/ *noun*, is the abbreviation for 'millimetre' and 'millilitre', i.e. a thousandth of a metre or a litre.

mill. /mɪl/ *noun*, is an abbreviation for 'million'. In financial circles, 'mill.' is an informal abbreviation for million: 'They paid ten mill. for that block of shares'. Note that the standard abbreviation for million is 'm.', as in '£30 m.'. As 'mil.' and 'mill.' are pronounced the same, there may be some confusion, and it does no harm to spell out in full which one is meant.

milli– /'mɪlɪ–/ *prefix*, means either thousand, as in the invertebrate animal 'millipede', literally a thousand feet, or in units of measurement, a thousandth part: 'There was a tiny gap of only 2 millimetres'.

kilo– /'kɪləʊ–/ *prefix*, means thousand in the metric system. In financial jargon, the abbreviation 'K' or 'k' is often used to mean thousand: 'London allowance, company car and salary of £35K'. Putting 'K' in front of ISO currency codes may be confusing. It is better to use the ISO currency code and write the figure in full: 'EUR 200 000', not KEUR 200.

MILLENNIUM, CENTURY

millennium /mɪˈlenɪəm/ *noun*, means a period of 1000 years: 'The millennium bug worried many people in late 1999'. Note that 'millennium' and the corresponding adjective 'millennial' are spelt with two 'l's and two 'n's. The plural is either 'millennia' or 'millenniums'.

century /'sentʃʊəri/ *noun*, means either a period of 100 years: 'Much of modern technology was invented during the past century'; or one of the periods of 100 years expressed as an ordinal number: 'He studied 18th century literature'. See **AD**, **BC**.

MILLION, MILLIONS

million /'mɪljən/ *adjective*, means a thousand thousands (10^6). 'Million' takes a singular verb when it is used in a unit of time, distance, money or temperature: 'Five million dollars is a lot of money'. 'Million' takes a plural verb when it follows a number or the words 'a', 'a few', or 'several': 'There are about six million cats in Britain'. The standard abbreviation is 'm'.

millions /'mɪljənz/ *noun*, is the plural of 'million' and refers to an inexact very large number. Often it has 'tens of' or 'hundreds of' in front. Thus 'millions' can range from a few 'million' to many 'million': 'The number of families in this country that own a pet is in the millions'. 'Millions' is sometimes followed by 'of' when, informally, it means very many: 'He has done this millions of times'. Note that 'millions' always takes a plural verb.

MINERˢ, MINORˢ

miner /'maɪnər/ *noun*, is someone who works in a mine: 'The miners in this area have faced a lot of hardship'.

minor /'maɪnər/ *noun & adjective*, is someone who is not legally termed adult. As an adjective, 'minor' means of less importance: 'They made only minor changes to the new limousine'. 'Minor' also has a special use in the context of music and education, where 'minor key' and 'minor subject' contrast with major ones. See **MAJOR** ➪ **LARGE**.

MINISTER, SECRETARY (POLITICAL)

minister /'mɪnɪstər/ *noun*, is the usual word to use for any of the elected members of the British government, including the department heads: 'The Health Minister is opening two hospitals next week'. Technically, a 'minister' is not the head of a department; that post is held by a Secretary of State. It is very rare, and nowadays almost impossible, for a member of the government in the UK not to be also a Member of Parliament.

secretary /'sekrətəri/ *noun*, is the title given to the head of a British or American government department, who, in Britain, may have several ministers reporting to him or her, such as: 'the Secretary for Defence'. Thus, in the UK there are a number of Secretaries of State. In the USA, however, there is only one Secretary of State, and this post is the equivalent of a Foreign Minister in other countries. The other members of the US government are also termed 'Secretary', and their deputies are Under Secretaries. Also in the USA, the Secretaries and their Under Secretaries are selected by the President, and are not allowed to be members of Congress.

MINUTE, MINUTES

minute /maɪ'njuːt/ *adjective*, means very small: 'It was a minute problem for the corporation that had such dramatic consequences'. Note that the stress is on the second syllable, which is pronounced 'newt'.

minute /'mɪnɪt/ *noun*, relates to time and geographical position. When referring to time, note that adjectival expressions, such as 'ten-minute break', are hyphenated. The symbol ' is used immediately after the number of 'minutes' when giving a geographical position: W 10° 35'.

minutes /'mɪnɪts/ *plural noun*, is the plural of 'minute' referring to time and geographical position. In another sense it is the written record of what is said and decided at a meeting: 'Who is taking the minutes today?' This is always used in the plural. The related verb is 'minute': 'Please do not minute that comment'.

MIS-⁵, MISS⁵

mis- /mɪs-/ *prefix*, can be added to a word to mean 'badly', as in: 'His misspent days as a student'. Never hyphenate words formed with 'mis'. Note the correct spelling of 'misspell'.

miss /mɪs/ *noun*, means an unmarried woman. This form is being replaced by 'Ms'. The plural of 'Miss' is 'Misses' so that the 'Misses Smith' can be used to refer to unmarried sisters, but the 'Miss Smiths' or the 'Ms Smiths' are more common alternatives. See **MS** ➪ **MR**.

MISTAKE, ERROR, FAULT, MALFUNCTION

mistake /mɪs'teɪk/ *noun*, is an action or judgement that is wrong or the result of being misguided: 'We made a mistake in buying that second-hand car'.

error /'erər/ *noun*, is a type of mistake that is often connected with calculations: 'There must be an error somewhere on this bill. It is much too high'. 'Error' also refers to misunderstanding or faulty judgement: 'Although there are errors in his argument, his essay shows a sound understanding of the historical background to the situation'. An 'error message' is one that indicates a problem in a computer program. 'Error' is more formal than 'mistake'.

fault /fɔːlt/ *noun*, means that something is wrong with a machine: 'There is a fault in this switch; there is no current'. It can also refer to a negative aspect of a person's character: 'Being intolerant is one of my worst faults'.

malfunction /mæl'fʌŋkʃn/ *noun*, means a failure in an item of equipment: 'Many programming errors are called computer equipment malfunctions'.
See **DAMAGE**. See **DEFECT**.

MOBILE, MOVABLE, MOVING

mobile /'məʊbaɪl/ *adjective*, refers either to something that is easy to move; or to something that can move by itself: 'They lived in a mobile home all summer'. The opposite, 'immobile', refers to a person or group that cannot or will not move.

mobile /'məʊbaɪl/ *noun*, is also used as a short form for a mobile cellular phone: 'I will call her mobile'. This is also called a 'cellphone', especially in AE. In another sense, a 'mobile' is a toy suspended above a child's cot, or from the ceiling, which rotates with the movement of the air.

movable /'muːvəbl̩/ adjective, refers to things that may be moved, but only with some effort. A wooden shed which can be taken down and re-erected elsewhere is 'movable' (i.e. can be moved by lorry). 'Moveable' is an alternative spelling. The opposite, 'immovable', refers to objects that cannot physically be moved, or attitudes or opinions that cannot be changed.

moving /'muːvɪŋ/ adjective, refers to something that changes place or position: 'Make sure that you keep your fingers clear of the moving parts on that machine'. It can also mean something sad that affects a person deeply: 'The funeral service was very moving'. The opposite, 'unmoving', refers to a person who is still, or to something that does not cause any emotion.

MOLTEN, MELTED

molten /'məʊltən/ adjective, refers to things that melt at very high temperatures: 'Molten lava started to move'.

melted /'meltɪd/ verb, is the past tense and past participle of the verb 'melt', and refers to things that go soft at moderate temperatures: 'The ice-cream melted while it was on the back seat of the car'.

MOMENT, MOMENTARY, MOMENTARILY

moment /'məʊmənt/ noun, means a brief period of time. Avoid using the cliché, 'at this moment in time'. Just say 'at present' or 'now'. See **NOW**.

momentary /'məʊməntəri/ adjective, means lasting only a moment: 'A momentary loss of concentration was enough to cause the crash'.

momentarily /'məʊməntərɪli/ adverb, means for a short time in BE: 'The train only stopped momentarily, and no one had time to get off'. In AE, 'momentarily', pronounced /məʊmən'terɪli/ means 'at any moment', or 'very soon'. Thus the BE and AE meanings of this word can cause some confusion.
See **EVENTUALLY**. See **NOW**. See **SOON** ⇨ **NOW**.

WE WILL BE LANDING MOMENTARILY IN DALLAS, TEXAS

WHERE ARE WE GOING AFTERWARDS?

MONOLOGUE, SOLILOQUY

monologue /'mɒnəlɒg/ noun, is a long speech by an actor when others are present. In a more everyday situation, a monologue means a long boring speech: 'The dictator's monologue lasted 4 hours'.

soliloquy /sə'lɪləkwi/ noun, means talking to oneself when thinking out loud, and is particularly used for a speech in a play: 'Hamlet's 'to be or not to be' speech epitomizes the soliloquy'.

MOONLIGHT, MOONLIT, MOONSHINE

moonlight /'muːnlaɪt/ noun & verb, as a noun means literally the light of the moon at night, and so by extension is used as an adjective to describe activities carried out on bright nights, such as 'moonlight skiing'. As a verb, 'moonlight' means to have a second job. This is often one that is kept secret from the tax authorities etc.: 'He is moonlighting as a taxi driver'. This is an informal term.

moonlit /'muːnlɪt/ adjective, is the visual effect of light from the moon: 'The beautiful moonlit sea stretched away to the horizon'.

moonshine /'muːnʃaɪn/ noun, is illegally made alcoholic spirits. In another sense it means a very foolish statement: 'I have never heard politicians speak so much moonshine'. This is an informal word.

 'Moonshine skiing' (On a student events programme, Scandinavia)

MORAL, MORALS, MORALE

moral /'mɒrəl/ *adjective & noun*, as an adjective, refers to the principle of right and wrong behaviour: 'They passed a harsh moral judgement on his action'. As a noun, a 'moral' is a lesson to be drawn from a story or an experience: 'The moral was never to go walking in the rain without a coat'.

morals /'mɒrəlz/ *noun*, are standards of conduct and behaviour: 'The company was fined for corruption of public morals'.

morale /mə'rɑːl/ *noun*, means the enthusiasm and confidence of a person or group: 'Morale in the political party was extremely high'. Note that the stress is on the second syllable.

MORTAL, FATAL, FATEFUL, DEADLY, DEATHLY, LETHAL

mortal /'mɔːtl/ *adjective*, means causing death, but is used only in formal contexts: 'Mortal combat was popular in Roman times'. The phrase 'mortal remains' refers to a dead body.

fatal /'feɪtl/ *adjective*, means both ruinous, as in: 'He made the fatal decision to accept a bribe', and causing death: 'a fatal accident'. 'Fatal' can only refer to unhappy events.

fateful /'feɪtfʊl/ *adjective*, means far-reaching and decisive. It has nothing to do with death and may refer to happy or unhappy events: 'The fateful meeting on that train to Berlin led to a happy marriage'.

deadly /'dedli/ *adjective & adverb*, as an adjective, means causing death, or having the potential to do so: 'A deadly weapon was found by the police'. As an adverb, 'deadly' can be combined with dull or serious to mean extremely: 'One glance at his face showed that he was deadly serious'.

deathly /'deθli/ *adjective*, refers to something that resembles death and is normally used figuratively: 'A deathly silence fell as the president's vast fortune was revealed'.

lethal /'liːθl/ *adjective*, refers to a substance capable of causing death: 'Lethal' is the word to choose in formal contexts: 'He swallowed a lethal dose of the drugs, but somehow survived'.

MOST OF, ALL OF

most of /'məʊst əv/ *determiner*, means nearly all, or the majority of: 'Most of the work was done'; 'Most of the votes were counted'. Note it is the noun following 'most of' that decides

whether the verb will be singular or plural. 'To make the most of something' means to take full advantage of it.

all of /'ɔːl əv/ *determiner*, means the whole quantity or amount. As with 'most of', 'all of' can be followed by a singular or plural noun, and it is this noun that decides whether the verb is going to be singular or plural. Note that in phrases with 'all of', the word 'of' can be omitted: 'All (of) my friends are coming to the party'.

MOTIF, MOTIVE

motif /məʊ'tiːf/ *noun*, is a distinctive feature in a work of music or literature, or a pattern: 'There was a delightful motif around the windows'. Note that the stress is on the second syllable.

motive /'məʊtɪv/ *noun*, means a reason for doing something, especially when it is hidden: 'The police tried to find the motive for the murder'.

MOTORWAY, DUAL CARRIAGEWAY, EXPRESSWAY, FREEWAY, THROUGHWAY, TURNPIKE

motorway /'məʊtəweɪ/ *noun*, means a major road in the UK with limited access, with two or more lanes in each direction. Access is restricted to numbered junctions, and stopping is not permitted anywhere along the carriageway: 'The M25 motorway is often humorously called the most expensive car park in London'. See **ROAD**.

dual carriageway /djuːəl 'kærɪdʒweɪ/ *noun*, means a road with two lanes in each direction, but without the restrictions of a motorway. Although all motorways are dual carriageways, not all dual carriageways are motorways. In the USA, this is often called a 'divided highway' or 'freeway'. See **CARRIAGEWAY ⟹ LANE**.

expressway /ɪks'presweɪ/ *noun*, means an urban motorway. The term is widely used in the USA.

freeway /'friːweɪ/ *noun*, is an AE term for a dual carriageway with limited access. The term 'free' means that such roads are without toll charges.

throughway /'θruːweɪ/ *noun*, is a general AE term for a main highway or motorway. An alternative spelling is 'thruway'.

turnpike /'tɜ:npaɪk/ *noun*, is an AE term for a motorway. 'Turnpike' was originally another term for tollgate. Thus it is used for a motorway where a road toll is charged.

MOUNTAIN, HILL
mountain /'maʊntɪn/ *noun*, means a steep and elevated area of land that rises over the surrounding countryside. In the UK, to be classified as a mountain, a land mass has to be 1000 feet above the surrounding level. The phrase 'to make a mountain out of a molehill' means to exaggerate the seriousness of a minor problem or difficulty.

hill /hɪl/ *noun*, is a rising area of land that is not high enough to be classified as a mountain. Steep slopes on roads are often called 'hills'. The informal phrase 'over the hill' means that a person is too old and no longer useful. 'As old as the hills' means extremely old.

MR, MS, MRS
Mr /'mɪstər/ is the BE spelling for the abbreviation of the title 'Mister' used before a surname or full name of a male adult: 'Mr Smith' or 'Mr George Smith'. It is normal to use 'Mr' for someone else, not for yourself. Note that in AE spelling, 'Mr.' (with a full stop) is normal. In AE, 'Mr.' is used in combinations such as 'Mr. President' and 'Mr. Ambassador'. Whether abbreviated or spelt in full, 'Mr' and 'Mister' are always capitalized. 'Messrs' /'mesəz/ is the plural of 'Mr': 'Messrs Brown and Smith'. This is used formally or in business English for the names of companies, but not elsewhere.

Ms /mɪz/ is a salutation in letters and emails; or when formally introducing or addressing a woman whose marital status is either not known, or not indicated. 'Ms' is recommended for use as a neutral alternative to 'Mrs' or 'Miss'. It is becoming the standard in many companies and organizations around the world. 'Ms.' is the AE spelling (with a stop).
See MISS ⇨ MIS-.

Mrs /'mɪsɪz/ is nowadays used with a married woman's surname: 'Mrs Smith' or full name: 'Mrs Mary Smith'. Traditionally, this was the style for a divorced or widowed woman, and under normal circumstances, her husband's name was used instead, i.e. 'Mrs John Smith'. This is now an old-fashioned custom, and tends only to be used on ceremonial occasions.

'Mrs' is not used with other titles, so that a woman doctor is Dr Jones and a woman mayor may be Madam Mayor. 'Mrs.' is the AE spelling (with a full stop). See SEXIST LANGUAGE.

MUCH, LOTS OF, A LOT OF
much /mʌtʃ/ *determiner*, refers to quantity, and is used with uncountable nouns: 'I do not have much money'. 'Much' is almost always used in negative or question sentences.

lots of /'lɒts əv/ refers to quantity, and is a common phrase in spoken English but is informal in written English. 'Lots of' can be followed by both countable and uncountable nouns, and it is the noun that determines whether the verb is singular or plural: 'Lots of money was wasted'; 'Lots of people were there'.

a lot of /ə 'lɒt əv/ *determiner*, means 'lots of', and is used with countable and uncountable nouns: 'A lot of people were there'. As with 'lots of', the subject-verb agreement is decided by the noun that follows 'a lot of'. 'A lot of' is common in spoken English but informal in written English.

MUNICIPALITY, LOCAL AUTHORITY, LOCAL COUNCIL
municipality /mju:nɪsɪ'pælɪti/ *noun*, means a town, or urban area governed by a locally elected body. It can also mean the group of people who govern an urban area, although 'local council/councillors' would be more common in this sense.

local authority /ləʊkḷ ɔ:'θɒrɪti/ *noun*, means an administrative body for local government. This is most commonly used in BE.

local council /ləʊkḷ 'kaʊnsḷ/ *noun*, refers to the elected officials in local government. See COUNCILLOR.

MUSLIM, ISLAM
Muslim /'mʊslɪm/ *noun*, is a follower of the religion of Islam. Most modern English dictionaries list this spelling for the religion and organizations such as the Muslim Brotherhood. Note that in the correct pronunciation, the first syllable rhymes with 'puss' and not with 'buzz'. 'Moslem' /'mɒslɪm/ is an older variant spelling.

Islam /'ɪslɑ:m/ *noun*, is the religion of those who follow the teaching of Mohammed. The two main branches of Islam are Sunni and Shia. Note that the first syllable is stressed and the second syllable rhymes with 'calm'. A related adjective is 'Islamic' /ɪsˈlæmɪk/ which is used in phrases such as 'the Islamic movement'. Note that the second syllable here rhymes with 'cam'.

MUTUAL, RECIPROCAL

mutual /ˈmjuːtjʊəl/ *adjective*, can mean actions or feelings that are experienced equally by two or more people: 'The mutual affection between mother and daughter was apparent'. 'Mutual' also refers to something that is shared by two or more people: 'Most of us are strangers, but the reason we are all here is because of our mutual friend, Robert'.

reciprocal /rɪˈsɪprəkl̩/ *adjective*, is used for something done or experienced in return for something similar done by another person. An act that is reciprocal involves repayment: 'She paid for lunch and looked forward to a reciprocal gesture by her friend'.

MYSTERIOUS, MYSTICAL, MYSTIQUE

mysterious /mɪsˈtɪərɪəs/ *adjective*, means puzzling, secretive or impossible to understand: 'I think Jane has got something important to tell me, as she was being very mysterious on the phone'. 'Mysterious' can also mean strange and fascinating: 'There were lights in the mysterious house across the bay'.

mystical /ˈmɪstɪkl̩/ *adjective*, means something difficult to understand that is related to spiritual and non-material feelings: 'Mystical events are part of many religions'.

mystique /mɪsˈtiːk/ *noun*, means fascination and awe for people or things which are regarded extremely highly: 'The mystique surrounding royalty in much of Europe is said to have almost disappeared'.

Nn

NAKED, NUDE, BARE

naked /ˈneɪkɪd/ *adjective*, refers to a person not wearing clothes, or, less commonly, a part of the body that is unclothed: 'He said that he could not answer the door because he was nearly naked'. It can also mean something that is unprotected by a covering, such as a 'naked flame' or 'naked sword'. 'Naked' can refer to extremely strong and uncontained emotions: 'His naked aggression was very intimidating'.

nude /njuːd/ *adjective & noun*, as an adjective, means wearing no clothes, and is used especially to describe a naked human form in art or photography: 'She once worked as a nude model for a famous artist'. As a noun, 'nude' means a 'naked' human form in a work of art. The expression 'in the nude', used after the verb, describes a person who is wearing no clothes. See **NATURIST ⇨ NATURALIST**.

bare /beər/ *adjective & verb*, as an adjective, means not covered by clothes, and is frequently used to refer to a part of the body: 'He walked across the room in his bare feet'. As a verb, 'bare' means to uncover: 'He removed his cap and bared his head'. It can also mean not decorated or empty: 'After we had moved our furniture out of the room it looked so bare'.

---

nationality words

There are no easy rules to learn for the derivation of nationality words from country names. In many cases, the adjective and language name have the same form, and often the noun describing a national of the country is also the same.

• Many adjectives end in **-(i)an**: *German, Ghanaian, Indian, Italian*. All South American nationality adjectives end in **-an** or **-ian**, for example *Brazilian, Ecuadoran, Peruvian* and *Venezuelan*, but note *Argentinian* (alternative *Argentine*). In other words, the way the country name ends does not determine the form of the nationality ending. The noun to describe nationals of almost all these countries is the same as the adjective form.

- A smaller group has adjectives ending in **-ese**: *Burmese, Chinese, Portuguese*. There is no noun for these nationalities, and a person from one of these countries has to be described as 'a person from ...' or 'a ...ese man/woman'.
- Many Asian nationality words end in **-i**: *Bangladeshi, Iraqi, Omani, Pakistani, Qatari*.
- Some mainly north-western European nationalities end in **-(i)sh**: *English, Irish, Welsh, Danish, Swedish, Turkish. French* and *Dutch* may be included here. In this group the noun form is always different: either add –man/woman to the –(i)sh form, or in some cases use a different word: *Dane, Swede, Turk. Scottish, Scots, Scotch* have particularly specialized uses. See **SCOTS**.
- Some country names ending in **-land** form the adjective by adding **-ic**: *Greenlandic, Icelandic,* and the nationality noun by adding **-er** (*New Zealander*). Exceptions: *Arab/Arabian/Arabic, Greek* and *Filipino*. See **ARAB**. See **GREEK**. See **FILIPINO ⇨ PHILIPPINES**.
- Nationality words are capitalized in English, and this also applies in fixed phrases where there is a clear connection with the country: *Russian roulette, French fries, Danish pastry*.

There are some combining forms which are used in hyphenated words to indicate bilateral relations between states: *Anglo-* (which in effect also means 'British'), *Dano-, Euro-, Franco-, Hispano-* (Spanish), *Indo-, Luso-* (Portuguese), *Russo-, Sino-* (Chinese): 'Dano-Norwegian language'; 'Hispano-Suiza cars'; 'Indo-European languages'; 'Sino-Soviet pact'. Note that both parts are capitalized. See **CAPITAL LETTERS**. See **FOREIGN PLACE NAMES**.

'This report considers hydropower research in the Turkey.'
(Student project)

NATIVE, INDIGENOUS

native /'neɪtɪv/ *adjective & noun,* as an adjective, means born in a certain place, or connected with a person's birthplace: 'I heard her speaking Russian, so I assumed that it was her native tongue'. When 'native' refers to plants or animals, it means originating or existing naturally. As a noun, 'native' means either someone who is born in a certain place, or who has a long association with it: 'She speaks Russian like a native'. The word 'native' was formerly used by Europeans about the people

who were living in countries before they were colonized. This is now considered offensive, although it is sometimes used humorously in colloquial BE to mean the local residents of a town or village: 'You really must visit us here. The village is lovely and the natives are friendly'. 'Native American' is an accepted way of referring to an 'American Indian'.

indigenous /ɪn'dɪdʒɪnəs/ *adjective,* is a formal equivalent of 'native', in the sense of originating or occurring naturally in a place. It can refer to people, plants or animals: 'The indigenous peoples of Africa are finding that their way of life is under threat'.

NATIVE AMERICAN, AMERICAN INDIAN

Native American /'neɪtɪv ə'merɪkən/ *noun,* is the politically correct term used officially today for the American Indians in the USA. Canadians use the terms 'Native Peoples' or 'Natives' in official contexts. See **BLACK**.

American Indian /ə'merɪkən 'ɪndɪən/ *noun,* is the preferred term for Native Americans used by the American Indians themselves and is a widely accepted term. An alternative is to refer to the specific people, for instance the Apache or Sioux. 'Red Indian' and 'redskin' are offensive terms for Native Americans and are only found in old history books.

NATURALIST, NATURIST

naturalist /'nætʃʊrəlɪst/ *noun,* is an expert or student of natural history, especially one who works out of doors rather than in a laboratory. In art or literature, a 'naturalist' is someone who depicts natural life realistically: 'Rousseau is often called the father of naturalist painting'.

naturist /'neɪtʃərɪst/ *noun,* is a term that is used especially in BE for someone who prefers to wear no clothes because they consider this practice to be more healthy and natural: 'Many beaches on this coast are reserved for naturists'. An alternative term is nudist. See **NAKED**.

NATURE, SCENERY, COUNTRYSIDE, LANDSCAPE

nature /'neɪtʃər/ *noun,* means all living things and natural characteristics of people or processes: 'Nature gives most insects a protective colour'. When 'nature' is used in this sense it is an uncountable noun, and does not take the definite article. Note that when describing the physical landscape, it is recommended to use 'countryside', 'scenery' or 'landscape', rather than 'nature'.

scenery /'si:nəri/ *noun,* means the natural features of a particular region or place, particularly when these form an attractive view: 'The scenery in the Alps in late spring is impressive'. It is an uncountable noun, and the related adjective is 'scenic'. 'Scenery' can also mean the painted hangings or movable set on the stage of a theatre.

countryside /'kʌntrɪsaɪd/ *noun,* means the land in a rural area. It often refers to farmed and settled land: 'We often go for a drive in the countryside at the weekend'. It is an uncountable noun. Note that the term 'the country' can be used to mean the same as 'countryside', but 'country' without the definite article has numerous other meanings.
See **COUNTRY ▷ STATE**.

landscape /'lændskeɪp/ *noun,* means all the features of an area of land that are visible, and usually refers to a rural environment: 'This landscape is very typical of the region'. 'Landscape' can be used adjectivally with other terms like 'landscape architect' and 'landscape gardening'. A landscape is also a painting of the countryside, and this has given rise to blend words such as 'seascape' or 'moonscape'.
See **BLEND WORDS**.

NATURE RESERVE, NATIONAL PARK, PROTECTED AREA, RESERVATION

nature reserve /'neɪtʃə rɪzɜːv/ *noun,* is an area of land set aside for the protection of plants, animals and the landscape. This may also be known as a 'wildlife sanctuary'.

national park /'næʃṇəl 'pɑːk/ *noun,* means an area of countryside protected by the State for the public to use and also for the welfare of the wildlife.

protected area /prəʊ'tektɪd 'eərɪə/ *noun,* is particularly used for land set aside to protect the landscape.

reservation /rezə'veɪʃṇ/ *noun,* has many meanings. In the context of land, it means an area set aside by treaty, for example for the use of Native Americans or Australian Aborigines in the USA and Australia, respectively.

NAVAL, NAVEL

naval /'neɪvḷ/ *adjective,* refers to the navy: 'He is a long-serving naval officer who commanded several ships'.

navel /'neɪvḷ/ *noun,* is the round, knotty depression in a person's belly: 'She had a diamond in her navel'. 'Navel' is also a type of orange.

 'Sapphire and naval-piercing jewellery.' (Web advert)

NB, SIC

NB /'en 'biː/ is used in writing to make a reader take special notice of something: 'NB This meeting room is closed all day on Monday'. It is an abbreviation of *nota bene* but is read as 'enn bee'. It may be punctuated as: N.B. Do not use an exclamation mark after NB.

sic /sɪk/ *adverb,* means 'as is written', and is used in brackets immediately after a typo or strange word to show that a quoted word or passage is what was written originally, and is not the present writer's mistake: 'The report said that the decline in standards of speling (sic) was alarming'. This is not an abbreviation, and thus should not be followed by a full stop.

NEAR, CLOSE, NEARBY

near /nɪər/ *preposition,* is used either before place names: 'She lives near Cairo', or for places a short distance away from the point of reference: 'He lives near the sea'.

close /kləʊs/ *adverb & adjective,* means only a short distance from the point of reference: 'He has always lived close to home'. 'Close' is less far away than 'near' and is also the word which should be used for emotional ties: 'A close friend'.

nearby /nɪə'baɪ/ *adjective & adverb,* means at a close distance to the person who is the subject of the sentence or clause: 'My father got caught in heavy rain, but managed to shelter in a nearby phone box'. Note that the adverb form can be spelt as one word or two: 'We camped in a field and washed our clothes in the river nearby/near by'.

negative prefixes

a-   is mostly used in formal or technical words to indicate lacking in or lack of: *amorphous* (lacking in shape), *amoral* (lacking in morals)

dis-   is also used with verbs, adjectives and nouns to form opposites: *dislike, disobedient, distrust*

dys-   is used with nouns and adjectives to mean bad or difficult: *dysfunctional, dyslexia*

il-   is used to form opposites before the letter l: *illegible, illogical*

im-   is used to form opposites before the letters **b**, **m**, **p**: *imbalance, immaterial, impossible*

in-   is used to form opposites, such as: *inaccurate, inexact*

ir-   is used to form opposites before the letter **r**: *irregular, irresponsible*

non-/non are two of the most used negative prefixes added to nouns, adjectives and adverbs to indicate an absence of something: *a non-drinker, a non-slip floor,* or *speaking non-stop*. Most of these *non-* words are hyphenated in BE: *non-cooperation, non-existent* but are spelt as one word in AE: *noncooperation, nonexistent*. See **HYPHENATION**.

un/un-   is added to adjectives and indicates the opposite quality from the positive word: *unexpected* = surprising, *unwise* = foolish.

The difference between *non-* and *un-* becomes clear if you compare *non-American* (a nationality which is not American) with *un-American* activities (being disloyal to America).

There are also some *false negative prefixes* which may be confusing.
See **INFLAMMABLE** ⟹ **FLAMMABLE**.
See **INHABITABLE** ⟹ **HABITABLE**.
See **INVALUABLE** ⟹ **VALUABLE**.

> 'The unorganized conference ... er, I'm sorry, the UN organized conference ...' (BBC Radio)

negatives: handling double and multiple negatives

• In standard English, two negatives in a phrase cancel each other and mean something positive. Phrases like: *Nobody has no skills* are complicated and really mean: *Everybody has some kind of skill*. The double negative is sometimes used as a rhetorical device to make a statement sound less definite, or to give a cautious confirmation: *It is not impossible to use a double negative*. Equally, in some BE and AE dialects the use of double or even multiple negatives is heard: *I didn't do nothing*. However, it is advisable in general to avoid using the double negative.

• In some languages, a negative word like *never* or *nobody* has to be used with a negative form like *not*. Avoid doing this in English as it may lead to misunderstandings.

• An easy trap to fall into is to use adverbs such as *hardly, scarcely,* and *rarely* that have a negative meaning in a phrase with a second negative, such as: *He rarely said nothing at planning meetings*, which means that this person spoke a lot at meetings.

... WHILE THERE ARE MANY CASES WHERE A DOUBLE NEGATIVE CONVEYS A POSITIVE, THERE IS NO CASE WHERE A DOUBLE POSITIVE CONVEYS A NEGATIVE

YEAH, YEAH

NEGLIGIBLE, NEGLIGENT

negligible /'neglɪdʒɪbl/ *adjective*, means of minor importance or not worth considering: 'The damage to the car was negligible'.

negligent /'neglɪdʒənt/ *adjective*, means either that someone has not done what was expected, or that proper care has not been taken: 'The authorities were negligent because of their lack of drug control'.

NETHERLANDS, HOLLAND, LOW COUNTRIES, DUTCH, FLEMISH

Netherlands /'neðələndz/ *noun plural*, is the official English name for this European country. Its name goes back to the times when they were literally 'the nether (i.e. low) lands' but nowadays it is not used with a capitalized definite article. However, as with other countries with a plural form, the lower case 'the' is still used in running text: 'She comes from the Netherlands'. See **DEFINITE ARTICLE**.

Holland /'hɒlənd/ *noun*, is often used as a synonym for the Netherlands. Strictly speaking this is incorrect as the name Holland refers only to the western provinces of the Netherlands.

the Low Countries /ðə 'ləʊ kʌntriz/ *noun plural*, is the historical name for the area covered by the present-day Netherlands, Belgium and Luxembourg, now frequently given the acronym Benelux.

Dutch /dʌtʃ/ *adjective & noun*, means the people of the Netherlands or their language. 'Double Dutch' is an informal expression meaning badly expressed spoken or written language that is difficult to understand. 'Going Dutch' means sharing the cost of a meal in a restaurant equally among those eating it.

Flemish /'flemɪʃ/ *adjective & noun*, refers to the people and culture of Flanders, an area of north eastern France, parts of Belgium and the Netherlands. Today the local Germanic language is called 'Dutch', not 'Flemish'.

NICE, DELIGHTFUL

nice /naɪs/ *adjective*, is a word with a broad range of meanings, including pleasant, delightful, agreeable, and satisfactory: 'Did you have a nice time?' Since 'nice' is a word that is often used without careful thought, it may be more appropriate to use other adjectives such as 'beautiful' or 'lovely' when expressing an opinion informally: 'Your hair looks beautiful'. Note that 'nice' is not generally used in formal writing, except in the sense of a very small, but important, distinction. See **CLICHÉ**.

delightful /dɪ'laɪtfʊl/ *adjective*, means very pleasant, agreeable and satisfactory and can often replace 'nice', especially in formal English: 'Thank you for a delightful meal'.

NO ONE, NONE

no one /'nəʊ wʌn/ *pronoun*, means no person, nobody: 'No one is teaching Russian well enough at this college'. 'No one' is more common in written English than 'nobody'. Note that 'no one' is followed by a singular verb. An alternative to 'no one' is 'nobody'. 'A nobody' is a person who is unremarkable, or of low status.

none /nʌn/ *pronoun*, means not one or not any: 'I went to the cupboard for some paperclips but there were none left'. 'None of' followed by a plural noun can take a singular or plural verb: 'None of the planes is/are available'. 'None' can refer both to uncountable nouns and plural countable nouns, when it means not one of three or more things: 'None of the cars were stolen'.

NORTH, NORTHERN, NORTHERLY

north /nɔːθ/ *adverb, adjective & noun*, is the direction of the North Pole. When it refers to a direction, 'north' is not usually capitalized: 'We travelled north'. It is capitalized when it is part of a continent, country or region. Thus, the sentence 'In England, we hired a car and travelled to the North' refers to the area defined as the 'northern' part of England. Note that there is no hyphenation in compounds such as North Dakota or North America. See **CAPITAL LETTERS**.

northern /'nɔːðən/ *adjective*, means located in the north or connected with the north in some way: 'There will be snow across northern Italy'. 'Northern' is only capitalized when it is part of a proper noun such as: Northern Ireland or Northern Territory.

northerly /'nɔːðəli/ *adjective*, means either in a direction towards the 'north': 'The birds were migrating in a northerly direction', or a wind that is blowing from the north: 'The ship started to roll when it was exposed to the northerly gale'. Note that 'northerly' is normally immediately followed by a noun.

NOTABLE, NOTICEABLE

notable /'nəʊtəbḷ/ *adjective*, means deserving attention: 'The students have made a notable improvement, and should be congratulated'. 'Notable' is a formal word.

noticeable /'nəʊtɪsəbḷ/ *adjective*, means clear and definite: 'The students have made noticeable progress, but there is still room for improvement'.

NOTE, NOTICE, MESSAGE, MEMO, MEMORANDUM

note /nəʊt/ *verb & noun*, as a verb, means to pay particular attention: 'He noted the teacher's expression'. The phrasal verb 'note down' means to record something briefly in writing, for future reference: 'He noted down the telephone number'. As a noun, 'note' means a few words written down, for example as a reminder: 'Make a note of that phone number'. See **BANKNOTE**.

notice /'nəʊtɪs/ *verb & noun*, as a verb, means to be aware of something: 'He noticed the teacher's expression'. As an uncountable noun, 'notice' means that attention is drawn to something: 'The teacher asked them to sit up and take notice'. It can also mean a warning that something is going to happen: 'We were given no notice of the roadworks'. As a countable noun, it means an announcement in a newspaper or on a sheet of paper: 'There is a notice on the door giving the office hours'.

message /'mesɪdʒ/ *noun*, means any sort of communication that is spoken or written, sent to, or left for, another person: 'I left a message on your answering machine this morning'.

memo /'meməʊ/ *noun*, means a written message, and is most often used in a professional context: 'Send me a memo on this next week'.

memorandum /memə'rændəm/ *noun*, means a note, but can formally mean a document which records agreed terms, as in a company's memorandum of association. 'Memoranda' and 'memorandums' /memə'rændə, -dəmz/ are the plural forms.

NOTHING, NOTHING BUT

nothing /'nʌθɪŋ/ *pronoun*, means not a single thing: 'Nothing was stolen from the office but there was a terrible mess'. 'Nothing' takes a singular verb, even when a plural noun follows:

'Nothing was learned from the experiments'. The phrase 'nothing to hope for' expresses a lack of possibilities.

nothing but /'nʌθɪŋ bʌt/ *pronoun & preposition*, is an emphatic expression which means only: 'Nothing but miles of snowy mountains was in front of him'. This also takes a singular verb.

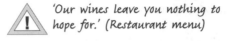

'Our wines leave you nothing to hope for.' (Restaurant menu)

NOW, CURRENTLY, AT PRESENT, PRESENTLY, SOON

now /naʊ/ *adverb*, means at the present time, but it never appears as the first word in a sentence in this sense: 'The peace negotiations have now been halted'. When 'now' is used initially, it is a way of making a contrast or drawing attention to something: 'Now what's the problem?'

currently /'kʌrəntli/ *adverb*, refers to the present time: 'The following car models are currently available'. See **CURRENT**.

at present /ət 'preznt/ *adverb*, also means 'now' or 'currently', and is the usual expression to be found at the beginning of a sentence: 'At present, the peace negotiations have been halted'. Never confuse 'at present' with 'presently', in the sense of 'soon'. See **EVENTUALLY**.

presently /'prezəntli/ *adverb*, refers to something that will happen after a short time: 'The doctor will be with you presently'. Note that this is a formal expression and that 'presently' comes at the end of a phrase. As this usage is typical of written English and is becoming old-fashioned in the spoken language, phrases like 'I will be with you presently' can be reworded, with 'presently' replaced by 'soon', 'in a moment' or 'in a minute'. In AE, 'presently' means 'now' or 'currently': 'They are presently on vacation in Mexico'. This usage is becoming established in BE.

soon /suːn/ *adverb*, means within a short time: 'We will soon be landing. Please fasten your seatbelts'. See **MOMENTARILY ⇨ MOMENT**.

NOWHERE, NO PLACE

nowhere /'nəʊhweər/ *pronoun*, means not anywhere: 'The customs officers were nowhere to be seen'.

no place /'nəʊ pleɪs/ *pronoun*, is an informal AE word that means the same as 'nowhere'.

NUMBER[5], NO.[5]

number /'nʌmbər/ *noun*, means an arithmetical value. 'A hundred is a good round number'. It is also used to express quantity: 'There were a large number of people waiting outside'. The expression 'number one' is used to emphasize a priority: 'We will make this a number 1 priority'.

no. /'nʌmbər/ *noun*, is an abbreviation for 'number' and is always read as 'number'. The plural of 'no.' is 'nos.'. In AE, the hash symbol # is often used instead of 'no.', for example in street addresses. 'No.' is often capitalized in English: 'The British Prime Minister officially lives at No. 10 Downing Street'.

'In case of emergency, say No.'
(Hotel notice by the phone)

A NUMBER OF, THE NUMBER OF

a number of /ə 'nʌmbər əv/ means several or some. It is followed by a plural countable noun, and takes a plural verb: 'A number of people <u>are</u> undecided'.

the number of /ðə 'nʌmbər əv/ means the size of the total. It is followed by a plural noun, but always takes a singular verb: 'The number of people outside <u>is</u> increasing'. One way to remember whether to use a plural or singular verb is the codeword 'PAST'. This stands for 'Plural with A number, Singular with The number'.

numbers

numbers in digits:

- 20/20 – means perfect eyesight without glasses or contact lenses: *The doctor said I still had 20/20 vision.*
- 24/7 – means 24 hours and 7 days a week. *That 24/7 shop might have some wrapping paper.*
- 4 x 4 – means a vehicle with four-wheel drive: *Even our car managed in the snow and it's no 4 x 4.* This is read *four by four.*
- 2.2 – is a decimal and is read as *two point two.* See **MEASUREMENTS**.
- Digits are used in various ways for expressing time, dates, and telephone numbers. See **TIME OF DAY**. See **DATES**. See **TELEPHONE NUMBERS**.

ordinal and cardinal numbers:

- Ordinal numbers mean 1st, 2nd, 3rd, and 4th etc., or first, second, third, fourth etc. These are used either to indicate rank: *He is second in command at the moment,* or the order of events: *The team managed to equalize in the 47th minute.* Ordinal numbers are also used in music to indicate the size of an interval between two notes: *major third, minor sixth.*
- Cardinal numbers mean 1, 2, 3, and 4 etc., or one, two, three, four etc. These are used when expressing size. See **DATES**.

Arabic and Roman numerals:

- Arabic numerals such as 1, 2, 3, 4 etc. are almost always preferred to Roman numerals like I, II, III, IV, etc. or i, ii, iii, iv, etc. which are only used in limited applications. These include designating the number of kings, queens, emperors, popes etc.: *Henry IV* and *Henry V* are also plays by Shakespeare' (read as *Henry the Fourth, Henry the Fifth*); giving dates of films, and paginating the numbers of introductory pages in books. When film-makers produce a sequel, the title is often written in Roman numerals (*Rocky II, Rocky III*, etc.) but is read as *Rocky Two, Rocky Three*, etc.

numbers in words:

- **decade** /'dekeɪd/ *noun*, is the normal word in English to refer to a period of ten years: *This has been around for a decade or more.* A decade expressed in numerals should be written *40s* with no initial apostrophe, or preferably *1940s*. If two or more *decades* are referred to, it is best to add the plural to each part: *In the 1970s and 1980s.*

- **ten years** /'ten ˈjɪəz/ *noun*, means the same as 'decade' but most people use *ten years* in informal English: *They have been here for about ten years*. When the number ten is important, use the more specific *ten years* rather than 'decade': *The money was paid over a period of nine or ten years*.
- **teens** /tiːnz/ *noun* means the period of a person's life between 13 and 19. The span can be narrowed by adding early or late to teens: *Even in their late teens they still enjoyed holidays with their parents*. The related adjectives are *teenage* and *teenaged*.
- **zero** or **nil** can be expressed in several ways depending on the context. See **ZERO**. See **APPROXIMATION**. See **INDEFINITE ARTICLE** .

twenties, thirties, forties, fifties, etc.:

- All describe temperature, age and sometimes coins or banknotes (note that a five-pound and ten-pound note are known in BE as a *fiver* and *tenner* respectively). For temperature, words like *low*, *mid* and *high* are added to show what part of the range is referred to: *The temperature in summer is always in the mid-twenties*. With age, words like *early*, *mid*, and *late* can be added: *Several of the teachers were in their early sixties*.

numbers in numerals or words:

- It is normal to write numbers as Arabic numerals in scientific and technical contexts. Otherwise, a general rule is to write numbers below 10 as words and larger numbers as numerals. Avoid mixing numerals and words in the same range: *The boys were from 7 to 15*, (not from seven to 15).
- Large numbers are written as words at the beginning of a sentence: *Seventy-two thousand people died in the war*. Beginning a sentence with *72 000 people* ... is generally considered poor written style. It can either be rephrased by adding *A total of* ... or by changing the syntax: *The war claimed 72 000 lives*.
- ISO standard 31-0 (1992), recommends using a space as the thousand/million/billion marker in numbers in English: 35 500 and 45 500. This standard is also followed by some standardization bodies at national level. A common convention is to use a space for thousands, millions, etc., only for numbers greater than 9999. The use of a comma here may be misleading, as many languages use the comma as a decimal marker. See **COMMA**.

numbers given by prefixes:

- It is often possible to work out what an unusual word means by looking at its prefix: For example, *the Pentagon is derived from a word meaning five-sided*. Here are some examples of prefixes that indicate a number and words that are formed in this way:

uni-/mono (one)	*unilateral negotiations* – one-sided
bi-/duo (two)	*bilateral negotiations* – two parties involved
tri-/trio (three)	*a triangle* – a three-sided plane figure
quad-/tetra (four)	*quadruplets* – four babies in one birth
quin-/penta (five)	*pentagon* – five-sided
sex-/hexa (six)	*sextet* – six musicians in a group
sept-/hepta (seven)	*September* – originally the 7th month in the Roman year
octo-/octa (eight)	*octopus* – animal with eight tentacles
nono-/nona (nine)	*nonagon* – nine-sided figure
deci-/deca (ten)	*decimal* – ten numeral system

NUMERATOR, DENOMINATOR

numerator /'njuːməreɪtər/ *noun*, is the part above the line in a fraction, so in 3/4, the numerator is 3.

denominator /dɪ'nɒmɪneɪtər/ *noun*, is the part below the line in a fraction, so in 3/4, the denominator is 4.

NUTRITIOUS, NUTRITIONAL

nutritious /njuː'trɪʃəs/ *adjective*, means food that is full of things that are good for the body: 'A fresh fruit salad is very nutritious'.

nutritional /njuː'trɪʃnəl/ *adjective*, means how efficiently nutrients in food are processed by the body: 'Doctors argue about the nutritional value of chocolate'. Note that food cannot be described as 'nutritional', but it can be described as 'nutritious'.

Oo

OBJECTIVE, GOAL, AIM, TARGET

objective /ɒb'dʒektɪv/ noun, often means the overall purpose of an action. This word is frequently used in reports and more formal types of English: 'The primary objective of this manual is to specify the correct installation of the equipment'.

goal /gəʊl/ noun, means the object of a precise ambition: 'The president had the goal of being re-elected'. Note that this is less formal that 'objective'.

aim /eɪm/ noun, means a direction or intention: 'His aim was to improve productivity in the company'.

target /'tɑːgɪt/ noun, means an aim, but it is often more specific as it frequently occurs in connection with other terms: 'target date', 'production target'. A value is often attached to 'target': 'Meeting our production target will bring a profit of €25 million'.

OBLIVIOUS, UNAWARE

oblivious /ə'blɪvɪəs/ adjective, means unaware of, or not concerned about something that is happening: 'He slept on, oblivious of the noise in the street'. 'Oblivious' can be followed by either 'of' or 'to'.

unaware /ʌnə'weər/ adjective, means not knowing or not realizing something: 'I was unaware that I needed to wear a jacket and tie'

OBNOXIOUS, NOXIOUS

obnoxious /əb'nɒkʃəs/ adjective, means extremely unpleasant: 'The right-wing politician made some obnoxious comments about immigrants'.

noxious /'nɒkʃəs/ adjective, means either poisonous: 'noxious fumes filled the lab', or very unpleasant: 'He came out with some noxious political ideas'. As 'noxious' in this sense is very unpleasant and 'obnoxious' is extremely unpleasant, there is only a shade of difference between them.

OBSERVATION, OBSERVANCE

observation /ɒbzə'veɪʃn/ noun, usually refers to watching someone or something carefully: 'He was in prison under close observation'. 'Observation' can also mean a remark or statement: 'He made a very clever observation about human nature'.

observance /əb'zɜːvəns/ noun, usually refers to the practice of obeying a ceremony, rule, or law: 'The observance of health, environment and safety regulations is mandatory'. It is a formal word. 'Following regulations' or 'respecting regulations' are more usual alternatives.

OBSOLESCENT, OBSOLETE

obsolescent /ɒbsə'lesnt/ adjective, means in the process of becoming outdated: 'This PC is obsolescent: it was not designed to work with Windows'.

obsolete /'ɒbsəliːt/ adjective, means outdated or no longer in use. Note that 'obsolete' is even more outdated than 'obsolescent': 'As they do not sell those large 5-inch floppy disks any more, that PC is obsolete'.

OBVIOUS, BLATANT

obvious /'ɒbvɪəs/ adjective, means clear or apparent: 'It was obvious from the first save he made that he was a brilliant goalkeeper'.

blatant /'bleɪtənt/ adjective, also means apparent or clear, but refers to hostile or unwelcome action that is performed openly and deliberately: 'The footballer kicked his opponent in what was a blatant foul'.
See FLAGRANT ⇨ FRAGRANT.

OCCUPIED, PREOCCUPIED

occupied /'ɒkjʊpaɪd/ adjective, means busy and active. 'Recently, she has been occupied in decorating the new house'.

preoccupied /pri'ɒkjʊpaɪd/ adjective, means thinking about a worrying problem and being oblivious of everything else: 'She was preoccupied all evening with worries about her tax returns'.

ODOUR, ODOROUS, ODIOUS

odour /'əʊdər/ noun, is a distinctive smell that is usually unpleasant: 'She wrinkled her nose at the odour of stale sweat'. 'Odour' is the BE spelling, but most words formed from it, such as 'odorous' and 'odorize', have no 'u' before the 'r'. An exception is 'odourless'. 'Odor' is the AE spelling of 'odour'. See –OR, –OUR SPELLINGS.

odorous /'əʊdərəs/ *adjective*, means having or emitting a smell that may be strong and unpleasant. The related noun is 'odour'.

odious /'əʊdɪəs/ *adjective*, means extremely unpleasant, repulsive: 'An odious scheme to rob the poor'. Note that this word has nothing to do with smell.

OFFENSIVE, AGGRESSIVE, FORCEFUL, VIGOROUS

offensive /ə'fensɪv/ *adjective*, refers to behaviour or language that causes hostility or distress. 'Offensive' can also mean disgusting if associated with an unpleasant smell. In military use, it can mean attacking: 'It has been proposed to turn NATO from a defensive organization into an offensive one'.

aggressive /ə'gresɪv/ *adjective*, means pushing certain aims and interests assertively and with determination. 'Aggressive' behaviour is likely to cause a negative reaction: 'We will follow an aggressive policy to establish our position in this market'. Alternatives to avoid these warlike associations include 'vigorous', 'active' and 'dynamic'; and any of these would have been suitable for a message on a greetings card, such as the one below.

forceful /'fɔːsfʊl/ *adjective*, means dynamic and assertive. It is commonly used about people: 'He is someone with a very forceful personality'.

vigorous /'vɪgərəs/ *adjective*, means very active and full of energy: 'Vigorous exercise can damage the body'. 'Vigorous' can be used together with words like measures and policies. Note that 'vigorous' is spelt with only one 'u'.

'We are an offensive organization and wish you all a Merry Christmas and a Happy New Year.' (Greetings card from a Scandinavian institution)

OFFICE STAFF, CLERK

office staff /'ɒfɪs stɑːf/ *noun*, is a general term for all the staff in offices. This is a wider term than 'clerk' as it covers secretaries, clerks, management and other office workers.

clerk /klɑːk/ (BE) /klɜːrk/ (AE) *noun*, in BE, is a person employed in an office or bank for administrative work. In AE, 'clerk' can mean someone at a sales service counter or in the reception of a hotel. Note that in BE this rhymes with 'dark', but in AE it rhymes with 'perk'. See **SHOP ASSISTANT ➪ SALESPERSON**.

OFFICIAL, OFFICIOUS

official /ə'fɪʃl/ *adjective*, means related to an authority or public body and its duty or position: 'The minister is here on official business'. It also means authorized: 'The official account is not the one in the newspapers'.

officious /ə'fɪʃəs/ *adjective*, means asserting authority in a pedantic and domineering way: 'He was an officious man whose favourite saying was "rules are rules"'.

OLD, ADVANCED AGE, ANCIENT

old /əʊld/ *adjective & noun*, as an adjective, means having lived or existed for a long time, or describes a person or thing as being no longer young. 'Old' can also be used informally for people where affection, not age, is indicated: 'How is my old friend today?' As a noun, 'old' can mean the aged: 'The old are not cared for adequately', and expresses age in combinations such as 'two ten-year-old boys'. Note how the plural form is used when 'boys' is omitted, as in: 'two ten-year olds'. See **AGED ➪ AGE**.

advanced age /əd'vɑːnst 'eɪdʒ/ *noun phrase*, means at a very old age. It often occurs in the expression 'He died at an advanced age'.

ancient /'eɪnʃnt/ *adjective*, refers to very old things that belong to the distant past, such as an 'ancient civilization'. Informally, it can refer in a humorous way to people who are considered old: 'My Dad's ancient: he's just had his thirtieth birthday'.

'Beef broth with ancient Bohemian meat balls.' (Restaurant menu)

ON BEHALF OF/ON SOMEONE'S BEHALF, ON THE PART OF/ON SOMEONE'S PART

on behalf of/on ...'s behalf /ɒn bɪ'hɑːf əv, ɒn '...z bɪ'hɑːf/ means behaving in someone's interests, or as their representative: 'The lawyer spoke on behalf of the prisoner/on the prisoner's behalf.' Both forms mean the same thing, and are interchangeable.

on the part of/on ...'s part

on the part of/on ...'s part /ɒn ðə 'pɑːt əv, ɒn '... z pɑːt/ implies responsibility by the person mentioned: 'Because of lack of attention on the part of the driver/on the driver's part, the car demolished the wall.' The two forms are interchangeable.

one, I, you

- *one* is the impersonal pronoun, and is used in two ways. First, when the speaker or writer either wants to avoid referring directly to him- or herself: *One does one's best* (meaning *I do my best*, but sounding more modest). Second, when talking about or referring to people in general: *When one has retired, one can enjoy getting up later in the morning.* This is a very formal usage, and in most contexts should be replaced by *I*, if referring back to the speaker or writer, or by *you*, when referring to people in general.

- In formal writing, neither *one* (too old-fashioned) nor *you* (too informal) may be suitable. Reword the sentence to refer to people in general:
At this stage, one may choose between two courses of action. (old-fashioned)
At this stage, you can choose between two courses of action. (too informal)
At this stage, two courses of action are possible. (good compromise)

- Sometimes *you* is inappropriate because it may be understood to be a personal comment rather than a general observation: *You always look scruffy in jeans.* This may be an insult to the person hearing it, or it may simply be the view of the speaker about jeans worn by anybody. If this problem arises, use *people* instead: *People always look scruffy in jeans.*

ONES^S, ONE'S^S

ones /wʌnz/ *noun*, is the plural of 'one': 'after six months at sea, he longed to return to his family and loved ones'.

one's /wʌnz/ *pronoun*, is either the genitive: 'To do one's best', or the contracted form of 'one is' and 'one has': 'We have three balloons: one's· blue, one's red, and one's got a hole in it'.

ONE–SIDED, LOPSIDED

one-sided /'wʌn'saɪdɪd/ *adjective*, means unfair and prejudiced: 'There began a one-sided argument about how to solve the problem of unemployment'. In competitive sport, 'one-sided' refers to opposing players of unequal abilities: 'The first round in the football cup was so one-sided that most of the spectators went home'.

lopsided /lɒp'saɪdɪd/ *adjective*, refers to someone or something with one side lower than the other: 'After the operation on his mouth, he had a lopsided grin'.

ONWARD, ONWARDS

onward /'ɒnwəd/ *adjective*, means going further in a journey or in time: 'The onward development of global warming is of great concern'.

onwards /'ɒnwədz/ *adverb*, means a continuing forward direction: 'From half-time onwards, the match was a walkover'. This is the BE spelling. 'Onward' is an alternative spelling, which is used especially in AE.

OPPORTUNITY, POSSIBILITY, CHANCE

opportunity /ɒpə'tjuːnɪti/ *noun*, means circumstances or a situation which may lead to achieving something. A person is given or gets an 'opportunity': 'Winning the lottery gave him a real opportunity to help the poor'.

possibility /pɒsɪ'bɪlɪti/ *noun*, means something that is capable of happening or being achieved. Although 'possibility' can be combined with 'of', it is more usually followed by 'that': 'There is a possibility that it might rain tomorrow'.

chance /tʃɑːns/ *noun*, is a more conversational alternative to 'possibility'. However, 'chance' can also express a probability or 'opportunity', on the condition of favourable circumstances. 'Chance' can be followed by 'of', 'that', or 'to': 'There is a good chance that we will win this match'.

OPTIC, OPTICS, OPTICAL

optic /'ɒptɪk/ *adjective*, describes the eye and sight. It is common in anatomical connections such as the 'optic nerve'. This is also used as a compound such as 'fibre-optic sensor'.

optics /'ɒptɪks/ *noun*, means the science that deals with visible and invisible light, and also vision. Use a singular verb with 'optics' when it means an academic subject: 'Optics is a subject for far-sighted students'. Another use of 'optics' is for the lenses, prisms and mirrors in an optical instrument. Here a plural verb is required: 'The optics of this telescope are handmade'. See –ICS.

optical /ˈɒptɪkl̩/ *adjective*, means applying the science or the principles of optics. It also relates to the eye and vision, such as 'an optical illusion'. An 'optical' specialist could mean someone working and researching in 'optics', or an optician, someone trained to make or sell glasses (BE), eyeglasses (AE) or contact lenses.

-or, -our spellings

- **-or** spellings are typical of AE in words such as *honor, favor, color*, where *honour, favour, colour* are the BE spellings. Some words, such as *error, pallor, tremor, horror, terror* that indicate a condition, have no *u* in BE or in AE. Also words that make a comparison like *minor, major* and *junior* only have the *-or* ending in BE and AE. See **–EE, –ER/OR NOUNS**.
- **-our** spellings are typical of BE in words such as *honour*, etc. but note that many such words that have a *u* in BE spelling, usually omit this *u* before *–ate, –ize* and *–ous*, as in: *invigorate, vaporize* and *humorous*.

ORIENT, ORIENTAL

orient /ˈɔːrɪənt/ *noun*, /ɔːrɪˈent/ *verb*, is capitalized as a noun, and means the East: 'The wonders of the Orient have attracted tourists for centuries'. As a verb, 'orient' is not capitalized and means to find the direction, as in 'orient the map', meaning using a compass and turning the map to the north. 'Orientate' /ˈɔːrɪənteɪt/ is an alternative form for the verb 'orient'.

oriental /ɔːrɪˈentl̩/ *adjective*, means characteristic of the Far East. It is offensive to use this term for a person from that region. It is recommended to use Asian or their nationality instead. See **ASIATIC ⇨ ASIAN**.

ORPHAN, FATHERLESS, MOTHERLESS

orphan /ˈɔːfən/ *noun*, means a child whose parents are both dead: 'The millionaire gave much of his wealth to orphans around the world'. This word should not be used for a child who has lost one parent.

fatherless /ˈfɑːðələs/, **motherless** /ˈmʌðələs/ *adjectives*, refer to a child who for some reason lacks a parent. Often, 'lost his father/mother' is used when it is clear that the death of the parent has occurred: 'She lost her mother at the age of six'.

OSTENSIBLE, APPARENT

ostensible /ɒsˈtensɪbl̩/ *adjective*, refers to something stated or appearing to be true but which may not be: 'The ostensible purpose of the meeting was to discuss housing. However, it became a demonstration against the council'. 'Ostensible' implies the deliberate intention to conceal something. This is a formal word, and 'apparent' is a less formal alternative.

apparent /əˈpærənt/ *adjective*, when placed before the noun, refers to something that appears to be true, but may in fact not be: 'His apparent success in politics was due to corruption'. When 'apparent' comes after the verb, it means obvious: 'After the trial, it became apparent that his success in politics was entirely due to corruption'. See **HIDDEN AGENDA ⇨ SCHEDULE**.

-ough

- This sequence of letters can be pronounced in several ways. There is no easy way of learning which pronunciation is needed for which word: they must be memorized individually.

bough	/baʊ/	rough	/rʌf/
cough	/kɒf/	thorough	/ˈθʌrə/
dough	/dəʊ/	through	/θruː/
hiccough	/ˈhɪkʌp/	thought	/θɔːt/

- There are many other words containing *-ough*, and it is best to look up each one in a dictionary to check which of these pronunciations is correct in each case.

OUTDOOR, OUTDOORS

outdoor /ˈaʊtdɔːr/ *adjective*, or 'out-of-door', means in the open air, as in: 'The healthy outdoor life appeals to most Scandinavians'.

outdoors /aʊtˈdɔːz/ *adverb*, or 'out of doors' means the same as 'outdoor' but is grammatically different: 'It is invigorating to go outdoors/out of doors when it is a crisp winter day'.

OUTWARD, OUTWARDS

outward /ˈaʊtwəd/ *adjective*, means in a direction going away from home. This is used before a noun as in: 'The outward voyage', or in the phrase 'outward-bound'.

outwards /ˈaʊtwədz/ *adverb*, means in a direction to the outside, as in 'the door opens outwards'. This is sometimes spelt 'outward'.

OVERFLOW, OVERFLY

overflow /əʊvə'fləʊ/ *verb*, /'əʊvəfləʊ/ *noun*, as a verb, refers mostly to water flowing over something, and has the past tense and past participle 'overflowed': 'The river overflowed its banks'. It is also used figuratively: 'The crowd overflowed into the streets'. As a noun, it means a pipe fixed in a tank, to prevent it becoming too full. Note the change in stress between the verb and the noun.

overfly /əʊvə'flaɪ/ *verb*, refers to aircraft flying over something. It has the past tense 'overflew' and the past participle 'overflown': 'The bomber has overflown enemy territory'.

OVERLOOK, OVERSEE, OVERSIGHT, OVERVIEW

overlook /əʊvə'lʊk/ *verb*, means either fail to notice: 'He overlooked the importance of this TV interview'; or refers to the view from a building: 'The house overlooked the village'.

oversee /əʊvə'siː/ *verb*, means to supervise a person or their work: 'The minister is extremely busy as she oversees two departments'. 'Oversee' is a formal term.

oversight /'əʊvəsaɪt/ *noun*, means an unintentional failure to notice something: 'We regret the delay in processing your order. It was due to an oversight'. This is a formal word.

overview /'əʊvəvjuː/ *noun*, means a general summary or review of a topic: 'Please give a quick overview of your plans'.

OVERTONE, UNDERTONE

overtone /'əʊvətəʊn/ *noun*, is originally a term from music. In its general sense, it means an additional effect or implication: 'There were unpleasant fascist overtones in the after-dinner speech'. Note that in this sense the word is nearly always used in the plural.

undertone /'ʌndətəʊn/ *noun*, is a subdued sound or colour. In another sense, it means an unsaid, but real feeling of unease: 'The whole bank and its staff felt undertones of despair'. Note that in this sense the word is nearly always used in the plural.

OXBRIDGE, IVY LEAGUE

Oxbridge /'ɒksbrɪdʒ/ *noun*, means the English universities of Oxford and Cambridge. There is no such physical place, being simply a blend of the two words. See **BLEND WORDS**. Note that graduates of Oxford University write *Oxon.* after their degrees: 'J. Smith, BA Oxon.' Similarly, graduates of Cambridge University write *Cantab.* after their degrees: 'M. Smith, BA Cantab.'

Ivy League /'aɪvi 'liːg/ *noun*, means the group of eight long-established and prestigious universities in the eastern United States. The group consists of Harvard, Yale, Pennsylvania, Princeton, Brown, Columbia, Dartmouth, and Cornell. The name may come from the ivy that traditionally grows on the walls of these institutions.

---

oxymoron /ɒksɪ'mɔːrɒn/

- An oxymoron is a word such as *firewater* that is self-contradictory. Frequently, oxymoronic terms like *old news* are used without us thinking about what we are really saying. A double classic is *fresh frozen jumbo shrimp*, where apart from its dubious freshness we have the problem of size when *jumbo* means very large, and *shrimp* means both a shellfish and also something very small.
- Oxymora are not necessarily mistakes or errors in speech or writing. They make effective titles and phrases as in Shakespeare's *parting is such sweet sorrow*. Some combinations may be the basis of satire, such as the story of the British officer who innocently called to his men in the heat of battle. *It's all right chaps, according to intelligence we are under friendly fire.* The term *military intelligence* is probably a good way to remember what an oxymoron is all about.
- Oxymora are the basis of clichés like: *half naked, small fortune, open secret, working holiday* and *living dead*. Even some foreign loan words are oxymoronic: *pianoforte* (soft-loud) and *sophomore* (wise fool).
- Perhaps the greatest problem with oxymora for careful writers is avoiding them. Here are some examples from trade names and elsewhere. *dry Martini elevated subway new classic plastic glass silent scream exact estimate tight slacks slack tights original copy bittersweet*
- Journalists often relish satirical oxymora like *the Senator's popularity soared like a lead balloon.* Here are some choice examples from the *Financial Times'* database: *English cuisine pleasant villain colourful accountant poor bookmaker*

 'Night security guards patrol this area 24 hours a day.' (Building site notice)

Pp

P., PP. (PAGES)

p. /peɪdʒ/, is an abbreviation that is used in two ways. First, for a page number in reports and references, when it is written before the number: 'p. 116'. Second, 'p.' indicates how many pages there are in a book cited on a reference list, when it is written after the number of pages: '75 p.' See **PENCE**.

pp. /'peɪdʒɪz/, is the plural form of 'p.' in its first use. Write 'pp. 11-16'. See **P.P.**

PAIR, PAIRS, COUPLE

pair /peər/ *noun*, can mean two similar objects, as in: 'You need to find two playing cards that make a pair.' It also refers to two people who share a connection: 'That couple we met were a friendly pair.' 'Pair' can be combined with 'of' to mean either two similar things such as 'a pair of expensive wine glasses', or one thing that has two parts joined, such as 'a pair of jeans/scissors'. The expression 'pair of' takes a singular verb: 'That pair of trousers I tried on was too small'. However, if 'pair of' is omitted, a plural verb is used: 'Those trousers I tried on were too small'. See **SCISSORS**.

pairs /peəz/ *noun*, is the normal plural of 'pair', and therefore means two or more sets of two things or people: 'The children must walk in pairs'. (Note that 'two pair' is substandard in BE.)

couple /'kʌpl/ *noun*, can mean two of the same objects, as in: 'I need ten tickets for the show but there are only a couple left'. It also refers to people who are living in an emotional relationship: 'We have never met the couple who live next door'. 'Couple' is often combined with 'of', to mean either exactly two or, informally, a small number: 'I will be back in a couple of minutes'. Note that in BE, 'couple' in all senses takes a plural verb, although it is possible to use a singular verb when the two things or people are considered as one unit. See **COLLECTIVE NOUNS**. See **FEW**.

PALATE⁵, PALETTE⁵, PALLET⁵

palate /'pælət/ *noun*, is the roof of the mouth, or the ability to distinguish between different flavours: 'Dry sherry may suit her palate'.

palette /'pælɪt/ *noun*, means a board on which an artist mixes paint: 'Her palette was a glorious mixture of various shades of brown'.

pallet /'pælɪt/ *noun*, is a portable platform for storing things or moving them, often by means of a forklift truck: 'All the pallets used by the company were made by prisoners'.

PARAFFIN, KEROSENE

paraffin /'pærəfɪn/ *noun*, is a light fuel oil produced by distilling petroleum. 'The cottage is lit by paraffin lamps'.

kerosene /'kerəusiːn/ *noun*, is both the AE term for what is known in BE as 'paraffin' and the standard term in all forms of English for a type of fuel oil in a technical sense. 'Kerosine' is an alternative spelling.

PARAMETER, PERIMETER

parameter /pə'ræmɪtər/ *noun*, in one sense means numerical or other measurable things that determine operational conditions: 'Density, temperature, and pressure are the main parameters of atmospheric measurements'. 'Parameter' is also used in the plural, as a more formal alternative to 'limits' or 'boundaries': 'We are working within the parameters of the budget'. See **BALLPARK FIGURE** ⇨ **ESTIMATE**.

perimeter /pə'rɪmɪtər/ *noun*, means the boundary of an enclosed area. It is only used in this physical sense: 'The perimeter of the army camp is heavily guarded'.

PARAMOUNT, SUPREME

paramount /'pærəmaʊnt/ *adjective*, means the most important factor or person, and therefore should not be combined with 'most'. 'Paramount' is used specifically in connection with overall power in a culture or society: 'He has been the country's paramount leader for more than a decade'.

supreme /sjuː'priːm/ *adjective*, means the most important factor or person, and therefore should not be combined with 'most'. 'Supreme' refers to the highest person or body in an organization or structure: 'The case is to go before the Supreme Court'.

PARENT, RELATIVE, RELATION, RELATIONS, CONNECTIONS

parent /'peərənt/ *noun*, is the biological mother or father: 'The state gives an excellent allowance for working parents'. Modern English distinguishes carefully between a 'step-parent', who is the husband or wife of a biological parent, but not in a biological relationship with the child, and a 'parent-in-law', who is the parent of a husband or wife.

relative /'rɛlətɪv/ *noun*, means a person in someone's family: 'That man over there is a relative of mine'. A relative can be either 'distant' or 'close'.

relation /rɪ'leɪʃn/ *noun*, is an alternative to 'relative', and can therefore be 'distant' or 'close'. Note that the expression 'poor relation' is used to refer to a thing or situation that is considered to be less of a priority: 'In terms of investment, inner-city housing is often the poor relation'. 'Relation' also means the way in which two things, people, groups or countries connect with each other: 'The statistics bear no relation to the reality of the situation'.

relations /rɪ'leɪʃnz/ *noun*, means both relatives and the way people or countries behave towards each other: 'Relations between the USA and Russia are changing'. Note that with the latter meaning, there is no article before 'relations'. It is also used in institutional terms such as 'industrial relations' and 'public relations'.

connections /kə'nekʃnz/ *noun*, are the relations, friends or acquaintances who are in a position of influence in society: 'Many people suspected that he had only got the job because of his connections'.

PARK, CAR PARK

park /pɑːk/ *verb & noun*, as a verb, means to drive a car into a space where it can stop temporarily: 'I parked behind the railway station'. In English, 'parking' is not used as a noun to mean the place where vehicles are parked, although it is combined with other words as in 'parking meter' and the AE 'parking lot'. As a noun, a park is an enclosed area for recreation usually in a town or city: 'Both Hyde Park and Central Park are integral features of London and New York respectively'.

car park /'kɑː pɑːk/ *noun*, means a place where cars can be parked. Multilevel buildings for car parking are called 'multi-storey car parks' in BE and 'multilevel parking lots' in AE.

PART (*NOUN*), PORTION

part /pɑːt/ *noun*, is a general term for a quantity taken from a whole: 'We spent part of our holidays in Wales'.

portion /'pɔːʃn/ *noun*, is a piece of something or part of a whole that is divided, such as: 'a portion of chicken' (= a helping) or 'her portion of the money' (= her share). Note that 'portion' is much more restricted than 'part'.

PART (*ADVERB*), PARTLY, PARTIAL, PARTIALLY

part /pɑːt/ *adverb*, means 'consisting of two things' or 'to some extent', and is commonly used in compounds, as in: 'He is part French and part Irish'.

partly /'pɑːtli/ *adverb*, means 'to some extent' or 'not completely'. 'Partly', not 'partially', is used for material things: 'The car is partly plastic'. 'Partly' is also combined with 'because of' or 'due to', to explain the reason for events or situations: 'We were delayed partly due to the traffic'.

partial /'pɑːʃl/ *adjective*, means 'not complete': 'We have only received partial payment of invoice no. 123 ACC'. 'Partial' also means one-sided: 'This was a very partial account of the conflict'. To be 'partial to' something means to be fond of it: 'They are partial to fish and shellfish'.

partially /'pɑːʃəli/ *adverb*, means 'to some degree', and is the word to use for physical conditions: 'He is partially deaf'.

PARTNER, BOYFRIEND, GIRLFRIEND

partner /'pɑːtnər/ *noun*, refers to either personal or business relationships. In the personal sense, it means someone a person is married to or is in a sexual relationship with: 'All the directors attended the dinner with their partners'. 'Partner' can also refer to someone sharing a common interest with another person, such as sport: 'I played, as his tennis partner was on holiday'. In the business sense, 'partner' means one of the owners of certain types of companies: 'All the senior partners in the law firm agreed with the new policy'.

boyfriend /'bɔɪfrend/ *noun*, means a male romantic or sexual partner, rather than a male friend. The term 'partner' is generally considered to be more sophisticated than 'boyfriend'.

girlfriend /'gɜːlfrend/ *noun*, can mean either a female romantic or sexual partner, or simply a woman's female friend. See **FRIEND**.

PARTY, SIDE (IN AGREEMENTS, CONFLICTS)

party /'pɑːti/ *noun*, is a formal word for a single person or a group of unspecified size. It is particularly used in legal contexts, as in: 'third-party insurance', and 'the guilty party'. 'Parties' is the plural form of 'party', meaning several individuals or groups: 'The parties to this agreement must all sign'.

side /saɪd/ *noun*, means a person or group opposing others in a conflict, dispute, sporting event, business deal or in politics: 'As any parent knows, there are two sides to every argument'. Note that the expression 'to take sides' means to support one party in a dispute.

PASS, PAST, SEND

pass /pɑːs/ *verb*, means to go past or along the side of something: 'As I passed the house I noticed that all the doors and windows were open'. 'Pass' also means to move an object towards someone: 'Could you pass me that pan, please'. In a formal sense, 'pass' can also mean to approve: 'The Act was passed this month'. The past tense and past participle of the verb is 'passed': 'We passed six villages and no pubs'. Note that 'passed' is pronounced the same as 'past'.

past /pɑːst/ *adjective, adverb, noun & preposition*, as an adjective, refers to something that has gone by in time: 'The past three weeks were very tiring'. As an adverb, it means travelling from one side to the other: 'The King drove past and waved'. As a noun, 'past' refers to a period of time that has elapsed: 'Life used to be harder in the past'. As a preposition, in BE, 'past' is used when telling the time: 'Ten past three'. The AE equivalent is often 'after': 'Ten after three'. See **TIME OF DAY**.

send /send/ *verb*, means to cause to go or be taken to a particular destination: 'Please send the order by registered mail'.

PASSER-BY, PASSERS-BY

passer-by /pɑːsə'baɪ/ *noun*, means someone who happens to go past something on foot: 'I couldn't find the post office so I asked a passer-by'.

passers-by /pɑːsəz'baɪ/ *noun*, is the plural form of 'passer-by'. As with other such hyphenated compounds, the plural 's' is added to the noun in the compound.
See **PLURAL NOUNS**.

PASSWORD, USER NAME (COMPUTING)

password /'pɑːswɜːd/ *noun*, means a series of letters and/or numbers that are typed into a computer to enable it to be used: 'After the holiday he completely forgot his password'.

user name /'juːzə neɪm/ *noun*, means the name that identifies a person and permits access to a computer or computer system: 'Type your user name into this box'.

PATENT, PATENTLY

patent /'pætənt/ *noun & verb*, as a noun, means the official sole right given to an individual or company to exploit an invention or to use a title, for a limited time: 'They filed a patent application for a kitchen device'. As a verb, 'patent' means to obtain the sole right to exploit an invention or to use a title.

patent /'peɪtənt/ *adjective*, can mean connected to a patent, as in 'a patent application'. It is also used to emphasize that something negative is obvious: 'The police regarded his story as a patent lie'. Note that 'patent' is also used in other contexts, like 'patent leather', or 'patent medicine'.

patently /'peɪtəntli/ *adverb*, means 'without doubt', and emphasizes that something negative is obvious: 'The police considered his story to be patently absurd'. 'Patently' is often used in the disapproving phrase 'patently obvious'.

PATIENCE[S], PATIENTS[S], PATIENT

patience /'peɪʃənts/ *noun*, means the quality of being peaceful and not irritated: 'The teacher had little patience with noisy students'. It also means a game of cards for a single player. This is called 'solitaire' in AE.

patients /'peɪʃənts/ *noun*, are people undergoing medical treatment in a doctor's care or admitted to hospital: 'All patients initially stay in the new hotel-wing adjoining the hospital'. The singular form is 'patient'.

patient /'peɪʃənt/ *adjective*, means the quality of being able to wait for a long time without irritation: 'The teacher told the children to be patient, and wait'.

PATRIOT, EXPATRIATE

patriot /'pætrɪət, 'peɪtrɪət/ *noun*, is a person who is proud of his or her country, and supports its actions: 'He was a true patriot, who defended his country's position at every opportunity'. The first pronunciation is more usual in BE, and the second in AE.

expatriate /ɪks'pætrɪət, ɪks'peɪtrɪət/ *noun*, is a person living away from his or her native country: 'He lost his right to vote when he moved to Canada and became an expatriate'. The first pronunciation is more usual in BE, and the second in AE. Note that the spelling 'expatriot' is not given in authoritative dictionaries, and could only mean a person who is no longer a supporter of his or her country.

PAVEMENT, SIDEWALK

pavement /'peɪvmənt/ *noun*, in BE means a paved or asphalt area for pedestrians or a path beside a road: 'Children must always walk on the pavement'. 'Pavement' in technical contexts and in AE generally means the hard surface of a road or airport runway: 'The pavement was good, even in the Rockies'. See **KERB**.

sidewalk /'saɪdwɔːk/ *noun*, is the AE term for the BE 'pavement': 'Many of the highways did not have sidewalks'.

'Traffic will be moved onto the new pavement in about three weeks.' (US Highway, Work Update)

PAY, SALARY, WAGE

pay /peɪ/ *noun & verb*, as a noun means financial compensation for work. It is a useful term for avoiding the social distinctions between 'salary' and 'wage'. 'Pay' is thus used in general contexts like 'pay claim' and 'rates of pay'. As a verb, note that the past tense and past participle are spelt 'paid', never 'payed': 'Have you paid for lunch?'

salary /'sæləri/ *noun*, means a fixed regular payment by an employer to employees typically made on a monthly basis but referred to as an annual total: 'The salary is $150 000'. In the UK, job adverts often refer to 'Salary £35k' (pronounced '35 kay') meaning £35 000. 'Salary' is the term used for 'pay' for professional people and white-collar workers such as staff in offices in the service or private sectors.

wage /weɪdʒ/ *noun & verb*, as a noun, is often used in the plural 'wages', and means a regular fixed payment on a daily or weekly basis by employers to employees such as manual and unskilled workers: 'Our wages are still too low'. 'Wages' is thus a term associated with blue-collar workers, such as those doing physical work in industry. Use 'wages' for payment for work, and 'wage' before nouns in phrases such as 'wage earner' and 'wage packet'. As a verb, 'wage' means to carry on a war or campaign: 'We are waging war on child prostitution'.

PAYMENT, REPAYMENT, REMITTANCE, SETTLEMENT

payment /'peɪmənt/ *noun*, means the act or process of paying money or settling an account or debt: 'There will be a 10% discount for cash payment'. 'Payment' can be in instalments, 'part payment', or in full: 'We enclose our cheque for €230 in payment of invoice XYZ'. The plural form is used for a series of financial transactions: 'Payments on the car'. Countries use the term 'balance of payments' to mean the difference between the amount paid for imports and received from exports in a given period.

repayment /ri:'peɪmənt/ *noun*, means the paying back of an amount that has been lent, in full or in instalments: 'Repayment is to be made by 31 December to the company account'. The plural form is used for a series of such payments: 'Repayments are to be made on a quarterly basis to the company account'.

remittance /rɪ'mɪtəns/ *noun*, refers to a sum of money that is sent, especially by post: 'We enclose our remittance for €230'. 'Remittance' is a formal word that is usually only used in this commercial sense; 'payment' is a more general term.

settlement /'setlmənt/ *noun*, in the financial sense means the act or process of paying an account. If someone is slow in paying, you can request 'settlement': 'Kindly arrange for settlement of this invoice within the next 10 days'. 'Settlement' is a formal word in this sense; 'payment' is a more general term. See **VILLAGE**.

PEACE^S, PIECE^S

peace /piːs/ *noun*, means calmness, and freedom from disturbance or conflict: 'He walked in the woods to get some peace and quiet'. If people ask to be 'left in peace', it means that they do not want to be disturbed.

piece /piːs/ *noun*, means part of something: 'Would you like a piece of cake?' 'Piece' also refers to the parts into which something divides: 'Some of the pieces in the jigsaw puzzle are missing'. However, note that 'a piece of paper' can also mean a whole sheet of paper: 'Can you give me a piece of paper so that I can make some notes?' 'Piece' in other contexts refers to a written or musical composition and a coin. In BE usage, 'piece' is the normal term to use with coins up to and including 50p, for example: 'a 10p piece', and 'coin' is used with non-paper money of £1 and higher denominations: 'She put four two-pound coins on the counter'. 'A piece of' is a useful alternative to 'some/any' when referring to uncountable nouns such as advice, information or news: 'I received an interesting piece of news this morning'.

PEACEFUL, PEACEABLE

peaceful /'piːsfʊl/ *adjective*, means both tranquil: 'A peaceful Sunday morning' and free from disturbance or violence: 'The students held a peaceful demonstration'.

peaceable /'piːsəbl/ *adjective*, means avoiding conflict and is used for people or their intentions: 'A peaceable settlement was reached, and the crisis was defused'.

PEAL⁵, PEEL⁵

peal /piːl/ *noun & verb*, as a noun, means a loud sound: 'Peals of laughter came from the hotel bar'. As a verb, it means the sound of bells ringing: 'All the bells started to peal'.

peel /piːl/ *noun & verb*, as a noun, means the skin of a fruit, and as a verb, the act of removing it. By extension, as a verb 'peel' is used to describe the way an outer coating of paint or layer of skin may become detached in strips: 'The wall had peeled during the hard winter'. To 'peel off' items of clothing is an informal expression that means to get undressed: 'He peeled off his track suit and took a shower'.

PEDAL⁵, PEDDLE⁵

pedal /'pedl/ *noun & verb*, as a noun, is a flat bar that each foot presses against when bicycling, or a foot lever for drums etc. As a verb, 'pedal' means using the feet to propel a bicycle.

peddle /'pedl/ *verb*, means to sell from house to house. 'Peddle' is formed from 'peddler', also spelt 'pedlar', which means someone who sells things, nowadays especially drugs: 'He is a convicted drug peddler'.

PEEK⁵, PEAK⁵

peek /piːk/ *verb*, means to have a quick look at something that you should not be looking at: 'Close your eyes and don't peek'. 'Peek' combined with 'out' can be used figuratively to mean 'become partly visible': 'If you have a hole in your sock, a toe may peek out'.

peak /piːk/ *noun & verb*, as a noun means the highest point of a mountain, or an achievement. As a verb, it means to reach a maximum point: 'Production peaked in March'.

PEER (*NOUN AND VERB*)

peer /pɪər/ *noun*, means an equal in age or social status. Sociologists use the term 'peer group' to mean a group of people with something in common, such as interests, age or social status. 'Peer pressure' means the influence exerted by a 'peer group' in terms of clothes, attitudes or behaviour: 'The lack of interest shown by some boys during lessons is often ascribed to peer pressure'. 'Peer review' means the evaluation of scientific or academic work by others working in the same field: 'All our research is to be subjected to peer review'. The phrase 'peer of the realm' refers to a person of noble rank in the UK.

peer /pɪər/ *verb*, means to look at something that cannot be seen clearly: 'He peered anxiously into the crowd, but could not see his children'.

PENCE, PENNY

pence /pens/ *noun*, is the plural of the smallest unit in the British monetary system: 'There are 100 pence to a pound'. When referring to the price of something both '20 pence' and the informal '20p' (pronounced 'pea') are used: 'That newspaper costs 20p'.

penny /'peni/ *noun*, is used to refer to the coin that is the smallest unit of currency in the British monetary system: 'You cannot buy anything for a penny any more'. 'Penny' has two plurals, 'pence' for the price of something and 'pennies' for the coins: 'She looked in her purse and found only pennies'. In AE, 'penny' is used informally to refer to a one-cent coin. Note that the BE expression 'the penny dropped' usually means that someone has grasped an idea. If someone is 'penniless', this means that he or she is very poor: 'Many people die virtually penniless'.

PENDANT, PENDING

pendant /'pendənt/ *noun*, is a hanging ornament worn around the neck: 'He bought her a beautiful pendant made of sapphires'.

pending /'pendɪŋ/ *adjective*, means waiting to be decided. This is a common term for business or official matters that are not processed: 'patents pending' is frequently seen on the labelling of new products. 'Pending' can also mean that something will happen soon: 'The election for the European Parliament is pending'.

PENINSULA^S, PENINSULAR^S

peninsula /pə'nɪnʃʊlə/ *noun*, is an area of land surrounded by water on three sides. The land mass of Spain and Portugal is referred to as the Iberian peninsula.

peninsular /pə'nɪnʃʊlər/ *adjective*, means something that happens on a 'peninsula'. Note this has a final 'r'. Do not confuse the two forms, even though they are pronounced the same. 'The French were defeated in the Peninsular War. This took place on the Iberian peninsula'.

PENSION, BOARD

pension /'penʃn/ *noun*, means a regular payment made by an employer or the State to people above retirement age. 'Pension' also means the rate or terms offered by a hotel or guest house. It is used in expressions like 'full pension' or 'half pension': 'Our rates include half pension', although this is now more often referred to as 'full' or 'half board'. The term 'pension' (also pronounced /'pãsjã/), can also mean a small, inexpensive hotel, usually outside Britain.

board /bɔːd/ *noun*, also refers to the rate or terms offered by a hotel or guest house. If all meals are provided, this is termed 'full board'. If only breakfast and an evening meal are provided, this is termed 'half board'. Note that in the context of hotel rates, 'board' is always used with a singular verb: 'The rate for full board is €100 a night'.

PENSIONER, SENIOR CITIZEN

pensioner /'penʃənər/ *noun*, means someone who receives a regular payment from the State, through a former employer, or from an insurance company. This is used particularly for those who receive a retirement pension: 'Special discounts for pensioners'. People in the UK who cannot work as a result of injury or other disability receive benefits, not pensions.

They are therefore referred to as being 'on disability benefit', rather than as 'pensioners'. Note that 'old-age pensioner', or OAP, is an informal term which is rather disrespectful.

senior citizen /'siːnɪə 'sɪtɪzn/ *noun*, means a person of retirement age or older. This term is considered to be more respectful than 'old-age pensioner': 'Many senior citizens have settled in warmer climates'.

PEOPLE, PEOPLES, PERSON

people /'piːpl/ *noun*, is the usual plural of 'person' in BE, and takes a plural verb: 'Those people are rich'. Note that 'people' takes a plural verb. When 'people' means a group united by race, religion, or nationality it is considered a single unit and has a singular determiner and verb: 'This peace-loving people is being driven off its land'. See **FOLK**.

peoples /'piːplz/ *noun*, refers to populations of different ethnic tribes, groups or nationalities: 'The peoples of Africa'; 'The Mediterranean peoples'.

person /'pɜːsn/ *noun*, means an individual, or someone unknown: 'There is a person outside who wishes to see you'. 'Person' is also used where references to an individual's sex might be considered inappropriate: 'We are looking for a person who can work well in a team'. When used in legal contexts: 'The crime was committed by person or persons unknown', 'person' means an unidentified individual. In AE, it is common to use the plural form 'persons', rather than 'people' if there are only a few of them. For example, 'There are three persons in the car'. 'Persons' becomes 'people' in AE for a large group.

PER, PR.

per /pɜːr/ *preposition*, means for each. Since it is not an abbreviation, a full stop is not used. 'Per' may be abbreviated to 'p.' in phrases such as *per annum (p.a.)*. 'Per' can also be combined with non Latin words, in phrases such as 'per room per night'.

pr. is a common abbreviation for 'pair', but is not used as an abbreviation for 'per'.

PER ANNUM, PER CAPITA, PER DIEM

per annum /pər 'ænəm/ *adverb*, means each year and is abbreviated 'p.a.': 'Her income is €30 000 p.a.' Recommended alternatives are 'a year' or 'annually', but avoid 'per year' in formal writing.

per capita /pə ˈkæpɪtə/ *adverb*, means for each person: 'The government calculated average income per capita'. 'Per capita' can be abbreviated 'p.c.', but this abbreviation is generally avoided due to possible confusion with PC meaning personal computer, police constable, and politically correct. The alternative 'a head' is sometimes possible, but 'per head' should be avoided in formal writing.

per diem /pə ˈdiːem/ *adverb*, means the daily allowance paid by an employer to an employee when travelling to cover hotel expenses and subsistence costs. This is often termed the travel allowance. Some companies use this term to refer to extra money to cover high living costs in large cities: 'We offer $10 000 p.a. in per diem to staff based in New York City'.

PER CENT, PERCENTAGE

per cent /pə ˈsent/ *adverb, adjective & noun*, means a specified amount in every hundred. In formal writing, the words 'per cent' are preferred to the % sign. The house style of Oxford University Press does not have space between the digit and the % sign: '33%'. 'Per cent' is written as two words in BE, but as one word in AE.

percentage /pəˈsentɪdʒ/ *noun*, is a rate for an amount that is so much in a hundred. 'Percentage' is followed by a singular or plural verb depending on the noun that it is governed by: 'Only a low percentage of his income is used for rent'; 'A high percentage of the houses are to be redecorated'. Do not use 'percentage' on its own to mean 'some' or 'a lot'. Use: 'a small/low percentage' or 'a large/high percentage'. Note that 'percentage' is written in one word in both BE and AE.

PERFECT, MORE PERFECT

perfect /ˈpɜːfɪkt/ *adjective*, is as good as something can be, and consequently 'less perfect', 'least perfect', 'more perfect' or 'most perfect' should be avoided. Recommended words to express near perfection include 'almost ~', 'nearly ~', and 'practically perfect'.

more perfect /ˈmɔː ˈpɜːfɪkt/ is used from time to time, but is not recommended in formal writing. Nevertheless, this phrase is found in the US Constitution which refers to a 'more perfect union': 'We, the People of the United States, in order to form a more perfect union ... establish this Constitution for the United States of America'.
See **ABSOLUTES AND FUZZY ABSOLUTES**.

PERHAPS, MAYBE, MAY BE

perhaps /pəˈhæps/ *adverb*, expresses uncertainty, and is used in both spoken and written English to avoid being too definite: 'A five per cent pay rise is perhaps going to be possible for the staff next year'. 'Perhaps' is more formal than 'maybe'.

maybe /ˈmeɪbiː/ *adverb*, conveys uncertainty and is more informal than 'perhaps'. 'Maybe' can always be replaced by 'perhaps' without any change in meaning: 'Maybe I'll visit Paris next year'. In formal English, it is better to write 'Perhaps I will visit Paris next year'.

may be /ˈmeɪ ˈbiː/ *verb*, expresses a possibility: 'I may be visiting Paris next year', meaning that this may or may not happen. Note that 'may be' consists of 'may' + 'be', followed by the present or past participle. It is important to stress both 'may' and 'be'.

PERIODIC, PERIODICAL

periodic /pɪərɪˈɒdɪk/ *adjective*, means appearing or occurring at intervals. There can be 'periodic' rumours about the end of the world. 'Periodic' is also used in academic and scientific terms such as the 'periodic table of elements'. See **–IC**.

periodical /pɪərɪˈɒdɪkl̩/ *adjective & noun*, as an adjective, can mean the same as 'periodic', but is used less frequently. As a noun, a 'periodical' is a magazine that is published at regular intervals.

PERMISSIBLE, PERMISSION, PERMISSIVE

permissible /pəˈmɪsɪbl̩/ *adjective*, means permitted and allowed, because no rules or laws are broken: 'It is permissible to address the jury now'. This is a formal word that may be replaced by 'allowed' or 'permitted'.
See **PERMIT ⟹ ALLOW**.

permission /pəˈmɪʃn̩/ *noun*, means being allowed to do something. 'Permission' is given by someone in authority: 'He asked for permission, and smiled when it was given'. In more formal English you may 'seek permission', and it may be 'granted'.

permissive /pəˈmɪsɪv/ *adjective*, means tolerant in the context of allowing great freedom of behaviour: 'We live in a permissive society'.

PERPENDICULAR, VERTICAL

perpendicular /pɜːpənˈdɪkjʊlər/ *adjective*, means at 90 degrees to a given line, plane or surface: 'The Leaning Tower of Pisa has never been perpendicular'.

vertical /'vɜːtɪkl̩/ *adjective*, means at 90 degrees to the horizon. This means there can be a 90-degree difference between these terms if a mountaineer climbing a vertical rockface leans on the ropes and stands perpendicular to the rockface.

See **ABSOLUTES AND FUZZY ABSOLUTES**.

ARE YOU VERTICAL OR PERPENDICULAR?

I DON'T KNOW — I'M JUST DIZZY

PERSECUTE, PROSECUTE

persecute /'pɜːsɪkjuːt/ *verb*, means to treat an individual or group cruelly and unfairly for racial, political or religious reasons: 'That minority group has been systematically moved off their land and persecuted by the rulers'. 'Persecute' can also mean to persistently annoy a person in order to make their life miserable: 'The football coach has resigned after being persecuted by the press'. The related noun is 'persecution'

prosecute /'prɒsɪkjuːt/ *verb*, means to start legal action and charge an organization or a person with a crime in a court of law. 'The company was very security conscious and has notices saying 'trespassers will be prosecuted' all round its premises'. The related noun is 'prosecution'.

PERSONAL, PERSONNEL

personal /'pɜːsn̩əl/ *adjective*, means something that belongs to an individual such as a PIN code (Personal Identification Number). It can also refer to someone's private life: 'He made some very personal remarks'. In a broader sense, 'personal' can mean designed for individual use: 'A personal computer'.

personnel /pɜːsn̩'el/ *noun*, usually means staff, and takes a plural when it means the staff employed in an organization: 'The personnel are all skilled in their own disciplines'. It takes a singular verb, however, when it refers to the part of an organization concerned with staff matters such as recruitment, discipline or welfare. Note that no determiner is used: 'Personnel was concerned at the small number of applicants for the post'. In the first sense, 'personnel' is a rather formal term, and may be replaced by 'staff' or 'employees', and occasionally 'team'. Many organizations are now abandoning the term 'personnel department' in favour of 'human resources department'.

PERSONAL IDENTIFICATION NUMBER, PIN

personal identification number /'pɜːsn̩əl aɪdentɪfɪ'keɪʃn̩ nʌmbər/ *noun*, means the number allocated to someone which is used to validate electronic transactions: 'He could not pay for the CDs because he had forgotten his PIN code'.

PIN /pɪn/ *noun*, is an abbreviation of 'personal identification number'. The expression 'PIN number' is commonly used, but as the 'N' in 'PIN' stands for 'number', many organizations use the expression 'PIN code'. See **TAUTOLOGY**.

PERSPECTIVE, PROSPECTIVE

perspective /pəs'pektɪv/ *noun*, is the way solid objects in space are represented on a flat surface. Figuratively it means a way of thinking about something that takes its relative importance into account: 'We need to put this matter into perspective before it turns into a huge problem'.

prospective /prəs'pektɪv/ *adjective*, is a formal word meaning likely to happen or to be expected: 'There are many prospective benefits in this new law'.

PERVERSE, PERVERT

perverse /pə'vɜːs/ *adjective*, means that a person is deliberate and obstinate and behaves in a way that most people find unreasonable or unacceptable: 'He took a perverse delight in harming small animals and pets'.

pervert /'pɜːvɜːt/ *noun* & *verb* /pə'vɜːt/, as a noun, means a person whose sexual behaviour is abnormal and unacceptable: 'He has become a complete pervert'. Note that the stress is on

the first syllable. As a verb, 'pervert' means to change something such as a system or behaviour so that the result is immoral or completely unacceptable: 'Many people fear that computer games have perverted some children's sense of violence'. Note that the stress is on the second syllable. The legal phrase 'to pervert the course of justice' means not to tell the truth, thus making it difficult for the police to investigate a crime.
See **SICK** ⟹ **ILL**.

A newspaper reported that 'the man was charged with attempting to pervert the court'.

PETROL, GAS, GASOLINE

petrol /'petrəl/ *noun*, is the BE term for refined petroleum used as fuel for cars: 'She filled her car up at the petrol station'.

gas /gæs/ *noun & verb*, as a noun, is an air-like fluid substance in BE. 'Gas' is a substance that can be used for cooking or heating. In AE, 'gas' has two meanings: the air-like substance as in BE and the short form for 'gasoline'. The plural is 'gases'. As a verb, this means to harm or kill with gas: 'Many of the coal miners were gassed to death in the accident'. Note the doubling of the 's' in the forms 'gassing' and 'gassed'.

gasoline /'gæsəli:n/ *noun*, is the AE term for 'petrol' and has the abbreviation 'gas' in AE. The AE equivalent of 'petrol station' is 'gas station'.

PHENOMENON, PHENOMENA

phenomenon /fɪ'nɒmɪnən/ *noun*, means a fact or situation that occurs or exists: 'We are looking at an interesting natural phenomenon on this reef'.

phenomena /fɪ'nɒmɪnə/ *noun*, is the plural of 'phenomenon'. Always write and say 'these phenomena are ...', not 'this phenomena is ...'. 'Phenomenons' is not an acceptable plural of 'phenomenon'.

PHILIPPINES, FILIPINO, FILIPINA

Philippines, the /'fɪlɪpi:nz/, is an island republic in the Pacific Ocean. Its official name in English is 'Republic of the Philippines'. Note the spelling with initial 'Ph-', and that the final syllable rhymes with 'beans'.
See **DEFINITE ARTICLE**.

Filipino /fɪlɪ'pi:nəʊ/ *noun & adjective*, is either a male native of the Philippines: 'Measures have been initiated to improve the employment situation among Filipinos', or the name of the national language: 'Do you speak Filipino?'

Filipina /fɪlɪ'pi:nə/ *noun & adjective*, is a female native of the Philippines: 'The Filipina singer was a great success'. Note that this nationality noun and adjective distinguishes between the sexes and that they are spelt with initial 'F'.

PHONE, CALL, RING

phone /fəʊn/ *noun & verb*, as a noun, is the standard short form of 'telephone' /'telɪfəʊn/, and should not be spelt with an apostrophe as in: 'phone. When giving a phone number in writing, the abbreviation 'tel.' is often placed in front. As a verb, this means to speak to someone on the phone: 'I'll phone you at 6'. Note that using 'telephone' as a verb is rather formal and is used mainly in BE.
See **TELEPHONE NUMBERS**.

call /kɔ:l/ *noun & verb*, as a noun, means a phone conversation: 'I'll take that call upstairs'. As a verb, 'call' means to speak to someone on the phone: 'I'll call a taxi for you'.

ring /rɪŋ/ *noun*, can have the meaning of a phone call in informal BE: 'Tell John that I will give him a ring tonight'.

ring (1) /rɪŋ/ *verb*. means to make a bell produce a sound, or (especially in BE), to make a phone call. It can also refer to the object making the sound: 'The phone/alarm clock is ringing'. The past tense is 'rang' /ræŋ/: 'He rang the bell', and the past participle is 'rung' /rʌŋ/: 'I have rung the bell'.

ring (2) /rɪŋ/ *verb*. means to encircle or surround: 'Please ring the correct answer on the exam paper'. It would be more common to say 'put a circle around' in this sense. This verb has the past tense and past participle forms 'ringed' /rɪŋd/: 'The field was ringed by security guards'.

PHOTOGRAPH, PHOTOGRAPHER, PHOTOGRAPHY

photograph /'fəʊtəgrɑ:f/ *noun*, means a picture taken by a camera. Often the abbreviation 'photo' (plural 'photos') is used in informal English: 'We got some good photos of the kids'. A photograph is always a thing, never a person.

photographer /fə'tɒgrəfər/ *noun*, means a person who takes photographs: 'Some eager photographers followed the Prince'. Remember to put the stress on the second syllable.

photography /fə'tɒgrəfi/ *noun*, is the art or process of taking a photograph: 'Digital technology has revolutionized photography'.

'The model said that she had been chased by many photographs.'

---

phrasal verbs

A **phrasal verb** is a verb combined with either a preposition or an adverb to create a new or extended meaning, which may appear to have little to do with the basic meaning of the verb. Some examples with *come* are *come in* (to enter or become fashionable), *come out* (to make an exit or admit to being gay), *come up* (happen), *come to* (wake up, especially after being unconscious rather than asleep), *come through* (to arrive or succeed).

PHYSICIAN, PHYSICIST

physician /fɪ'zɪʃn/ *noun*, is the normal term used in AE for someone who is qualified to practise medicine and should be used for a medical doctor who does not carry out surgery. In BE the term is used in the names of institutions such as the Royal College of Physicians, but otherwise, use doctor or GP (general practitioner): 'If you continue to feel unwell, you should visit your GP'.

physicist /'fɪzɪsɪst/ *noun*, means an expert in physics. 'She is a brilliant nuclear physicist'.

PHYSICS, PHYSIQUE

physics /'fɪzɪks/ *noun*, is the academic study of the nature and properties of matter and energy particularly phenomena such as heat, light, sound and electricity. Like other academic subjects ending with '-ics', 'physics' takes a singular verb when it means the discipline: 'Physics is her favourite subject'. See **-ICS**.

physique /fɪ'ziːk/ *noun*, is the form, size and development of a person's body. 'He had a well-developed physique'.

> ⚠️ 'She studied physiques and spent many hours in the lab.' (Student essay)

PICTURESQUE, PICARESQUE

picturesque /pɪktʃʊ'resk/ *adjective*, means visually attractive and charming: 'This is a picturesque village'. Language can also be termed 'picturesque' if it is vivid and unusual.

picaresque /pɪkə'resk/ *adjective*, is an epic style in literature that presents the adventures of a dishonest but likeable hero: '*The Adventures of Tom Jones* and *Tristram Shandy* are two 18th century examples of English picaresque novels'.

PINCERS, PLIERS

pincers /'pɪnsəz/ *noun*, are tools for grasping things that have sharp rounded jaws with a circular space between them: 'He gripped the nail head firmly in the pincers'. This takes a plural verb.

pliers /'plaɪəz/ *noun*, are also tools for grasping things that have long and somewhat tapering jaws to bend or cut wire: 'The wire was twisted into a circle using the pliers'. This takes a plural verb. See **PAIR**.

PITIFUL, PITIABLE

pitiful /'pɪtɪfʊl/ *adjective*, means shameful, and not worthy of respect: 'The firm paid pitiful wages'.

pitiable /'pɪtɪəbl/ *adjective*, means in poor condition and worthy of compassion: 'The poor old man was in a pitiable state'.

PLACE, PUT

place /pleɪs/ *verb*, means to position something carefully or exactly in a particular situation: 'We placed the table by the window'. It can be used figuratively, as in: 'This placed the government in a difficult situation'. 'Place' is often used as an alternative to 'put', especially in written English.

put /pʊt/ *verb*, means almost the same as 'place', but when something is 'put' in a position this implies less care and neatness than 'place': 'She put her heavy bag down'. 'Put' is less formal than 'place', and is the basis of many phrasal verbs.

PLAIN^S, PLANE^S

plain /pleɪn/ *noun & adjective*, as a noun, means a large area of flat country like the Great Plains in the USA. As an adjective, 'plain' can mean insignificant: 'She wore plain clothes and was a typical ordinary girl'. The expression 'to make something plain' means to make it clear, and 'plain sailing' refers to a situation that develops without any difficulties: 'I found the first exam question hard, but after that it was plain sailing'. See **ORDINARY ⇨ USUAL**.

plane /pleɪn/ *noun*, means a level surface. In a figurative sense, it means a different level: 'On a spiritual plane'. 'Plane' is also an abbreviation for 'aeroplane' (BE), and 'airplane' (AE). See **AIRCRAFT**.

PLAN, PLANNING

plan /plæn/ *noun*, means a detailed proposal for how to do something: 'We drew up a training plan'. 'Plan' also means intention, and in this sense, it is often used in the plural: 'What are your plans for the future?' The associated verb is also 'plan'.

planning /ˈplænɪŋ/ *noun*, is the process of making plans. Both 'plan' and 'planning' may be the cause of tautology, as a 'plan' must refer to the future. Thus 'future plans' or 'future planning' should be used with care, unless there is a contrast with 'present plans' or 'earlier plans'. See **TAUTOLOGY**.

PLATFORM, BAY, GATE (TRANSPORT)

platform /ˈplætfɔːm/ *noun*, means the raised area in a railway station where trains can be boarded: 'The train now approaching Platform 4 is the 13.20 for Nottingham'. This is termed 'track' in AE.

bay /beɪ/ *noun*, is used for coach services in a bus terminus to show where the different coaches or long-distance buses depart from: 'The service to Cambridge departs from Bay 6'.

gate /geɪt/ *noun*, is used in airports to show where planes depart from: 'BA flight 126 to Amsterdam is now boarding from Gate 16'.

PLC, LTD

Plc and **PLC** /ˈpiː el ˈsiː/ are BE abbreviations for **p**ublic **l**imited **c**ompany. A British company which is eligible for listing on the London Stock Exchange always has 'plc' after its name. See **COMPANY ⇨ BUSINESS**.

Ltd. /ˈlɪmɪtɪd/ (BE), /ˈel tiː ˈdiː/ (AE), is short for 'limited', and is used by incorporated companies which are not listed on the Stock Exchange: 'The liability of the owners of limited companies is limited to the amount of their shareholding'.

PLEASE, PLEASE FIND ENCLOSED..., ENCLOSED PLEASE FIND

please /pliːz/ *exclamation*, is a polite way of asking for something. The word has little significance except for showing politeness: 'Please pay attention'; 'Two beers, please'.

Please find enclosed or **enclosed please find** are old-fashioned business English expressions sometimes found as an opening phrase in a letter. It is better to use: 'I enclose' or 'We enclose'. Note that enclose is used for letters, but 'attach' is frequently used with emails.

plural nouns

standard formation:

- Most English plurals are formed by adding an *s* to the singular form. There are some irregular plurals that have survived from Old English. These include:
  brother ~ brethren (only for religious orders); *child ~ children*; *foot ~ feet*; *goose ~ geese**; *louse ~ lice*; *man ~ men*; *mouse ~ mice*; *ox ~ oxen*; *tooth ~ teeth*; *woman ~ women* (/ˈwʊmən ~ ˈwɪmɪn/)
  * but note that the plural of *mongoose* is *mongooses*.

- There are many examples of plural nouns which have no singular form:
  cattle   clergy   gentry   police   vermin

• Those that represent groups of people can often be made singular by adding *a member of*, for example *a member of the clergy/gentry*.

compound nouns:

• Compound nouns are formed by adding *s* to the most significant word, which is not necessarily the last word. Examples: *deputy judges; lieutenant colonels; trade unions; attorneys at law; lords lieutenant; daughters-in-law; goings-on; passers-by; hangers-on.*

foreign plurals:

• Many nouns of foreign origin have adopted the English plural *-s*: *piano ~ pianos; kilo ~ kilos, sauna ~ saunas*, but nouns borrowed from the classical languages (Latin and Greek) and French often retain the plural spellings of their origins.

nouns of Latin origin:

• *-a* becomes *-ae* (some nouns have an alternative in *-as*)
alumna ~ alumnae; antenna ~ antennae (zoological use) / *antennas* (radio aerials); *formula ~ formulae/formulas*. Note that the plural of *agenda* must always be *agendas*.

• *-ex* becomes *-ices* (some nouns have an alternative in *-exes*)
index ~ indices/indexes; vertex ~ vertices; vortex ~ vortices

• *-is* becomes *-es*
analysis ~ analyses; axis ~ axes; basis ~ bases; crisis ~ crises; hypothesis ~ hypotheses; oasis ~ oases; parenthesis ~ parentheses; synopsis ~ synopses; thesis ~ theses

• *-ix* becomes *-ices* (some nouns have an alternative in *-ixes*)
appendix ~ appendices/appendixes; helix ~ helices; matrix ~ matrices; radix ~ radices

• *-um* becomes *-a* (some nouns have an alternative in *-ums*)
consortium ~ consortia; curriculum ~ curricula/curriculums; datum ~ data; equilibrium ~ equilibria; erratum ~ errata; forum ~ forums/fora (only in the archaeological sense of a Roman marketplace); *medium ~ media* (in most senses)/*mediums* (intermediaries with the spirit world); *memorandum ~ memoranda/memorandums; referendum ~ referenda/referendums* (different meanings); *stratum ~ strata; symposium ~ symposia/symposiums.*

• *-us* becomes *-i* (some nouns have an alternative in *-uses*)
alumnus ~ alumni; focus ~ focuses/foci; nucleus ~ nuclei; radius ~ radii/radiuses; stimulus ~ stimuli; syllabus ~ syllabuses/syllabi (rare); *terminus ~ termini*

• *-us* becomes *-ra* with change of preceding vowel
corpus ~ corpora; genus ~ genera; opus ~ opera (but *opera* is also a singular noun for a staged musical work, with plural *operas*)

• *-us* becomes *-uses*
crocus ~ crocuses; omnibus ~ omnibuses; octopus ~ octopuses
Note these are the only standard plurals of these words.

nouns of Greek origin:

• *-a* may become *-ata* with alternative *-as*
dogma ~ dogmas; stigma ~ stigmas/stigmata

• *-on* becomes *-a*
criterion ~ criteria; oxymoron ~ oxymora; phenomenon ~ phenomena

nouns of French origin:

• *-eau* becomes *-eaux* (some nouns have an alternative in *-s*)
bureau ~ bureaux/bureaus; château ~ châteaux; gateau ~ gateaux/gateaus
See **AGREEMENT BETWEEN SUBJECT AND VERB**.
See **-F, -FE ENDINGS IN NOUNS**.

POLITICAL, POLITICS, POLICY

political /pəˈlɪtɪkl/ *adjective*, means relating to the State or public affairs: 'These political plans might be successful'. When used of a person, 'political' means interested in politics: 'Her experience as a staff representative made her very political in her outlook'.

politics /ˈpɒlɪtɪks/ *noun*, means governing, debating about how to manage a country or relations between states: 'The mayor is a leading figure in local politics'. Use a plural verb when you mean political sympathies: 'John's politics are a matter for him, not for me'. Use a singular verb elsewhere: 'Global politics is becoming a key issue'. See **-ICS**.

policy /ˈpɒlɪsi/ *noun*, means a course or principle for action by a government, party or company: 'We have a clear policy on environmental issues'. 'Policy' may also be an insurance contract.

POPULAR, POPULOUS[S], POPULACE[S], POPULATION

popular /'pɒpjʊlər/ *adjective*, means someone or something that is liked or admired by many people: 'Television has made some sports incredibly popular'. It is also used to refer to ideas, beliefs or opinions that are shared by many people: 'His campaign quickly gained popular support'.

populous /'pɒpjʊləs/ *adjective*, refers to an area where a large number of people gather or live: 'Some of the most populous parts of Asia are exposed to the danger of flooding'. A less formal alternative is 'highly populated'.

populace /'pɒpjʊləs/ *noun*, means all the ordinary people living in a country or area: 'Some western journalists never seem to grasp the views of the populace in this part of the world'. Note that the definite article is normally used with 'populace'. A less formal equivalent is 'the general public', or 'people'.

population /pɒpjʊ'leɪʃn̩/ *noun*, means all the citizens of a country or area, regardless of their status or social rank: 'The rural population is increasing in size'.

PORE[S], POUR[S]

pore /pɔːr/ *noun & verb*, as a noun, means a minute opening in a surface, commonly the skin. As a verb, this means to study with great attention: 'She pored over her textbooks'.

pour /pɔːr/ *verb*, means to cause a liquid to flow rapidly: 'They poured the sour milk down the drain'. It is also used in figurative idioms such as: 'It never rains, but it pours'.

PORTABLE, TRANSPORTABLE

portable /'pɔːtəbl̩/ *adjective*, means an object that is lighter than a standard object and can be easily carried: 'A portable television'.

transportable /træns'pɔːtəbl̩/ *adjective*, means something that can be moved or transported, but not with the ease of a portable unit: 'A transportable power unit'.

POSITIVE, NEGATIVE

positive /'pɒzɪtɪv/ *adjective*, refers to feelings of hope and encouragement: 'They are extremely positive about developments'. It can also mean to be certain about something: 'Are you positive you saw her?' In a scientific sense, a test which is 'positive' shows that some substance is found to be present: 'The athlete tested positive for steroids'.

negative /'negətɪv/ *adjective*, refers to something that is harmful: 'The teacher's racist jokes had a very negative influence on the children'. It can also mean discouraged, and looking on the bad side: 'She is a difficult person because she is always so negative about everything'. If an answer is 'negative' that means it is a 'no': 'We expected an affirmative answer about that bank loan, but instead we got a negative one'. In a scientific sense, a test which is 'negative' shows that some substance is not found or is not present: 'The pregnancy test was negative'.

POSTCODE, ZIP CODE

postcode /'pəʊstkəʊd/ *noun*, is a sequence of letters and numbers assigned to addresses in countries such as Britain to enable post to be sorted automatically. The initial letters give some indication of the nearest large town, city, or in the case of London, the postal district. This is also called the 'postal code'.

zip code /'zɪp kəʊd/ *noun*, is the five- or nine-digit number given to locations in the USA to assist in the sorting of post. The numbers run east to west, so that locations in Maine begin with 0 and those in Hawaii with 9. 'Zip' is an acronym for **z**one **i**mprovement **p**lan.

POTENT, STRONG

potent /'pəʊtənt/ *adjective*, means both strong and powerful. 'Potent' is restricted to contexts such as medicine, drink and argument: 'He had a very potent argument for the new licensing laws'. Note that calling a drink 'potent', focuses on its effect. 'Potent' is often used for liquids that taste or smell very strong: 'She was wearing a very potent fragrance'.

strong /strɒŋ/ *adjective*, refers to the power to move heavy objects or do physically demanding tasks: 'He lifted the twins in his strong arms'. 'Strong' is also used about a person or object that can withstand pressure or wear: 'The strong nerves of the teacher helped him to survive'; 'Strong, durable cloth'. Note that calling a drink 'strong', focuses on its intense flavour or concentrated volume of alcohol.

POUND, OUNCE

pound /paʊnd/ *noun*, is a unit of weight in the imperial system (0.45 kg). This is abbreviated to 'lb'. 'Pound' is also the unit of currency in several countries including Britain (pound sterling). The recommended abbreviation for the British currency is the ISO currency code GBP. Otherwise, the symbol '£' is also used. This is read as 'pound'. The origin of both 'lb' and '£' is the Latin 'libra' (pound).

ounce /aʊns/ *noun*, is also a unit of weight in the imperial system (1 ounce equals about 28g). It is used figuratively to mean the last bit: 'We pushed the car and used every ounce of strength'. 'Oz.' is the abbreviation and is read as 'ounce'.

P.P., SIGNED BY

p.p. is used when someone signs a letter by authority or proxy because his or her superior is not available: 'Yours sincerely, John Jones p.p. Charles Baker'. 'p.p.' is the abbreviation for the Latin 'per pro' which is never used. See **P**.

signed by ... in the absence of ... is common in AE and is the equivalent of 'p.p.'.

PRACTICAL, PRACTICABLE

practical /'præktɪkl̩/ *adjective*, means useful or sensible, as opposed to theoretical. Things which are 'practical' are connected with real situations, not ideas: 'The new tax was a practical solution to air pollution'. The negative forms of 'practical' are 'impractical' and 'unpractical'.

practicable /'præktɪkəbl̩/ *adjective*, means feasible, able to be done, possible, or capable of being put into practice. It can also mean easy to use. Consequently a plan, method, or suggestion may be both 'practical' and 'practicable'. The negative form of 'practicable' is 'impracticable'.

PRACTICE⁵, PRACTISE⁵, PRACTITIONER

practice /'præktɪs/ *noun*, means the use of an idea or method: 'He put the principles of work organization into practice'. 'Best practice' is a term that is used to comment on a high quality method or approach. 'Practice' is the spelling of the noun in BE and AE. But note that in AE, 'practice' is also the common spelling of the verb: 'Practice your American spelling'.

practise /'præktɪs/ *verb*, usually means to repeat actions in order to become more skilled: 'He had to practise his part every day before the concert'. Fully qualified professionals, such as doctors and lawyers, are said to 'practise' their profession: 'How long have you been practising medicine?' This spelling with an 's' only occurs in BE.

practitioner /præk'tɪʃənər/ *noun*, means a person who works in a profession such as law, medicine or dentistry. The expression 'general practitioner' (GP) means a medical doctor in BE who is in direct contact with his or her patients.

PRECEDENCE, PRECEDENT

precedence /'presɪdəns/ *noun*, means to be more important and to be given priority: 'His wish to remain in power took precedence over his family responsibilities'. Note that 'order of precedence' involves ranking: 'The guests were seated in order of precedence'. This is a formal word.

precedent /'presɪdənt/ *noun*, is an earlier event or decision that may serve as an example or rule for a later one: 'The judge's ruling has set a precedent'. This is also a formal word.

PRECEDING, EARLIER

preceding /prɪ'siːdɪŋ/ *adjective*, refers to what comes immediately before: 'In the preceding entry it was shown how to handle 'precedent''. Note that the indefinite article cannot be used before 'preceding'. Never confuse this word with 'proceeding'. 'Preceding' is a formal word. See **PROCEED**.

earlier /'ɜːlɪər/ *adverb*, means before. Note that this word is not as precise as 'preceding', as it does not give the exact context. Compare 'an earlier section of this report' (no exact reference given) to 'the preceding section' (the section immediately before this one).

PRECIPITOUS, STEEP

precipitous /prɪ'sɪpɪtəs/ *adjective*, means very steep, and implies a sharp descent or drop: 'The group moved away from the edge because of the precipitous slope'.

steep /stiːp/ *adjective*, means sharply rising or falling: 'We noticed a steep drop in temperature in the room'. It can also be used to refer to a sharp gradient: 'The cliff is too steep to climb without the proper equipment'.

In informal English, 'steep' can mean unreasonable when referring to prices. In this sense it is usually modified by 'rather', 'pretty', or 'a bit': 'Fifteen pounds to mend a pair of shoes seems a bit steep'.

PREFIX, SUFFIX, AFFIX

prefix /'priːfɪks/ *noun*, means a letter or group of letters added to the beginning of a word, such as 'co', 'in', 'un' in words like 'cooperate', 'independent', and 'unhappy'. BE dictionaries may separate the two parts by hyphens in order to avoid confusion, for example, 're-cover' (to cover again) and 'recover' (to get better after an illness). See **HYPHENATION IN INDIVIDUAL WORDS**. See **NEGATIVE PREFIXES**.

suffix /'sʌfɪks/ *noun*, means a letter or group of letters added to the end of a word, such as 'ly', 'less' and 'ness' in words like 'quickly', 'careless', and 'goodness'.

affix /'æfɪks/ *noun*, means a letter or group of letters added to the beginning or end of a word to change its meaning. Thus 'affix' means both 'prefix' and 'suffix': For instance, the word 'independent' has the prefix 'in', and 'suddenly' has the suffix 'ly'. Both 'in' and 'ly' are affixes.

PREMIER, PREMIERE

premier /'premɪər/ (BE), /prɪ'mjɪr/ (AE) *noun & adjective*, as a noun, means the first minister, or prime minister. As an adjective, this means foremost: 'England's premier racing driver'. However, this use is fairly restricted. Alternatives are 'desirable', 'superior' or 'attractive'.

premiere /'premɪeər/ *noun*, means a first public performance: 'The premiere attracted most of Berlin society'. 'Premiere' is not spelt with an accent in modern English.

PREMISE, PREMISES

premise /'premɪs/ *noun*, means the underlying basis of an argument: 'The fundamental premise of the report is wrong'. It also means something that can be assumed: 'Detectives are working on the premise that the criminal is a local man'. A less formal alternative in the latter case is 'assumption'.

premises /'premɪsɪz/ *noun*, means both the plural of 'premise' and also a house, site, block of offices, or building occupied or owned by a person or company. 'Licensed premises' mean a pub in BE.

prepositions

A **preposition** is a function word that indicates either the relationship between somebody or something and its position in time and space, or a method of doing something. Although the use of prepositions is often difficult, this book has listed many of the common ones in groups. Prepositions are also used in many phrasal verbs. See **PHRASAL VERBS**.

PRESCRIBE, PROSCRIBE

prescribe /prɪ'skraɪb/ *verb*, is to lay down a rule, to advise or specify: 'The doctor prescribed a course of injections'. Its related noun is 'prescription'.

proscribe /prəʊ'skraɪb/ *verb*, means to prohibit: 'Doctors have proscribed this new drug, because it is very dangerous'. The corresponding noun is 'proscription'. A less formal alternative is 'prohibit'.

PRICE, COST

price /praɪs/ *noun*, means the amount of money that has to be paid for something in order to buy it: 'The average price of a house has risen by 15% this year'.

cost /kɒst/ *noun*, also means the amount of money needed to pay for an object but it is also used to refer to the price of services and processes, such as the 'cost of living' and 'production costs'. 'Cost' in a broader sense can mean the effort or loss involved in doing something: 'The cost of industrial pollution to the environment has been enormous'.

PRIMARY SCHOOL, JUNIOR SCHOOL, SECONDARY SCHOOL

primary school /'praɪməri skuːl/ *noun*, in Britain means a school where young children are taught from the age of five. In the USA, 'primary school' often refers to the first three or four years in grade school and even the kindergarten. There is also a good deal of variation in the UK and the USA about the use of this term.

junior school /'dʒuːnɪə skuːl/ *noun*, is part of the compulsory education system in England and Wales and is typically for pupils aged between 7 and 11.

secondary school /'sekəndri skuːl/ *noun*, is the general term used in the UK for education from 11 to 16: 'The local secondary school is one of the best in the area'. See **SCHOOL**.

PRIMEVAL, PRIMITIVE

primeval /praɪˈmiːvəl/ *adjective*, refers to the earliest ages in the history of the world: 'The landscape was like a primeval forest'.

primitive /ˈprɪmɪtɪv/ *adjective*, means at an early stage of evolution or historical development: 'Primitive tools from the first settlers were found on the island'.

PRINCIPLE⁵, PRINCIPAL⁵

principle /ˈprɪnsɪpl/ *noun*, means a fundamental truth or course of action: 'We respect the basic principles of racial equality'. 'Principle' can also mean a belief or moral standard: 'He was a man of principle who never compromised his values'.

principal /ˈprɪnsɪpl/ *noun & adjective*, as a noun, means someone in authority. The principal of a school or college in AE is known as 'the head teacher', or simply 'the head' in BE. As an adjective, 'principal' means the main or most important: 'My principal role in this company is to oversee the budget'.

⚠️ *George Smith, Principle Scientist (On a business card)*

PRIVATE SCHOOL, PUBLIC SCHOOL

private school /ˈpraɪvɪt ˈskuːl/ *noun phrase*, means a school run by an individual or company, often for profit, and funded from fees paid by the pupils' families. Often many or all of the pupils live (or 'board') at the school, and 'boarding school' is an alternative name in the UK. Another name for 'private school' in England and Wales is 'independent school'. This contrasts with 'state school', which is publically funded.

public school /ˈpʌblɪk ˈskuːl/ *noun phrase*, in most parts of the English-speaking world except England and Wales, means a school paid for by the State. In England and Wales, however, a public school is an independent school that is mainly funded by fees paid by parents. There are about 200 public schools in England and Wales and traditionally many of the male leaders and public figures in Britain were pupils or 'old boys' of public schools such as Eton and Harrow. Today, most of the public schools in England and Wales admit boys and girls.

PRIZE⁵, PRISE⁵

prize /praɪz/ *noun*, means something awarded for winning a contest or competition: 'He was awarded the Nobel Peace Prize'. It can also mean outstanding, as with 'a prize bull'. However 'a prize idiot' means a complete idiot.

prise /praɪz/ *verb*, means to use force to open something with difficulty: 'If we can't get in through the door we will have to prise the window open'. It also means to obtain with force: 'It is difficult to prise any information out of them'. In AE this is spelt 'prize'.

PRO, CON

pro /prəʊ/ *noun*, means the arguments for. The idiomatic expression 'pros and cons' means the arguments both for and against a proposal.

con /kɒn/ *noun*, means the arguments against and is an abbreviation of *contra*.

PROCEED, PRECEDE, PROCEEDINGS

proceed /prəʊˈsiːd/ *verb*, means to pursue a course of action: 'The two governments are now proceeding with the peace negotiations'. It can also mean to move forward, or advance: 'Passengers are asked to proceed to Gate 11'. In this second sense, 'proceed' is a formal word.

precede /prɪˈsiːd/ *verb*, means to be in front of someone or something: 'That matter was discussed in the preceding meeting'. In another sense, 'precede' means go ahead of: 'The howls from the dogs preceded the earthquake'.

proceedings /prəʊˈsiːdɪŋz/ *noun*, means events, or the minutes of a formal meeting. In conferences, the proceedings are the written record that includes the papers and presentations given. In a legal sense, 'proceedings' means what happens in a court of law to settle a dispute: 'Unless payment is received by 31 January, we will bring legal proceedings against you'.

PRODIGY, PROGENY

prodigy /ˈprɒdɪdʒi/ *noun*, means an exceptionally skilled person, usually a child: 'The Chinese gymnast was a child prodigy'.

progeny /ˈprɒdʒəni/ *noun*, means offspring or descendants and may take either a singular or plural verb: 'The progeny of mixed English and Scottish marriages often has/have a problem deciding its/their sporting loyalties'. This is a formal word.

PRODUCE, PRODUCT, PRODUCTION

produce /'prɒdjuːs/ *noun* & /prə'djuːs/ *verb*, as a noun, means things made or grown in large quantities. 'Produce' is usually associated with farming: 'A lot of dairy produce is being imported'. Note that the stress is on the first syllable. As a verb, 'produce' means to grow something or to manufacture it: 'The factory produced all kinds of furniture'. Note that the stress is on the second syllable.

product /'prɒdʌkt/ *noun*, is a thing that is grown or produced for sale such as farm products. 'Products' can also be the result of industrial manufacturing such as steel products. It is also used about people to mean the result: 'The minister was regarded as a typical product of the upper class'. Various types of product from the same source make up a 'product range', and secondary products of a reaction or industrial process may be termed 'by-products'. See **BY-**.

production /prə'dʌkʃn/ *noun*, is the process of growing food or manufacturing things: 'The production of biological weapons should be banned'. Apart from its use in agriculture and manufacturing, the entertainment industry also uses the term 'production': 'That talk-show was a controversial production'.

PROFESSOR, PROF.

professor /prə'fesər/ *noun*, in BE is a university academic with the highest rank. 'Professorships' are also called chairs. In AE, 'professor' is used for almost all university teachers.

prof. is an informal abbreviation of 'professor' and should be avoided by careful writers and speakers.

PROGRAMME[S], PROGRAM[S]

programme /'prəʊgræm/ *noun* & *verb*, as a noun, means a plan, a course of study, instructions or a TV/radio performance: 'The research programme will include methods of human resources development'. As a verb, 'programme' means to plan, cause action or give instructions: 'The committee will programme its research work'. This is the BE spelling. The AE spelling for the noun and verb forms is 'program'.

program /'prəʊgræm/ *noun* & *verb*, as a noun, means software. As a verb, this means the programming of software: 'To program a computer'. Note that the person doing the computer programming is spelt 'programmer'.

PROHIBIT, FORBID

prohibit /prəʊ'hɪbɪt/ *verb*, means to stop someone from doing something by law: 'It is strictly prohibited to serve alcohol to those under 18'. It also refers to a situation that makes something impossible: 'The high cost of land prohibits the building of a new golf course'. The associated adjective and noun forms are 'prohibitive' and 'prohibition'.

forbid /fə'bɪd/ *verb*, means not to allow and usually relates to actions or personal authority: 'We can't get married because my parents have forbidden it'.

PRONE, PROSTRATE

prone /prəʊn/ *adjective*, means lying facing downwards: 'The gunman was found lying in a prone position'. 'Prone' combined with 'to' means likely to do something badly, or to suffer from something: 'Footballers are prone to knee injuries'.

prostrate /'prɒstreɪt/ *adjective* & /prɒs'treɪt/ *verb*, as an adjective, means lying down, but often has the added meaning of feeling weak through shock or illness: 'The severe attack of pneumonia left him prostrate for a month'. As a verb, this term is used if someone is lying down in order to express adoration or submission: 'He prostrated himself before the paramount chief'. Note that the position of the stress changes between the adjective and verb.

PRONOUNCE, PRONUNCIATION

pronounce /prə'naʊns/ *verb*, means to make the sound of a letter or word: 'It is difficult to pronounce the name of that village correctly'. 'Pronounce' also means to make a formal public declaration, for which the associated noun form is 'pronouncement'.

pronunciation /prənʌnsi'eɪʃn/ *noun*, is the way sounds or words are produced in a language: 'His Spanish pronunciation needs some correction'. Note the differences in spelling, pronunciation and stress in these two words.

> Two tourists in Wales were getting off a bus at a town called Pwllheli. They said to the driver: 'Can you pronounce where we are, very slowly?' The driver replied: 'Bussssssss Staaaaaaaaationnnnnn'.

PROPAGANDA, PUBLICITY

propaganda /ˌprɒpə'gændə/ *noun*, means the organized spreading of information to form public opinion by false or misleading news. Propaganda always takes a singular verb: 'A lot of hostile propaganda was written about the party'. See **SPIN**.

publicity /pʌb'lɪsɪti/ *noun*, means the organized spread of information, but is a neutral term compared with 'propaganda'. Like 'propaganda', it also takes a singular verb: 'Publicity does amazing things to people'.

PROPHECY, PROPHESY

prophecy /'prɒfəsi/ *noun*, means the prediction of what will happen in future, usually in connection with religion or magic: 'He made a prophecy about a new age'.

prophesy /'prɒfəsaɪ/ *verb*, means to say what will happen in the future. Note the spelling and pronunciation differences between these two words.

PROPOSAL, PROPOSITION

proposal /prə'pəʊzl̩/ *noun*, means a plan that is put forward for consideration, particularly in a formal context: 'The party presented a controversial proposal to raise sales taxes'. A 'proposal' is also an offer of marriage: 'She politely turned down his proposal'.

proposition /ˌprɒpə'zɪʃn̩/ *noun*, means a suggestion or scheme to be considered, particularly in business and investment: 'Buying that TV station could be an attractive proposition'. A proposition also means something that is problematic. 'Getting across town in the rush hour is a real proposition'.

PROVED, PROVEN

proved /pruːvd/ *past participle*, is one of the past participles of 'to prove', and is the more common past participle form in BE: 'Can it be conclusively proved that he stole the money?'

proven /'pruːvən/ *past participle*, is one of the past participles of 'to prove', and is only used as a past participle form of 'to prove' in AE and for the Scottish legal verdict 'not proven'. In BE 'proven' is only used as an adjective: 'He has a proven sales record'. (Note that 'proved' cannot be used here.)

PUBLIC, AUDIENCE, CONGREGATION, SPECTATORS, ONLOOKERS

public /'pʌblɪk/ *noun*, means people as a whole and is always used with 'the': 'This library is open to the public all year round'. 'Public' can also refer to people with a common interest in a specific activity: 'The theatre-going public still enjoy Shakespeare'. Note that 'public' can take either a singular or a plural verb. See **COLLECTIVE NOUNS**.

audience /'ɔːdɪəns/ *noun*, means a group of people who are watching a cultural event (theatre, show, cinema, concert, TV etc.) or readership: 'She is a novelist with a wide audience'. The audience is nearly always inside a building: 'The audience in the TV studio had to be told when to clap'. Note that 'audience' can take either a singular or a plural verb. See **COLLECTIVE NOUNS**. See **VIEWER**.

congregation /ˌkɒŋgrɪ'geɪʃn̩/ *noun*, only refers to the gathering at a religious service: 'He addressed the congregation in a straightforward manner'. Note that 'congregation' can take either a singular or a plural verb. See **COLLECTIVE NOUNS**.

spectators /spek'teɪtəz/ *noun*, means a group of people at a sporting event or a show who intend to watch the event: 'There was a large crowd of interested spectators at the match'.

onlookers /'ɒnlʊkəz/ *noun*, means people who watch something but do not get as involved as an audience or spectators: 'A crowd of onlookers gathered to watch the two women arguing in the street'.

PUBLIC HOLIDAY, BANK HOLIDAY

public holiday /pʌblɪk 'hɒlɪdeɪ/ *noun phrase*, means any national holiday (New Year's Day, Christmas Day) which may be on any day of the week.

bank holiday /bæŋk 'hɒlɪdeɪ/ *noun phrase*, in the UK means a holiday on a weekday, generally a Monday, when banks, public offices, and most other businesses, are officially closed: 'Are you going anywhere for the bank holiday?' In AE, a 'bank holiday' is a weekday when banks are closed, usually on special instructions from the Federal Administration.

PUNCTUAL, PRECISE

punctual /'pʌŋktʃʊəl/ *adjective*, means doing something or meeting at the agreed time: 'He is so punctual that you can set your watch by him'.

precise /prɪˈsaɪs/ *adjective*, means exact and accurate: 'There were several people in the court, eight to be precise'. Note that 'precise' is not used about time in the sense of a person being on time or punctual.

QUALITY ASSURANCE, QUALITY CONTROL

quality assurance /ˈkwɒlɪti əˈʃʊərəns/ *noun*, means managing the way that goods are manufactured or services delivered to ensure high standards: 'Quality assurance is implemented in all stages of production and upon the delivery of a product'. In business English the normal abbreviation is QA.

quality control /ˈkwɒlɪti kənˈtrəʊl/ *noun*, is a system for maintaining high standard products: 'Quality control is often based on comparing samples of the final output from a manufactured process against the specification'. In business English the normal abbreviation is QC.

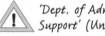 *'Dept. of Administrative Qulity Support' (University web site)*

QUILT, EIDERDOWN, DUVET

quilt /kwɪlt/, and **eiderdown** /ˈaɪdədaʊn/ *nouns*, are alternative names for bedclothing placed on the top of a bed over the other bedclothes: 'A feather quilt is always warm and snug'. The two names reflect differences in their manufacture: 'quilting' means keeping the filling between two layers of cloth in place by sewing sections separately, while 'eiderdown' refers to the down (soft inner feathers) of the eider duck originally used in the best quality quilts.

duvet /ˈduːveɪ/ *noun*, is a type of quilt with a removable cover, and replaces the top sheet, blankets and eiderdown on a bed.

QUITE, QUIET

quite /kwaɪt/ *adverb*, means either to some degree: 'He swims quite well for his age', meaning about average; or to the greatest possible degree or absolutely: 'He swims quite magnificently for his age', meaning much better than average. Note that the indefinite article comes after 'quite' when it is followed by an adjective and a noun: 'It was quite a large village', not 'a quite large village'. 'Quite' is pronounced as one syllable and rhymes with 'white'. See **FAIRLY**.

quiet /'kwaɪət/ *adjective & noun,* means the absence of noise or bustle and activity caused by many people: 'An excellent property for those in need of peace and quiet'. 'Quiet' may also refer to a person who does not speak much, or always behaves calmly: 'He's quite a quiet person'. Note that 'quiet' is pronounced as two syllables, and rhymes with 'riot'.

 'Excellent property for those in need of piece and quite.' (Estate agent's advert)

QUOTE, QUOTATION, QUOTA

quote /kwəʊt/ *noun & verb,* as a noun, means quotation: 'Do you remember that quote from Shakespeare about a summer's day?' In the plural, 'quote' means 'quotation marks': 'In this book all example sentences are set off by quotes'. As a verb, 'to quote' means either to recite poetry, or to give the price of something, particularly on the stock exchange: 'Brent oil is quoted at $20 a barrel for delivery in the spring'. See **CITE**. See **INVERTED COMMAS**.

quotation /kwəʊ'teɪʃn̩/ *noun,* means an exact extract from a printed work or from a speech: 'A quotation from Tolstoy'. 'Quotation' is used on the stock exchange for the prices of shares: 'We have received a quotation of $25 a share'.

quota /'kwəʊtə/ *noun,* means a limited number of people or things: 'Some countries refused to take their full quota of refugees'. It also means a share of something that has been allocated: 'We have received a quota of one hundred shares in the company'.

Rr

RADIO, WIRELESS

radio /'reɪdiəʊ/ *noun & verb,* as a noun, is the preferred term for the device used for receiving sound broadcasts: 'We tuned in the radio to the BBC World Service'. The plural is 'radios'. As a verb, 'radio' is used with the meaning of transmitting sound: 'The firefighters radioed for help'.

wireless /'waɪələs/ *noun & adjective,* as a noun, is a now old-fashioned term for radio. 'Wireless' as an adjective refers to a network or computer peripheral that is operated by means of infrared signals rather than wires: 'Many airports are installing wireless connections so that passengers can use PCs anywhere in the main building'.

RAILWAY, RAILWAYS, RAILROAD

railway /'reɪlweɪ/ *noun & adjective,* as a noun, means a track with rails used by trains: 'This railway has not been used for years'. As an adjective, 'railway' is used to describe specific parts of the system for the transport of passengers and goods, as in: 'railway line' and 'railway worker'. Sometimes train-operating companies have 'railway' as part of their name, as in Great Western Railway.

railways /'reɪlweɪz/ *noun,* means the entire system required to operate train services – the tracks, staff, organization and the trains themselves: 'My grandfather worked on the railways all his life'.

railroad /'reɪlrəʊd/ *noun & verb,* is the main AE term for 'railway'. The term is only used in BE as a verb, meaning to force someone or something to decide or act quickly without allowing time for thought: 'Many complained that they had been railroaded into accepting the new conditions'.

RAIN, DRIZZLE, HAIL

rain /reɪn/ *noun,* means water that descends from the clouds as water droplets: 'They were soaked in the pouring rain'. In Britain, the rain traditionally comes in showers, but can also be torrential or light. 'Rain' is an uncountable noun, so it can never be immediately preceded by 'a'. However, the indefinite article can be used before compounds such as 'a rainstorm' or 'a raincoat'. The plural form 'rains' refers to the season of heavy rain in tropical regions. See **RAIN CHECK ⇨ ADJOURN**.

drizzle /'drɪzl̩/ *noun*, means fine light rain: 'The steady drizzle fell all morning'. This is also an uncountable noun.

hail /heɪl/ *noun*, means small drops of ice that fall as rain: 'The hail stung our faces'. Although 'rain' evaporates, 'hail' melts: 'The hail on the grass melted slowly'. 'Hail' is an uncountable noun. The indefinite article can be used before compounds such as 'hailstone' or 'hailstorm'.

RAINFALL, PRECIPITATION

rainfall /'reɪnfɔːl/ *noun*, is the total amount of rain that falls in a specific area during a defined period of time: 'The average annual rainfall here is 85 cm'. This is an uncountable noun.

precipitation /prɪsɪpɪ'teɪʃn̩/ *noun*, in this context is the technical term that covers all types of moisture that falls to the ground as rain, snow etc. 'Precipitation' is also the term used to express the amount over a period: 'Monthly precipitation figures for July and August'. As 'rainfall' is only part of the total 'precipitation' in some areas of the world, the term 'precipitation', rather than 'rainfall', is recommended when giving annual totals. This is also an uncountable noun. See **SNOW**.

RAPTˢ, WRAPPEDˢ

rapt /ræpt/ *adjective*, means paying very careful attention, engrossed: 'The President's speech was received in rapt silence'. 'Rapt' is normally only used in written English.

wrapped /ræpt/ *past participle*, is from the verb 'wrap', and means enclosed or packed: 'The gift was wrapped in shiny paper'. Note that to be 'wrapped up in' refers either to an object that is contained within paper or soft material: 'The gift was wrapped up in brown paper', or figuratively, to a person who is engrossed in something: 'He can't hear the phone ringing because he's completely wrapped up in that football match'.

RARE, SELDOM

rare /reər/ *adjective*, refers to an event or situation which is uncommon. Things that are rare are often valuable: 'He has some extremely rare stamps in his collection'. 'Rare' can also mean not often: 'He paid a rare visit to his parents'.

seldom /'seldəm/ *adverb*, is equivalent to the adverb 'rarely': 'A species that is seldom seen this far north'; 'There were seldom any visitors to the village'. See **SCARCITY**.

RAW MATERIAL, COMMODITY

raw material /rɔː məˈtɪərɪəl/ *noun*, means the basic material from which a product is made: 'Using aluminium as the raw material in car bodies has several environmental advantages'. 'Raw material' can also be used figuratively: 'Working in Paris provided enough raw material for three short stories'.

commodity /kəˈmɒdɪti/ *noun*, means a raw material or primary agricultural product that can be bought and sold: 'Two attractive commodities are coffee and copper'. The London International Financial Futures and Options Exchange is a major world market for commodity trading. A 'commodity' also means something that is useful and valuable: 'Fresh air is a precious commodity in some highly polluted cities'.

reˢ, re/re-ˢ

re /riː/ *abbreviation*, is used in the headlines of letters and emails to introduce a reference: *Re: Order no. 78/NH-18/204.* See **CF**.

re /riː-/ *prefix* is combined with a verb to mean doing something again. In modern English these are usually not hyphenated: *recreate, reopen* and *retouch* (for paintwork). Some exceptions are listed below. The prefix carries some stress.

re /rɪ-, re-/ *prefix* occurs within some verbs which have no sense of doing something again. In this case, the prefix is pronounced differently as in: repair /rɪ'peər/ and represent /reprɪ'zent/. Never stress the prefix with such words.

There are two cases where *re-* is used with a hyphen:

• When the main verb starts with e. Examples: *re-elect, re-enter, re-examine.* This is standard in BE, but AE does not have hyphenation here.
  See **HYPHENATION IN INDIVIDUAL WORDS**.

• When a hyphen is necessary to distinguish between two verbs with the same spelling but different meanings. Examples with entries in this book are: *recover, reform, resign, resort.* A few nouns also have the *re* prefix. See **RECREATION**.

READ, SKIM, STUDY, PERUSE

read /riːd/ *verb*, means both to understand a written text and also to speak the words aloud to one person or a few people: 'The charges were read to him'. In BE, to 'read' a subject at a university, means to study it: 'He read Economics at Glasgow'. This form is not used in AE. Note that the past form and past participle are spelt the same as the present, but these are pronounced /red/.

skim /skɪm/ *verb*, means to read something quickly: 'He skimmed through the paper in 10 minutes'.

study /'stʌdi/ *verb*, means to read, devote time and attention, so as to master an academic subject, or to read something carefully: 'She studied the instruction manual carefully'.

peruse /pə'ruːz/ *verb*, means the same as 'study' in its second meaning, i.e. read thoroughly and carefully: 'The lawyers required three weeks to peruse the draft contract'. Many people misunderstand this formal term. 'Peruse' never means to glance at a text or skim through it. See **SCRUTINIZE**.

READABLE, LEGIBLE

readable /'riːdəbl/ *adjective*, refers to the quality of a text. It means that something is interesting to read and not boring or too difficult to understand: 'The wording of the regulations has been simplified, and they are now much more readable'. Note that documents that are scanned by modern technology are termed 'machine-readable'. See **UNREADABLE ⇨ ILLEGIBLE**.

legible /'ledʒɪbl/ *adjective*, means that something is clear and can be read: 'The copies of the fax were barely legible'. See **ILLEGIBLE**.

REAL, REALLY, TRUE, TRULY

real /rɪəl/ *adjective*, means actually existing and not imaginary: 'King John was a real person, but I'm not so sure about Robin Hood'. 'Real' can also mean genuine: 'The sofa is made of real buffalo hide'.

really /'rɪəli/ *adverb*, is used to emphasize the truth of a situation: 'What really happened on the bridge of the Titanic?' 'Really' can also mean very or thoroughly: 'That is a really stupid thing to say'. In this sense, AE slang uses 'real stupid'.

true /truː/ *adjective*, means correct or connected with facts, rather than invented: 'It's true that the team isn't very strong, but the players have done their best'. Both 'true' and 'real' can be used to describe the quality of something. 'The elections will be a real/true test of democracy'.

truly /'truːli/ *adverb*, means 'very much so', and is used to emphasize the sincerity or correctness of something: 'The company is truly sorry'. 'Yours truly' is used as an ending in formal letters in AE. See **LETTERS AND EMAILS**.

RECEIPT, RECEIPTS, REVENUE

receipt /rɪ'siːt/ *noun*, means written proof that you have received something or paid for it: 'On receipt of payment, we will send the goods'. This means receiving notification of payment. In general contexts, it is more usual to say 'Once we have received payment ...'.

receipts /rɪ'siːts/ *noun*, mean earnings in a given period by a government, organization or business: 'Box office receipts are dropping and the play may not last the month'.

revenue /'revənjuː/ *noun*, means money or income received by the State, the local authorities or a large company. The tax authorities in Britain are called the 'Inland Revenue'. In the US they are called the 'Internal Revenue Service' (IRS).

RECENT, LAST, LATEST

recent /'riːsnt/ *adjective*, refers to something that happened only a short time ago: 'This was her most recent play'. The time reference can also cover a longer period: 'The weather has been better in recent years'.

last /lɑːst/ *determiner*, means either final as in 'His last words are very famous', or the most recent of a series that is considered complete: 'I lived in Paris last year'. Note that in the second sense, the noun following 'last' must be singular, and the main verb must be in the simple past. However, 'last' combined with 'few' is used with a plural noun, to indicate a time in the past which leads up to the present: 'I have lived in Paris for the last few years'. Note the change in tense.

latest /'leɪtɪst/ *adjective*, means the most recent of a series that is expected to continue: 'Have you read his latest book?' In the context of producing things, 'latest' or 'most recent' is used for the newest version, and 'last' or 'previous' for the one before that: 'His latest play is being produced next week. Let us hope that it is better than his last/previous one'.

RECIPE, PRESCRIPTION

recipe /'resɪpi/ *noun*, means a set of instructions for making a dish or meal: 'He used the traditional recipe for fish soup'. Figuratively, 'a recipe for' means a situation that has a predictably successful or disastrous result: 'Sharing a flat with Jane and Sarah would be a recipe for disaster'.

prescription /prɪ'skrɪpʃn̩/ *noun*, means a written order from a medical doctor to a chemist regarding medicine that is only to be taken under medical supervision: 'The over-prescription of penicillin is becoming a problem'.

RECORD, REGISTER, REGISTRATION

record /'rekɔːd/ *noun*, can mean many things including a written account: 'The company keeps a record of all phone calls'. 'Record' also refers to the setting of a standard: 'He broke the long-standing world record in the high jump'. It should only be combined with 'new' if it is clear that there is a contrast to an old or earlier record. If it is a 'record', it must be a new one. In music, a record can be a thin plastic disc or a CD.

record /rɪ'kɔːd/ *verb*, means deliberate storage and permanent registration: 'The police recorded the details'; 'The group recorded a new single'. Note the difference in pronunciation between the noun and verb.

register /'redʒɪstər/ *noun & verb*, as a noun, means an official record: 'The register of marriage settlements'. As a verb, this means to record data on an official list: 'The company was registered in the Channel Islands'. When recording measured data, 'register' is the automatic and temporary storage of a reading: 'The vehicle's speed was registered on the dial'.

registration /redʒɪs'treɪʃn̩/ *noun*, is the act of making an official record of something: 'The compulsory registration of voters starts next month'. In BE, a vehicle has 'registration plates' or 'number plates' ('license plates' in AE). See LICENSE ⇨ LICENCE.

RECOUNT, RETELL

recount (1) /rɪ'kaʊnt/ *verb*, means to tell someone about a story or situation, especially from personal experience: 'He vividly recounted his early life as a Hollywood actor'. It is pronounced with a short first vowel.

recount (2) /riː'kaʊnt/ *verb &* /'riːkaʊnt/ *noun*, as a verb, means to count something once again, especially votes in an election: 'The margin was so narrow that the votes had to be recounted'. There is no hyphenation in modern BE, but the first syllable is pronounced with a long vowel. 'Recount' may also be used as a noun in this sense: 'The vote was so close that three recounts were necessary'. Note the difference in stress between the noun and the verb.

retell /riː'tel/ *verb*, means to tell a story once more. This may not have been something experienced personally: 'She retold the entire story for the benefit of those who had missed the beginning'. 'Retell' is pronounced with a long first vowel, and both syllables are stressed.

RECOVER, RE-COVER

recover /rɪ'kʌvər/ *verb*, means to return to a normal state of health: 'The economy was doing well and share prices recovered'. A second meaning is to find or regain possession of something: 'That was when the painting was recovered'. It is pronounced with a short first vowel.

re-cover /'riː'kʌvər/ *verb*, means to cover something again or put on a new cover: 'I think we will re-cover both sofas'. This is hyphenated. The first syllable is pronounced with a long vowel.

RECREATION, RECREATE

recreation (1) /rekri'eiʃn̩/ *noun*, means a leisure activity, something done out of working hours: 'His only physical recreation was walking the dog'. The first syllable is pronounced 'wreck'.

recreation (2) /'riːkri'eiʃn̩/ *noun*, means the process of creating something again: 'The police arranged an accurate recreation of the scene of the crime'. The first syllable is pronounced 'ree'.

recreate /'riːkri'eit/ *verb*, means to make something again from the beginning: 'After his computer was stolen, he had to recreate all the files'. The first syllable is pronounced 'ree'.

REDECORATE, RESTORE, REFURBISH, RENOVATE, REHABILITATE

redecorate /riː'dekəreɪt/ *verb*, means to paint the inside of a flat, house or office and/or put new wallpaper up. Note that the first time this is done is 'decorating', and 'redecorating' is used for the second or subsequent times.

restore /rɪ'stɔːr/ *verb*, means to bring back to a previous state or condition. Buildings, works of art, and pieces of furniture are typical objects that are 'restored': 'The stolen painting had to be restored after being left in a barn for 3 months'. The phrase 'restore to its former glory' means to make something as beautiful as it was previously. 'Restore' is also used more widely than simply to refer to objects. The health, confidence and faith of people can all be 'restored': 'The speech restored public confidence in the government'.

refurbish /riː'fɜːbɪʃ/ *verb*, means to redecorate and modernize a building. Note that 'refurbish' is often limited to superficial redecoration, such as replacing wallpaper and carpets: 'The hotel by the beach has been completely refurbished'. This is a formal word.

renovate /'renəveɪt/ *verb*, means to modernize and restore an old building to a good condition. Note that 'renovate' involves more extensive work than 'refurbish', such as new windows or roof tiles: 'We are going to renovate the façade in this street next summer'.

rehabilitate /riːhə'bɪlɪteɪt/ *verb*, means to restore an area of buildings to a better standard or a good state and can refer to whole urban areas: 'The housing in the slums was going to be rehabilitated'. It is also used for people who have been imprisoned, or who have lost privileges and are being helped to get a job, or back into their former status: 'The prison service set up a programme to rehabilitate former prisoners'.

REDUNDANT, JOBLESS, UNEMPLOYED

redundant /rɪ'dʌndənt/ *adjective*, means superfluous, no longer needed or useful. In BE, 'to make someone redundant' means to abolish a position because it is no longer required. This reflects the fact that the cause is changes in a company, a sector or an entire economy. See **DISMISS**. See **RETIRE**.

jobless /'dʒɒbləs/ *adjective*, refers to the status of a person who does not have a job in the workplace. It may be either a temporary or permanent state: 'He had been on the jobless register for ten years'. This is an informal term.

unemployed /ʌnɪm'plɔɪd/ *adjective*, also refers to the status of a person who does not have a job, but is looking for one: 'He entered a retraining programme for unemployed miners'. This is a more formal term than 'jobless'.

REFEREE, UMPIRE, JUDGE

referee /refə'riː/ *noun*, means a person appointed to see that the rules of a game are observed and also settle any disputes. Referees are found in American football, basketball, billiards, boxing, hockey, rugby, snooker, soccer, and wrestling. 'Ref' is used in this sense as an abbreviation. Outside sport, a referee is a person who is willing to make a statement about the character or ability of someone who is applying for a job: 'He asked his teacher to be a referee'. See **REF** ⮕ **CF**.

umpire /'ʌmpaɪər/ *noun*, means a referee in certain sports. Umpires are found in American football, badminton, baseball, cricket, hockey, table tennis, tennis, and volleyball. When there is both a referee and an umpire, as in American football, the referee is in charge of the game and the umpire controls the behaviour of the players. In hockey, both terms are used. Outside sport, an umpire is used to arbitrate between two parties in dispute and try to bring them to an agreeable settlement.

judge /dʒʌdʒ/ *noun*, is a public officer appointed to decide cases in a law court. A judge can also be someone who decides the result of a competition, or if a ball is in or out in tennis: 'The line judge must have been asleep'.

REFERENDUM, REFERENDUMS, REFERENDA

referendum /refə'rendəm/ *noun*, means either a vote by all the voters in a country on an important political question: 'The referendum is a well-known element in Swiss democracy', or the issue to be decided: 'The issue was not well formulated in the text of the referendum'.

referendums /refə'rendəmz/ *noun*, is the plural form for the first meaning of 'referendum': 'Referendums were held in several countries to decide whether to join the single currency'.

referenda /refə'rendə/ *noun*, is the plural form for the second meaning of 'referendum': 'In a Swiss referendum, there may be many referenda on the ballot paper'.

REFORM, RE-FORM

reform /rɪ'fɔːm/ *verb*, means to make a change: 'Education has been reformed and this has cost too much'. The first syllable has a short vowel.

re-form /'riː'fɔːm/ *verb*, means to form again: 'The demonstrators re-formed when the soldiers marched away'. This is hyphenated. The first syllable is pronounced with a long vowel.

REFUSE, DECLINE, DENY, REFUTE

refuse /rɪ'fjuːz/ *verb*, indicates that you are not willing to do something: 'She categorically refused to reveal who was the father of her child'.

decline /dɪ'klaɪn/ *verb*, can mean refuse, but is a formal and more polite term: 'She firmly declined the invitation to put the father's name on record'. 'Decline' in another sense means to decrease gradually in size, especially as regards quantity or value: 'Support for the party declined dramatically'.

deny /dɪ'naɪ/ *verb*, means to say that something is not true: 'She denied (the fact) that John was the father'. It can also mean disallow, especially in connection with permission, opportunity and access: 'He was denied entry to the country'.

refute /rɪ'fjuːt/ *verb*, means to disprove something: 'Many attempts have been made to refute Einstein's theory'. A second meaning is to strongly deny or reject something: 'I completely refute your slanderous comments'. 'Refute' is only used in formal English. See **DISPROVE**.

REGARDING, IN REGARD TO/WITH REGARD TO

regarding /rɪ'gaːdɪŋ/ *preposition*, means about or concerning something: 'Do you have any news regarding the pay claim?' Alternatives are concerning and respecting.

in regard to/with regard to /ɪn rɪ'gaːd tə/wɪð rɪ'gaːd tə/ *prepositional phrase*, means as concerns, or in respect of something. These expressions are more formal than 'regarding', but are normal in some business contexts: 'This letter is in regard to your complaint about slow delivery'. Note that it would be unsuitable to use 'regarding' here.

REGARDLESS, IRREGARDLESS

regardless /rɪ'gaːdləs/ *adverb*, means without paying attention to or caring about the results: 'They heard the weather forecast, but carried on regardless'. 'Regardless' is often combined with of: 'They paid a pension, regardless of the length of service'.

irregardless is informal and is often not included in dictionaries, as it is not usually considered an acceptable English word. *The New Oxford Dictionary of English* lists it, but recommends that 'regardless' should be used instead. 'Irregardless' is a blend of two words 'irrespective' and 'regardless'.

REGRETFUL, REGRETTABLE

regretful /rɪ'gretfʊl/ *adjective*, means feeling or showing sadness for something you have or have not done: 'He was dismissed and the manager was genuinely regretful about having to write the notice of dismissal'. This is a formal word.

regrettable /rɪ'gretəbl̩/ *adjective*, refers to a situation that gives cause for sorrow or regret: 'He lost his job, and at the age of 55 found himself in a highly regrettable position'.

RELAID[S], RELAYED[S]

relaid /'riː'leɪd/ *verb*, is the past tense and past participle of the verb 'relay' in the sense of lay again: 'We relaid the turf on the football pitch'.

relayed /'riːleɪd/ *verb*, is the past tense and past participle of the verb 'relay' in the sense of retransmit: 'The speech was relayed all over the world by satellite'.

 'His words were relaid all over the world.' (Student essay)

REMEMBER, RECOLLECT, RECALL, REMIND

remember /rɪ'membər/ *verb*, means to bring something to mind, and often implies a faster process than 'recall': 'He tried to remember whether he had locked the front door'. 'To remember to do something' means not to forget: 'He always remembered to take the dog out'.

recollect /rekə'lekt/ *verb*, means to remember something especially by making an effort: 'She could not recollect her music teacher's name'. It is a formal word, and a less formal alternative is 'remember'. Note that the first syllable rhymes with 'wreck'. 'Recollect' also means to collect again, and in this sense the verb is pronounced /ˌriːkə'lekt/.

recall /rɪ'kɔːl/ *verb*, means to try to bring a memory or event back to mind, especially when recounting the event to others: 'Can you recall the colour of the getaway car'. 'Recall' also means to officially order someone or something to be returned: 'The car manufacturer had to recall all 2003 models for a safety check'.

remind /rɪ'maɪnd/ *verb*, means to generate a memory and help someone to remember something important: 'I am sure that I do not need to remind you about the date of payment'.

REMEMBRANCE, MEMORY, REMINISCENCE, RECOLLECTION

remembrance /rɪ'membrəns/ *noun*, is the act of recalling an event or a thing, particularly in a serious or solemn context: 'The remembrance service for the avalanche victims will be in the church on Sunday'.

memory /'meməri/ *noun*, means the ability to remember things: 'His memory was damaged as a result of the head injuries he received'. In this sense, 'memory' is an uncountable noun. It also means an individual thing remembered from the past: 'My earliest memories are of playing in the garden'. In this sense, it is a countable noun.

reminiscence /remɪ'nɪsəns/ *noun*, means a pleasant memory of the past: 'His curious reminiscences of growing up in Texas were amusing'. This is most often used in the plural. The related verb is 'reminisce'.

recollection /rekə'lekʃn̩/ *noun*, means something remembered or called to mind, often with some effort: 'My recollection is that the car was not speeding before the crash'.

RENT, HIRE, LET, LEASE

rent /rent/ *verb & noun*, as a verb, means to pay some money in order to use an object for a specified (often long) period: 'We rented a cottage for the summer'. Note that in AE, 'rent' can be used for a short period, and this use is also now seen in BE. As a noun, this means the amount paid to the owner of a flat by a tenant: 'The rent for the last three months is overdue'.

hire /haɪər/ *verb & noun*, as a verb, means renting specific objects for a short period: 'He hired a dinner jacket for the weekend'. When 'hire' is used for engaging people to do some work, in BE this is for a short engagement: 'We have hired a babysitter for the evening'. For a long-term contract, engage or employ is used. In AE, 'hire' is the normal word for employing or engaging staff: 'The bank has hired three new managers'. As a noun, this means the amount paid for the short-term use of an object: 'The hire of the dinner jacket will cost £15'.

let /let/ *verb & noun*, as a verb, means to rent out a property: 'We let (out) the cottage for 6 weeks to some visitors from Denmark'. As a noun, it means a property rental: 'This house is available as a short-term let'. For another meaning of 'let', see **ALLOW**.

lease /liːs/ *verb & noun*, as a verb, means to enter into a contract where one person uses property, land or an object such as a car belonging to another for a specified period, in return for a regular rent or fee: 'They have leased the property from the local council'. As a noun, this means the contract for the use of property, a car, etc., in return for rent: 'This lease will run for five years'.

REPEAT, REITERATE, REPETITIVE

repeat /rɪ'piːt/ *verb*, means to say or write something again, often word by word: 'He regularly repeated that passage from Shakespeare'.

reiterate /ri'ɪtəreɪt/ *verb*, means to repeat something a number of times for emphasis or to make things clear: 'He reiterated the government's position on taxation'. This is a more formal word than 'repeat'.

repetitive /rɪ'petɪtɪv/ *adjective*, refers to saying the same thing many times, often using an unnecessary number of words: 'The speech was an ordeal, extremely repetitive and lasted for three hours'. This is usually a negative word.

REPEL, REPULSE, REPULSIVE

repel /rɪ'pel/ *verb*, means to fight attackers back successfully and drive them away: 'The guards repelled the first wave of attackers'. 'Repel' can also imply aversion and disgust: 'She disliked him and was repelled by his stale, unwashed smell'. A related adjective is 'repellent'. Fabrics that repel moisture are termed 'water repellent'.

repulse /rɪ'pʌls/ *verb*, means to feel disgust or strong dislike: 'The unnecessary violence on TV repulsed many viewers'. It also means to drive back an attack or repel it: 'The mob was repulsed by the armed forces'. 'Repulse' is a more formal word than 'repel'.

repulsive /rɪ'pʌlsɪv/ *adjective*, means disgusting and causing extreme distaste: 'She was repelled by his appearance and found his behaviour repulsive'. 'Repulsive' is a stronger word than 'repellent'.

repetition of words

- repeat a keyword again rather than use another term such as *it* that might be misunderstood:
  The malfunction started before the last inspection, a month before the blowout. It was an obvious human error. (*It refers to what? The malfunction, inspection or blowout?*)

- avoid placing similar sounding words together if they have different meanings:
  Our research showed *that the temperature* showed *an increase* (use *indicated, had increased*)
  These clear effects *will* affect *our budget* (use *effects, influence*)
  The study has proved *that the matter is* proven (use *proved, decided*)

- avoid repetition of several words containing the same sounds:
  There is to be no variation *in* hyphenation *and* capitalization (use *in the use of hyphens and capitals*)
  Many major man-machine manifestations may ... (rewrite)

- Although repetition is often boring, it can be used for special effect. An example is one of Churchill's speeches in World War II: *We shall fight on the beaches, we shall fight on the landing grounds, we shall fight in the fields and in the streets, we shall fight in the hills; we shall never surrender.*

REPLY, ANSWER, RESPONSE

reply /rɪ'plaɪ/ *noun & verb*, as a noun, means a reaction to someone or to a specific question or issue: 'The company's reply to my letter arrived today'. As a verb, 'reply' means to give a reaction: 'The company replied to my letter today'. Note that 'reply' is followed by 'to' both as a noun and a verb. See **FEEDBACK**.

answer /'ɑːnsər/ *noun & verb*, as a noun, means a reply to a specific question or issue: 'The new hydrogen-powered car is a possible answer to the problem of environmental pollution'. As a noun, 'answer' is followed by 'to'. As a verb, 'answer' means to reply: 'You have not answered our last letter'. Note that as a verb, 'answer' is not followed by 'to'.

response /rɪs'pɒns/ *noun*, means both a reply and an answer, but is more formal than both of these words: 'We are still waiting for your initial response to our questionnaire'. It is also the result of a stimulus: 'The audience's enthusiastic response to his music was incredible'. The related verb is 'respond'. Both 'respond' and 'response' are followed by 'to'.

REPORT, RAPPORT

report /rɪ'pɔːt/ *noun & verb*. As a noun, this means a written study or presentation of research findings: 'This extensive report on air pollution took six months to complete'. As a verb, it means to give information: 'I am sorry to have to report this bad news'.

rapport /ræ'pɔːr/ *noun*, means a close and harmonious relationship: 'The teacher established close rapport with his students from day one'. Less formal alternatives to 'rapport' are 'relationship' and 'working relationship'.

REQUISITE, PREREQUISITE, PRECONDITION, REQUIREMENTS

requisite /'rekwɪzɪt/ *noun*, means something necessary to meet a specific purpose: 'A high, bushy hedge is a requisite for peace and privacy in the garden'. Physical objects are sometimes termed 'requisites': 'Why not call a spade a spade instead of a garden requisite?' This is a formal word.

prerequisite /priː'rekwɪzɪt/ *noun*, means a prior condition or something necessary prior to a specific event or purpose: 'A pass in mathematics and physics at school are two prerequisites for this course at university'. This is also a formal word.

precondition /priːkən'dɪʃn̩/ *noun*, means that something must exist before something else can be achieved: 'Adequate funding is a precondition for building the new State'.

requirements /rɪ'kwaɪəmənts/ *noun*, means demands that must be met: 'The requirements for this type of work are drive, team spirit, and a keen sense of humour'. Here, 'requirements' could have been replaced by 'requisites' or 'prerequisites', although these words are not always interchangeable.

RESIDENCE, RESIDENCY

residence /'rezɪdəns/ *noun*, is a formal word that means a large house that gives the impression of grandeur: 'That estate agent has a number of attractive residences near London, if you can afford them'. The phrase 'take up residence' is a formal way of saying that someone has moved into an area: 'The royal couple have now taken up residence in Paris'. See **HOUSE**.

residency /'rezɪdənsi/ *noun*, is another formal word that means a building or country where someone lives: 'He was finally granted permanent residency in New Zealand'. Students often have to follow special regulations about how much time is to be spent at university. These are called 'residency requirements'. In AE, 'residency' can also refer to time a doctor spends in hospital undergoing advanced medical training. See **RESIDENT ⇨ INHABITANT**.

RESIGN, RE-SIGN

resign /rɪ'zaɪn/ *verb*, means to voluntarily leave a job or position, usually as a way of resolving a difficult situation: 'The club's main coach resigned before he was fired'. 'To resign oneself' to a situation means to accept being in a position that cannot be changed. See **DISMISS**. See **REDUNDANT**. See **RETIRE**.

re-sign /'riː'saɪn/ *verb*, means to sign a document again. In the world of sport, a player or coach who re-signs enters into a new contract with his or her employer: 'The club's main coach re-signed for two more seasons'. Note the hyphenation here in modern English.

RESORT, RE-SORT

resort /rɪ'zɔːt/ *noun*, means a popular holiday location: 'Cannes is always a relaxing holiday resort'. 'Resort' also means a last or final effort: 'He was short of money and started gambling heavily as a last resort'.

re-sort /'riː'sɔːt/ *verb*, means to sort something once more: 'He re-sorted the papers on his desk, but there were still three piles'. Note that this is hyphenated and that the first syllable is pronounced with a long vowel.

RESPECTABLE, RESPECTFUL

respectable /rɪ'spektəbl/ *adjective*, means acceptable and proper: 'They lived perfectly respectable lives and wore extremely respectable clothes but were really rebels at heart'. If someone's work is 'respectable' this usually means that it is better than might be expected: 'Despite having no artistic background, he produced a very respectable pen-and-ink sketch'.

respectful /rɪ'spektful/ *adjective*, means showing or feeling respect: 'The congregation listened in respectful silence'.

RESPECTIVE, RESPECTIVELY

respective /rɪ'spektɪv/ *adjective*, means belonging or referring to two or more people separately: 'At Christmas they returned to their respective families'.

respectively /rɪ'spektɪvli/ *adverb*, means separately and in the order already referred to. It is used when referring to a list of items: 'The three children selected new T-shirts, in small, medium, and large, respectively'. Note that 'respectively' usually comes after such a list, not before it.

RESPONSIBLE, ACCOUNTABLE

responsible /rɪ'spɒnsɪbl/ *adjective*, means reliable: 'That child is remarkably responsible and mature'. A person who is in a position of authority is said to be 'responsible for' other people, actions or things in his or her care: 'The project manager is responsible for meeting the agreed targets'. 'Responsible for' can also refer to a person who is the cause of something unpleasant or criminal: 'I want to know who was responsible for this terrible decision'. If someone is 'responsible to' a person or organization, this indicates a line of command: 'Even the President is responsible to the Senate'.

accountable /ə'kaʊntəbl/ *adjective*, means that a person or organization is required or expected to justify actions or decisions. If someone is 'held accountable' for something, it means that he or she has to pay for damage that was done by others: 'Someone must be held accountable for this terrible mistake'. 'Accountable to' is similar to 'responsible to'.

REST, REMAINS, REMAINDER, REMNANT, BALANCE

rest /rest/ *noun*, means something left. The 'rest (of)' is the remaining part: 'What do you want to do for the rest of the summer?' Note that it is the noun to which 'rest' refers that determines whether a singular or plural verb should be used: 'The rest of the money is in the bank', but 'the rest of the refugees are arriving tomorrow'.

remains /rɪ'meɪnz/ *noun*, means the parts left over after something has been eaten or used, and are therefore in a poor state: 'The remains of the paella were given to the dog'. 'Remains' also means historical relics: 'They visited the Roman remains'. A dead animal or corpse can also be referred to as 'remains': 'The dog's remains were removed from the road'.

remainder /rɪ'meɪndər/ *noun*, means the part of a whole that has not yet been used, and can refer to both abstract and physical nouns: 'We got some of the information straight away, but the remainder was hard to locate'. Unlike 'remains', the word 'remainder' implies nothing about the quality of what is left. Note that it is the noun to which 'remainder' refers that determines whether a singular or plural verb is used: 'After he sold some of his paintings, the remainder were donated to the local art gallery'.

remnant /'remnənt/ *noun*, means a small remaining part of a whole with the same quality as the rest: 'This is the remnant of the great beech forest'. In the plural, 'remnants' means a quantity remaining which has declined in quality: 'After the fire, the family looked helplessly at the remnants of their home'.

balance /'bæləns/ *noun*, means numerous things. In the context of something remaining, the 'balance' is the outstanding amount that is to be paid: 'We paid 40% of the bill when we ordered the furniture and agreed to pay the balance within 30 days'. A 'balance' is also a type of scales that is used for weighing things and in this sense contrasts two related categories such as earnings and spending: 'It was a great holiday, but unfortunately my bank balance is not too healthy now'. Similarly, 'balance sheet' is a written record of the income and expenditure for a company. Here, the 'balance' means the difference between these amounts.

RESTAURANT, CAFE, DINER

restaurant /'restərɑːnt/ *noun*, means a place where people can buy and eat meals: 'The curries in that Indian restaurant are to be recommended'. The owner of a restaurant is formally called a 'restaurateur' /restərə'tɜːr/. Note that this word has no 'n'.

cafe /'kæfeɪ/ *noun*, means a place to buy light meals and snacks. Cafes in the UK and USA are often not licensed to sell alcoholic drinks: 'We had milkshakes at the pavement cafe down the road'. Note that the French spelling 'café' (with an acute accent) is not recommended in most modern English dictionaries.

diner /'daɪnər/ *noun*, means a customer in a restaurant. In the USA it also means a roadside cafe or a dining car on a train: 'The company has its own diner just down the road'. The decor of a diner often resembles a traditional dining car. See **BUFFET**.

RESULT, RESULTS, OUTCOME

result /rɪ'zʌlt/ *verb*, can be combined in a number of phrases. 'Result from' points back to the cause or reason that was responsible for an event: 'Many accidents result from drunk driving'. 'Result in' focuses on the consequences: 'The accident resulted in a break up of the family'.

results /rɪ'zʌlts/ *noun*, means the things that are successfully achieved or not: 'She smiled when she saw the exam results'.

outcome /'aʊtkʌm/ *noun*, means the result of a series of events: 'The outcome of the interviews was that no one was appointed'.

RETIRE, RETREAT, WITHDRAW, PULL BACK

retire /rɪ'taɪər/ *verb*, means to withdraw from working life because of age or state of health: 'Although the normal retirement age is 65, in our company people retire at 60'. In formal English, 'to retire for the night' means to go to bed. In a military context, if soldiers 'retire' in the face of the enemy, this means they make a planned and orderly withdrawal.
See **REDUNDANT**. See **RESIGN**.

retreat /rɪ'triːt/ *verb*, means to draw back from danger when things are going badly or to move away: 'The villagers were pleased when the flood waters retreated'. In a military context, 'retreat' means to move back from the enemy. The related noun is also 'retreat'.

withdraw /wɪð'drɔː/ *verb*, means to cease to participate in an activity, often applying to armed conflict. 'Withdraw' also means to remove support: 'They withdrew the offer to help'. It can also mean leave a contest: 'He withdrew from the elections'. The related noun is 'withdrawal'.

pull back /pʊl 'bæk/ *verb*, means to move something away or to the side with one's hand: 'She pulled the child back from the edge of the road'. It also means to stop oneself from doing something: 'He pulled back from calling me a liar'. In a military sense, it means to 'withdraw' soldiers. 'Pull back' is also used in soccer to mean a positive change in the situation after a goal: 'United pulled the match back to 2–1 just before half time'. There is no noun form in standard English. The word 'withdrawal' is used instead.

REVENGE, AVENGE

revenge /rɪ'vendʒ/ *noun*, means the harm done to someone in return for an injury or wrong done by them earlier: 'The family said that it was an act of revenge'. Note that 'revenge' is an uncountable noun.

avenge /ə'vendʒ/ *verb*, means to take revenge for something that has been done: 'He wanted to avenge the murder of his brother'. 'Avenge' is a more literary word than 'revenge' and is often used in constructions like 'seek to avenge'. The related noun is 'vengeance'. Note that a person who carries out 'revenge' is an 'avenger'.

REVERENT, REVEREND

reverent /'revərənt/ *adjective*, means feeling or showing deep respect: 'The atmosphere in the church was one of reverent silence'. The related noun is 'reverence'. Both 'reverent' and 'reverence' are formal words.

Reverend /'revərənd/ *adjective*, refers to a person to be revered, and is used as a title for the clergy. The correct form of address in BE is 'Reverend John Smith' or 'the Reverend J. Smith'. In AE, the Christian name is omitted: 'Reverend Smith'. The abbreviation is 'Rev.' or sometimes 'Revd.' These should always be capitalized, since 'rev.' is an abbreviation for 'revolutions'. Note that the final letter in Reverend is pronounced with a 'd'.

REVERSAL, REVERSION

reversal /rɪ'vɜːsl/ *noun*, means a change in the opposite direction: 'Many are expecting a total reversal in share prices'.

reversion /rɪ'vɜːʃn/ *noun*, means a change back to a previous state or condition: 'There was a reversion to open ethnic conflict in the area'. In property law, 'reversion' means transferring property back to a former owner: 'The reversion of Hong Kong to China took place in 1997'. This is a formal word.

REVERSE, INVERSE, OBVERSE

reverse /rɪ'vɜːs/ *noun & adjective*, as a noun, means the opposite of the previous state: 'The company had expected huge profits. As it turned out, the reverse was the case'. As an adjective, it refers to the other side of an object: 'The reverse side of the sculpture'. 'Reverse' is a more general and useful term than 'inverse' and 'obverse'. Note that a coin has its secondary design on the 'reverse' side. In everyday English this is known as 'tails'. See **BACK ⇨ BACKSIDE**.

reverse /rɪ'vɜːs/ *verb*, can mean to overturn a previous decision: 'The judge totally reversed the verdict of the lower court and the suspect was freed'. It can also mean to go backwards: 'The car reversed slowly down the street', or to exchange two things. 'The father reversed the traditional roles in the home'.

inverse /ɪn'vɜːs/ *adjective*, means something that is opposite or contrary in position, direction or order: 'The results obtained from many space probes have been in inverse proportion to their cost'. 'Inverse' is often linked to terms such as ratio and relationship, particularly in mathematics and statistics.

obverse /'ɒbvɜːs/ *noun*, is a technical term that means the side of a coin carrying the head and the main inscription. In everyday English this is known as 'heads'. In formal English, 'the obverse' is the opposite of a fact or truth.

REVIEW⁶, REVUE⁷

review /rɪ'vjuː/ *noun*, means an examination or assessment of something to see if changes are required: 'There will be a comprehensive review of government spending'. A 'review' can also be a critique of literary or artistic work: 'The film got a bad review in the press'. See **REFER**.

revue /rɪ'vjuː/ *noun*, means entertainment on stage with dancing, songs and sketches: 'A typical revue should have topical humour and satire'.

REVOLT, REBELLION, RIOT, RISING

revolt /rɪ'vəʊlt/ *noun & verb*, as a noun, means an uprising against political rulers in order to take over control: 'The large-scale, popular revolt lowered the rate of taxation'. As a verb, 'revolt' has two meanings: first, to rise up in opposition, and second, to disgust: 'The violence on the TV news completely revolts me'. In the present continuous, 'revolt' can be ambiguous: 'The students are revolting'. If they were not disgusting, it would be better to say 'rebelling'.

rebellion /rɪ'beljən/ *noun*, means various degrees of opposition to established power. The seriousness of the opposition depends on which word 'rebellion' is combined with. At one end of the scale it can mean armed revolution, and at the other end, mild opposition to a teacher or parent: 'Typical teenage rebellion'.

riot /'raɪət/ *noun*, means a violent and local disturbance of the peace by a crowd: 'The police arrived and stopped the prison riot'.

rising /'raɪzɪŋ/ *noun*, means a widespread armed protest against authority, a rebellion: 'Many Dubliners are still proud of the Easter Rising'.

RIGHT, RIGHTLY, CORRECT, RIGHT–HAND, RIGHT–HANDED

right /raɪt/ *adjective, adverb & noun*, all refer to the side of a person or thing which is facing east when that object or person is facing north: 'Turn right, and you will see the cinema on the right'. In a political context, 'right' means connected with conservative groups or ideas: 'He used to be a socialist, but is now on the right of the political spectrum'. The adjective form can also mean 'morally justified': 'She was unsure of the right way to behave in the circumstances'. The expression 'to be right' means to be proved correct: 'You were right about his potential. He has become one of the best students we have ever had'. As an adverb, 'right' is also found in a variety of expressions, such as 'right away', meaning immediately, and 'right ahead', meaning straight in front.
See **WRITE**.

rightly /'raɪtli/ *adverb*, means either for a good reason or correctly: 'He was rightly fined by the police'. Note that 'rightly' is usually placed just before a verb or adjective.

correct /kə'rekt/ *adjective*, means either without mistakes: 'The figures in the report were completely correct', or 'right' in the sense of doing things in the approved way: 'The

president dressed in a very correct manner'. The term 'politically correct' refers to behaving and using words that will not cause offence to specific groups of people.

right-hand /'raɪt hænd/ *adjective*, only refers to the direction or position 'right', and never means 'correct'. Note that 'right-hand' as an adjective is hyphenated: 'This car has a right-hand drive', and can only come before a noun.

right-handed /raɪt 'hændɪd/ *adjective*, refers to people who use their right hand more naturally than their left: 'A right-handed boxer is called orthodox'.

RIGHTWARD, RIGHTWARDS

rightward /'raɪtwəd/ *adjective*, means a movement to the right: 'They took a rightward turn in the dark'. Note that this is usually placed before a noun.

rightwards /'raɪtwədz/ *adverb*, also means a movement to the right: 'They looked rightwards'. Note that this usually occurs after a verb. This is sometimes spelt 'rightward'.

RIGOUR^S, RIGOR^S

rigour /'rɪgər/ *noun*, means the quality of being strict and inflexible: 'The sentence passed by the judge shows the full rigour of the law'. This is a formal word. In the plural, 'rigours' mean harshness and strain: 'They were exposed to the rigours of a winter storm'.

rigor /'rɪgər/ *noun*, means muscular stiffness as in 'rigor mortis'. In BE this may also be pronounced /'raɪgər/, especially by medical people. In AE, 'rigor' is the spelling of 'rigour'. The related adjective is spelt 'rigorous' in both BE and AE. See **-OR, -OUR SPELLINGS**.
See **STRICT**.

RISE, RAISE

rise /raɪz/ *noun & verb*, as a noun, means an upward movement or an increase in quantity or quality: 'The company experienced a substantial rise in profits'. In another sense a 'rise' can be a movement to get more power or importance: 'The rise and fall of the Roman Empire'. As a verb, 'rise' has the past tense 'rose' and the past participle 'risen'. 'Rise' never has an object: 'The sun rises'. Note that 'rise' in BE can mean an increase in pay. This is called a 'raise' in AE. See **ASCENT**. See **WAKE**.

raise /reɪz/ verb, means to lift something to a higher position. 'Raise' has the past tense and past participle 'raised'. 'Raise' always takes an object: 'Please raise your right arm'. In AE, 'raise' can mean to rear children and animals. In BE, 'raise' in this sense is informal, and 'bring up' (for children) and 'breed' (for animals) are standard.

ROAD, STREET, AVENUE, BOULEVARD, ALLEY, LANE

road /rəʊd/ noun, means a highway that connects places and is sometimes named after the place it goes to: 'London Road'.
See MOTORWAY.

street /striːt/ noun, is a road in towns and cities with buildings on either side: 'Regent Street'. There are many exceptions to this basic distinction between 'road' and 'street', such as 'King's Road' in Chelsea, London. 'High Street' means the main shopping street in towns in the UK, and is often its official name. The AE equivalent is 'Main Street'. 'Street' is abbreviated as 'St' (BE), and 'St.' (AE) which are both read as 'street'. See SAINT.

avenue /'ævənjuː/ noun, originally meant a wide, tree-lined street: 'Where have all the trees gone in Shaftesbury Avenue?' 'Avenue' is also used in cities in the USA for the grid-patterned streets: '5th Avenue' and in BE and AE outside urban areas to mean a tree-lined road: 'Follow the avenue of beech trees'.
See ADDRESSES IN LETTERS.

boulevard /'buːləvɑːd/ noun, means a broad avenue such as Sunset Boulevard in Hollywood.

alley /'&li/ noun, means a narrow passageway in a town between or behind buildings. 'Tin Pan Alley' is a district in New York where many songwriters and producers used to live or work, not one specific alley.

lane /leɪn/ noun, means a small narrow street between buildings in a town, or in BE a narrow country road: 'I love to ride my bicycle down winding country lanes'.

ROAST, FRY, GRILL, BROIL

roast /rəʊst/ verb, adjective & noun, as a verb, usually means to cook food such as meat or vegetables in an oven or over a fire: 'The meat on the spit was roasted over an open fire'. Although the past tense and past participle are 'roasted', the adjective, unusually, is 'roast': 'Duck and roast potatoes is a speciality here'. As a noun, 'roast' means a joint of roast beef

or other meat. Figuratively, 'a roasting' is used informally in the sense of criticizing severely or very intensively: 'They knew the CEO would get a roasting at the shareholders' meeting'.

fry /fraɪ/ verb, means to cook food in oil/fat in a shallow pan: 'Fry the meat quickly'.

grill /grɪl/ verb, means to cook food under a very strong heat. 'Grill' is also used figuratively to mean question someone closely: 'The police were unhappy with the suspect's first answers, and spent several hours grilling him'. See GRILL.

broil /brɔɪl/ verb, is the usual AE term for the BE 'grill' in the sense of cooking.

'Foreign diplomat grilled for six hours.'

ROB, STEAL, BURGLE, BURGLAR

rob /rɒb/ verb, means to take property from a person or place by force or threat of force: 'The gang robbed the bank at lunchtime'. Note that 'rob' refers to public acts of theft.

steal /stiːl/ verb, means to take property belonging to a person or place without any legal right to ownership: 'He stole $300 000 from his company before he left'. The thing that is taken is 'stolen', not 'robbed'. If a person or thing is 'stolen', this means it is physically removed: 'The cash machine was stolen by a gang using a fork-lift truck'. Note that 'steal' refers to acts of theft done furtively or secretly. 'Steal' also means to move quietly: 'She stole silently out of the room'.

burgle /'bɜːgl/ verb, means to enter a house or building illegally, usually by forcing open a door or window, in order to steal something: 'We were burgled three times last year'. 'Burglarize' /'bɜːgləraɪz/ is an AE alternative to 'burgle'.

burglar /'bɜːglər/ *noun*, means a person who enters a house or building illegally, usually by breaking in, in order to steal: 'The burglar was caught red-handed inside the house after the alarm went off'.

ROCK, BOULDER, STONE, PEBBLE

rock /rɒk/ *noun*, means a continuous layer of mineral or one that has been eroded into smaller pieces: 'The rocks by the river were very slippery'. In AE, 'rock' also refers to small stones, unlike in BE, where a 'rock' usually requires two or more people to lift one. Thus some British speakers are surprised that Americans are strong enough to throw 'rocks' at crows. This lighter use of 'rock' is starting to become established in BE.

boulder /'bəʊldər/ *noun*, means a very large rock typically associated with mountainous country: 'The boulders on the mountains were very loose'.

stone /stəʊn/ *noun*, means any piece of mineral that is larger than a pebble and smaller than a rock: 'Stones are small enough to throw'.

pebble /'pebl/ *noun*, means a small round stone that is usually found in or near water: 'Pebble beaches can be quite uncomfortable to walk on in bare feet'.

RODE^S, ROWED^S

rode /rəʊd/ *verb*, is the past tense of the verb 'ride': 'They rode all night' (on horses or motorbikes). The past participle is 'ridden'.

rowed /rəʊd/ *verb*, is the past tense of the verb 'row': 'They rowed all night' (in a rowing boat). The past participle is also 'rowed'.

ROLE^S, ROLL^S

role /rəʊl/ *noun*, means an actor's part, or a function that has to be carried out: 'He fitted into the role of teacher very smoothly'.

roll /rəʊl/ *noun & verb*, as a noun, means a list of names: 'The candidate consulted the electoral roll before giving his speech'. It can also mean a small cylindrical loaf of bread, or paper wrapped round a tube. As a verb, 'roll' describes movement, usually turning: 'He rolled over in bed'.

ROOM, HALL, CHAMBER

room /ruːm/ *noun*, refers to the basic unit in a house, flat or building used for accommodation: 'She was given a delightful room at The Savoy'.

hall /hɔːl/ *noun*, is the entrance or passage inside the front door of a building. 'Hall' is also a large room for public meetings.

chamber /'tʃeɪmbər/ *noun*, is a hall in a public building. 'Chamber' also means a legislature: 'The House of Commons is the chamber of real power in Parliament'.

ROUTE, ITINERARY, SERVICE

route /ruːt/ *noun*, means a way or course taken to get to a destination: 'We took what was called the scenic route'.

itinerary /aɪ'tɪnərəri/ *noun*, means a plan of a route or journey. This is often worked out for a single trip: 'Their itinerary was timed in six-hour stages'. Note that both 'r's in the word should be pronounced.

service /'sɜːvɪs/ *noun*, in this sense means a travel system providing bus, coach, train, air or coastal connections on a regular basis: 'The local bus service starts the summer timetable on 15 May'.

RUCKSACK, BACKPACK

rucksack /'rʌksæk/ *noun*, means a bag with shoulder straps worn by a modern hiker: 'All he needed for the walk was in his rucksack'.

backpack /'bækpæk/ *noun*, is a synonym for 'rucksack' that originated in AE. The verb form 'backpacking' describes a person who is travelling with their possessions in a rucksack or backpack.

RULE, REIGN^S, REIN^S

rule /ruːl/ *verb*, means to exercise or impose ultimate power in a region, country or a family: 'It is a question of who really rules this country'.

reign /reɪn/ *verb & noun*, means to hold royal office or to be supreme. In modern English, 'reign' implies less power than 'rule': 'The king's reign lasted for nearly fifty years'.

rein /reɪn/ *noun*, is a long leash for controlling horses: 'The horse was given a freer rein'. In figurative use, 'rein in' means to start to control activities more closely: 'The Finance Minister reined in public spending'. Confusion between the soundalikes 'reign' and 'rein' sometimes leads to mistakes in writing.

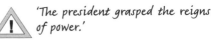

'The president grasped the reigns of power.'

RUMOUR, TALE, STORY

rumour /'ruːmər/ *noun,* means a story or report where both the origin and accuracy may or may not be true: 'There was a false rumour about devaluation'. 'Rumor' is the AE spelling of 'rumour'.

tale /teɪl/ *noun,* means an imaginative story or an exciting description which may or may not be true: 'It was a rambling but amazing tale of adventure'.

story /'stɔːri/ *noun,* means a description of events by a writer or speaker. In some contexts as in a newspaper's 'exclusive story' or 'lead story', this may be accurate and true. In other contexts, such as a 'children's story', or a 'hard luck story', many elements are invented. The word 'story' should be handled with care: if someone tells 'the story of their life', it may be completely true, but if someone is 'telling stories' they are probably untrue; and a 'tall story' is utter fantasy.

Ss

SAFETY, SECURITY

safety /'seɪfti/ *noun,* means protection from harm or the risk of injury: 'The police cannot guarantee the safety of the villagers'. 'Safety' is often used to modify a noun, such as 'safety belt' and 'safety valve'. 'Safety' also means the state of not being dangerous: 'The new safety guidelines will improve the company's record'.

security /sɪ'kjʊərɪti/ *noun,* means the state of being or feeling free from danger or a threat: 'In times of high unemployment, job security is vital'. For a company or state, 'security' is a matter of protection against espionage, terrorism and theft: 'We need to tighten up security measures'. Policies about 'security' in a company are often stipulated in 'security regulations'. 'Security' is also an item of value that acts as a guarantee when applying for some types of financial loan. If something of value is not available to back the loan, then it is termed an 'unsecured loan'. In the plural, 'securities' means stocks and bonds: 'Heavy trading in government securities followed the Finance Minister's announcement'.

SAINT^S, ST^S

saint /seɪnt, sṇt/ *noun,* is capitalized when referring to someone who is formally canonized: 'Saint Peter'. It is not capitalized when it means saint-like behaviour: 'The nurse was a real saint to the injured'. The first pronunciation is appropriate when the word 'saint' is used on its own, while the second one /sṇt/ is used when a name follows: 'Saint Paul'.

St /seɪnt, sṇt/ *noun,* is the abbreviation of 'Saint'. Note that the full stop is omitted in modern BE: 'St Bernhard Pass'. 'St' is read as 'saint'. Sometimes 'saint' is abbreviated to 'S' (plural 'SS'). 'St' is also the usual abbreviation of street. See **STREET** ⇨ **ROAD**.

SALESPERSON, SALES REPRESENTATIVE, SHOP ASSISTANT

salesperson /'seɪlzpɜːsṇ/ *noun,* means someone whose job is to sell or promote goods or services. 'Salesperson' is a neutral alternative to 'salesman' when referring to a man. In BE, these terms together with 'saleswoman' can be ambiguous as they mean both 'sales representative' and 'shop assistant'.

sales representative /'seɪlz reprɪˌzentətɪv/ *noun*, means a person who visits businesses in an allotted sales district to get orders for goods. This is often abbreviated to 'representative', or informally, 'sales rep.'. Companies use a variety of terms for sales representative including 'account executive' and 'marketing executive'. See **EXECUTIVE**.

shop assistant /'ʃɒp əsɪstənt/ *noun*, means someone working in a shop to assist customers. In AE, such a person is termed a 'sales clerk' /'seɪlz klɜːrk/. See **CLERK** ⇨ **OFFICE STAFF**.

SALON, SALOON

salon /'sælɒn/ *noun*, means a business establishment for a hairdresser ('hairdressing salon'), or beautician ('beauty salon').

saloon /sə'luːn/ *noun*, means a public room or a special-purpose building such as a 'billiard saloon'. In BE it means a lounge bar in a country pub. A comfortable room for passengers on a ship is also termed 'saloon' and a vehicle with two or four doors and a boot that is designed for a family is sometimes called a 'saloon car' ('sedan' in AE).

SALTWATER, SALT WATER, SALINE, SALTY

saltwater /'sɔːltwɔːtər/ *adjective*, usually refers to fish or plants that live in sea water as opposed to fresh water: 'The saltwater crocodiles are dangerous in this estuary'.

salt water /'sɔːlt ˌwɔːtər/ *noun phrase*, is the phrase used to refer to sea water: 'They measured the percentage of salt water in the river'. Note that the noun is written as two words, while the adjective is written as a single word.

saline /'seɪlaɪn/ *adjective*, is a technical term that means something containing salt: 'He rinsed his contact lenses in a saline solution'. The related noun is 'salinity' /sə'lɪnɪti/.

salty /'sɔːlti/ *adjective*, refers to a substance that contains or tastes of salt: 'They could not eat the soup because it was just too salty'. The related noun is 'saltiness'.

SANCTION, SANCTIONS

sanction /'sæŋkʃən/ *noun & verb*, as a noun, means official approval: 'The Pope gave his official sanction to the appointment'. As a verb, 'sanction' is ambiguous as it can mean both to give approval: 'The act was sanctioned by the assembly', and the opposite, to impose a penalty: 'The United Nations agreed to sanction that country for having broken the agreement'.

sanctions /'sæŋkʃənz/ *noun*, usually plural, is an attempt by one state or body to force another to behave in accordance with its wishes. It is commonly used with the verbs 'impose' and 'lift': 'The sanctions that were imposed on that country are to be lifted'.

SATISFIED, SATISFYING, SATISFACTORY

satisfied /'sætɪsfaɪd/ *adjective*, means pleased because something has been achieved, or because an event has occurred. However, it can also mean certain or convinced, and it is therefore necessary to use 'satisfied' with caution where there might be any ambiguity. The infinitive is 'satisfy'. See **CERTAIN**.

satisfying /'sætɪsfaɪɪŋ/ *adjective*, is a positive word that means giving fulfilment or pleasure: 'The volunteers said that the work was very tiring but thoroughly satisfying'.

satisfactory /sætɪs'fæktəri/ *adjective*, usually means acceptable, meeting the requirements but not more: 'The work was not altogether satisfactory but I paid the builders anyway'. 'Satisfactory' can also mean completely acceptable: 'A perfectly satisfactory answer'.

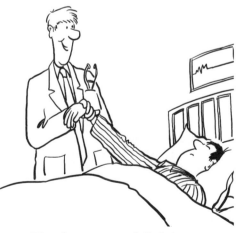

'The doctor was satisfied that the patient was dead.'

SAUCE, GRAVY

sauce /sɔːs/ *noun*, means a thick liquid added to food to give moisture or flavour: 'The brown bottle contained a spicy sauce not chocolate sauce'.

gravy /ˈgreɪvɪ/ *noun*, means a sauce made from the fat and other juices of meat. In AE slang, 'gravy' means money, so 'getting on the gravy train' means to earn money easily. However, the 'gravy boat' is just a jug used for serving gravy during a meal.

SAWN, SAWED

sawn /sɔːn/ is the past participle of the verb 'to saw' in BE: 'The trees were sawn down'. 'Sawn' is also an adjective in BE, as in: 'He pointed a sawn-off shotgun at us'.

sawed /sɔːd/ is the past tense of 'saw', as in: 'They sawed down the maples'. 'Sawed' is also used as the past participle in AE, and forms the adjective too, as in: 'He pointed a sawed-off shotgun at us'.

SAY, TELL

say /seɪ/ *verb*, means to speak, and is often used to report a person's words: "Here I am', he said hastily'. 'Say' also means to express feelings: 'I am going to say what is on my mind'; or state an opinion: 'Say what you like'. Note that 'say' never has a person as the object, so that 'say him' is always wrong. Use 'tell him'.

tell /tel/ *verb*, means to explain facts, instructions or a story: 'Please tell me how to get to the station'; 'I am going to tell you the story'. Note that 'tell' always has a person as the object, often with a 'that' clause: 'I want to tell you that it is raining'.

SCARCITY, SHORTAGE, LACK, NON-AVAILABILITY, NON-EXISTENCE

scarcity /ˈskeəsɪtɪ/ *noun*, means an insufficient amount of common, useful things such as food, money or resources. This may be temporary: 'After that wet summer, there will be a scarcity of wheat this winter'. This means that there are supplies in some places but they are inadequate in others. See **RARE**.

shortage /ˈʃɔːtɪdʒ/ *noun*, means a state of not having enough of the things or people that are required: 'The desperate shortage of energy resulted in severe industrial problems for the country'. This means that there is not enough of a key resource.

lack /læk/ *noun*, means that there is not enough of something: 'The project was cancelled due to a lack of volunteers, after only one person came forward'.

non-availability /ˈnɒn əveɪləˈbɪlɪtɪ/ *noun*, means a temporary situation where no examples of a given product or service can be supplied at that particular moment: 'The car production line stopped because of the general non-availability of tyres'.

non-existence /nɒn egˈzɪstəns/ *noun*, means there is nothing: 'They died because of the complete non-existence of any outside help'. Note that both 'non-availability' and 'non-existence' always have 'the' before them or a linked adjective.

SCEPTIC, SCEPTICAL, SEPTIC

sceptic /ˈskeptɪk/ *noun*, means someone who doubts accepted opinion: 'One can convince sceptics or try to prove them wrong'. This is the BE spelling. Note the pronunciation, despite the spelling with initial 'sce-'. 'Skeptic' is the AE spelling.

sceptical /ˈskeptɪkl̩/ *adjective*, corresponds to the noun 'sceptic' in BE: 'She remained sceptical about her husband all her life'. The AE spelling is 'skeptical'.

septic /ˈseptɪk/ *adjective*, refers to a wound that is infected by bacteria. In a house, the 'septic tank' refers to a local drainage system and tank: 'They have a septic tank in the garden'.

SCHEDULE, TIMETABLE, AGENDA, HIDDEN AGENDA

schedule /ˈʃedjuːl/(BE) /ˈskedjuːl/(AE) *noun*, means a plan for the tasks and dates of future work: 'We are working to a tight schedule and budget this year'. In AE, 'schedule' is the equivalent of 'timetable' in BE, as in 'bus schedule' ('bus timetable' in BE). See **DIARY**.

timetable /ˈtaɪmteɪbl̩/ *noun*, means a list of times of planned events, for instance arrival and departure times of public transport or planned teaching in school: 'The timetable for the next school year has just been printed'. Note that in AE, 'schedule' is used in this context.

agenda /əˈdʒendə/ *noun*, means matters to be discussed, usually in a meeting: 'I'm sorry, the agenda for this meeting is rather long'. Note that although 'agenda' is a Latin plural, in modern English it is a singular noun and takes a singular verb.

hidden agenda /ˈhɪdn̩ əˈdʒendə/ *noun*, means a secret or ulterior motive: 'The kind of questions she was asking suggested that she had a hidden agenda'. This is a disapproving term.

SCHOLARSHIP, GRANT, STIPEND

scholarship /ˈskɒləʃɪp/ *noun*, means financial support usually related to paying the fees for a place to study. In this sense it has normal singular and plural forms. 'Scholarship' in the sense of leading academic performance can be used only in the singular and means the achievements of a scholar: 'His thesis was an eminent piece of scholarship'. 'Scholarship' also means a body of academic knowledge: 'The scholarship of the ancient Greeks'.

grant /grɑːnt/ *noun*, means financial support from organizations for a variety of educational purposes. 'Government grants' mean financial support from the state to a university. Examples of types of grant are a 'travel grant' and a 'research grant'.

stipend /ˈstaɪpend/ *noun*, in BE, means a sum of money (such as a salary) regularly paid to a member of the clergy. 'Stipend' in AE means a sum of money such as a scholarship paid to any category of student.

SCHOOL, COLLEGE, UNIVERSITY

school /skuːl/ *noun*, generally covers the institutions for compulsory education. In both BE and AE, a school can also be a specialized part of a university, such as the London School of Economics; or it can be a vocational training establishment such as 'secretarial school'. 'School' is often used in AE where in BE 'college' or 'university' are more usual: 'He was working his way through school'. In BE, this means pre-university level, but in the AE sense it could mean any level. In AE, 'universities' such as Yale and Harvard are widely called 'schools'.

college /ˈkɒlɪdʒ/ *noun*, in BE, can be the name of an independent secondary school such as Harrow College. 'College' in adult education and higher education can refer to vocational training institutions, such as: 'art college', or non-specialized units within a university such as: King's College, Cambridge. Some professional bodies in the UK also use the term 'college': Royal College of Surgeons. In AE, 'college' is used for institutions in adult education and higher education, and usually refers to vocational training institutions, or

specialized units within a 'university': 'college of engineering' (in BE this would often be 'department' or 'school' of engineering). See **HIGH SCHOOL**.

university /juːnɪˈvɜːsɪti/ *noun*, is an institution that offers the highest level of education. In BE this level is known as tertiary education, and universities offer courses that lead to a degree (BA, BSc, etc.). See **GRADUATE**.

SCISSORS, PAIR OF SCISSORS

scissors /ˈsɪzəz/ *noun*, is a hand-held device for cutting. This is a plural noun, and takes a plural verb in phrases like: 'Where are the scissors?'

pair of scissors is used to express one unit, and thus it takes a singular verb: 'I need a pair of scissors that cuts through cardboard easily'. This is one of a number of objects that refer to two things joined together. For other examples, see **AGREEMENT BETWEEN SUBJECT AND VERB**.

SCOTS/SCOTTISH, SCOT, SCOTCH

Scots/Scottish /skɒts, ˈskɒtɪʃ/ *adjectives*, mean people from Scotland, who are generally termed 'Scots' or 'Scottish'. 'Scots' is used particularly for 'Scots pine', and 'Scots accent', while 'Scottish' is the more general term. As a noun, 'Scots' is used to refer to the distinctive Germanic language of Scotland, which has many grammatical as well as lexical differences from the English of England. See **GAELIC ⇨ FRENCH**.

Scot /skɒt/ *noun*, means a person who comes from Scotland. This is the only word in this group that can be used as a noun in this way: 'Although he had been born in New Zealand, he felt himself to be a Scot through and through'.

scotch /skɒtʃ/ *adjective & noun*, nearly always means whisky and to call the people of Scotland 'the Scotch' is likely to insult both drinkers and teetotal Scotsmen and Scotswomen alike. The word 'Scotch' is used in a few set phrases such as 'Scotch broth' and 'Scotch egg'. Note that there is at least one brand of 'scotch' which includes 'Scots' in its name. See **FERMENT**.

SCRUTINIZE, EXAMINE

scrutinize /ˈskruːtɪnaɪz/ *verb*, means to look closely and carefully at something: 'The lawyer closely scrutinized the fine print in the contract'. See **PERUSE ⇨ READ**.

examine /ɪgˈzæmɪn/ *verb*, means to look at a person or thing in detail, usually in a medical context: 'The doctor said that he would carefully examine the patient's chest'. 'Examine' also means to consider an idea in an academic context: 'In this essay, I shall examine the historical background to this conflict'. In another sense, 'examine' means to test: 'Students will be thoroughly examined in English proficiency'.

SEA, SEAS, OCEAN

sea /siː/ *noun*, means both the expanse of water that covers most of the Earth's surface, and defined areas covered by salt water such as the South China Sea, North Sea and the Black Sea: 'As they moved into the open sea, it became very rough'. See **SEASIDE ⇨ BEACH**.

seas /siːz/ *noun*, means either the plural of 'sea' as in: 'They sailed the high seas' or it means waves, particularly large waves: 'They were rocked by the heavy seas'.

ocean /ˈəʊʃn̩/ *noun*, means very large expanses of sea. There are five oceans: Atlantic, Pacific, Indian, Arctic and Antarctic. 'The Barents Sea borders the Arctic Ocean'. Otherwise, when describing an expanse of water, BE uses 'sea' and AE often uses 'ocean'.

SEASONABLE, SEASONAL

seasonable /ˈsiːznəbl̩/ *adjective*, means usual for a particular time of year: 'We enjoyed the delightful seasonable temperature in New Zealand last December'.

seasonal /ˈsiːznəl/ *adjective*, means happening or relating to a particular season: 'The refugees were only offered seasonal employment in the orchards'. The phrase 'seasonal greetings' is often used by large organizations on Christmas cards to avoid using Christian terminology like 'Merry Christmas'. See **CHRISTMAS**.

seasons

In some parts of the world there is a *dry/rainy* season distinction. In others, *summer/winter* seasons are sufficient. In Europe, there are four seasons: *spring, summer, autumn* and *winter*. In AE, the word *fall* is used instead of *autumn*. To talk about what happens during the seasons use, for example, *in (the) summer*, or more formally *during the summer months*. *Seasons* tend to

approach or *arrive*. Some useful phrases when talking about the seasons are *height of summer*, or *mid-summer* and the *depths of winter*, or *mid-winter*. See **AUTUMN**.

SECULAR, SECTARIAN

secular /ˈsekjʊlər/ *adjective*, refers to activities and attitudes that are not religious, sacred or spiritual: 'The new church was criticized for the secular appearance of its buildings'.

sectarian /sekˈteərɪən/ *adjective*, means involving religious sects or denominations: 'Northern Ireland has a history of sectarian violence'.

SEMI-, DEMI-, HEMI-

semi- /ˈsemi-/ means either half, as in 'semicircle', or partly, as in 'semiconscious'. In BE, a 'semi' means a 'semi-detached' house. See **DETACHED HOUSE**. 'Semi-' is of Latin origin. Note that 'semi-' is the only one of these words that is freely available for making new words, such as: 'semigovernmental'. The pronunciation /semi-/ is normal in BE, while /semaɪ-/ is standard in AE.

demi- /ˈdemi-/ means half or partly. It is generally used in connection with words of French origin such as 'demi-pension' and 'demi-sec'.

hemi- /ˈhemi-/ means half and is used in connection with terms sharing its Greek origin such as 'hemisphere'.

semicolon (;)

• Use a semicolon to separate parts of a long sentence that already have commas. This is particularly useful in lists:
In France, 34% were in favour; the figure in Germany was 35%; in Spain, 42%; and in all the other member states, the figures were between 45% and 55%.

• In formal usage, the semicolon can join two clauses instead of using words like *and* or *but*:
The train was late; I hoped that I would not have to stand all the way home

SENSIBLE, SENSITIVE, INSENSIBLE, INSENSITIVE

sensible /ˈsensɪbl̩/ *adjective*, refers to the ability to make good reasonable judgements: 'The director resigned which was a very sensible way to avoid a scandal'.

sensitive /'sensɪtɪv/ *adjective*, means how easily or quickly someone or something responds to changes: 'This sensor is highly sensitive to slight changes in temperature'. Sensitive also means easily upset: 'He is terribly sensitive about his baldness'. 'Sensitive' things can be harmed or damaged: 'The environment of Antarctica is too sensitive for mass tourism'. A person's skin can also be 'sensitive'. Companies and governments often term commercial or government secrets, 'sensitive information'.

insensible /ɪn'sensɪbl̩/ *adjective*, means without feeling: 'He jumped into the icy water, completely insensible to the cold'. 'Insensible' can also mean unconscious: 'The boxer was knocked insensible'. Note that even though it has the prefix 'in', this word is not the opposite of 'sensible'. For the opposite, use 'not sensible'.

insensitive /ɪn'sensɪtɪv/ *adjective*, means not knowing or caring how someone feels: 'He grew insensitive and did not care what other people thought'. 'Insensitive' can also mean not influenced by something: 'It would be dangerous to be totally insensitive to pain'.

 'The spy got hold of some very sensible information.'

SENSUAL, SENSUOUS

sensual /'senʃʊəl/ *adjective*, refers to physical pleasure connected particularly with sex: 'She had sensual lips'. The words commonly used with 'sensual' reinforce this meaning: 'sensual desire' and 'sensual appearance'.

sensuous /'senʃʊəs/ *adjective*, traditionally means related to the senses not the intellect: 'The sensuous experience of walking on the beach'. As 'sensual' and 'sensuous' are commonly confused in modern English, it is often safer to use 'stimulating' or 'enjoyable'.

SERGEANT, LIEUTENANT

sergeant /'sɑːdʒənt/ *noun*, is a non-commissioned officer in the army below staff-sergeant or the rank between constable and inspector in the police in Britain. A spelling tip is to remember 'serge'+'ant'.

lieutenant /lef'tenənt/ (BE Army), /lʊ'tenənt/ (BE Navy and AE) is a rank in the army and navy below captain. In the US it is the police rank above sergeant. A spelling tip is to remember 'lieu'+'tenant'.

SERIES, STRING (OF), SUCCESSION (OF), SEQUENCE OF EVENTS, TRAIN OF EVENTS

series /'sɪəriːz/ *noun*, means a number of similar things or events that occur one after the other but not necessarily close in time: 'The series of lectures on computer science started last year'. A TV or radio series is a regular programme that is broadcast one or more times a week: '*Star Trek* is a TV series that has been running for decades'. The word 'series' is the same in both singular and plural.

string (of) /'strɪŋ (əv)/ *noun*, means either a series of similar items occurring close together: 'He owns a string of shops', or similar events that occur very close together: 'She has published a string of best-sellers'. Note that 'string (of)' stresses both the similarity and closeness in time or place. This is a less formal word than the others in this group.

succession (of) /sək'seʃn̩ (əv)/ *noun*, means a number of people or things that follow in time or place: 'An Englishman now joins the succession of foreign football managers who have gone to that country'. Note that 'a succession of' can suggest that there are too many: 'The rock star had a succession of girlfriends'.

sequence of events /'siːkwəns əv ɪ'vents/ *noun*, means a series of related events that occurs in a particular order: 'The police are trying to determine the sequence of events that led to the murder'.

train of events /'treɪn əv ɪ'vents/ *noun*, means a series of events where each action causes the next to occur: 'The fall of the Berlin Wall started an incredible train of events in Central and Eastern Europe'.

SERVE, SERVICE

serve /sɜːv/ *verb*, means many things including to give somebody food or drink, usually in a restaurant: 'Serve these customers immediately'. 'Serve' also refers to the provision of services such as shops and transport: 'The city is well served by buses'. In formal contexts, 'serve' means that a person has worked for a company, organization, or country: 'He served his country loyally'.

service /'sɜːvɪs/ *verb*, is a less general word than serve. It means to examine a vehicle or machine, repairing it if necessary: 'My car has just been serviced but still uses too much oil'. In business English, the expression to 'service a debt' means to pay interest on money borrowed: 'Several developing countries were struggling to service their debts to the international banking community'. See **ROUTE**.

SEW^s, SOW^s

sew /səʊ/ *verb*, means to make stitches with a needle. The past tense of 'sew' is 'sewed', and the past participle either 'sewn' or 'sewed': 'She sewed her wedding gown herself'. 'Sew' combined with 'up' is an informal phrase that means to arrange things in a satisfactory way: 'We sewed up the contract last night'. Note that 'sew', 'sewn' and 'sewed' are pronounced the same as 'sow', 'sown' and 'sowed'. A related noun is 'sewer' /'səʊər/, a person who sews clothes. This rhymes with 'lower' and must not be confused with 'sewer' /'sjuːər/ in the drainage sense.

sow /səʊ/ *verb*, means to plant seeds: 'Sow the grass seed thinly'. The past tense is 'sowed', and the past participle is either 'sowed' or 'sown'. A figurative meaning of 'sow' occurs in the idiom to 'sow the seeds of', meaning to try to spread ideas or feelings that may cause trouble: 'He carefully sowed the seeds of hatred that later destroyed the party'.

SEWAGE, SEWER, SEWERAGE

sewage /'sjuːɪdʒ/ *noun*, means waste material and excrement that are transported in a sewer: 'Raw sewage was pumped and mixed with treated sewage'. A 'sewage farm' is a processing plant and a 'sewage works' is usually designed for recycling sewage.

sewer /'sjuːər/ *noun*, is the underground piping through which sewage is removed. Do not confuse this with 'sewer' /'səʊər/, meaning a person who sews clothes.

sewerage /'sjuːərɪdʒ/ *noun*, means the total system that provides drainage by sewers and treatment and processing of 'sewage'.

SEX, GENDER

sex /seks/ *noun*, is used for the physical activity and biological differences between males and females. Otherwise 'sex' is combined with numerous other terms such as: 'safe sex', 'sex discrimination', which have carefully defined meanings. It is always best to consult an authoritative dictionary before using such terms.

gender /'dʒendər/ *noun*, is a grammatical term used to name classes of nouns. Other parts of speech, such as pronouns, take the gender of the noun they refer to. In English, unlike many other languages, pronouns agree only with the sex of the noun they stand for, and gender has no relevance: male creatures are 'he', female ones are 'she', and all inanimate objects are 'it', with the rare exception of ships, and occasionally favourite land or air vehicles, which may be referred to as 'she'. Even this is dying out. Living creatures whose sex is either irrelevant or unknown may be called 'they', in order to avoid attaching a sex label to them. 'Gender' is also used otherwise to emphasize the social and cultural aspects of being a male or female. Thus 'gender gap' and 'gender roles' are phrases that stress culture, not biology.

> 'It is strictly forbidden on our camping site that people of different sex, for instance, men and women, live together in one tent unless they are married to each other for that purpose.'
> (Sign in campsite)

sexist language

- Sexist language is to be avoided in politically correct, modern English. Here are some of the problem areas and solutions.

- *Generic terms* like **mankind** and **man** when used to mean people of both sexes are criticized because they are old-fashioned, and also because they make males more central than females. One solution is to use *people*, *humanity* and *humankind* instead. Some find *humankind* a strange term, but it has existed since the 17th century. So before you entitle a book or paper *Industrial Man* or *Political Man*, consider *Industrial Life* or *Politics* instead. If you do mean *woman* and *man* as in Sheila Rowbotham's *Woman's Consciousness, Man's World*, there is no problem. Today, *mankind* should be used for males exclusively.

- It follows from this that *the man in the street* could be replaced by *the average person*; *a man-machine interface* could be *a human-machine interface*; *manpower* could be *workforce*, *workpower*, *personnel* or *human resources*; *man's achievements in space* could be *human achievements*. When *man* occurs in expressions such as *time and tide wait for no man* this could be rephrased into *time and tide wait for nobody*.

- **-man** also occurs in some occupations or roles. Here *The New Oxford Dictionary of English* suggests that unless you mean a male and only a male, *businessman* becomes *business person*, *chairman* becomes *chair/chairperson* (*chair* is now the official designation adopted by some British societies), *fireman* becomes *firefighter*, *foreman* becomes *supervisor*, *layman* becomes *layperson*, *policeman* becomes *police officer*, *postman* becomes *postal worker*, and *sportsman* becomes *sportsperson*, and so on. Even though *a Frenchman and Frenchwoman are present* is lengthy, it is better than using *Frenchman* for both sexes; another solution is writing *two French people are present*.

- The verb **to man** is more difficult to replace by a single standard accepted alternative. Unless you are referring only to males, it should be avoided. Here are some suggestions. An office can be *staffed*, an emergency phone can be *answered*, not *manned*. Avoid *manning a ship* by rephrasing and use *the ship's crew*.

- **-ess** is a feminine suffix which has never been used widely, and is losing ground all the time. *Actor-actress, author-authoress, steward-stewardess* are all pairs which are being replaced, either by *actor, author* (whether a man or a woman) or by another term completely, such as *flight attendant* for *air steward(ess)*. The pairs *host-hostess* and *governor-governess* still show useful distinctions in meaning and there is no real masculine equivalent for the term *seamstress*.

See **AUTHOR**. See **GOVERNOR**. See **HE, SHE, THEY**. See **HOST**.

Examples of sexist writing and how to avoid it:

- *Man and his intellectual development*. (Use: *People and their intellectual development.* Alternatively: *Intellectual development in humans*.)
- *Man's search for methods of food preservation has led him*; (Rewrite: *The search for methods of food preservation has led us ...* Alternatively, use: *People have always looked for methods of food preservation. This search has led them ...*)
- This phenomenon has been demonstrated in rats, monkeys and *men*. (Change *men* to *humans*.)
- *There were nine men and three females in the ship's crew.* (Rewrite: *The ship had a crew of 12.* Alternatively, to avoid the non-parallel *men and females*, use: *nine men and three women* or *nine males and three females* – perhaps even reverse the traditional order.)

- *The men and girls in the office.* (Use parallel terms: *men* and *women*, or *boys* and *girls*, perhaps even reverse the traditional order.)
- *The girls at the reception desk.* (Use: *secretaries, office assistants* or just *staff*.)
- *Woman doctor, lady lawyer.* (Use: *doctor, lawyer.* If it is necessary to mention the sex of the person, use *female doctor* and *female lawyer*.)
- *The child may notice his surroundings.* (Change *his* to *its*.)
- *Each person was interviewed and his statement was checked.* (Use the plural: *people ... their statements were*. Otherwise, keep the singular and use *his or her*.)
- *The individual often sees these political issues as nothing that concerns him.* (Use the plural: *individuals often see ... them*.)
- *Research scientists often neglect their wives.* (Replace *wives* by *partners* or *spouses*.)
- The traditional use of *Mr and Mrs James Green* may be found in wedding invitations and other very formal contexts. (Otherwise use *Mr and Mrs Green* or *James and Mary Green* in less formal contexts.)
- The traditional use of *Mrs James Green* may be found in wedding invitations and other very formal contexts. (Otherwise use *Mrs Green*, if she uses 'Mrs'. If not, *Ms Green*, or *Mary Green*, which is the most informal of these.)

See **MR, MS, MRS**.

SHADE, SHADOW

shade /ʃeɪd/ *noun*, means a place of darkness and coolness sheltered from the sun: 'There was only one patch of shade on the beach'. 'Shade' is also used to distinguish colour differences: 'The room was painted in different shades of blue'; and for objects that reduce the intensity of light such as 'lampshade' and informally 'shades' (sunglasses).

shadow /ˈʃædəʊ/ *noun & verb*, as a noun, means either a dark area or a clear shape made by the shade of someone or something. Note that a shadow is sharply defined, but shade is a more general area of relative darkness. People and objects cast shadows, not shades. As a verb, 'shadow' means to follow: 'He was carefully shadowed by the police'.

SHALL, WILL

shall /ʃæl/ *verb*, is becoming less common in modern English. Traditionally, 'shall' was the natural choice for expressing the future in the first person singular and plural, but nowadays 'shall' is used most commonly when making offers and suggestions: 'Shall I see who is at the door?' The contracted form of 'shall not' is 'shan't' /ʃɑːnt/.

will /wɪl/ verb, together with 'going to' and the present tenses, is a way of talking about the future: 'We will talk about this later'. It is most often used to make predictions, firm decisions, and to give a refusal. 'Will' is more and more frequently being used instead of 'shall' in the first person singular and plural. However, it is essential to use 'shall' when making offers and suggestions. Note the difference between: 'Shall we get a drink?' (Would you like one?) and 'Will we get a drink?' (Do you know whether they will give us one?). The contracted form of 'will not' is 'won't' /wəʊnt/. See **CONTRACTIONS**.

SHARP, SHARPLY

sharp /ʃɑːp/ adjective & adverb, as an adjective, means either having a fine edge: 'sharp knife', or a sudden rise or fall: 'A sharp drop in share prices'. If someone is 'sharp', they are quick to understand and react: 'He had razor-sharp intelligence'; or they can be angry: 'Her teacher was rather sharp'. 'Sharp' as an adverb is an informal way of referring to exactness in directions or timekeeping: 'Turn sharp right' (abruptly to the right). It can also mean 'punctual' when used with a specific time: 'Be there at 9 sharp'.

sharply /ʃɑːpli/ adverb, means harshly and distinctly as in: 'The minister was sharply criticised for his role in the matter'.

SHEAR⁵, SHEER⁵

shear /ʃɪər/ verb, means either to cut the wool off sheep, or to break off something such as a metal, as a result of structural strain: 'The wing sheared off the plane'. The past tense form of both uses is 'sheared', and the past participle forms are 'shorn' and 'sheared' respectively.

sheer /ʃɪər/ adjective & verb, as an adjective, means 'incredible', and is used to emphasize the impact of something: 'They were astonished by the sheer size of Australia'. 'Sheer' also means utter or complete: 'Buying that house was sheer stupidity'. As a verb, 'sheer' means to swerve or change course quickly: 'The car sheered off the track'.

SHELF, SHELVE

shelf /ʃelf/ noun, means a flat length of wood on a wall or some furniture for placing books or ornaments on. Note that the plural is 'shelves'. If something is 'off the shelf' that means it is standard: 'Off-the-shelf software'. If a person is 'on the shelf' this is an informal expression that means no longer useful or wanted, or too old to get married. 'Shelf life' means how long something can be kept in a shop before it is no longer able to be used or consumed. See **–F, –FE ENDINGS IN NOUNS**.

shelve /ʃelv/ verb, means to decide not to continue with a plan or to put things aside: 'We have been forced to shelve our plans to hire new staff'. If the ground 'shelves', it slopes gently downwards. Matters that are 'shelved' may be just postponed or forgotten. See **TABLE**.

SHORT, SHORTLY

short /ʃɔːt/ adjective & adverb, as an adjective, refers to a small distance, measurement or duration: 'They took a short walk before dinner'. A person who is 'short' may be below average height or may use few words to show anger: 'He was extremely short on the phone'. 'To be short of' means to not have enough of something. 'To be short for' means that a word, name or group of letters are an abbreviated form of a longer word or expression: 'plc is short for public limited company'. As an adverb, 'short' is only used in such phrases as 'cut short' and 'stop short'. Compare 'to cut someone's hair short' (long hair becomes short hair) with 'to cut someone's hair' (hair of any length becomes shorter).

shortly /ʃɔːtli/ adverb, means 'soon' or 'a short time': 'They arrived shortly after dinner'. 'Shortly' also means 'in an angry way', although the word 'sharply' is more commonly used in this sense.

SHOULD, OUGHT, MUST, HAVE TO

should /ʃʊd/ verb, is used to say that something is right, to give advice or to say which action is best and appropriate: 'You should stop smoking'. Note that 'should' can be used to give instructions politely: 'You should always use safety glasses when operating this machine'. 'Should' can be used to talk about something that is expected to happen: 'He should arrive at 6 o'clock if the train is on time'. It is followed by the infinitive without 'to'.

ought /ɔːt/ *verb*, usually combined with 'to', is used in exactly the same way as 'should', but is less common: 'You ought to see that film'.

must /mʌst/ *verb*, is also used to give advice, especially when speaking persuasively and enthusiastically about something: 'You must see that film. It's fantastic!' However, 'must' is also used when the speaker is giving someone an order or instruction. It is therefore often used in notices: 'Children must be accompanied by an adult'. 'Must' is followed by the infinitive without 'to' : 'must be', 'must have', etc. Note that 'must' can only be used in the present. Use different tenses of 'have to' when giving an order or instruction in the past or future.

have to /'hæv tə/ *verb*, is used to stress that an action must be done because circumstances make it necessary, rather than expressing the personal authority of the speaker: 'I can't go out tonight, because I have to revise for my exams'. 'Have to' is followed by the infinitive without 'to'.

SHOUT, SCREAM

shout /ʃaʊt/ *verb*, means to say something in a loud voice either to make someone hear or because the speaker is angry: 'She shouted hysterically at the dog's owner'.

scream /skriːm/ *verb*, also means to make a loud noise, but this is a loud and piercing cry and the result of pain, fright or excitement: 'Both the children started screaming their heads off'.

SIDE, HAND

(on one) side /(ɒn 'wʌn) saɪd/ usually means a specific position, such as 'The sun shone on one side of the valley'. If you want to contrast this, use 'the other side': 'The other side of the valley was in the shadow of the mountain'. See **PARTY**.

(on the one) hand /(ɒn ðə 'wʌn) hænd/ expresses the general idea of a contrast: 'On the one hand, I think that he should have resigned, but on the other (hand), he was probably following the orders of his superiors'.

SIGN, SIGNAL

sign /saɪn/ *noun*, means an event or action that indicates the existence of something now or in the future: 'These flowers are the first distinct sign of spring'.

signal /'sɪgnəl/ *noun*, means both an event or action that gives a sign of something, and a movement or sound to give information, a warning, etc. Consequently, 'sign' and 'signal' can overlap, but while there may be no reaction to a sign, a positive reaction to a signal is expected: 'After he drove past the stop sign, the police made a clear signal that he had to pull over'.

SILICON, SILICONE

silicon /'sɪlɪkən/ *noun*, is a non-metallic solid element (chemical symbol Si), from which computer chips are made: 'Silicon Valley produces computer products, not silicon'.

silicone /'sɪlɪkəʊn/ *noun*, is any of a group of malleable plastics used in polishes, or for implants used in cosmetic surgery.

SILK, SILKY

silk /sɪlk/ *noun*, means things that are made of the fibre produced by silkworms: 'She wore a delicate silk dress'.

silky /'sɪlki/ *adjective*, is used for things that look or feel like silk: 'He stroked the cat's black, silky fur'. A person's voice can be termed 'silky' if it is smooth.

SIMILAR, LIKE, ALIKE, AS IF

similar /'sɪmɪlər/ *adjective*, means having a resemblance to a thing or person without being identical. 'Similar' is combined with 'to' when followed by a noun or pronoun: 'This part of Europe is very similar to New Zealand'. 'Similar' is more formal than 'like'.

like /laɪk/ *preposition & conjunction*, as a preposition, means having the same characteristics or qualities as some other person or thing: 'Now he was eighteen, he wanted to be treated like a grown-up'. 'Similar to' could not be used here. However, as a conjunction, 'like' means 'similar to'. In standard usage, 'like' is not followed by a clause: 'He looks like Napoleon'. Careful writers avoid non-standard usage, such as 'He looks like he's just won the lottery' (use 'as if' here).

alike /ə'laɪk/ *adjective & adverb*, as an adjective, means that two or more people, animals or things are similar: 'The girls looked remarkably alike'. As an adverb, it means in a similar way, without discrimination, and follows the object: 'The King talked to the managers and workers alike'.

as if /əz 'ɪf/ *conjunction*, indicates a comparison about the way something is done or happens: 'He looks as if he's just won the lottery'. Always use a verb after 'as if'.

SIMPLE, SIMPLISTIC

simple /'sɪmpl̩/ *adjective*, means easily understood, plain and uncomplicated: 'KISS is short for "keep it short and simple"'.

simplistic /sɪm'plɪstɪk/ *adjective*, means oversimplified and treating complex ideas as if they were 'simple' ones. 'Simplistic' is thus a negative term. As it contains the idea of being oversimple, it is best to use 'simplistic' rather than 'oversimplistic': 'The director presented a highly simplistic account of why the two companies had to merge'.

SINK, SUNKEN

sink /sɪŋk/ *verb*, means to go below the surface or move towards the bottom. This has the past form 'sank': 'The ferry sank in the river'. The past participle is 'sunk', which means, for a boat, that it has suffered damage making it 'sink' below the surface: 'The ship was sunk by the enemy'.

sunken /'sʌŋkən/ *adjective*, means being submerged in water or being below its usual level, such as 'sunken ship' or 'sunken garden'.

'If the ship sinks, walk quickly to the liferafts. Do not swim.' (Notice in steamer)

SIR, DAME

Sir /sɜːr, sər/ is the English title of a male who has been knighted and who is formally addressed by his first name and surname: 'Sir Alex Ferguson', or just 'Sir' with the first name: 'Sir Alex'. It is incorrect to omit the first name: not 'Sir Ferguson'. 'Sir' (sometimes capitalized) is used as a polite form of addressing a man who is in a position of authority. It should not be used among equals. 'Sir' is also used as a salutation in formal business letters. The female equivalent is 'madam'.
See **LETTERS AND EMAILS**. See **MADAM**.

Dame /deɪm/ is the female equivalent to 'Sir'. Like 'Sir', 'Dame' is placed before a first name: 'Dame Mary', or before the whole name: 'Dame Mary Smith', but it is not used before the surname without the first name: not 'Dame Smith'.

SIZE, SIZED, SIZEABLE

size /saɪz/ *noun*. When talking about shoes or clothes, 'size' means one of a range of standard measurements: 'What size do you take?' Avoid 'large in size' or 'large-sized'. Just use 'large'. See **TAUTOLOGY**.

size and **sized** /saɪzd/ refer to measurements or dimensions and are used with compound adjectives. One or the other may be normal in particular combinations, such as: 'outsize dress' and 'life-size painting'.

sizeable /'saɪzəbl̩/ *adjective*, means large and this word can be spelt either with or without 'e' in mid position: 'She was earning a sizeable income'.

SKILFUL, SKILLED

skilful /'skɪlfʊl/ *adjective*, means being good at something that needs ability or special training both practically and theoretically: 'The strike was finally over thanks to the efforts of a skilful negotiator'. This is the BE spelling. 'Skillful' is the AE spelling of 'skilful'.

skilled /skɪld/ *adjective*, suggests knowledge, ability and training in a craft, and can apply to professional as well as manual work: 'The number of skilled carpenters is decreasing'.

SLACK, SLACKEN

slack /slæk/ *adjective*, either means loose: 'The rope was taut, then went completely slack'; or refers to a low level of business: 'This has been a slack season for all the hotels'. In a third sense 'slack' means lazy: 'The manager told his team that they were too slack, and needed to work harder'.

slacken /'slækən/ *verb*, means to make something less tight, or to slow down progress: 'Can we slacken the pace of this meeting a little?' In business, the phrase 'slacken off' means that something becomes less active or stops growing: 'The rise in shares slackened off'.

SLIGHT, SLIGHTLY, MARGINAL, MARGINALLY

slight /slaɪt/ *adjective*, means small in degree: 'The glare of the sun caused a slight headache'. A person who is small and thin can have a 'slight figure'.

slightly /'slaɪtli/ *adverb*, means a little: 'He offered them a slightly more expensive car'. A 'slightly built' person means someone who is small and thin.

marginal /'mɑːdʒɪnəl/ *adjective*, means connected with or located at the edge of something: 'This is classified as marginal agricultural land – nothing will grow here'. 'Marginal' also means slight, low, or of minor importance. In economic terminology, a 'marginal profit' means close to making a profit or not: 'This product will only make a marginal profit'.

marginally /'mɑːdʒɪnəli/ *adverb*, means not very much: 'Prices only rose marginally last year'. 'Marginally' can always be replaced by 'slightly', but note that 'slightly' cannot always be replaced by 'marginally', e.g. 'a slightly built person'.

SLOW, SLOWLY

slow /sləʊ/ *adjective & adverb*, as an adjective, means with delay, not busy or not moving fast: 'They were stuck on the motorway in the slow lane'. As an adverb, 'slow' is often used with 'go', as in 'go slow', meaning doing something at a slow tempo.

slowly /sləʊli/ *adverb*, means not fast and is used in expressions like: 'Please drive slowly'. Note that 'please drive slow' is informal, and many people would consider it to be incorrect.

SMELL, STINK, STENCH

smell /smel/ *noun*, means an odour or scent. A smell can either be pleasant: 'The smell of roasting coffee beans always makes my mouth water', or unpleasant: 'There was a musty smell in the room'. See **FRAGRANT**. See **ODOUR**.

stink /stɪŋk/ *noun*, means a very unpleasant smell: 'This room has an overpowering stink of unwashed clothes'. Figuratively, 'to cause a stink' means to cause trouble.

stench /stentʃ/ *noun*, means a strong, very unpleasant smell: 'He was greeted by the nauseating stench of rotten fish'.

SNOW, SLEET, SLUSH

snow /snəʊ/ *noun*, means either the soft white flakes of frozen water or the layer formed by such flakes that is lying on the ground. In some cultures there are dozens of names for the different types of snow. In English, it may only be skiers who are familiar with terms like 'fine, powdery snow'. Figuratively, 'snow' is an indicator of purity and expressions like: 'Her conscience was white as snow' describe cleanness.

sleet /sliːt/ *noun*, means a mixture of rain and snow falling from the sky. If sleet settles, this layer will be described as ice. See **RAIN**.

slush /slʌʃ/ *noun*, means partly melted snow and ice on the ground. This is usually dirty: 'The roads were salted and drivers had to cope with 3 cm of grey slush'.

SO-CALLED, IN NAME ONLY

so-called /'səʊ 'kɔːld/ *adjective*, means that something or someone is described inappropriately: 'His so-called humour'. Avoid overusing 'so-called', as it shows a personal view that others may disagree with. The term that is 'so-called' is sometimes enclosed by inverted commas: 'His so-called "humour" and "jokes" bored us all'.

in name only /ɪn 'neɪm 'əʊnli/ means generally recognized, but not genuinely valid. This is a more formal way of implying the same idea as 'so-called': 'Everybody in the country knew that it was a university in name only'.

SOCIABLE, SOCIAL

sociable /'səʊʃəbl̩/ *adjective*, refers to those who enjoy spending time with others: 'They are very sociable in this part of Europe'.

social /'səʊʃl̩/ *adjective*, can mean sociable. However, in this context, 'social' is usually found in fixed expressions connected with sociable activities, such as: 'social club' or 'social events': 'They have a very limited social life'. 'Social' can also be a neutral word that means connected with society, as in 'social reform' and 'social class'.

SOCIAL SCIENCE, SOCIAL STUDIES

social science /'səʊʃl̩ 'saɪəns/ *noun*, means the study of people in society, and the 'social sciences' include academic subjects such as sociology, political science and economics: 'Social science has a good reputation at this university'. The term is used in phrases such as 'a social science degree'; or 'a degree in the social sciences'.

social studies /'səʊʃl̩ 'stʌdɪz/ *noun*, is the study of human society. This is more broadly based and often less advanced than social science: 'Social studies is well taught at this school'. Note that it is followed by a singular verb.

SOLVABLE, SOLUBLE, SOLUTION

solvable /'sɒlvəbl̩/ *adjective*, means able to be solved and is used in reference to problems: 'This puzzle must be solvable'. Note that the negative form is 'unsolvable'.

soluble /'sɒljʊbḷ/ adjective, means able to be dissolved, such as some substances in liquids: 'Salt is soluble in water'. 'Soluble' in informal use can also mean 'solvable' and is used to refer to problems and challenges. Note that the negative form is 'insoluble'.

solution /sə'lj uːʃn/ noun, is a means of solving something such as a problem or dispute: 'We must find a quick solution, otherwise there will be fighting'. 'Solution' in another sense means a liquid in which a solid is dissolved: 'A concentrated solution of acid was spilt on the workbench'.

SOME, ANY

some /səm, sʌm/ determiner & pronoun, as a determiner, means an indefinite amount or number of things: 'I have still got some furniture from last year'. When 'some' is followed by a number, the number should be an approximate figure, usually ending in a zero: 'Some 500 soccer fans', not 'some 498 fans'. 'Some' can also indicate certain groups etc.: 'Some people still think that the earth is flat'. Note that in this sense the pronunciation is always the strong form with a full vowel. Informally, 'some' can be used in an emphatic sense to convey enthusiasm: 'That was some party. One of the best I've ever been to'. As a pronoun, 'some' is used in affirmative statements, and in questions where the expected answer is 'yes', or when a 'yes' answer is being encouraged: 'I've got some /səm/ champagne in the fridge. Would you like some /sʌm/?' See **APPROXIMATION**.

any /'eni/ determiner & pronoun, as a determiner, means an indefinite amount or number of things. It is usually used in negative statements and general questions: 'I haven't got any scissors, so you will have to use a knife'. Note that 'any' can be combined with negative words like 'hardly', 'never' and 'without': 'You have never/hardly done any cleaning in the house'. However, on its own, 'any' does not have a negative meaning: 'Which can I have?' 'Any'. As a pronoun, 'any' is used in questions where the expected answer is 'no': 'We've run out of champagne. I hope you didn't want any?'

SOMEONE, SOMEBODY

someone /'sʌmwʌn/ pronoun, means a person who is unspecified or unknown: 'Someone is at the door'. The difference between 'someone' and 'anyone' is the same as for 'some' and 'any'. Note that 'someone' always takes a singular verb. See **ANYONE**. See **NO ONE**.

somebody /'sʌmbədi/ pronoun, means the same as 'someone', but is considered slightly more informal. The difference between 'somebody' and 'anybody' is the same as for 'some' and 'any'. However, 'a somebody' informally refers to a person who is remarkable, or of high status: 'He thinks he is a real somebody'. Note that 'somebody' always takes a singular verb.

SOMETIME, SOMETIMES, SOMEDAY

sometime /'sʌmtaɪm/ adverb, means at some unspecified time. 'Some time' is an alternative spelling: 'They will arrive sometime/some time soon'. 'Some time' also means that a job may require many hours or days: 'Reading that report will take some time'. (Note there is a double stress here: /'sʌm 'taɪm/.)

sometimes /'sʌmtaɪmz/ adverb, means 'occasionally': 'They sometimes had to wait for the train for five hours'.

someday /'sʌmdeɪ/ adverb, means at a future, but not specified time: 'We will be back someday'. This is sometimes spelt 'some day' and this may stress a specific day: 'We will be back some day next week'.

SOMEWHERE, SOMEPLACE

somewhere /'sʌmhweər/ adverb, means an unspecified place: 'See you somewhere, sometime'; as well as an unspecified amount or a range of time, distance, etc.: 'They offered somewhere around £250 000 for the house'. Note that 'somewhere' is used in positive sentences or questions where the expected answer is 'yes', unlike anywhere, which occurs in negative sentences and questions. See **ANYWHERE**.

someplace /'sʌmpleɪs/ adverb, means 'somewhere' and is used more widely in AE than in BE. It is an informal word: 'We are still trying to find someplace to live'.

SORE[S], SOAR[S]

sore /sɔːr/ adjective, means painful: 'He had a sore heel after the long walk'. 'Sore' is also used figuratively in the expression 'a sore point'. The phrase 'to stick out like a sore thumb' is a criticism, and refers to a thing or person that is unpleasantly and noticeably different.

soar /sɔːr/ *verb*, means to reach a high level very smoothly and quickly: 'The gulls soared above the cliffs'. Figuratively, it means to increase in value: 'Prices soared dramatically when war was declared'. If a person's 'spirits soar', this means that he or she is happy and pleased about something.

SOUND, NOISE

sound /saʊnd/ *noun*, is a general word for things that can be heard: 'There was the faint but unmistakable sound of a waterfall in the distance'. Although 'sound' can be used with a negative adjective like 'awful', it is not as critical as calling something 'noise'. 'Sound' is countable, except in technical contexts such as: 'sound engineer' and 'sound quality'.

noise /nɔɪz/ *noun*, is a loud and unpleasant sound that is unwelcome. Consequently, 'noise' is frequently used together with words that are negative, such as 'horrible'. In a technical context, 'noise' is unwanted signals: 'This noise is creating snow on the monitor'. 'Noise' can be uncountable, as in: 'The children are making a lot of noise'. It is not correct to use 'sound' here.

SOUTH, SOUTHERN, SOUTHERLY

south /saʊθ/ *noun & adjective*, is the direction to a person's right when facing the rising sun. When it refers to a direction, 'south' is not usually capitalized: 'The wind was blowing from the south'. It is capitalized, but not hyphenated, when it is part of a continent or country: 'South Korea'; a regional name: 'South of France'; or a defined region, for example within the USA: 'She returned to the South', meaning the SE part of that country.
See **CAPITAL LETTERS**.

southern /'sʌðən/ *adjective*, means located in, or connected with, the south: 'There will be warm weather across the whole of southern England'. 'Southern' is only capitalized when it refers to a proper noun such as: 'Southern Alps'.

southerly /'sʌðəli/ *adjective*, means in a direction towards the south: 'The birds were migrating in a southerly direction'. It also refers to a wind that is blowing from the south: 'The ship stopped rolling when it reached an area with southerly winds'. Note that 'southerly' is normally immediately followed by a noun and that it rhymes with 'motherly'.

SPECIALITY, SPECIALISM

speciality /speʃɪ'ælɪti/ *noun*, means a product or food that is characteristic of a company, person or region: 'Plum pudding is a speciality in this restaurant in December'. Someone who has a specific skill or is an expert also has a speciality: 'He is a good singer, but playing the drums is his speciality'. 'Specialty' /'speʃlti/ is an AE alternative to 'speciality'.
See **ESPECIAL/ESPECIALLY**.

specialism /'speʃlɪzm̩/ *noun*, means an area of academic study or work that someone has specialized in: 'This degree has a specialism in biotechnology'.

SPECIES, STRAIN

species /'spiːʃɪz/ *noun*, means a group of the same type. It is normally used for plants and animals. Note it is unchanged in the singular and plural forms: 'This species is rare, but those species are rarer'.

strain /streɪn/ *noun*, means a variety or stock of plant or animal developed by breeding: 'They successfully marketed a new strain of rice in South East Asia'. See **STRESS**.

SPEED, SPED, SPEEDED

speed /spiːd/ *noun & verb*, as a noun, is the rate of progress and is given as a number, so that 'speed' cannot be 'fast' or 'slow', only 'high' or 'low': 'His speed was too high for such narrow roads'. As a verb, 'to speed' means to go too fast, generally over the speed limit: 'He was fined for speeding last year'. 'Speed up' means to go faster: 'Whenever I try to overtake that car, it speeds up'. 'Speed up' is also used figuratively: 'We will need to speed up the negotiations if we are to find a solution quickly'.

sped /sped/ *verb*, is the past tense and past participle of 'to speed'. 'Sped' is often used with an adverb, to mean move fast: 'He quickly sped home'.

speeded /'spiːdɪd/ *verb*, is also the past tense and past participle of to 'speed'. 'Speeded' is used in connection with traffic limits: 'He speeded all the way home' (broke the speed limit). 'Speeded up' is the past tense of 'speed up'.

SPELL, SPELT, SPELLED

spell /spel/ *noun & verb*, as a noun, means a period of time. Weather is typically described in terms of 'spells': 'Next week there will be spells of thundery weather'. 'Spells' can also be magic, as in fairy stories. As a verb, 'spell' is connected with spelling or is used to indicate something bad or unfortunate: 'The fog on the roads spelt danger'. 'To spell something out' means to clarify something by explaining it in detail: 'I will now spell out the details in the contract'.

spelt /spelt/ *verb*, is the past tense and past participle of the verb 'to spell'. 'Spelt' is the BE form: 'He spelt most of the words wrong'.

spelled /speld/ *verb*, is an alternative spelling for the past tense and past participle of 'spell', and is the only AE form.

spelling – some typical problem words

• Here are some words that often cause difficulty:
accommodate, acknowledge, allege, argument, calendar, cemetery, committee, concede, conscience, consensus, embarrass, exceed, February, foreign, gauge, government, harass, inoculate, language, library, millennium, necessary, neighbour, occasion, parliament, persuade, precede, privilege, proceed, professor, pronunciation, pursue, recede, recommend, reference, science, secretary, succeed, supersede, surprise, suspicious, therefore, Wednesday.

See **PLURAL NOUNS**. See **–ES, –S AFTER NOUNS ENDING IN –O**.

SPIN, SPIN DOCTOR

spin /spɪn/ *noun*, means the presentation of information in a way that puts a favourable bias or angle on one particular standpoint: 'The Minister's advisers put some spin on the events'. In a figurative context this is uncountable.

spin doctor /'spɪn dɒktər/ *noun*, means a spokesperson who is skilled in presenting information to the media that favours one organization or group: 'He used to be a government spin doctor'. See **PROPAGANDA**.

SPIRITUAL, SPIRITED

spiritual /'spɪrɪtjʊəl/ *adjective*, refers to that which affects the spirit or soul. It also means non-material: 'More attention to our spiritual needs is required'.

spirited /'spɪrɪtɪd/ *adjective*, means full of energy, enthusiastic and determined: 'Despite all the odds, this spirited politician became the next president'.

split infinitives

• *Split infinitives* are verb forms in which a word has been inserted between the infinitive marker and the verb stem, such as between *to* and *make*, as in *to really make*. This has often been regarded by purists as one of the deadly sins in English. Many modern authoritative books about English such as *The New Oxford Dictionary of English* point out that this 'rule' is probably misguided as it is said to be based on practice in Latin. As Latin writes its infinitives, such as *amare* (to love) in one word, it is a very strange argument.

• Inserting a word, usually an adverb, between *to* and the following infinitive may result in greater precision such as: *His only wish was to really sleep* (sleep very well and undisturbed). Compare this with: *His only wish really was to sleep* (means just to sleep, nothing about the quality of sleep). This example of an adverb splitting an infinitive is natural in many cases. *I wish to flatly forbid* sounds more natural than *I wish to forbid flatly* or *I wish flatly to forbid*. *Always, finally, fully, nearly, really* and *simply* are typical adverbs that naturally split infinitives today. On the other hand, a lengthy gap between *to* and the following infinitive is not recommended and *He wanted to completely and comprehensively redesign the training programme*, should be rephrased.

• The splitting of infinitives is a natural part of modern English and there is nothing wrong in writing *to always use* or *to really remember*.

SPOUSE, HUSBAND, WIFE

spouse /spaʊs/ *noun*, means a husband or wife when considered in relation to their partner: 'Let us invite all our friends and their spouses'. This is a formal or legal term, and an expression such as 'She decided to take her spouse out for a meal' is not everyday English.

husband /'hʌzbənd/ or **wife** /waɪf/ should always be used instead of 'spouse' whenever it is possible.

STAFF, MAID, AU PAIR (DOMESTIC)

staff /stɑːf/ *noun*, in a house means residential, domestic employees. 'Servant' is no longer a suitable word. See **EMPLOYEE**.
See **PERSONNEL ⇨ PERSONAL**.

maid /meɪd/ *noun*, is a domestic helper. The term is disliked in BE, but not in AE. Hotels use the term 'chambermaid'.

au pair /əʊ ˈpeər/ *noun*, means a young foreign person, often female, who is paid to help in the house.

STAND, GRANDSTAND, STADIUM, ARENA

stand /stænd/ *noun*, means a seated, tiered construction in a stadium for spectators to sit in to watch football matches and similar sporting events. A 'stand' can also be a raised platform for musicians, called a 'bandstand', or a small structure from which food, drink or clothing are sold, especially in the street: 'Can you go to the hot-dog stand for me?'

grandstand /ˈɡrændstænd/ *noun*, is a large covered structure with seats at a football stadium or racetrack. A 'grandstand view' means the best view possible.

stadium /ˈsteɪdɪəm/ *noun*, means an athletics or sports ground with rows of seating and food and drink stands for spectators: 'The track events will be in the new stadium'. The plural is 'stadiums'. The alternative plural, 'stadia' /ˈsteɪdɪə/ refers to the site of Roman chariot races.

arena /əˈriːnə/ *noun*, means an enclosed area which is flat in the centre and has seats around it, that is used for people to watch a sporting event or entertainment: 'That was the last concert in the arena before it was rebuilt'. 'Arena' can also be used figuratively to mean an area of activity, particularly involving dispute, as in: 'He won the election and became central in the political arena'.

STATE, COUNTRY

state /steɪt/ *noun & verb*, as a noun, means a country or government. This emphasizes the political organization: 'The member states in the EU'. 'State' in BE means the government and public administration at national level, but in AE it only refers to government in any of the fifty states in the USA. 'State' is often written without a capital: 'The welfare state does not work very well'. 'State' is capitalized in the titles of countries, or organized political entities or parts of a federal republic: 'The State of California'. Also some proper nouns containing the word are capitalized such as 'State Registered Nurse'. 'The States' is normally understood as an informal reference to the USA. 'State' in another sense means a condition: 'The company was in a poor financial state'. As a verb, 'state' means to express something definitely and clearly in speech or writing: 'They were asked to state their opinion clearly'. See **GOVERNMENT**.

country /ˈkʌntri/ *noun*, means either an area of land with its own government: 'The country has just celebrated the 50th anniversary of its independence'; or an area of land with distinctive features: 'This is real mountain country'. In this second sense, 'country' usually follows an adjective. When people refer to 'the country' this generally means an area that is not a town or city: 'They bought a small cottage in the country'. See **COUNTRYSIDE** ⇨ **NATURE**.

STATE OF THE ART, CUTTING EDGE

state of the art /ˈsteɪt əv ði ˈɑːt/ *adjective*, means the newest ideas, most up-to-date features or the most recent stage in product development: 'This equipment is state of the art'. Note that hyphens must be used when 'state of the art' is used in front of a noun: 'This PC has state-of-the-art design'.

cutting edge /kʌtɪŋ ˈedʒ/ *noun & adjective*, means the latest or most advanced stage of development. It can also be used for pioneering and/or innovative research: 'This work is at the cutting edge of marine cybernetics'. Note that a hyphen is required when 'cutting edge' is used as an adjective in front of a noun: 'This is cutting-edge technology'. Apart from describing research, the term can also be used for speech or writing that is sharp and direct: 'Sir Winston's humour was renowned for its cutting edge'.

STATIONARY[S], STATIONERY[S]

stationary /ˈsteɪʃn̩ri/ *adjective*, means without movement or change in condition: 'The car was completely stationary'.

stationery /ˈsteɪʃn̩ri/ *noun*, means writing paper and envelopes. 'Office supplies' is a more general term that includes staplers, ring binders, paper clips and tape dispensers: 'We now have our business stationery and office supplies'.

STATUE, STATUTE

statue /ˈstætjuː/ *noun*, means a figure of a person or animal that is made in stone, metal, wood, etc. and is often life-size or larger: 'The huge bronze statue stands in the market square'. A related word is 'statuette', meaning a small statue.

statute /ˈstætjuːt/ *noun*, means a law that has been passed by a parliament and written down: 'This law is now on the statute book'. 'Statutes' usually means the written and formal rules of an association or company: 'The statutes of the club were changed to admit female members'.

STEP, STAGE, PHASE

step /step/ *noun*, means one of a series of events in making progress towards a goal: 'Wanting to learn to swim is the first step towards success or failure'. The phrase 'a step in the right direction' means a positive move.

stage /steɪdʒ/ *noun*, means a period or state passed through when in training or making progress: 'We have now reached the stage where the children can swim with small buoyancy tanks'. A 'stage' can also be a distinct part of a predetermined process: 'The insect was in its larval stage'; or a raised area in a theatre for actors to perform on. This can also be extended to mean all types of acting: 'He went on the stage at the age of sixteen'.

phase /feɪz/ *noun*, means either a stage in a process of development: 'They have finished the design phase for the lightweight car battery'; or a changed situation such as a new phase of life: 'After he left home, he had a phase when he drifted from town to town'. The shape of the moon and characteristics of electronic signals can be described in phases.

STEPS, STAIRS

steps /steps/ *noun*, means a series of flat surfaces outside a building, and an alternative term is a 'flight of steps': 'Take care with the steps by the garage, the stones are loose'. 'Steps' is also a truncated form for 'stepladder', a device in two parts for climbing short heights to assist in painting ceilings, etc.

stairs /steəz/ *noun*, means a flight of steps inside a building or structure: 'Take that flight of stairs up to the second floor'. An alternative term is 'staircase'. This means that in a large aircraft, passengers can be asked to take the 'staircase' and go 'upstairs' or 'downstairs'. However, when a plane is on the ground it may be boarded by going up or down the 'steps'.

 'Hot and cold water running up and down the stairs.' (Hotel brochure)

STIMULUS, STIMULANT, STIMULATION, SIMULATION

stimulus /'stɪmjʊləs/ *noun*, refers to things that produce a reaction in a person, plant or animal: 'The heavy rain acted as a powerful stimulus upon plant and animal life'. A 'stimulus' can also

be a means of helping development or an incentive: 'Early retirement provided a major stimulus'. The plural of 'stimulus' is 'stimuli' /'stɪmjʊlaɪ/.

stimulant /'stɪmjʊlənt/ *noun*, is something that quickens bodily action or a mental process: 'Coffee is a good stimulant'. A stimulant has a short life, but a stimulus can continue for years. The plural of stimulant is 'stimulants'.

stimulation /stɪmjʊ'leɪʃn/ *noun*, means the process or state that encourages interest or activity in something: 'The writing course provided sufficient stimulation to produce three novels'. Note that 'stimulation' is a more general term than 'stimulus' or 'stimulant'.

simulation /sɪmjʊ'leɪʃn/ *noun*, means an artificially created condition which represents a real-life situation for study or experimentation: 'The pilot-training unit has a real-life simulation of landing a plane in heavy rain'. In another sense, it can mean action or behaviour that attempts to deceive others: 'The jury all agreed that her tears in court were just simulation'.

STOCK, STOCKPILE, STORE, STORAGE

stock /stɒk/ *noun*, means goods or materials for sale that are kept on the premises of a shop or a warehouse: 'We have this size in stock'. Often 'stocks' is used to mean all the goods: 'Stocks of milk are running low'. 'Stocks' can also mean shares in a company, or in BE, government stocks which are traded like shares on the 'stock market'.

stockpile /'stɒkpaɪl/ *noun & verb*, as a noun, means a large supply of food, oil, materials or weapons that is kept for future use: 'We have a large stockpile of grain at the moment'. As a verb, 'stockpile' means to build up and maintain a large supply: 'Most countries in Europe stockpile oil for the winter'.

store /stɔːr/ *noun & verb*, as a noun, means a quantity or supply of something: 'The store of nuts was getting low'. A store can be a large shop with many departments: 'Harrods is the only real department store for many people'; or a local village shop. The plural 'stores' followed by a singular verb is the place where military supplies are kept. When followed by a plural verb, 'stores' are either the supplies themselves or, in AE, a number of shops. As a verb, 'store' means to keep something for future use or reference: 'The database had millions of entries stored on six servers'.

storage /ˈstɔːrɪdʒ/ *noun*, means the process of keeping something for future use: 'The crops were put in cold storage'. However, unlike 'stockpile', the quantity of items is not relevant. In computing, 'storage' and retrieval of data are two critical issues: 'What is the available disk storage now?' Note that 'storage' is an uncountable noun.

STORM, GALE

storm /stɔːm/ *noun*, means very bad weather which may include strong winds and rain or snow: 'The raging storm was approaching'. 'Storm' can be combined with nouns such as 'sand', 'snow,' and 'thunder': 'I just heard on the news we are in for a thunderstorm'. In figurative use, 'storm' means a display of strong feeling: 'The minister provoked a storm of protests with her new plans'.

gale /geɪl/ *noun*, means a very strong wind: 'There was a howling gale outside'; 'The ship was rolling in the gale-force winds'. Note that 'gale' is a measurement of wind speed on the Beaufort Scale that runs from force 0 (calm) to force 12 (hurricane): 'It was either a force 8 or force 9 gale outside'. See **HURRICANE**.

STRAIGHT[S], STRAIT[S]

straight /streɪt/ *adjective & adverb*, as an adjective, means in a line: 'He had a straight back'. As an adverb, 'straight' means immediately, directly or without deviation: 'Go straight there'. A sports team can have three 'straight wins', meaning three consecutive wins.

strait /streɪt/ *noun & adjective*, means a narrow stretch of water: 'They sailed through the strait'. In some proper names the plural form is used as in: 'The Straits of Gibraltar'. 'To be in dire straits' means to be in serious difficulty. As an adjective, 'strait' means narrow, or restricting. A 'straitjacket' is a garment that restrains someone who is mentally unstable and likely to become violent.

STRANGER, FOREIGNER, ALIEN

stranger /ˈstreɪndʒər/ *noun*, is a person not known to the speaker, even if he or she lives in the next street. Although the phrase 'Don't talk to strangers' warns children not to talk to unfamiliar people, the expression 'Hello stranger' is an ironic greeting used when meeting a friend who has not been seen for a long time.

foreigner /ˈfɒrənər/ *noun*, is a person of a different nationality from oneself. Informally, 'foreigner' may refer to someone of the same nationality but who is an outsider, or a stranger to a particular group: 'We don't like foreigners from London here in Birmingham'.

alien /ˈeɪlɪən/ *adjective & noun*, as an adjective, means something unfamiliar or distasteful. As a noun, it is a technical word used by the authorities in various countries to mean 'foreigner', but it now also means a creature from another planet – an extraterrestrial.

STRATEGY, TACTICS

strategy /ˈstrætədʒi/ *noun*, means an overall plan to obtain a major objective: 'He designed a corporate strategy that is very promising'. A 'strategist' is a person who is skilled in devising 'strategies'.

tactics /ˈtæktɪks/ *noun*, are the methods or detailed procedures involved in carrying out a strategy. This word is usually plural but 'tactic' refers to a single action: 'That strike was a poor tactic'. A 'tactician' is a person who is skilled in working out tactics.

STRENGTH, POWER, FORCE

strength /streŋkθ/ *noun*, means the quality of being physically or mentally strong. The context generally indicates which is understood: 'Sorry, I have not got enough strength to push that car'. The 'strength' of a rope is its ability to hold a certain weight. The related adjective is 'strong'.

power /ˈpaʊər/ *noun*, in terms of a person's physical strength, is limited to the capacity of a part of their body: 'He has great power in his legs'. 'Power' in a machine or energy carrier is the energy within that can be applied: 'We can use the power in this river to generate electricity'. 'Power' when applied to people or groups is often a state or condition of having influence or authority: 'I do not have the power to make that decision'. The related adjectives are 'powerful' and 'potent'. See **POTENT.**

force /fɔːs/ *noun*, means the physical strength or energy that is used to do something: 'The building was completely wrecked by the force of the explosion'. Note that 'force' is used to describe the application of physical strength, action, or power, whereas both 'strength' and 'power' are qualities that do not have to be used. As a result of this, 'force' is a word that is often combined with terms such as 'centrifugal', 'driving', or 'magnetic'. The related adjective is 'forceful', which is often used to describe the way one puts across an argument. See **VIGOUR**.

STRESS, STRAIN

stress /stres/ *noun & verb*, as a noun, means mental or physical pressure: 'Too many people are working under stress today'. 'Physical stress' also relates to pressure or tension on objects such as buildings or bridges. Note that 'stress' can be both countable and uncountable. The adjective form is 'stressful'. As a verb, 'stress' means to place emphasis on something that is said or written: 'The minister stressed the importance of saving energy'. Informally, a person can feel 'stressed (out)', when they are feeling under pressure.

strain /strein/ *noun & verb*, as a noun, means general anxiety and tension, caused by having too many problems to deal with: 'The strain of repaying the debt caused his nervous breakdown'. 'Physical strain' usually refers to the pressure on objects such as a rope or cable under great tension: 'The ship started to drift when the rope broke due to the strain'. Note that 'strain' can be both countable and uncountable, and has no adjective form. A pressurized situation can be described as 'a strain'. As a verb, 'strain' means to injure a part of one's body such as a muscle: 'He fell off the branch and strained his wrist when he landed'.

STRICT, HARSH, RIGOROUS, HARD, SEVERE, TOUGH

strict /strikt/ *adjective*, means demanding that rules and behaviour are obeyed: 'She says that all the teachers at her new school are very strict'.

harsh /hɑːʃ/ *adjective*, means both too strong and bright, as in: 'the harsh light of dawn', and also cruel and unkind: 'He was a harsh, despotic chairman'. 'Harsh' is also used to describe a climate that is unpleasant and hostile.

rigorous /'rɪgərəs/ *adjective*, means precise and explicitly stated: 'The company has rigorous production standards'. This is a formal word. See -OR, OUR SPELLINGS. See RIGOUR

hard /hɑːd/ *adjective*, means solid and firm and not easily broken. A person described as 'hard' is physically and mentally strong, and does not show weakness or fear: 'The typical American action film hero is a hard man'. It can also mean strong or intense, as in 'hard liquor'. See **HARD** (adverb).

severe /sɪ'vɪər/ *adjective*, means unkind or very difficult: 'The prisoner told of his severe upbringing'. 'Severe' means very bad when used to describe negative concepts such as damage or loss.

tough /tʌf/ *adjective*, can also mean difficult, or causing problems: 'I have some tough decisions to make'. Tough also means firm in order to ensure rules are followed, and is a less formal alternative to 'strict'. A useful expression is 'to get tough on/with' someone or something: 'The prime minister said that his government would get tough on crime'.

STRIKE, STRICKEN

strike /straɪk/ *verb*, means to hit, often hard or with force. The past tense and past participle is 'struck'. This is used in phrases such as 'The chance of winning the lottery is about the same as being struck by lightning'.

stricken /'strɪkən/ *adjective*, means hit or afflicted, generally by poverty or disease: 'I was stricken by flu all last week'. This is a fairly formal word. 'Suffer from' or 'hit by' are alternatives. 'Stricken' also occurs in compounds like 'panic-stricken' and 'horror-stricken'.

STUDENT, EXTERNAL STUDENT, GRADUATE, PUPIL

student /'stjuːdnt/ *noun*, in BE is reserved for young adults at college or university. In AE, the age-range of student goes right down to high school. Though this sometimes occurs in BE today, it is best avoided in formal contexts. Thus the term 'university student' is often used in English to add precision. An extra complication is that many English-speaking countries use 'undergraduate' for a university student taking a first degree (BA, BSc or equivalent).

external student /ɪks'tɜːnəl 'stjuːdnt/ *noun*, means a student who takes examinations at a university where he or she is not a regular member: 'There are several external students taking this subject'.

graduate /'grædjʊət/ *noun &* /'grædjʊeɪt/ *verb*, as a noun, means a university student who has passed a first degree. Note that in BE, the term 'graduate' is often used alone: 'A graduate of Oxford', while AE uses 'graduate student' to mean someone who continues to study after a first degree: 'A graduate student from Yale'. As a verb, 'graduate' in BE refers to the award of a university degree. In AE, this has a wider use meaning to successfully leave senior high school, college or to be awarded a university degree. Note the difference in pronunciation between the noun and verb.
See **DOCTORAL DEGREE**. See **MASTER'S DEGREE**.

pupil /'pju:pl̩/ *noun*, in BE usage means a schoolchild. A person of any age being directly instructed by a barrister, musician, or painter can also be termed a 'pupil': 'Several of her singing pupils were over thirty'.

SUBSCRIPTION, MEMBERSHIP FEE

subscription /səb'skrɪpʃn̩/ *noun*, means a sum of money paid in advance in order to get a service, such as a subscription to a magazine or newspaper: 'I am going to take out a subscription to my local newspaper'. It also means an annual fee that is paid in order to belong to a club.

membership fee /'membəʃɪp fi:/ *noun*, means an amount of money paid on a regular basis to an association by its members: 'The membership fee for the tennis club is becoming too expensive'. Note that in BE, one pays a fee for membership of a club. In AE, the fee is for membership in a club.

SUBSIDE, SUBSIDENCE, SUBSIDY

subside /səb'saɪd/ *verb*, means to sink or cave in: 'After the rain, the road may easily subside'. 'Subside' also means to become less intense: 'The strong wind subsided during the night'.

subsidence /'sʌbsɪdəns, səb'saɪdəns/ *noun*, is what happens to a building when the ground beneath falls in, causing the building to sink. The second pronunciation is to be preferred if there is any danger of the word being confused with 'subsidy'.

subsidy /'sʌbsɪdi/ *noun*, is money granted by the state or a public body to assist industry: 'The telecommunications sector may soon need a government subsidy'. See **SCHOLARSHIP**.

SUBSTITUTE, REPLACE

substitute /'sʌbstɪtju:t/ *noun & verb*, as a noun, means that one person or thing takes the place of another person or thing: 'Wealth was not a substitute for happiness'. As a verb, 'substitute' can be followed by 'by', 'with,' or 'for'. However, note the use of these prepositions in the following two sentences: 'She substituted the black scarf for the red one' and 'The red scarf was substituted by/with the black one'. In both cases, the same scarves are substituted, but in the former, the agent of the action is mentioned. Note that 'by' can also introduce the agent: 'The scarves were substituted (by her)'.

replace /rɪ'pleɪs/ *verb*, also means that one thing or person takes the place of another. 'Replace' is immediately followed by 'by' or 'with': 'Alcohol was replaced by/with water'. Note that 'by' can also introduce the person doing the action: 'The glasses were replaced (by me)'.

SUGGESTIVE, EVOCATIVE

suggestive /sə'dʒestɪv/ *adjective*, means bringing something to mind: 'The wine expert claimed the taste of the latest vintage was suggestive of blackberries'. A 'suggestive remark' is one that has sexual connotations. Do not confuse 'suggestive' with 'suggestible', which means easily influenced by others.

evocative /ɪ'vɒkətɪv/ *adjective*, means creating an atmosphere that brings something pleasant to mind: 'His description of the village cricket match was evocative of warm summer afternoons before the war'. This is a formal word.

 'Suggestive views from every window.' (Hotel brochure)

SUIT, SUITE

suit /sju:t/ *noun*, means a matching jacket and trousers for a man. For a woman, a suit can either be a 'trouser suit' (BE) or 'pantsuit' (AE). A woman's matching jacket and skirt is also a 'suit'. In other contexts, 'suit' is also used for one of the four 'sets' in a pack of playing cards, or for a 'lawsuit'. See **CLOTHES**.

suite /swi:t/ *noun*, means a set of rooms, a set of matching furniture, or a piece of music made up of three or more parts. Note that this is pronounced 'sweet'. An 'en suite bathroom' is one which is connected to a bedroom.

SUPER-, SUPRA-

super- /'sjuːpər/ *prefix*, means above, over, such as: 'superstructure'; to a greater extent: 'supercool'; or of a higher kind: 'superhuman'.

supra- /'sjuːprə-/ *prefix*, means above in the sense of going beyond, as in 'supranational law', meaning law that has international validity.

SUPERMARKET, HYPERMARKET, MALL, SHOPPING CENTRE

supermarket /'sjuːpəmaːkɪt/ *noun*, means a self-service shop that may not be very large, and often sells only one type of goods, such as food.

hypermarket /'haɪpəmaːkɪt/ *noun*, is a very large supermarket outside a town or city that sells a wide range of consumer goods. This is typically a BE term.

mall /mɔːl/ *noun*, is a large facility built for shopping outside town or city centres. It is a typical AE term for a 'shopping centre' or 'hypermarket' but is used internationally. The above pronunciation, which rhymes with 'all', originated in AE but is commonly heard in BE in this sense.

shopping centre /'ʃɒpɪŋ 'sentər/ *noun*, is a BE term for mall. 'Shopping centres' may be either in the centre of towns and cities or outside these centres: 'The nearest shopping centre is several miles out of town'.

SUPPLY, PROVIDE, PROVISION, DELIVER

supply /sə'plaɪ/ *verb & noun*, as a verb, means to make something that is needed available, often on a large scale: 'The pipeline supplies 25% of the gas to this part of the country'. As a noun, 'supply' means the quantities available for use: 'The supply of oil is still a political issue'. Note that 'supplies' (only plural) refer to food, medicine etc. required by expeditions and troops: 'Medical supplies are arriving tomorrow'.

provide /prə'vaɪd/ *verb*, means give something, or make it available for somebody to use: 'The refugees were provided with food and shelter'. Note that 'supply' and 'provide' refer to similar activities, the difference being in the scale and size of the operation.

provision /prə'vɪʒn/ *noun*, means the supply of food, particularly to the armed forces or expeditions. To make provision means to supply or distribute services, benefits or even money: 'They made provision for the education of the village children'.

deliver /dɪ'lɪvər/ *verb*, means to bring and hand over something to one person or to many people from time to time. The focus is on the handing over of something: 'The parcel was delivered to her house, but no one was at home'.

SURNAME, FAMILY NAME, LAST NAME

surname /'sɜːneɪm/ *noun*, means the hereditary name for members of a family, in contrast to given name(s), first name(s) or Christian name(s). See **FIRST NAME**.

family name /'fæmɪli neɪm/ *noun*, is an alternative to 'surname' and is sometimes used on printed forms in English to make sure that everyone understands which name is required.

last name /'laːst neɪm/ *noun*, also means a surname but is a term to avoid as it may not be understood. This is because some cultures and languages reverse the order of the given and family names (e.g. Hungarian, Korean, Chinese, Japanese).

SUSPECT, SUSPICIOUS

suspect /'sʌspekt/ *noun & adjective*, as a noun, means a person or thing that is not to be trusted: 'The butler was the obvious murder suspect'. As an adjective, this refers to something that cannot be relied upon or which is thought to be dangerous: 'The police removed the suspect package, which was later found to be harmless'.

suspect /səs'pekt/ *verb*, means to have a feeling that something bad is likely to happen: 'The blue smoke from the car made him suspect that he had an oil leak'. It also means to be suspicious about somebody without being able to prove it: 'She suspected his motives in taking a month's business trip to Paris'.

suspicious /səs'pɪʃəs/ *adjective*, means showing or feeling distrust: 'She was suspicious of/about his motives in taking a month's business trip to Paris'

SWEET, SWEAT, PERSPIRE

sweet /swiːt/ *noun & adjective*, as an adjective, refers to something that contains, or tastes as if it contains, a lot of sugar: 'A sweet wine'. It can also mean something pleasant. Smells and sounds are often described as 'sweet': 'The sweet smell of summer'; 'The sweet singing by the choir'. As a noun, 'sweet' means either a piece of sugary confectionery: 'Let's buy a bag of sweets to eat in the cinema'; or a final dessert course to a meal: 'There were ice cream, treacle pudding and apple pie on the sweet menu'. 'Sweet and sour' is a type of sauce often used with food from parts of Asia.

sweat /swet/ *noun & verb*, as a noun, means the drops of liquid on someone's skin caused by heat, fear, or illness: 'The tennis player wiped the beads of sweat from his forehead'. Informally, 'sweat' can also mean hard work. The informal expression 'no sweat' means a job is being done and everything is under control: 'Mike just said, "No sweat: I'll get the report finished".' As a verb, 'sweat' means either to produce drops of liquid on the skin or informally to work very hard: 'John was sweating blood to get his part of the report finished'. In this sense, 'sweat' is less formal than 'perspire'.

perspire /pəs'paɪər/ *verb*, means to sweat: 'The dancers were perspiring after the performance'. 'Perspire' is a formal word.

A traditional hint about how these words are used, is the saying that horses sweat, men perspire and ladies glow.

 'Fried wanton in sweat and sour sauce.'
(Chinese restaurant menu)

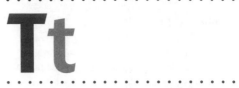

TALK, SPEECH, LECTURE, ADDRESS

talk /tɔːk/ *noun & verb*, as a noun is an informal type of presentation and does not have to be prepared. When 'talk' is used without an article it means the process of communication: 'Careless talk costs lives'.

speech /spiːtʃ/ *noun*, is a presentation that is prepared and designed to gain support or present an argument, often in politics and diplomacy. An 'after-dinner speech' can vary a lot in standard and length, but it is supposed to be prepared. When 'speech' is used without an article it means language: 'Three years after the accident his power of speech returned'.

lecture /'lektʃər/ *noun*, is a prepared presentation for teaching purposes: 'He always gives well-prepared, interesting lectures'.

address /ə'dres/ *noun & verb*, in the sense of an oral presentation means a very formal prepared speech. As a noun, 'address' is often combined with the verbs 'give', 'deliver', and 'listen to': 'The US President gave a short televised address'. Note that 'address' is always spelt with a double 'd' in English. In BE, the second syllable is stressed in both the noun and the verb, but in AE the first syllable is stressed when 'address' is used as a noun /'ædres/.

⚠️ *'English well talking.' (Shop sign)*

TALKS, DISCUSSION

talks /tɔːks/ *noun*, means formal occasions of serious talking, often between government representatives: 'The three groups have agreed to hold peace talks'.

discussion /dɪs'kʌʃn̩/ *noun*, means a talk with a serious purpose, usually where speakers consider a subject from different angles: 'I saw a good discussion on the TV last night'. See **CONVERSATION**.

TASTEFUL, TASTY, TASTELESS, DELICIOUS

tasteful /'teɪstfʊl/ *adjective*, means selected and chosen by those with taste, such as: 'Both the furnishings and the dining-room were extremely tasteful'.

tasty /'teɪsti/ *adjective*, means having a pleasant taste when referring to food, but 'a tasty bit of gossip' means a scandal.

tasteless /'teɪstləs/ *adjective*, is the opposite of both 'tasteful' and 'tasty'. Use this word with care as 'tasteless' can refer to a lack of tact. 'That was an extremely tasteless thing to write'.

delicious /dɪ'lɪʃəs/ *adjective*, means very pleasant to the taste or smell: 'The delicious smell of home-baked bread wafted into the room'.

TAUGHT[S], TAUT[S]

taught /tɔːt/ *verb*, is the past tense and past participle of 'to teach': 'They had been taught how to use a gun when they were in the army'.

taut /tɔːt/ *adjective*, means tight or stretched: 'The rope was getting taut because of the rain'. People can also be 'taut' if they are anxious or tense: 'The teacher's face was taut with anger'. See **TIGHT**.

tautology

- Tautology means the unnecessary repetition of the same idea, in the same phrase, often using synonymous words or expressions, where just one is sufficient. Here are some examples that careful writers should try to avoid:
  bisect in two both twins final end future plans large in size past history puzzling mystery red in colour
- Tautology also appears in expressions like:
  each and every in this day and age
- There are occasions when such phrases are not tautologous, but necessary for the sense: *Only one of the twins was a good pianist, but both twins were excellent tennis players.*
- Sometimes, tautology occurs because writers do not remember what the last letters in acronyms and abbreviations stand for. Common examples include: *LCD display* (liquid crystal display), *HIV virus* (human immunodeficiency virus), *PIN number* (personal identification number) and *OPEC countries* (Organization of Petroleum Exporting Countries). Reports and papers often contain tautology caused by combining *such as, like* and *examples include* with *etc.* or *and so on* at the end. Example: *Traffic such as: lorries, trucks and vans etc.* Combining foreign words with English sometimes leads to tautology. Examples: *and etc.* and *RSVP, please reply.*

'We ask people to be short, brief and to the point.' (BBC Radio)

TEACH, TRAIN, LEARN

teach /tiːtʃ/ *verb*, means to give instruction or information about a subject, which can be on an informal basis: 'I am teaching him how to swim'; or professionally: 'My brother teaches mathematics in school'. See **INSTRUCTION**.

train /treɪn/ *verb*, means to teach a person or an animal specific behaviour or a skill by practice and instruction over a period of time: 'We trained the dog to jump through a paper-covered hoop'.

learn /lɜːn/ *verb*, means to receive teaching, training or instruction or gather experience by practice and instruction over a period of time: 'She is learning how to drive'; 'Jane is learning French'. See **LEARNED**.

TECHNICAL, TECHNIQUE, TECHNOLOGY

technical /'teknɪkl̩/ *adjective*, means relating to a subject, craft or applied science: 'He bought a dictionary of technical terms in computer science'.

technique /tek'niːk/ *noun*, means the way of doing something, especially using artistic or scientific methods: 'The most advanced technique on the market'. An AE spelling of 'technique' is 'technic', which is pronounced /'teknɪk/ or /tek'niːk/.

technology /tek'nɒlədʒi/ *noun*, means the practical application of scientific knowledge especially in industry: 'Information and communication technology is one of the leading businesses'.

TEEM[S], TEAM[S]

teem /tiːm/ *verb*, usually combined with 'with', means be full of: 'The beaches were teeming with small children'.

team /tiːm/ *noun & verb*, as a noun, means an organized group of people: 'The marketing team did well last week'. As a verb, 'team up with' means to join a group for a specific reason: 'That Italian company has just teamed up with a British engineering design firm'.

TEETH, TEETHE

teeth /tiːθ/ *noun*, is the plural of tooth: 'She has beautiful teeth: they are so white'. See **PLURAL NOUNS**.

teethe /tiːð/ *verb*, means to grow teeth: 'The baby is starting to teethe'. Note that this rhymes with 'breathe'.

telephone numbers

reading telephone numbers:

- When giving telephone numbers, native English speakers tend to group them in 2s, 3s or even 4s. There is also a tendency to use a rising intonation at the end of each group, and for the intonation to drop at the end.
+44 20 7437 4514 (or, within the UK, 020 ...)
+4´42´07´43´74´51´4
- In English, no number above 9 is normally used in a telephone number (34 is *three, four* not *thirty four*).
- 0 is pronounced *oh* in BE and usually *zero* in AE. Two O's together are pronounced *double oh* in BE, and *zero zero* in AE.

writing telephone numbers:

- According to international standards, telephone numbers should be written in pairs, without hyphens between digits:
+33 1 46 57 11 00
+32 16 23 90 96
- the + sign means the international code, which is usually 00 today.
- A common format for writing mobile telephone numbers is:
+46 721 23 500
- In Britain, telephone numbers are usually divided into two or three parts, the first is the area code (e.g. 01865), and the second is the local number, which may be six, seven, or eight digits. If it has 6 digits, they are written together, e.g. 556767. If there are seven or eight digits, the last four are written apart from the first three or four, e.g. 020 7765 4305, or 0131 554 1923.

TEMERITY, TIMIDITY

temerity /təˈmerɪti/ *noun*, means with great confidence and daring. This is a formal word and an informal equivalent is 'cheek': 'He had the temerity to invite the princess for tea'.

timidity /tɪˈmɪdɪti/ *noun*, means a lack of confidence and being easily frightened: 'The timidity of the kittens was surprising'.

TEMPERATURE, FEVER, COLD

temperature /ˈtempərətʃər/ *noun*, means the degree of heat or excitement. If someone is said to 'have a temperature', this means a temperature that is above normal: 'She stayed in bed for the day because she had a temperature'. If people discuss a topic excitedly, this can be called a 'heated debate'. Note that careful writers avoid saying 'hot/cold temperature', because 'temperature' is a measure of heat or cold and should be indicated by a number: 'The temperature is 5 degrees above average for this time of year'. Use 'hot water', not 'a hot water temperature'.

fever /ˈfiːvər/ *noun*, means an abnormally high body temperature: 'Several local people have died of a fever'. 'Fever' can also mean great excitement: 'Election fever'. A related adjective is 'feverish': 'The candidate was feverish with excitement as the election results were announced'.

cold /kəʊld/ *noun*, is any one of a large number of viral infections which may cause either a runny nose or a blocked nose, coughs or sneezes, or a temperature: 'She had to stay in bed for two days because of a heavy cold'.

TENDER, BID

tender /ˈtendər/ *noun*, means an offer to carry out work or supply goods at an agreed price. The group that wants the work done invites tenders or, more formally, it can issue an invitation to tender. The tenderers, the companies that try to get the work, put in a tender (or, more formally) submit a tender. The process is often called 'competitive tendering' based on the tenderers sending either sealed tenders or open tenders.

bid /bɪd/ *noun & verb*, as a noun, means either tender, which is mostly used in AE in this context, or an attempt to win something: 'George's bid for the party leadership was unsuccessful'. As a verb, 'bid' means to make an offer to buy something and the past tense of the verb is 'bid': 'He bid £50 000 for the painting'. 'Bid' can also be found in expressions such as 'bid farewell'. See **WISH**.

TERMINABLE, TERMINAL, TERMINUS

terminable /ˈtɜːmɪnəbl̩/ *adjective*, means can be ended after a time: 'This contract is terminable at three months' notice'.

terminal /ˈtɜːmɪnl/ *adjective*, means leading to death, as in 'terminal cancer'. If the cancer was 'terminable' this would mean that the cancer could be ended.

terminal /ˈtɜːmɪnl/ *noun*, means a building for passengers at an airport, or a place where journeys by sea, rail or road begin or end: 'The international ferry terminal opens next month'. In another sense, a terminal is a piece of computer equipment, usually a keyboard and screen connected to a central computer: 'All students have their own terminal that is connected to the college server'.

terminus /ˈtɜːmɪnəs/ *noun*, is the end of a route, such as a railway terminus. The plural is either 'termini' /ˈtɜːmɪnaɪ/ or 'terminuses' /ˈtɜːmɪnəsɪz/.

THANKFUL, GRATEFUL

thankful /ˈθæŋkfʊl/ *adjective*, is used either to show relief about the outcome of a potentially difficult situation: 'I am extremely thankful that there were no floods', or to show relief that something negative did not happen: 'We are thankful that the hurricane changed direction and moved away from the coast'.

grateful /ˈɡreɪtfʊl/ *adjective*, is used to express gratitude and thanks to a person: 'I am deeply grateful to Jim Smith for his assistance'.

that, which, who

- A defining relative clause is one that is essential to the meaning of a sentence. It is not separated by commas. The relative pronouns *which* and *that* can be used interchangeably in defining clauses to refer to things: *The hotel which/that is by the beach is expensive. Who* and *that* can be used interchangeably to refer to people: *My psychiatrist is the only one who/that understands me.*
- When the relative pronoun is the object of the defining relative clause, these relative pronouns are often omitted, especially in informal language: *The hotel (which/that) you told me about is closed.* Also: *The woman (who/that) I met in the supermarket is Sarah's sister.*
- A non-defining relative clause gives additional information about a noun. It always appears within commas. Only *which* (for things) and *who* (for people) can be used. It is not possible to use *that*, or to omit the relative pronoun: *The islands, which are privately owned, are very beautiful.* Also: *The new secretary, who speaks excellent German, works in the office upstairs.*

- A simple rule of thumb is to use *that* for defining clauses and *who* or *which* for non-defining clauses.

THERE, THEIR, THEY'RE

there /ðeər/ *adverb*, can mean not here, but in the direction indicated: 'Let's move over there out of the wind'.

their /ðeər/ *possessive determiner*, means associated with those already mentioned: 'The French are renowned for their cuisine'. See **HE**.

they're /ˈðeɪər/ is the short form of 'they are': '"They're here," he cried'. See **CONTRACTIONS**.

THESIS, DISSERTATION

thesis /ˈθiːsɪs/ *noun*, means an original piece of work that is part of a doctoral degree in British universities. In American universities, a thesis is a piece of work submitted for a lower or master's degree: 'After working on her thesis for two years, she finally submitted it'. The plural of 'thesis' is 'theses' /ˈθiːsiːz/. The second syllable is pronounced 'seas'.

dissertation /dɪsəˈteɪʃn/ *noun*, means, in most British universities, the lengthy piece of work that is written as part of a lower degree or master's degree. 'He was delighted when the completed dissertation could be presented'. In American universities, a 'dissertation' is what in BE would be termed a doctoral 'thesis'.

THIN, SKINNY, SLIM

thin /θɪn/ *adjective*, is a general word to describe people who are underweight. It may be negative and suggest weakness: 'He is so incredibly thin, he doesn't look strong enough to lift the freezer'. 'Thin' can also be used to describe objects: 'I need a thin piece of card and some scissors'. 'Bony' is an adjective which refers to the body or to parts of the body, and is an alternative to 'thin'.

skinny /ˈskɪni/ *adjective*, means very thin, unattractive and also suggests lack of strength: 'She looks terribly skinny'. Note that 'skinny-dip' means to swim without clothes and has nothing to do with being skinny.

slim /slɪm/ *adjective & verb*, as an adjective, means attractively thin and slender: 'The model was so tall and slim that she could wear anything'. As a verb, 'slim', or more commonly 'slim down', means to become thinner by changing one's diet and/or exercise regime: 'She has really slimmed down recently'. Note also that 'slimming down' describes the process by which industry sheds jobs.

thing words

- *Thing* is one of the most abused words in English and means literally anything and everything. As *thing* is so vague it is often best to avoid using it or at least add another element to it. *Something, anything, everything* and *nothing* are all more explicit.

- Other alternatives are: *attribute, characteristic, feature, issue, matter, subject, topic*

- By not using *thing*, the concept being described can be made more interesting and precise. Thus, a sentence such as 'An important thing about English is its rich vocabulary', can be improved by rewriting it as: *An important attribute of/ characteristic of/ feature of/ English is its rich vocabulary.* Over the course of time, words can change their status. This has happened to the everyday word *thing*. Originally it meant the court of advisers to a king and *ting* is still used in this sense in some Scandinavian languages today.

THOUSAND, THOUSANDS

thousand /ˈθaʊznd/ *adjective*, means a number, and is the term that is used following an exact number or the words 'a', 'a few' or 'several': 'Several thousand people have already gathered'. When 'thousand' is used in a unit of time, distance, money, temperature, or such like, it takes a singular verb: 'Fifty thousand dollars is required'. Otherwise, a plural verb is used: 'Fifty thousand people were watching the football match'.

thousands /ˈθaʊzndz/ *noun*, means an inexact number ranging from a few 'thousand' to many 'thousand' and is often followed by 'of': 'Thousands of people took part in the demonstration'. 'Thousands' is often used informally to exaggerate a point: 'I have asked you to tidy your room thousands of times'.

THROUGH, THOROUGH

through /θruː/ *preposition & adverb*, means from one side of something to the other. This can refer either to an object or physical barrier: 'It was difficult to walk quickly through the long grass'; or to some other type of obstacle: 'She had to get through the exam'. When someone connects a caller on the telephone, it is normal to say 'I'm putting you through now'. Note that 'through' can mean 'finished' in AE: 'When you're through, can you help me in the kitchen?'

thorough /ˈθʌrə/ *adjective*, means complete in all details: 'The doctor carried out a thorough medical examination'. This is a positive meaning. 'Thorough' can also be used negatively: 'The teachers agreed that the students were a thorough nuisance'.

TIGHT, TIGHTLY

tight /taɪt/ *adjective & adverb*, means held firmly in position: 'She kept a tight hold of his hand'; fitting closely: 'His shoes were too tight'; or controlled very strictly: 'The manager kept extremely tight control of his budgets'. 'Tight' is also used to refer to a shortage of time: 'We seem to have a tight schedule today'. As an adverb, 'tight' is often used as an informal alternative to 'tightly', and immediately follows the verb: 'The case was packed tight'.

tightly /ˈtaɪtli/ *adverb*, means firmly and closely: 'The case was tightly packed'. When not used in a compound, 'tightly' generally comes after the object: 'He packed the cups and plates tightly'.

TIMBER, LUMBER, WOOD

timber /ˈtɪmbər/ *noun*, means wood prepared for building and carpentry: 'A timber-frame house is being built down the road'.

lumber /ˈlʌmbər/ *noun*, in BE means any furniture or other large objects that are unused and being stored. In AE, 'lumber' means 'timber', and is commonly used in the term 'lumberjack'.

wood /wʊd/ *noun*, is the material that is found in the trunk and branches of trees. 'Wood' is used in building or making things. When used for fuel, a sawn-up branch of a tree is called a log: 'A log fire'. 'Wood' is a more general term: 'A wood-burning stove'.

time of day

As the time of day may be written in several different ways in English, it is easy to cause confusion. There are three systems to choose among when presenting the time of day and they should never be mixed. The o'clock and a.m./p.m. systems are both based on the 12-hour clock, and there is also the **24-hour** system.

- **o'clock**: In formal writing, use *o'clock* with words, not figures: *six o'clock*, not *6 o'clock*. Do not use *o'clock* with *a.m.* or *p.m.* As it is incorrect to write *nine o'clock a.m.*, use *in the morning/afternoon/evening* and *at night* after *o'clock*: *nine o'clock in the morning* and *ten o'clock at night*. The expression comes from the days of the town crier: 'Three of the clock'. *O'clock* is only used for the whole hour. To express fractions of an hour: *a quarter to one* and *a quarter past one* are used. These are correct in both British and American English, but Americans also say *a quarter of one* (= BE *quarter to one*) and *a quarter after one* (= BE *quarter past one*). The informal BE way of expressing half hours *half twelve* is short for *half past twelve*, and means *12.30* in English, not *11.30* as in the other Germanic languages.

- **a.m./p.m.** system for hours or fractions of an hour uses figures, not words: *8 a.m.* or *9.15 p.m.*, not *eight a.m.*. If minutes are included in a time, use figures and either the *a.m./p.m.* system or the *24-hour clock* system. The abbreviation *a.m.* means *before noon* (Latin: ante meridiem) and is the period from midnight to noon; *p.m.* means 'after noon' (Latin: post meridiem) and is the period from noon to midnight. (Note that the Latin terms are never used.) An easy way to remember this is that *a.m.* comes before *p.m.* alphabetically. With this system, write and say: *8.35 a.m.* and *4.20 p.m.* In AE, a colon is used instead of a stop, and *a.m.* and *p.m.* are sometimes written in small capitals: *8:35 A.M.* and *4:20 P.M.*. There is often confusion between *12 a.m.* which is midnight, and *12 p.m.* which is noon. Consequently it is recommended to use *midnight* or *12 midnight* and *noon* or *12 noon* instead. The *a.m./p.m.* system is commonly used for conference programmes etc., and often a schedule can omit *a.m.* and *p.m.* if it is obvious when the events are taking place: *9.15 Opening, 10.30 Coffee, 1.00 Lunch, 5.15 Closing Session*. A careless error is combining *in the morning/afternoon/evening* and *at night* with *a.m.* or *p.m.*, as in *8.30 a.m. in the morning*. See **TAUTOLOGY**.

- **24-hour clock** system is common in transport timetables and military use. Only four-digit numbers are used in this system and there is no combination with *o'clock* or *a.m./p.m.* The time may be written with or without a stop between the hour and minutes: *13.25* or *1325*. Note that *12.00* means 12 noon and *24.00* is 12 midnight. In military contexts, the time in the 24-hour clock system is read as *oh one hundred hours* (*0100*), *thirteen hundred hours* (*1300*).

'We serve 5 o'clock tea at all hours.' (Restaurant notice)

TOILET, LAVATORY, WC, LOO, BATHROOM, PUBLIC CONVENIENCE

toilet /'tɔɪlət/ *noun*, is both a room and the object in that room for disposing of bodily waste. This is the most widespread word in BE. Go to and use are the two most common verbs combined with 'toilet': 'Ask the children if they need to go to the toilet'. In AE, it is usual to say 'go to/use the bathroom'. In a formal context this could be termed a 'comfort break'. The expression 'toilet water' is a kind of perfume. An extra toilet in a house near the front entrance is usually called a cloakroom. See **CLOAKROOM**.

lavatory /'lævətri/ *noun*, is also sometimes used to mean 'toilet' in BE: 'The lavatory had a basin, lavatory bowl and lavatory paper in exactly the same colour'.

wc /'dʌbljuː'siː/ *noun*, is an abbreviation for 'water closet'. Although this is considered a dated term, 'WC' is used on maps and signs, and in other places to save space.

loo /luː/ *noun*, is a popular informal BE word for toilet: 'Excuse me, can I use your loo?'

bathroom /'bɑːθruːm/ *noun*, means a room in a house or hotel where there is a bath/ shower, a washbasin and often a toilet. In AE, this means a room in which there is a toilet, washbasin, and sometimes a bath/shower. This may also be called a washroom in AE, although this is now old-fashioned. Outside the USA these terms may be misunderstood.

public convenience /'pʌblɪk kən'viːnɪəns// *noun*, means a room or small building containing several toilets for anyone to use. In BE, the words Ladies and Gents are the usual terms for a 'public convenience'. In AE, this may be termed a men's room, women's room or even rest room.

'Our toilets are undergoing repair. In the meantime, use Platform 6.' (British Rail notice)

TONIGHT, LAST NIGHT

tonight /tə'naɪt/ *adverb*, means the evening or night of the present day: 'Tonight will be an event to remember'.

last night /lɑːst 'naɪt/ *adverb*, means the previous night: 'There was too much noise outside last night'.

TONNE⁵, TON⁵

tonne /tʌn/ *noun*, means 1000 kg. The tonne may be referred to as the metric ton or alternatively, metric tonne.

ton /tʌn/ *noun*, needs to be specified closely. In weight it means either the 'short ton' which is the American system (2000 lb or 907.19 kg) and is used a lot in the oil industry, or the 'long ton' in the imperial system (2240 lb or 1016.5 kg) which may still be used in parts of the English-speaking world. 'Ton' in informal English is used to mean a great quantity or a lot: 'I've got a ton of work to do'. It is also used in the plural: 'There were tons of people there'. The phrase 'to hit someone like a ton of bricks' means to have a strong impact.

TOTAL, SUM

total /'təʊtl/ *noun & adjective*, as a noun, means the final amount after adding a series of numbers, people or things together: 'From all the divisions, a total of 25 000 employees were sacked'. The phrase 'a total of' is often useful in front of a number at the beginning of a sentence to avoid writing long numbers in words. See **NUMBERS IN NUMERALS OR WORDS**. As an adjective, 'total' means the final amount of something counted together: 'Our total profit for the year is $16 million'. 'Total' also means complete, and is used in phrases such as 'total eclipse' and 'total stranger': 'The party was a total disaster'. See **ABSOLUTES AND FUZZY ABSOLUTES**. See **COMPLETE**.

sum /sʌm/ *noun*, means an amount of money: 'The investor contributed only a tiny sum'. It can also mean an elementary mathematical problem usually of addition: 'The company got its sums wrong', or the 'total' arrived at by adding numbers together: 'The sum of 21 and 7 is 28'. Note that a singular verb is used here. The expression 'sum total' can suggest disapproval of a small amount: 'A 90-page novel was the sum total of the writer's output'.

TOWARDS, TOWARD, UNTOWARD

towards /tə'wɔːdz/ *preposition*, means in the direction of, and is the BE spelling: 'He had a positive attitude towards life'. A plane may fly 'towards' a direction, but goes 'to' its destination: 'We are now flying to Prague'.

toward /tə'wɔːd/ is the AE spelling of 'towards': 'We drove toward the mountains'.

untoward /ˌʌntə'wɔːd/ *adjective*, means unexpected, inappropriate and unpleasant: 'His book sold badly due to untoward comments about the traditional role of women'. It is commonly used in the expression 'anything/nothing untoward': 'He is late. I hope that nothing untoward has happened'. 'Untoward' is a fairly formal word.

TOWER, SPIRE

tower /taʊər/ *noun*, is a tall, relatively narrow building, often part of a castle or church: 'The Tower of London is one of the oldest buildings in the capital'.

spire /spaɪər/ *noun*, is a tapering structure on top of a building, often on top of a tower: 'The spires of Oxford are a wonderful sight'.

TRACK, TRAIL, PATH

track /træk/ *noun & verb*, as a noun, means the marks or signs left by the passage of a person, animal or vehicle. This is normally used in the plural: 'The tracks left by the tanks were still clearly visible'. A track can also be a rough unsurfaced road: 'We followed a cart track up the mountain'. Informally, 'to make tracks' means that it is time to leave: 'Thanks for the coffee. Now it's time to make tracks'. The verb 'track down' means to try to locate a person, animal or, informally, an object, which is difficult to find: 'I'm trying to track down a couple of very rare books'.

trail /treɪl/ *noun & verb*, as a noun, means marks or signs left by someone or something: 'The trail of cigarette butts and empty beer bottles showed where the party was'. A trail can also be a narrow track in the countryside: 'They built a nature trail'. As a verb, it means to follow someone or something by keeping them in sight: 'They trailed the escaped prisoners over the marshes'.

path /pɑːθ/ *noun*, means a way or narrow track that is either created deliberately, or made by people's feet through the action of walking: 'If you follow that path, you will get up the mountain in two hours; take the track and you will need at least three hours'. The informal expression 'to lead someone up the garden path' means to give a person misleading information: 'The director was leading the shareholders up the garden path when he painted a rosy picture of profitability'.

TRADEMARK, BRAND NAME

trademark /'treɪdmɑːk/ *noun,* means the name, symbol, or design that is registered or established by a company to represent the types of products it sells: 'Every company wants its name to become the generic trademark - the Hoover of the vacuum cleaners'. A trademark usually has an upper case initial letter, such as Biro or Bic. However, where the trademark has come to be used as a verb, it begins with lower case, as in: 'to hoover', meaning to use a vacuum cleaner, and 'to xerox', meaning to photocopy. A trademark can also mean a particular characteristic of an individual, especially in terms of their style of dress: 'She looked as I remembered her, with her trademark long, red, curly hair'.

brand name /'brænd neɪm/ *noun,* means either the name given by a manufacturer to a particular product or its range of products: 'Research has shown that shoppers are very loyal to brand names'.

TRADE UNION, LABOR UNION

trade union /treɪd 'juːnɪən/ *noun,* means an organized association of workers in a trade or profession. This is a BE term. An alternative is 'trades union': Trades Union Congress (TUC).

labor union /'leɪbə juːnɪən/ *noun,* is the AE expression that is equivalent to 'trade union': 'The Teamsters is the only labor union that these drivers listen to'. Note the difference in stress pattern between the BE and AE forms.

TRAILER, CARAVAN

trailer /'treɪlər/ *noun,* means an unpowered vehicle towed behind a car or truck: 'They moved the boat on a trailer'. In AE, 'trailer' can also mean a mobile home or office that can be towed and parked in a 'trailer park'. See **TRUCK**.

caravan /'kærəvæn/ *noun,* means an unpowered vehicle towed behind a car that is used for holidays and temporary accommodation: 'The caravan site needed tidying up'. In AE this is termed a 'camper'.

TRANSFER, RELOCATE, RESETTLE, MOVE

transfer /træns'fɜːr/ *verb,* means to move a person or thing to another location or group: 'After the reorganization, he was transferred to the Personnel Department'; 'A considerable amount of money was transferred to Dublin'. Phone calls are also 'transferred': 'Please hold while I transfer the call'.

relocate /'riːləʊ'keɪt/ *verb,* means to move to a new place. It is frequently used in business instead of just saying 'moving': 'The firm has relocated to Scotland'.

resettle /'riː'setl/ *verb,* means to find a new place to live. The word is used for people or population groups: 'When the Berlin Wall fell, many Germans from the eastern part resettled in the west'.

move /muːv/ *verb,* is a more general term that covers all the words that it is grouped with here, but with 'move' the focus is on the movement rather than the result. An object can be 'moved', and people can be 'moved along' by the police if they seem to be causing an obstruction. When a family goes to live in a new home, they are said to 'move house'.

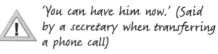

'You can have him now.' (Said by a secretary when transferring a phone call)

TRANSMIT, BROADCAST

transmit /trænz'mɪt/ *verb,* refers to electrical signals that are sent, or to a radio/TV programme that is broadcast. A fax or email is transmitted, but many people use the more informal term send. 'Transmit' has a variety of other meanings connected with passing one thing on to another. These can be diseases or feelings such as fear: 'Mothers can transmit their own anxiety to their babies'.

broadcast /'brɔːdkɑːst/ *verb,* refers just to radio or TV programmes that are being transmitted: 'Many BBC programmes are broadcast by other stations as well'. Note that the past tense and past participle are spelt the same as the infinitive form.

TRANSPARENT, TRANSPARENCY, SLIDE, OVERHEAD

transparent /træns'pærənt/ *adjective,* refers to something such as clear window-glass that allows light through and the objects on the other side to be seen clearly. 'Transparent' is also used figuratively to mean clear and understandable: 'Our policy is to achieve more transparent measures in government'.

transparency /træns'pærənsi/ *noun,* means three things. First, a sheet of plastic film for making overheads on printers and photocopiers that can be viewed on an overhead projector. Second, a transparent photograph that is printed on glass or plastic and can be viewed using a device such as a slide projector: 'This high-speed film should produce excellent transparencies'. Third, the term 'transparency' means clarity in terms of an idea or policy: 'The decision-making process needs to have greater transparency'.

slide /slaɪd/ *noun*, means in the context of photography a mounted transparency that can be placed in a slide projector and viewed on a screen: 'You are warned, Jim is having one of his three-hour holiday slide shows tonight'.

overhead /'əʊvəhed/ *noun*, in the context of business presentations or teaching means a transparency designed for use with an overhead projector. The term 'overhead' often refers to the projector as well: 'I can illustrate our plans with a couple of overheads, if I can find out how to turn the overhead on'. Some people use the term 'overhead transparency' when referring to sheets of plastic film: 'All the overhead transparencies for our standard presentation are supplied in transparent pockets'.

TRANSPORT, TRANSPORTATION

transport /'trænspɔːt/ *noun &* /træns'pɔːt/ *verb*, as a noun, means the system of vehicles used for moving people and goods: 'The general ordered the soldiers to organize the transport'. 'Transport' is commonly found in the names of British companies and institutions, such as: London Transport. As a verb, this means to convey physical things: 'Most of our gas is transported along these pipelines'. Note the stress in the verb is on the second syllable.

transportation /trænspɔː'teɪʃn̩/ *noun*, in BE is occasionally used as an alternative to 'transport' but in a historical sense means the act of sending convicts out of England to settle new territories: 'The transportation of convicts to the colonies ended in 1868'. In AE, 'transportation' means 'transport'.

TRAVEL, JOURNEY, TRIP, TOUR, VOYAGE

travel /'trævl̩/ *noun & verb*, as a noun, refers to movement from place to place, especially abroad, rather than a specific journey: 'Travel is said to broaden the mind, but many find long business trips tiring'. 'Travel' is uncountable, and is often used in terms such as 'air travel' and 'business travel'. 'Travel' has a plural form, but this is only used in a literary sense to mean many long, exotic trips: 'He is off on his travels

again'. Note that in BE, the verb forms are spelt 'travelled' and 'travelling': 'We have travelled a lot'. In AE, the equivalents are spelt 'traveled' and 'traveling'.

journey /'dʒɜːni/ *noun*, means the act of travelling from one place to another: 'We had a long, hard journey ahead of us'. A journey may be short, if it is taken regularly: 'He only had a fifteen-minute journey to work'. In AE, 'trip' may be used in this sense.

trip /trɪp/ *noun*, means a specific journey, often for pleasure: 'The whole class was looking forward to this trip'. A 'business trip' is a journey with a commercial objective

tour /tʊər/ *noun & verb*, means a journey for pleasure where several places are visited: 'He is going on a tour of the Far East'. 'Tour' is also used in the context of sport and entertainment, to refer to a route taken around a country or countries in order to perform in several places: 'The Royal Ballet's tour of Europe was a great success'.

voyage /'vɔɪ.ɪdʒ/ *noun*, means a long journey by sea or in space: 'He set off on a voyage around the world'. 'Voyage' often has literary associations. A more common word in everyday English is 'journey'.

TREATY, ACCORD

treaty /'triːti/ *noun*, means a formal ratified agreement between states, such as the Treaty of Rome. NATO, for example, stands for the North Atlantic Treaty Organization.
See **AGREEMENT**.

accord /ə'kɔːd/ *noun*, often means a diplomatic agreement between states, and thus is less formal than a treaty. An example is the Camp David Accord.

TREBLE, TRIPLE

treble /'trebl̩/ *verb & determiner*, as a verb, means to increase by three times: 'She bought shares and trebled her savings in five years'. As a determiner, 'treble' means three times as much: 'Earnings were treble the level in Britain in 2002'. Note that this is used before a noun.

triple /'trɪpl̩/ *verb & adjective*, as a verb, means to increase three times: 'Oil prices may triple by 2015'. As an adjective, 'triple' means either three times as much: 'Average earnings are triple those in Britain', or being in three parts: 'A triple-glazed window'.

TRUCK, LORRY

truck /trʌk/ noun, means, in BE, a small lorry that is usually open, or an open wagon for goods on the railway. In AE, 'truck' is the normal term for the BE term 'lorry'.

lorry /'lɒri/ noun, means a large vehicle for goods transport by road. It is a BE term: 'A large articulated lorry is called a juggernaut'. Informally, if something is said to have 'fallen off the back of a lorry', it means it is stolen.

truncated words

As the purpose of all speech is to convey the maximum amount of sense with the minimum amount of effort, many words and phrases have been shortened in order to save time and energy. These truncated words are the spoken equivalent of abbreviations and acronyms in written language. Sometimes the beginning of the word has been lost: *loudspeaker* has become *speaker*, *omnibus* has been shortened to *bus*, *telephone* to *phone*; but more often it is the end of the word that has disappeared: *cabriolet* to *cab*, *microphone* to *mike* (or *mic*), *taximeter* to *taxi*, *television* to *telly*. The last of these is already a truncated phrase, as *television* is properly the technology, and the box in the corner of the room a *television set*. Other phrases which have been truncated to a single word include *immersion* (from *immersion heater*), *mobile* (from *mobile phone*) and *overhead* (from *overhead projector*).

TRUTH, VERACITY

truth /truːθ/ noun, means the true facts, not invented. 'Truth' is usually combined with 'the': 'Having established the truth, the judge said he must face up to it'. However, it can also be a countable noun: 'We hold these truths to be self-evident ...' (US Declaration of Independence).

veracity /vəˈræsɪti/ noun, means the quality of truthfulness, or telling the truth: 'My solicitor admitted that he questioned the veracity of the allegation'. This is a formal word. Both 'truthfulness' and 'accuracy' are less formal alternatives.

TRY, ATTEMPT, STRIVE, ENDEAVOUR

try /'traɪ/ verb, means to make an effort to do something: 'It's a bit late to ring them, but I'll try'. When great effort is indicated, 'try' is often combined with 'best' or 'hardest': 'I will try my best/hardest in the exam'. 'Try' can be followed by 'to' plus the infinitive, as in: 'Try to remember what she said'. An informal alternative is 'try' followed by 'and' plus the infinitive: 'The car won't start. Try and get some help, will you?' In this sense, 'try and' cannot be used in the past or continuous tenses. A separate use of 'try and' is to link two separate ideas: 'I tried and I succeeded'. This is clearly not the same as saying: 'I tried to succeed'. 'Try and' is used in everyday speech and in informal contexts to link 'try' to another verb: 'The car won't start, try and get some help'. 'Try to' means the same but is used in writing and in more formal contexts: 'We will try to get some help because the car won't start'. Note that only 'try to' can be used in the past.

attempt /əˈtempt/ noun & verb, as a noun, means the act of trying to do something difficult, often without succeeding: 'There have been several attempts to re-commence negotiations'. As a verb, 'attempt' means to carry out such an action, again, without success: 'They attempted to climb Mont Blanc last winter'.

strive /straɪv/ verb, means to try very hard to achieve something: 'We are striving to help the children in these slums'. 'Strive' is often used to stress a competitive element: 'Over 50 nations were striving to win that gold medal'. This is a formal word.

endeavour /enˈdevər/ verb & noun, as a verb, also means to try very hard to do something but is a more formal word than 'strive'. As a noun, this means the 'attempt' to do something that is new or difficult: 'The United Nations will make every endeavour to remove the cause of poverty in these slums'. 'Endeavour' can be used in the plural: 'I wished him well in his endeavours.' This is the BE spelling; the AE equivalent is 'endeavor'.

TYPE IN, KEY IN, WRITE IN, ENTER, OVERWRITE (COMPUTING)

type in /taɪp 'ɪn/ verb phrase, means to type characters on a typewriter and is now used for writing something on a keyboard.

key in /kiː 'ɪn/ verb phrase, means to enter data or write on a computer keyboard: 'He keyed in the commands and password'. Note that 'key in' is used for short commands.

write in /raɪt 'ɪn/ verb phrase, means to enter text, and is associated with both word processing and handwriting.

enter /'entər/ *verb & noun*, means to write information into a computer: 'Enter your password, and then press return'. This is used for short series of keystrokes, and may even mean simply 'Press enter'.

overwrite /əʊvə'raɪt/ *verb*, means to replace data that has already been entered in a file or on the screen of a computer: 'Note that overwriting this file will delete the previous version'.

TYPE OF, KIND OF, SORT OF

type of /'taɪp əv/ *noun phrase*, indicates a group of items: 'Caravans are a type of vehicle'. Note that 'type' can be both singular and plural, and should be used with the corresponding form of the verb: 'Those types of books are difficult to read'. In the singular, 'type of' is followed by a singular noun: 'He had a special type of hearing-aid'.

kind of /'kaɪnd əv/ *noun phrase*, also indicates a group of items, but this phrase is only used in informal contexts. 'Kind' can be both singular and plural, but should be used with the corresponding form of the verb: 'These kinds of dogs are very obedient'. In AE, 'kind of' (pronounced /'kaɪndə/) is widely used in informal speech as a way of making something sound less harsh: 'The store detective let the two youths go and said, "I had to, I felt kind of sorry for them"'.

sort of /'sɔːt əv/ *noun* phrase, is another general way of indicating a group of items, and is similar to 'kind of': 'She is the sort of woman who always gets what she wants'. 'Sort' can be both singular and plural, and should be used with the corresponding verb form: 'Those sorts of people always cause trouble'.

TYPICAL, TYPICALLY, CHARACTERISTIC

typical /'tɪpɪkl̩/ *adjective*, refers to the distinctive qualities of a particular type of person or thing: 'This is a typical Alpine village'. This word is sometimes overused by non-native speakers of English. An alternative is 'traditional', as in 'There are many traditional inns in this part of the country'.

typically /'tɪpɪkl̩i/ *adverb*, refers to something that happens in a predictable way. It may be used to describe an adjective or a whole sentence: 'Her tone of voice was typically sarcastic'.

characteristic /kærəktə'rɪstɪk/ *adjective*, is combined with 'of' to mean typical of a particular person, group, place or thing: 'It was very characteristic of the British delegate to speak only English during the meeting'.

TYPO, MISPRINT

typo /'taɪpəʊ/ *noun*, means a typographical error. Examples of this are dividing the word 'legends' into 'leg-ends'. 'Typo' is used informally and often too broadly to include mistakes in books which do not come from the printers: 'Many typos in newspapers are caused by reporters not the print shop'.

misprint /'mɪsprɪnt/ *noun*, means a mistake in spelling when a document or book is printed. One misprint to avoid is 'mispell', which correctly has double 's': 'misspell'.

'The driver was found guilty of carless driving.'
(Newspaper report)

Uu

UNBALANCED, IMBALANCE

unbalanced /ʌnˈbælənst/ *adjective*, refers to a lack of symmetry or balance in someone or something: 'He became mentally unbalanced and needed medical attention'. In a report or similar presentation, this means being inaccurate or biased: 'This is an extremely unbalanced account of agricultural policy'.

imbalance /ɪmˈbæləns/ *noun*, means a lack of proportion or relation between corresponding things: 'There is an imbalance of power between the two regions'.

---

uncountable nouns

- One of the many ways in which nouns can be subdivided is into those that can be counted (*a/one cat, two cats*, etc.) and those that cannot, and which only have a singular form, such as *information*. This group is known as *uncountable nouns*. Uncountable nouns cannot be made plural, and cannot have the indefinite article before them. They should not be confused with countable nouns that have the same form in the singular and plural, such as *sheep*. Uncountable nouns are often the names of qualities, such as *fear* or *hatred*, or of substances of indeterminate amount, such as *beer, hair, information, oil, tea, wheat*.

- If the sense of the sentence requires some sort of singular concept with an uncountable noun, then a longer phrasing must be used: *a grain of rice, a piece of information, a cup of tea, a feeling of hatred*.

- There is one exception to the rule that uncountable nouns have no plural: instead of saying 'two cups of tea', or any other drink, it is permissible to say *two teas*. This can also mean two varieties of tea, for example Earl Grey and Lapsang Souchong.

See **AGREEMENT BETWEEN SUBJECT AND VERB**.

' I have brown eyes and a black, bushy hair...'

UNEATABLE, INEDIBLE

uneatable /ʌnˈiːtəbḷ/ *adjective*, means not good enough to be eaten: 'These bananas are so soft they are completely uneatable'. See **EATABLE**.

inedible /ɪnˈedɪbḷ/ *adjective*, also means not good enough to be eaten, but has a secondary meaning of not suitable as food. 'People who pick mushrooms must avoid those that are totally inedible as some of them are poisonous'. See **EDIBLE** ⟹ **EATABLE**.

UNFAIR, UNJUST

unfair /ʌnˈfeər/ *adjective*, usually refers to a situation or behaviour that is not based on the principles of equality. 'Unfair' is the word to use when referring to personal relationships: 'The manager was so unfair to the staff that he lost his job'.

unjust /ʌnˈdʒʌst/ *adjective*, means based on what is morally incorrect. 'Unjust' is a formal word and often applies to social structures: 'The cutting of pensions was a very unjust measure'. See **JUST**.

UNILATERAL, BILATERAL, MULTILATERAL

unilateral /juːnɪˈlætərəl/ *adjective*, refers to an action by one group or country without reference to others: 'The market position forced unilateral action on the government'.

bilateral /baɪˈlætərəl/ *adjective*, refers to an action or agreement that affects two groups or countries: 'Bilateral trade talks were planned between the USA and the EU'.

multilateral /mʌltiˈlætərəl/ *adjective*, refers to an action or agreement that affects three or more groups or countries: 'Multilateral environmental discussions take place every year'.

UNINTELLIGIBLE, INCOMPREHENSIBLE

unintelligible /ʌnɪnˈtelɪdʒɪbl̩/ *adjective*, refers to spoken or written language that is impossible to understand: 'The loudspeaker system was so badly tuned that the speech was completely unintelligible for most of the audience'. See **ILLEGIBLE**.

incomprehensible /ɪŋkɒmprɪˈhensɪbl̩/ *adjective*, refers to an act, reaction or other non-verbal behaviour that cannot be understood: 'It is utterly incomprehensible that you have cut down those trees'.

UNINTERESTED, DISINTERESTED

uninterested /ʌnˈɪntrɪstɪd/ *adjective*, means not showing any interest in someone or something: 'I thought the museum was fascinating, but the children were completely uninterested'.

disinterested /dɪsˈɪntrɪstɪd/ *adjective*, means impartial, and not influenced by any personal benefit that might result from a situation: 'To maintain impartiality, all advice will be given by disinterested parties'. Less formally, it can also mean 'uninterested', but careful writers will avoid using 'disinterested' in this sense.

UNIQUE, REALLY UNIQUE

unique /juːˈniːk/ *adjective*, is an absolute term, which means that there is only one of a thing, and it is therefore incorrect to use comparatives like 'more' and 'most' together with 'unique'. Careful writers never use 'unique' as a synonym for exceptional, rare, or unusual, and avoid expressions like 'the most unique city/vehicle/ball-point pen'. As 'unique' has a consonant sound at the beginning, the indefinite article is always 'a', never 'an'.

really unique means remarkable or most unusual. This is a case of the secondary meaning of 'unique' being used in less formal English as something very special: 'A really unique opportunity'. Such developments are cultivated by advertisers and ignored by careful users of English. See **ABSOLUTES AND FUZZY ABSOLUTES**.

A small town in Europe claimed in a tourist guide that it was 'the most unique city in the world.'

UNPAID, OUTSTANDING

unpaid /ˈʌnˈpeɪd/ *adjective*, means not paid for. This can either refer to debts: 'They came back from holiday to find a pile of unpaid bills'; or to work without pay: 'A housewife is someone who does unpaid work in the home'.

outstanding /aʊtˈstændɪŋ/ *adjective*, means either exceptionally good: 'The actors gave an outstanding performance'; or 'unpaid', in connection with debts: 'They had many bills outstanding'. In this sense it usually follows the noun it refers to.

URBAN, URBANE

urban /ˈɜːbən/ *adjective*, means relating to or characteristic of a town or city: 'The authorities have increased the budget for urban renewal by 25%'. Note that 'urban' can only be used before a noun.

urbane /ɜːˈbeɪn/ *adjective*, refers to a man who appears relaxed and confident in social situations: 'He is delightful company, both witty and urbane'.

USE, UTILIZE, USAGE

use /juːs/ *noun &* /juːz/ *verb*, as a noun, means the employment of something for a specific purpose: 'The explosion in the use of electronic communications is changing office life'. Note that 'use of' takes a singular verb. As a verb, 'use' means to employ a tool or method for a specific purpose: 'Have you used a lawnmower like this before?' In another sense, it means the consumption of a liquid or substance: 'This car uses a lot of petrol'. Note that as a verb, 'use' rhymes with 'clues'.

utilize /ˈjuːtɪlaɪz/ *verb*, means to put to practical and effective use: 'We are trying to utilize solar energy to convert sea water to fresh water'. 'Utilize' occurs very frequently now in BE, but often the more general verb 'use' is a better choice. See **DEVELOP**.

usage /ˈjuːsɪdʒ/ *noun*, means the action of using something, or the extent to which it is used: 'Electricity usage is increasing, to the concern of environmentalists'. In connection with language, 'usage' is the way words and phrases are employed: 'Many details about English are explained in reference books on usage'.

USED TO, BE USED TO

used to /'juːstə/ *verb*, refers to things that happened regularly in the past, but which do not happen now. 'Used to' is followed by the infinitive without 'to': 'We used to play tennis three times a week when we lived in the village'.

be used to /biː 'juːstə/ *adjective*, means to be accustomed to something or someone that was once unfamiliar or strange and which is now part of everyday life. 'Be used to' is followed either by a noun or the '–ing' form: 'I am used to having three meals a day'. To gradually become accustomed to something, we say 'become used to', or, more conversationally, 'get used to': 'It took some time to get used to that new software'.

USUAL, CUSTOMARY, COMMON, NORMAL, ORDINARY

usual /'juːʒʊəl/ *adjective*, means habitual or occurring frequently: 'He sat in his usual seat on the bus'; 'He asked for his usual table in the restaurant'. The phrase 'business as usual' means carrying on as if no difficulties had occurred. This can also refer to some kind of business, such as a shop that has suffered fire damage but is continuing to trade. Alternatively, it can refer to any situation which carries on as normal after an interruption: 'There was an unexpected cease-fire, but after two weeks it was business as usual'.

customary /'kʌstəməri/ *adjective*, refers to customs that are usual, habitual and typical of specific social groups or places: 'It is customary to be polite in business life'. 'Customary' is a slightly more formal word than 'usual'.

common /'kɒmən/ *adjective*, refers to things that occur or are done very often: 'It is common to catch a cold in the spring'. 'Common' also refers to a lack of high rank or status: 'He was just a common soldier'. Things that are seen as being in poor taste are also described as 'common': 'The hotel was decorated in a very common way'.

normal /'nɔːml/ *adjective*, means typical and as to be expected: 'Feeling tired on Monday morning is quite normal'.

ordinary /'ɔːdɪnri/ *adjective*, refers to a person who is plain or a thing with no special features: 'It is just an ordinary redbrick house'. Since 'ordinary' is often associated with things that are commonplace and uninteresting, it can be an unfavourable word. Compare: an 'ordinary' girl (uninteresting); a 'common' girl (low status); with the neutral, a 'normal' girl. See **PLAIN**.

'v' and 'w': pronunciation tips

It is always important in English to distinguish between the way the *v–* and *w-sounds* are pronounced, especially at the beginning of words. The *v-sound* is pronounced by lightly touching the bottom lip with the upper front teeth and breathing out as you say a word like *very*. Few people have problems with the *w-sound*. This is just a matter of pursing the lips to blow a kiss, keeping your teeth out of the way, then breathing out as you say a word like *well*. Practise with *very well*.

VACANT, AVAILABLE, FREE, FREELY, ACCESSIBLE

vacant /'veɪkənt/ *adjective*, refers to a position at work, a hotel room or a seat on a train/bus/plane that is empty. Jobs and hotel rooms are advertised as 'vacancies'. When asking someone if a particular object such as a seat on a train or plane etc. is available, a typical expression is 'Is this seat vacant?'

available /ə'veɪləbl/ *adjective*, refers to a person who is not otherwise occupied: 'He will ring you as soon as he becomes available'. 'Available' in another sense refers to things that are obtainable: 'The TV series was readily available throughout the world'.

free /friː/ *adjective*, means at liberty: 'The prisoner was suddenly a free man', or unrestricted: 'Free speech is a democratic right'. 'Free' can mean unoccupied. It is used as a less formal alternative to 'available', for people who are not busy: 'Are you free for lunch tomorrow?'. 'Free' is also a less formal alternative to 'vacant', for objects that are not in use: 'Excuse me. Is that chair free?' In a third sense, 'free' means without payment: 'The children were given free pencil cases on their first day at school'. The phrase 'for free' is often seen, but should be avoided in formal writing. The expression 'to give someone a free rein' means to allow them to act however they wish.

freely /'friːli/ *adverb*, means openly, candidly, or without restriction. It is not connected to the idea of payment. Children educated 'freely' receive a liberal education. This may or may not involve the paying of school fees. Children educated 'free', on the other hand, do not pay for their schooling.

accessible /æk'sesɪbl̩/ *adjective*, refers to places that can be reached and entered: 'This part of the coast is accessible only by boat'. People who are easy to know and talk to are also accessible: 'The students were surprised that the professor was so casual and accessible'.

VALUABLE, INVALUABLE, VALUE CREATION, VALUELESS, WORTHLESS,

valuable /'væljʊəbl̩/ *adjective*, means something worth a great deal of money, or that is extremely useful or important: 'His research is a valuable contribution to our knowledge of the topic'.

invaluable /ɪn'væljʊəbl̩/ *adjective*, means extremely useful or very valuable: 'I would not have been able to do this without you – your help has been invaluable'. Note that the opposite of 'valuable' is 'valueless' or 'worthless', never 'invaluable'.

value creation /'vælju: kri.eɪʃn̩/ *noun*, means the development of profitable activities for a company or organization, often as a result of applied research: 'The company CEO stated that value creation was their number one priority'.

valueless /'vælju:ləs/ *adjective*, means without value or importance. This is a formal word which is the opposite of 'valuable': 'Much agricultural land became valueless following contamination by radioactive pollution'.

worthless /'wɜ:θləs/ *adjective*, means having no practical or financial value. In this sense it is a less formal alternative to 'valueless': 'The damaged crops are utterly worthless'. When referring to a person who has no value, 'worthless', not 'valueless', should be used: 'His run of bad luck made him feel completely worthless'.

VAPOUR, VAPORIZE

vapour /'veɪpər/ *noun*, means a substance suspended in the air: 'A cloud of petrol vapour hung over the tanker'. This is the spelling in BE. 'Vapor' is the AE spelling of 'vapour'.

vaporize /'veɪpəraɪz/ *verb*, means to turn into gas: 'The particles that were emitted were vaporized'. Note that there is no 'u' in the second syllable. See **-OR, -OUR SPELLINGS**.

VEGETABLE, SALAD, LETTUCE

vegetable /'vedʒətəbl̩/ *noun*, means a plant or part of a plant that can be eaten: 'He sliced some seasonal vegetables, and then steamed them'. A person who is physically alive but incapable of mental activity is informally described as a 'vegetable': 'The car crash turned him into a vegetable'. Use 'vegetable' in this sense with great care. 'Severely mentally disabled' is often a better alternative. See **INVALID**.

salad /'sæləd/ *noun*, means a cold dish that is a mixture of vegetables, often with cold meat, eggs or shellfish: 'They served a crisp green salad'. As a dessert, a 'fruit salad' is a mixture of fruit. Note that the expression 'in one's salad days' has two meanings: either focusing on youth and lack of experience, or being at the peak of one's ability.

lettuce /'letɪs/ *noun*, is a green vegetable cultivated for its edible leaves: 'We washed and chopped some lettuce for the salad'.

VENDING MACHINE, SLOT MACHINE

vending machine /'vendɪŋ məʃi:n/ *noun*, is a machine from which soft drinks, sweets and other items can be bought when money or tokens are inserted: 'After 11 p.m. the only place to buy snacks was from vending machines'.

slot machine /'slɒt məʃi:n/ *noun*, is used for amusement, gambling and games machines: 'He lost £5000 on the slot machines'. This is also an alternative term to 'vending machine' in BE. Thus 'slot machine' may be an ambiguous expression.

VERBAL, ORAL[S], AURAL[S]

verbal /'vɜ:bl̩/ *adjective*, means relating to words: 'He swore at the parking meter attendant and was prosecuted for verbal abuse'. 'Verbal' is often used for spoken words, in contrast to written words. This can be confusing as a 'verbal agreement' may mean one that is only spoken and not written down. As the main meaning of 'verbal' is to do with words (both written and spoken), the solution is to use 'oral' for spoken words and 'written' for writing, and avoid 'verbal' altogether.

oral /'ɔ:rəl/ *adjective*, refers to speech and the mouth: 'In an oral examination, students are tested on their ability to demonstrate their knowledge in discussion with the examiners'. A dentist is concerned with 'oral hygiene'.

aural /'ɔːrəl/ *adjective*, refers to ears and hearing. Tests designed to assess a student's listening comprehension skills are often called 'aural comprehension tests', as distinct from 'oral tests', which evaluate a learner's proficiency in speaking the language. Note that 'oral' and 'aural' are pronounced the same.

verbiage

This is the use of too many words, or of more difficult words than are required, to express an idea. The following are examples of verbiage, with some suggested alternatives:

all of - Except with pronouns, *of* is unnecessary.

as to whether, whether or not - Whether is usually sufficient.

at an earlier date - Use *before, previously*.

in character - This is often redundant, as in *the work was demanding in character*.

commence, initiate - Use *begin* or *start*.

due to the fact that/in view of the fact that - Use *because* or *since*.

end result - Use *result*.

fact - All facts are true and actual, so it is redundant to say *actual fact* or *true fact*.

in order to - Simply use *to*.

in some cases - Use *sometimes, often*.

in the final analysis - Use *finally*, or omit.

in view of the fact that - Use *because*.

irregardless - This is incorrect in formal English, use *regardless*.

knots per hour - *Per hour* is redundant: a *knot* means 1 nautical mile (1 852 m) per hour.

-speaking - This is a rather clumsy way of saying *from a ... perspective*

subsequent to - Use *after*.

unique - Means without equal, the only one of its kind. As this is rarely the case, it may be better to use *special*. See **ABSOLUTES AND FUZZY ABSOLUTES.**

utilize - *Use* is often preferable.

-wise - Not recommended as a home-made ending. *Clockwise* is standard. *Costwise* is not. See **TAUTOLOGY.**

VIA, BY MEANS OF

via /'vaɪə/ *preposition*, means by way of: 'We travelled from London to Moscow via Copenhagen', and is commonly used for electronic communications: 'Reply via email'; 'Broadcast via satellite TV'.

by means of /baɪ 'miːnz əv/ *prepositional phrase*, refers to the means or methods used to achieve something: 'Our financial problems can only be solved by means of a huge win on the lottery'. 'By means of' is often just written as 'by': 'Freight is sent by air or rail'.

VICE[s], VICE-[s]

vice /vaɪs/ *noun*, can mean criminal activities, immorality, or bad habits: 'The police from the Vice Squad'; 'He indulged in his vices of fast cars and gambling'.

vice- /vaɪs-/ *prefix*, means next in rank to, and a deputy of: 'Vice-president and former vice admiral'. Note that 'vice-president' has a hyphen, but many other words with 'vice' are written without a hyphen, as two words, 'vice chancellor'.

VICIOUS, VISCOUS

vicious /'vɪʃəs/ *adjective*, means violent and evil. It is used in expressions like 'vicious circle', a chain of evil and danger that repeats itself: 'The vicious circle of heroin addiction'.

viscous /'vɪskəs/ *adjective*, means thick and sticky: 'The seagull's feathers were full of a black viscous oil'. This word is normally used in technical expressions.

VICTIM, CASUALTY, DEATH TOLL

victim /'vɪktɪm/ *noun*, means a person who is affected, harmed, injured or killed as a result of a crime or accident: 'The villagers who fled were the helpless victims of the war'. A victim can also be someone who has been tricked: 'He was the unfortunate victim of some clever blackmailers'.

casualty /'kæʒʊəlti/ *noun*, means a person who is injured or killed in a war or accident: 'The troops suffered heavy casualties'. The 'casualty unit' or 'casualty ward' is the part of a hospital where people requiring emergency treatment are taken. This part of the hospital is also known in BE as 'Casualty': 'I cut my hand very badly and was taken to Casualty', or 'A & E' (Accident and Emergency), and in AE as the Emergency Room

death toll /'deθ təʊl/ *noun*, means the number of casualties as a result of a war or disaster: 'The full death toll was never revealed'.

VIEW, OPINION, THINK

view /vjuː/ noun, means both what can be seen from a particular place and a subjective way of considering something. The expression 'in view of the fact that' is an example of verbiage and can usually be replaced by 'because' or 'since'. See SIGHT. See VERBIAGE.

opinion /əˈpɪnjən/ noun, means a view or judgement by the speaker, or by people in general. However, an opinion is more considered and formal than a view: 'The politicians held conflicting opinions about ecological policy'. The term 'a second opinion' means a professional statement made by an expert: 'The patient was not happy with the diagnosis and decided to seek a second opinion'. 'Opinion' can be uncountable when referring to opinions held by a large number of people: 'Public opinion was turning against him'.

think /θɪŋk/ verb, is used to enquire about someone's opinion or belief: 'What do you think about the scandal in London?' This is a request for a reaction, an opinion about the scandal. The related noun is 'thought': 'What are your thoughts on the subject?'

VIEWER, WATCHER

viewer /ˈvjuːər/ noun, means someone who watches a TV programme: 'A number of viewers called the TV station to complain about the programme'. See PUBLIC.

watcher /ˈwɒtʃər/ noun, means a person who observes or studies something regularly: 'She changed jobs and became a trend-watcher'. This word usually appears in compounds, such as 'bird-watcher'.

VILLAGE, SETTLEMENT

village /ˈvɪlɪdʒ/ noun, means a group of houses and other buildings in a country district that is smaller than a town. It can also be a self-contained unit or community inside a town or city, such as a student village.
See TOWN ➪ CITY.

settlement /ˈsetḷmənt/ noun, means a place where people have made their homes, that previously was uninhabited: 'A settlement in the Australian outback'.

VISIBLE, VISUAL, VISUAL ARTS

visible /ˈvɪzɪbḷ/ adjective, refers to things that can be seen: 'The fog has lifted and the airport is now clearly visible'.

visual /ˈvɪzjʊəl/ adjective, means of, or related to, seeing, as in: 'He suffered visual disturbances after the accident'. 'Visual aids' are pictures or videos used in education or training in order to assist learning.

visual arts /ˈvɪzjʊəl ˈɑːts/ noun, means activities such as painting, sculpture and film. This is often combined with the definite article, 'the visual arts': 'The budget for the visual arts has unfortunately been cut'.

VISIT, STAY, CALL ON, DROP IN

visit /ˈvɪzɪt/ verb & noun, means to go to see someone at home or at work for a short time: 'We looked forward to visiting your country'. In BE one visits people; in AE one visits with them. As a noun, 'visit' is often used in the expression 'pay a visit'.

stay /steɪ/ verb & noun, means to spend some time as a guest in another person's house or in a hotel: 'We are staying at The George Hotel'. The noun form occurs most frequently in the phrase: 'I hope you enjoy your stay'.

call on /ˈkɔːl ɒn/ verb, means to visit someone for an official purpose: 'A representative of the company will call on you next week'. 'Call in' is informal and refers to a short visit on the way to somewhere else: 'We could call in later when you are less busy'. There is no noun form. Use 'visit' instead.

drop in /drɒp ˈɪn/ verb, means to make a casual visit. It is similar to 'call in', but is even more informal: 'Drop in whenever you are passing'. There is no noun form.

VOUCHER, COUPON

voucher /ˈvaʊtʃər/ noun, means a piece of paper that enables the holder to buy goods without money: 'As the company does not have a canteen, it gives all its staff luncheon vouchers'. A 'gift voucher' is a token that allows someone to buy goods in a specific shop. This is called a 'gift certificate' in AE.

coupon /ˈkuːpɒn/ noun, means a piece of paper that is used to get a reduction in the price of goods: 'He cut the coupon out of the newspaper and received a 10% discount in the supermarket'. This may be termed a 'discount voucher'.

Ww

WAIT, AWAIT

wait /weɪt/ verb, means to remain where one is or postpone an action until something happens: 'I'm sorry to have kept you waiting'. Note that 'wait' usually has no object. The phrase 'wait for' means that someone is waiting until a person arrives or a particular event occurs: 'They are waiting for their exam results'.

await /ə'weɪt/ verb, means to wait for an event and is a more formal word. 'Await' always takes an object: 'We are anxiously awaiting the announcement of the World Cup draw'.

WAIVEˢ, WAVEˢ

waive /weɪv/ verb, is a formal word meaning not to use the rights one has: 'We waive our rights to any future commercial exploitation'. As 'waive' means to not exercise a right, it cannot be combined with 'aside' or 'away' in standard English.

wave /weɪv/ verb, means to move the hand as a signal or greeting: 'He turned and waved to the reporters'.

WAKE, AWAKE, AROUSE, ARISE

wake /weɪk/ verb, means to stop sleeping or to make someone else stop sleeping: 'I don't want to wake the baby'. 'Wake up' is a very commonly used alternative, which, when combined with 'to', can also mean to realize the truth of a situation: 'They need to wake up to what is going on in this company'.

awake /ə'weɪk/ verb & adjective, as a verb, is a formal word that means to arouse from sleep and is most commonly used in writing in the past tense 'awoke': 'The family suddenly awoke to the sound of thunder'. 'Awake' as an adjective means not being asleep, or, when combined with 'to', being aware of the situation: 'He was awake to the commercial possibilities of the software'.

arouse /ə'raʊz/ verb, means to generate or awaken a feeling, a response or interest: 'The heavy bag aroused the suspicion of the customs officer'. 'Arouse' also means to wake someone up, and in this sense it is a formal word. In another sense, aroused can mean sexually stimulated.

arise /ə'raɪz/ verb, means to become apparent or develop: 'Our customer relations staff are good at dealing with conflicts that arise between customers and the company'. Both 'occur' and the informal 'crop up' could replace 'arise' in this context. It is only now in poetic contexts that 'arise' means to get out of bed. The past tense is 'arose' /ə'rəʊz/.

'Work Experience: Dealing with customers' conflicts that arouse.' (From a CV)

WALK, HIKE, HITCH-HIKE, MARCH

walk /wɔːk/ noun & verb, means travelling by foot. It is a general word covering a variety of different types of pace and distance, from a stroll (a leisurely walk to stretch one's legs), to a long hike: 'He walked briskly for two miles every day on his doctor's orders'.

hike /haɪk/ noun & verb, means walking in hilly country or across country: 'We hiked across the mountains'. A 'hike' is more strenuous than a 'walk'.

hitch-hike /'hɪtʃ haɪk/ verb, means to travel by getting free lifts from passing motorists. It may be shortened to 'hitch', but never to 'hike': 'They hitched to town and back last night'.

march /mɑːtʃ/ verb & noun, means to walk with a regular step, often in a military style: 'The soldiers marched for three days'. 'March' can also convey angry intentions: 'She marched into the shop and demanded to speak to the manager'. As a noun, 'march' means a long, tiring journey on foot: 'The march through the mountains exhausted them'.

'Do not march on the grass.' (Park notice)

-WARD, -WARDS

-ward /-wəd/ adjectival suffix, is used to indicate direction: 'The homeward journey'.

-wards /-wədz/ adverbial suffix, also indicates direction 'We are moving northwards'. This adverbial suffix is sometimes spelt '-ward', thus 'we are moving northward' is acceptable. This distinction applies to similar words including: 'eastward/eastwards' and 'southward/southwards'.

WARM, HOT

warm /wɔːm/ *adjective*, means at a fairly high temperature. It also means comfortable: 'A warm summer evening'. 'Warm' is also used about colours such as red, yellow or orange: 'The house was decorated in various warm shades'. Figuratively 'warm' means friendly, as in 'a warm welcome' or 'a warm smile'.

hot /hɒt/ *adjective*, means at a high temperature: 'After lunch it was just too hot to sit outside'. 'Hot' is used for food, which can mean either very warm in temperature or strongly spiced: 'He likes very hot curries'. 'Hot' is used in many contexts ranging from lust, anger, high activity to a topical issue often called a 'hot potato', meaning one that is controversial, and therefore difficult to handle. 'Hot news' means very recent and important news.

WASH, WASH UP, WASH DOWN

wash /wɒʃ/ *verb*, means to make things clean, usually by using soap and water: 'I'm going to wash the car this afternoon'. 'Wash' can be used in set phrases to mean numerous things that are often only indirectly connected to making things clean, such as 'wash one's dirty linen in public' which means to reveal personal, and potentially embarrassing, affairs to others in public.

wash up /wɒʃ ˈʌp/ *verb*, means, particularly in BE, to wash the dishes. This is also called 'doing the dishes' in both BE and AE. In AE, 'wash up' also means to wash one's face and hands. If a person is feeling 'washed up' it means tired out. When this phrase is used about public figures, it means they are finished: 'He used to be a VIP in Congress, but now he is washed up as a politician'.

wash down /wɒʃ ˈdaʊn/ *verb*, means either to clean a surface usually with water: 'We washed down the paintwork before we started redecorating', or informally to have a drink with a meal: 'He washed down his meal with a pint of beer'.

WASTE^S, WAIST^S

waste /weɪst/ *noun*, means using something or spending carelessly, without thinking economically: 'His new yacht is a waste of money'. 'Waste' also means material that is not wanted, or a by-product. If one specific type is referred to, there is a singular verb: 'Nuclear waste is to be treated with great care'. In the plural, wastes either means different types of material that are not wanted: 'Industrial wastes are sometimes valuable'; or a large area of uninhabited land: 'The Antarctic wastes of snow and ice'.

waist /weɪst/ *noun*, means the area around the middle of the body just above the hips: 'These shorts have a 50 cm waist'. 'Waistline' refers to the measurement of the body around the waist: 'The size of the average waistline is increasing'.

 'Reduce your waste line.'
(Slimming advert)

WATERPROOF, WATERTIGHT

waterproof /ˈwɔːtəpruːf/ *adjective & noun*, as an adjective, refers to something that cannot be penetrated by water or washed away by it: 'Waterproof ink'. As a noun, a jacket and trousers made from waterproof fabric may simply be called 'a set of waterproofs': 'Their waterproofs were muddy and torn after the long hike'.

watertight /ˈwɔːtətaɪt/ *adjective*, means made or sealed so that water cannot get in or out: 'The ship had ten watertight compartments'. 'Watertight' is also used for a justification or alibi that cannot be disproved. A 'watertight agreement' is drawn up so that there is no chance of anyone misunderstanding it.

–WAYS, –WISE

–ways /-weɪz/ *suffix*, is added to adjectives and adverbs to indicate the direction or manner of doing something: 'They moved lengthways'. It can also be combined with 'edge-' and 'side-'.

–wise /-waɪz/ *suffix*, means in the manner or direction of something. An example is 'clockwise', which means moving in the same direction as the hands of a clock: 'Turn the handle clockwise'. '–wise' also means 'with regard to', when added to other words to form adverbs, such as 'likewise', meaning 'similarly', or 'otherwise', meaning 'apart from that'. The formation of some new words with the '-wise' ending has been criticized, and 'timewise' and 'newswise' are best avoided in formal writing. See **VERBIAGE**.

'we': tips for authors

- Academic papers and doctoral theses in English written by a single author should use the word *we* with care. *We* is a tiny, but powerful word as it sets the tone. At worst, *we* can irritate readers into thinking the writer has an inflated opinion of him or herself as it conveys the impression that this is the opinion of the entire department or research group. At best, it can rivet the reader's attention to a valuable contribution to knowledge.

editorial 'we':

* This use of *we* is only suitable when it refers to the view of an editorial board or a collective body: *We recommend this paper for publication*. It is recommended that sentences like *As we have indicated in Section 2.3* should be avoided. Instead use either *as indicated in Section 2.3* or *as I indicated in Section 2.3*. In formal writing, many single authors are afraid of using *I*, but the use of anything but *I* is unnatural in the Acknowledgements and Preface in this type of writing.

'we' for reader involvement:

* In order to bring the reader into the discussion, many style guides encourage the use of *us* and *we* in contexts like: *Let us consider these results in detail ... .We now turn to the applications of this school of thought ....* This appeals to the reader's involvement and is encouraged as a means of drawing attention to a piece of academic writing. The trick is to make sure the *we* refers to the reader and the author, not a single author. It is also acceptable to use *we* to refer to a nation or humanity in general: *We need to look after the environment.*

royal 'we':

* Referring to oneself as *we* is known as the *royal we*. This used to be a way to distance the monarch from the people. Nowadays this is avoided, even in formal contexts, by the British monarch. When this is not done, it is likely to hit the headlines of the British press, as when Margaret Thatcher, the then prime minister, declared: *We are a grandmother.*

WEALTH, RICHES, AFFLUENCE

wealth /welθ/ *noun,* means having an abundance of valuable possessions or money: 'His wealth is measured by his cars, boats and expensive homes'. 'Wealth' can also mean a large amount of something that has been acquired: 'She brought a wealth of experience to the company'. Note that 'wealth' is an uncountable noun.

riches /'rɪtʃɪz/ *noun,* means an abundance of valuable possessions or money. However this word is normally used in poetic and literary contexts: 'She would not kiss him, not even for all the riches in Arabia'. 'Riches' can also be used to refer to the wealth of a geographical area: 'The riches of the Mediterranean'. This word is only used in the plural.

affluence /'æfluəns/ *noun,* is the state of being rich. It is normally used for a social group or a district or region, unlike 'wealth', which refers to an individual. The 'affluence' of a region refers to the situation where the average person is comfortably well off in material terms. Those who have 'wealth' in the West are the truly rich.

WEATHER⁵, WHETHER⁵

weather /'weðər/ *noun,* means the meteorological conditions, such as temperature, wind, rain, cloud, or sun: 'What terrible weather for the time of year'. Note that 'weather' is uncountable. See **HURRICANE**. See **RAIN**. See **SNOW**. See **STORM**.

whether /'weðər/ *conjunction,* is used to make a choice between alternatives: 'She did not know whether to laugh or cry'. It can also express doubt: 'It's doubtful whether I'll come'. See **WHETHER ⇨ IF**.

WEB PAGE, WEB SITE, HOME PAGE, WEBMASTER, WORLD WIDE WEB

web page /'web peɪdʒ/ *noun,* means a document of one or more pages connected to the World Wide Web, that may be accessed by others connected to the Internet: 'I will put a bookmark on this web page'.

web site /'web saɪt/ *noun,* means a location on the Internet where one or more web pages are collected by theme or provider: 'Our organization now has 50 000 pages on its web site'.

home page /'həʊm peɪdʒ/ *noun,* means two things: first, the introductory starting page for a web site on the Internet where an individual or organization gives the structure and links to other web pages and web sites; second, the screen that appears on a PC when the Internet browser is opened.

webmaster /'webmɑːstər/ *noun,* means a person responsible for a particular web site on the Internet. A 'webmaster' may be either male or female.

World Wide Web /'wɜːld waɪd 'web/ *noun*, is a widely used information system on the Internet which enables information to be accessed. Documents are marked by hypertext and can be found by these links. The World Wide Web was developed by CERN in Switzerland in 1991 to enable physicists all over Europe to share information. 'Web', 'WWW,' and 'W3' are all abbreviations for the World Wide Web. It is recommended that all of these terms are pronounced as 'w, w, w' /'dʌbl̩juː 'dʌbl̩juː 'dʌbl̩juː/ when giving an address on the Internet.

web addresses in English

- When giving someone a web address over the phone, it is important to use terms so that everybody understands what you mean. *World Wide Web* is written as *www* and read aloud as 'w, w, w' /'dʌbl̩juː 'dʌbl̩juː 'dʌbl̩juː/.
- **Slash** is the / sign. Slashes are used to indicate directories and subdirectories in World Wide Web addresses. Because the top of the slash leans forwards, it is sometimes called a *forward slash*. If there are two, call them *double slash*. (Note that web addresses never contain a *backslash* \.)
- **Dot** is the term for the full stop punctuation mark in web addresses and email addresses.
- **Dash** is the mid-position short horizontal line. Thus *t-de* is read as *t, dash, d, e.*
- **Underscore** is the term to use for letters or spaces that are underlined. Thus *h_c* is read as *h, underscore, c.*

- **Tilde** /'tɪldə/ is the sign from Spanish and Portuguese that looks like ˜. Thus ˜*xy* is read as *tilde, x,y.*
- A full web address like http://www.oup.com is read as: *h, t, t, p, colon, double slash, w, w, w, dot, o, u, p, dot, kom.*

See **EMAIL ADDRESSES.**

WEIGH, WEIGHT, WEIGHTING

weigh /weɪ/ *verb*, means to find the weight of something: 'Weigh the ingredients carefully'. 'Weigh up' is used in a figurative sense to mean to consider something carefully: 'The company weighed the use of video-conferencing against face-to-face meetings'. 'Weigh down' means either to use a heavy object to keep something in its place, or to make someone feel worried. In this sense, it is often used in the passive: 'He was weighed down with financial problems'.

weight /weɪt/ *verb & noun*, as a verb, means either to give importance to something: 'The housing allowance for executives sent abroad was heavily weighted in favour of the Middle East'; or to load: 'The plane was incorrectly weighted'. 'Weight' is commonly used in the passive. As a noun, 'weight' means how heavy something is in terms of a unit of measurement such as tonnes or kilos: 'Is your baby gaining weight?'

weighting /'weɪtɪŋ/ *noun*, means an allowance or adjustment to compensate for something: 'The more difficult questions carry an extra weighting of 20%'.

ONE AT A TIME PLEASE

SPEAK YOUR WEIGHT

PLEASE PUT THE OTHER FOOT ON

SPEAK YOUR WEIGHT

WELCOME, GOOD TO SEE YOU

welcome /'welkəm/ *exclamation & verb*, when used as a greeting, is a friendly way to meet guests: 'Welcome to our city'. A more formal way of greeting someone is to use 'welcome' as a verb: 'I am extremely honoured to welcome our distinguished guests to our city'.

welcome /'welkəm/ *noun & adjective*, is the reception of a person: 'He was given a warm welcome'. A formal greeting may also include 'welcome' as a noun: 'I extend a welcome to ... '. When 'welcome' is used as an adjective, it can mean different things. For example: 'You are welcome to come to the party with us' means to be happy for someone to do something if they want to. Compare it with: 'This has been a very unreliable car. You are welcome to it', which means to be happy to return or get rid of something because it is not wanted. Note that the common idiom 'You're welcome' is used when replying to somebody who has just said 'thank you'. An alternative phrase is 'Please don't mention it'.

good to see you /'gʊd tə 'siː juː/ is an informal greeting for guests to one's home or for meeting colleagues: 'Great to see you' is an alternative greeting.

'If this is your first visit to the country, you are welcome to it.'
(Hotel notice)

WELL, GOOD, HEALTHY

well /wel/ *adverb & adjective*, means in a good or satisfactory way. 'Well' is mainly used as an adverb: 'He skied very well for a beginner'; 'The prisoners were well treated'. 'Well' can also be an adjective meaning fit and in good health at a particular time: 'They looked well after six months in jail'. 'As well as' is a phrase which gives more information: 'He sings as well as dances'. Note that: 'He sings as well as he dances' is a comparison of his singing and dancing skills.
See **HYPHENATION IN COMPOUNDS**.

good /gʊd/ *adjective*, means in a pleasant or satisfactory way. 'Good' should never be used as an adverb: 'He skied very good' is non-standard English. 'Good' means in satisfactory shape. Thus : 'He looked good after six months in jail' refers to his appearance, while: 'He looked well after

six months' would refer to his state of health. The phrase 'to be good' refers to satisfactory conduct: 'The teacher told the children to be good while he was out of the classroom'.

healthy /'helθi/ *adjective*, means being in a physically good state. Thus, it can refer both to a person who is rarely ill and to activities that promote good health, such as a lot of outdoor exercise and balanced diet: 'She is so healthy that she hasn't had a day off work since 1995'. Figuratively, 'healthy' can be used for having a lot of something: 'Following his operation, he developed a healthy appetite'. See **ILL**.

WEST, WESTERN, WESTERLY

west /west/ *noun*, is the direction of the sunset. When 'west' refers to a direction it is not usually capitalized: 'The sun sets in the west'. 'West' is capitalized when it is a defined unit: 'The West and its high technology'; a part of a continent or country: 'West Indies'; a regional name: 'West Bank'; or a defined region: 'They moved West', meaning the western part of the USA. See **CAPITAL LETTERS**.

western /'westən/ *adjective*, can mean a region of a country to the west: 'There will be rain across western Scotland'. It is not usually capitalized in this case. 'Western' also means a characteristic of life in the West, such as: 'western rock music'. 'Western' is usually only capitalized when it is a part of proper nouns: 'Western Isles', 'Western Sahara'. 'Western' is also often capitalized when referring to living in Europe and North America: 'Western lifestyle'. See **EASTERN ⇨ EAST**.

westerly /'westəli/ *adjective*, means either in a direction towards the west: 'The animals were moving over the plains in a westerly direction'; or a wind that is blowing from the west: 'The ship started to roll when it was exposed to the westerly gale'. Note that 'westerly' is normally immediately followed by a noun.

WHERE EVER[s], WHEREVER[s]

where ever /hweər 'evər/ *adverb*, is sometimes written in two words when it means: 'Where ever did you go?' The stress is on 'ever'.

wherever /hweər'evər/ *adverb*, is the more usual form meaning in what ever place: 'You must take this purse back to wherever you found it'.

WHILE, WHILST, WHEREAS

while /ʰwaɪl/ *noun & adverb*, as a noun, means a period of time: 'We drove for a while in silence'. As an adverb, it means at the same time: 'The political situation was stable while the President was in hospital'.

whilst /ʰwaɪlst/ *adverb*, is a common alternative to 'while' and is used mostly in formal BE: 'Whilst the minister was speaking in Parliament, the lights failed'. 'Whilst' is rarely used in AE.

whereas /ʰweər'æz/ *conjunction*, is used to emphasize contrast: 'Roses will grow anywhere, whereas rhododendrons require special soil conditions'.

WHITE-COLLAR, BLUE-COLLAR

white-collar /'ʰwaɪt kɒlər/ *adjective*, refers to those working in an office, rather than on a factory floor: 'The white-collar workers were all given an extra holiday'. This term must be followed by a noun.

blue-collar /'blu: kɒlər/ *adjective*, refers to those doing physical work in industry: 'The candidate toured the industrial areas to get the blue-collar vote'. This term must also be followed by a noun.

WHITE PAPER, GREEN PAPER

white paper /'ʰwaɪt 'peɪpər/ *noun*, means a government report that is used to give a brief statement of policy before a law is introduced: 'The Commission laid out its plans for education in the new European White Paper'.

green paper /'gri:n 'peɪpər/ *noun*, means a government report that is distributed for public comment before drafting a new law: 'The Green Paper on social security is likely to provoke a lot of opposition among the general public'.

WHITSUN, PENTECOST

Whitsun /'ʰwɪtsən/ *noun*, is the Christian festival on the seventh Sunday after Easter. 'Whit' is an abbreviation for 'Whitsun' and is used in 'Whit Sunday' and 'Whit Monday': 'Many people in Europe still enjoy a public holiday at Whitsun'.

Pentecost /'pentɪkɒst/ *noun*, is either an alternative Christian name for the Whitsun festival, or a Jewish festival 50 days after the second day of Passover. Use 'Pentecost' when the intention is to emphasize the religious aspects of the festival: 'The devout family always considered Pentecost to be the highlight of their year'.

who, whom, who's, whose

- **who** /hu:/ *pronoun*, refers to people not things and is increasingly used in spoken English today to replace *whom*, as in *Who am I speaking to?* which was previously *To whom am I speaking?* Note that when *who* replaces *whom* in such questions, *to* is moved to the end of the sentence. *Who* is also used instead of *that* and *which* in relative clauses. See **THAT**.

- **whom** /hu:m/ *pronoun*, is the object of a verb or preposition but is only used in modern English in formal written contexts. *Whom* is always used after prepositions: *To whom it may concern*. This is a typical salutation in a letter of recommendation where the addressee is unknown.

- **who's** /hu:z/ is a contraction of *who is* (*who's speaking?*) or *who has* (*who's arrived?*). See **CONTRACTIONS**.

- **whose** /hu:z/ *pronoun*, is the possessive form of *who*: *Whose book is this? Whose* is also used to link a characteristic or possession to the person who owns it: *He's a footballer whose skill I admire*.

- Avoid confusing the soundalikes **who's** and **whose** in questions like: *Who's this?* asking about a person's identity, and *Whose is this?* which is a way of asking who owns something.

WIDE, WIDELY, BROAD

wide /waɪd/ *adjective*, means of greater than average width: 'A wide road' or to the full extent: 'His eyes are wide open'. It is also used in expressions like the World Wide Web.

widely /'waɪdli/ *adverb*, means in or to many places: 'Many students have travelled widely'. It can also mean to a large extent or by many people: 'This is a widely accepted viewpoint'. Note that when used in this sense, 'widely' often comes before the verb.

broad /brɔ:d/ *adjective*, means having a distance that is greater than average from side to side. 'Broad' is always the best word to choose when describing parts of the body: 'He had broad shoulders'; or when writing about features of the countryside: 'A broad expanse of grassland'. 'Broad' is used to describe things that are general and not detailed. Here 'wide' cannot be used: 'He gave a broad outline of the status of the peace negotiations'.

WINK, BLINK

wink /wɪŋk/ verb, means to close and open one eye as a signal which may imply humour, affection or that something is secret: 'The TV presenter was seen by millions winking to his colleague during the programme'.

blink /blɪŋk/ verb, means to open and shut both eyes in order to clear them of tears or dust: 'He was nervous and blinked throughout the interview'. 'Blink' can be used negatively to indicate a lack of surprise: 'He did not blink at the price they wanted for the house'. The related noun 'blinkers' is an alternative term for the indicators on a car: 'The blinkers were flashing left when he turned right and crashed'.

WISH, WANT, WOULD ... LIKE, DESIRE, BID

wish /wɪʃ/ noun & verb, as a noun, means a feeling that something should be done: 'She always had a wish to help others'. It can also mean something that a person wants to have: 'I know that your wish will come true one day'. As a verb, 'wish' means to hope that something will happen: 'I wish I had not pressed that button in the lift'. In formal BE, it is sometimes used in phrases like: 'You can have this room overlooking the park, if you wish'. (Informally, this could be 'if you want to').

want /wɒnt/ verb & noun, as a verb, means to have a wish for something: 'He has always wanted to live on a farm'. 'Want' can also be used to ask others what they would like, as in informal questions like: 'Do you want a coffee?' As a noun, 'want' is rather formal, and can mean a need or lack of something: 'There is a great want of cheap housing in rural areas today'. However, in this sentence, 'a lack of ' or 'a need for' would be more natural.

would ... like /wʊd ... laɪk/ verb, also refers to what a person wants or likes. It is used in questions as a more formal alternative to 'want': 'Would you like a cup of coffee?' Note that the phrase 'would you care for some tea?' sounds very old-fashioned today.
See CARE FOR ➪ CARE ABOUT.

desire /dɪˈzaɪər/ noun & verb, as a noun, means a strong feeling about something: 'They had a tremendous desire to buy just that house'. This is a formal word. As a verb, 'desire' means to have a strong feeling about something. This verb should be used with care, as expressions like 'We desire the pleasure of your company' is old-fashioned and classified as archaic English. 'We request' could be an alternative here.

bid /bɪd/ verb, means to wish, but only in formal expressions of greeting. The past tense is 'bade', pronounced /bæd/: 'He bade the members welcome'. See TENDER.

WITH, BY

with /wɪð/ preposition, is used in many different contexts such as doing things in the presence of another person: 'She built the boat together with her son'; or by the use of an instrument: 'They painted the boat with a spray device'. When emotion is to be expressed, 'with' is used for pleasure, fear, satisfaction etc.: 'The stranger shook with rage'. 'With' also means accompanied by: 'Who were you with at the party?' In another sense, 'with' can mean having a particular characteristic: 'He is a tall man with brown eyes'.

by /baɪ/ preposition, also has countless meanings, but is often used to show who or what is responsible for an action: 'The man was knocked down by a bus'. 'By' is also found in expressions such as 'by accident' and 'by chance'. See BY. See PREPOSITIONS. See VIA.

'The tunnel was measured with engineers.'

WITNESS, TESTIFY

witness /ˈwɪtnɪs/ verb & noun, as a verb, means either to see an event such as a crime or an accident: 'A passer-by witnessed the robbery'; or to be present in a figurative sense: 'The 1990s witnessed the acceptance of the Internet by the general public'. One cannot be asked to 'witness' in court: the correct term is 'testify'. As a noun, 'witness' is used in the expression 'bear witness' (in court), which means to give evidence. The person testifying is also called a 'witness'.

testify /'testɪfaɪ/ *verb*, means to give evidence as a witness in court: 'The judge agreed that she could testify behind closed doors'.

WORK (*VERB, COUNTABLE AND UNCOUNTABLE NOUN*)

work /wɜːk/ *verb & uncountable noun*, as a verb, means to be employed, often in a specific field: 'She works in the City and he works in education'. 'Work' as a verb can also refer to how something operates: 'How does this computer work?' 'Work on' means to be engaged in something: 'He is working on the computer problem'. 'Work with' refers to the tool used: 'He still works with pen and paper'. As an uncountable noun, 'work' means a place of employment and the activity that generates income: 'He is looking for work'. 'Work' can also be the result of physical or intellectual effort: 'Work by the scientific community needs better coordination'. See **JOB**.

work /wɜːk/ *countable noun*, means a literary, artistic, or musical composition: 'This is a work by Rembrandt'. In the plural, 'works' therefore means the complete artistic output of a writer, artist or composer: 'The collected works of William Shakespeare would make a good present for someone'. 'Works' can also refer to building operations and repairs; the parts of a machine; or a factory or installation. If the definite article is used, 'works' can take a singular or plural verb: 'The engineering works is/are finished'. 'Works' in this sense is usually restricted to manufacturing industry and this use of the word is mainly found in BE.

WORK EXPERIENCE, INTERN, PLACEMENT

work experience /'wɜːk ɪkspɪərɪəns/ *noun*, means the total work or jobs done in a person's career: 'Salary is not dependent on the work experience of staff'. In BE, 'work experience' is the period of time a student or young person spends in a company on a training scheme: 'Three months of work experience was required as part of the engineering degree'.

intern /'ɪntɜːn/ *noun*, is an AE term that means a student or new graduate who is getting work experience in a company of any type, particularly during the summer holiday: 'The

insurance company had positions for six interns'. It applies particularly to medical students in the final stages of their education. A related noun is 'internship'.

placement /'pleɪsmənt/ *noun*, means a job in business or industry that is integrated with a course at college or university in order to give the student work experience: 'The university called this a sandwich course as Year 2 is spent working on an industrial placement'.

WORKFORCE, MANPOWER

workforce /'wɜːkfɔːs/ *noun*, means the number of people working or available to do a job: 'Our manufacturing workforce is very well trained'. See **EMPLOYEE**.

manpower /'mænpaʊər/ *noun*, is an alternative to 'workforce' that is now avoided because of its sexist appearance. See **SEXIST LANGUAGE**.

WOUND, INJURE

wound /wuːnd/ *noun & verb*, means physical damage to the body by a knife or bullet cutting the flesh. A wound is a result of deliberate action, often in battles and surgery: 'Three are seriously wounded'. In a figurative sense it means emotional pain caused by what is said or done to a person. Note that one can 'wound' someone's pride but never 'injure' it.

injure /'ɪndʒər/ *verb*, refers to physical damage to one's own or another person's body often in an accident: 'Ten people were seriously injured in the crash'. One can 'injure' a reputation, but not 'wound' it. 'The reputation of the US Presidency was injured several times in the late 20th century'. If the same body had been wounded, this would be the result of a violent physical attack. See **DAMAGE**.

WRECK, DESTROY, SMASH

wreck /rek/ *verb & noun*, as a verb, means to damage something severely: 'This attack threatens to wreck all attempts to bring peace to the area'. As a noun, 'wreck' means the loss of or severe damage to something such as a ship at sea, a plane or road vehicles. 'Wreck' can also apply to people who are in a bad mental condition: 'He was a nervous wreck'.

destroy /dɪs'trɔɪ/ *verb*, means to completely ruin something: 'The house was destroyed by the storm'. When something is 'destroyed' there is nothing left.

smash /smæʃ/ *verb & noun*, as a verb, means to break something, such as a window, violently: 'Another smash-and-grab raid on a jewellery shop'. As a noun, 'smash' can mean physical violence, and, as the sound of the word implies, loud noise is involved. The related adjective 'smashing' is used in informal BE to mean excellent and enjoyable.

WRITE^S, WRIGHT^S, RITE^S

write /raɪt/ *verb*, means to put words on paper: 'A person who writes advertising text or copy is called a copywriter'. See **TYPE IN**.

wright /raɪt/ *noun*, means a maker or builder. However, the word is classified as archaic when it is used alone. 'Wright' is still alive in combinations such as 'playwright' and 'shipwright'.

rite /raɪt/ *noun*, means a religious ceremony or other ceremonial act, event or even custom: 'Every culture has devised some kind of funeral rites'.

X-RAYED, X-RATED

x-rayed /'eks reɪd/ *verb*, means photographed or examined using X-rays: 'All baggage is X-rayed before being loaded on the aircraft'.

x-rated /'eks reɪtɪd/ *adjective*, refers to something that is pornographic, violent or otherwise indecent. It usually relates to films or videos that should only be seen by adults: 'The newspapers concluded that the film was X-rated because of its black humour'.

⚠️ *The airline tightened security and told its passengers that 'All baggage would be X-rated.'*

Yy

-y, -ies (for plural nouns)

- Nouns ending in -y form their plural by adding -s if the y has a vowel immediately before it: *attorneys, monkeys*.
- The y is replaced by -ies if the y has a consonant immediately before it: *pony ~ ponies, supply ~ supplies*.

YEA, NAY, AYE, NO (POLITICS)

yea /jeɪ/ *noun*, means an affirmative answer and is also used in special circumstances such as voting in the US Congress to approve a motion: 'Will the yeas vote now'.

nay /neɪ/ *noun*, means a negative answer: 'The Government has said both yea and nay on this issue'. 'Nay' is an old-fashioned word whose usage is limited to meaning 'if not', in sentences such as: 'She is going to be annoyed, nay furious, when she hears about this'. It is best avoided.

aye /aɪ/ *noun*, means an affirmative answer, and is used in the British Parliament to indicate support for a motion: 'Those in favour say "Aye"'. 'The ayes have it' means the 'yes' vote has won.

no /nəʊ/ *noun*, means a negative answer, and is used in the British Parliament to indicate rejection of a motion: 'The noes have it', means the 'no' vote has won.

YEAR-OLD, YEARS OLD

year-old /jɪər əʊld/ *adjective* phrase, is always preceded by a number and states the age of someone or something. This is used in phrases such as: a 'nine-year-old girl'. If it is clear who or what is being referred to, the noun may be omitted: 'a nine-year-old'. As it is always incorrect to add an 's' to an adjective, 'a nine-years-old girl' is wrong. The parts of this adjective phrase are hyphenated.

years old /jɪəz ˈəʊld/ *noun phrase*, also means the age of someone or something. Here year is a noun and takes a plural 's', except, of course, when the preceding number is 'one'. Thus 'he is one year old; she is nine years old' are both correct. There are no hyphens between the words in this usage.

YET, STILL, ALREADY, ALL READY

yet /jet/ *adverb*, refers to something that is planned but has not happened: 'Have you eaten yet?' 'Yet' is used mostly in negative sentences and in questions, but is sometimes found in affirmative statements: 'I have yet to meet a Scot who does not like whisky'. Another way of phrasing this would be to say: 'I have not yet met a Scot ...'.

still /stɪl/ *adverb*, refers to something that is ongoing and unfinished: 'We have been here for 30 minutes and are still waiting for our meal'. 'Still' can also be used to make a comparison: 'July was hot, but August was warmer still'.

already /ɔːlˈredi/ *adverb*, refers either to something that has happened before now: 'The waiter said that he had already spoken to the chef about the delay', or before a time in the past: 'We got to the supermarket at 6, but it had already closed'. Note that the stress is only on 'ready'.

all ready /ˈɔːl ˈredi/ *adverb*, means that everyone in a group is now prepared for an activity: 'The chef explained about the fire, but now his staff were all ready to start making the food'. 'All ready' is written as two words. Note that both of them are stressed.

YOUNG, YOUTH

young /jʌŋ/ *adjective*, means having lived or existed for a short time: 'It was a relatively young democracy'.

youth /juːθ/ *noun*, means a young male when used for individuals. It often has negative connotations in this sense: 'These youths are always hanging around this cafe'. As a collective noun for young people of both sexes, 'youth' is most frequently found in the expression 'the youth of today': 'The youth of today are more affluent than young people were fifty years ago'.

you/You, your/Your

Some languages capitalize the words that are equivalent to the polite forms of *you* and *your* in correspondence. It is incorrect to transfer this custom to English and write *You* or *Your* with initial capitals, unless in first position in the sentence. Capitalization in such words vanished from English a few hundred years ago. However, note that *Your* does begin with a capital letter in some titles, such as *Your Majesty*, and occasionally in religious texts when referring to God.

–YSE⁵, –YZE⁵

-yse /-aɪz/ is the BE spelling of the ending of a small group of verbs such as 'analyse' and 'paralyse'.

-yze is the AE spelling of the ending of verbs such as 'analyze' and 'paralyze'.

Although a lot is written about '-ize' and/or '-ise' in BE, when it comes to these endings there are no exceptions: '-yse' is the BE spelling and '-yze' is the AE spelling. See **–IZE, –ISE**.

Zz

z (pronunciation)

- The BE pronunciation of the letter *z* is /zed/, and the AE pronunciation of *z* is /ziː/.

- As this is the only letter of the alphabet where there is a clear difference in pronunciation between AE and BE, care should be taken to pronounce proper nouns or names correctly: *The President asked ZZ Top* (read *zee zee top*) *to play at the White House.*

ZERO, OH, NOUGHT, NIL

zero /'zɪərəʊ/ *noun & verb,* as a noun, is used in BE for temperature and numerical amounts: 'How many zeroes did you say?' Except for scientific writing, there is no reason to add zeroes when referring to the time or money. For example, 5 p.m. is better than 5.00 p.m. in most contexts. Also for whole units, write €25, not €25.00. In AE, 'zero' is widely used for the number 0 in both written and spoken language. For telephone numbers, the number 51 12 04 00 would be 'five one, one two, zero four, double zero' in AE and a decimal is 'zero point two'. The plural of the noun is either 'zeros' or 'zeroes'. The forms of the verb are: 'zeroes', 'zeroed', 'zeroing'. The phrase to 'zero in' on something means to focus on the main issue: 'Parliament has finally zeroed in on the question of European expansion'. See **ZOOM**.

oh /əʊ/ *noun,* is widely used in BE, where AE uses 'zero'. In BE, a decimal mentioned by itself is 'oh point two'. In telephone or bank account numbers, the number 51 12 04 00 would be 'five one, one two, oh four, double oh'. 'Oh' is not used in written language.
See **TELEPHONE NUMBERS**.

nought /nɔːt/ *noun,* means 'zero' in BE in mathematical references: 'The class was asked to multiply six by eight, and then add five noughts'. Nought is also used to refer to a range: 'His motorbike could do nought to sixty in seven seconds'.

nil /nɪl/ *noun,* is used in some team sports to indicate no score: 'Liverpool won 1-0' (read as 'one nil'). Other sports have various names to express the same thing, e.g. 'love' in tennis, 'duck' in cricket.

ZOOM, WHIZ, ZIP

zoom /zuːm/ *verb & noun,* as a verb, is an onomatopoeic word that resembles a low engine noise, or the rapid, noisy sudden movement of a jet aircraft: 'The jets zoomed low over the farm and terrified the animals'. The phrase to 'zoom in' is used in photography to mean take a close-up photo. Figuratively and informally this means to focus closely on a particular issue: 'The press zoomed in on corruption in local government'. 'Zoom' as a noun is also a type of camera lens designed to focus quickly on distant objects: 'The reporter used his longest zoom lens'. In aeronautics, 'zoom' also means a steep climb.

whizz /hwɪz/ *verb,* is also an onomatopoeic word that resembles a high whistling noise: 'An arrow whizzed over our heads'. An alternative spelling, especially in AE, is 'whiz'.

zip /zɪp/ *verb & noun,* describes fast movement, but without noise. It refers to doing things quickly: 'There was little traffic and we zipped along the motorway'. A zip is also a fastening mechanism, especially for suitcases, dresses and trousers. In computing, a zip file is one in which data is compressed in order to allow the transfer of large files between computers to be carried out more quickly. See **POSTCODE**.

Bibliography

Allen, R. (ed.). 2000. *The New Penguin English Dictionary* 2nd edition. Harmondsworth, England: Penguin Books.

Bryson, B. 1987. *The Penguin Dictionary of Troublesome Words* 2nd edition. Harmondsworth, England: Penguin Books.

Burchfield, R.W. (ed.) 1996. *The New Fowler's Modern English Usage* 3rd edition. Oxford: Oxford University Press.

Clark, S. 2001. *Getting Your English Right* 2nd edition. Trondheim, Norway: Tapir Academic Press.

Clark, S. 2002. *Put ikke foden i munden ...* 2002. Copenhagen: Gads Forlag.

The Economist 2000. *The Economist Style Guide* 6th edition. London: The Economist/Profile Books.

Greenbaum, S. and **J. Whitcut** 1988. *Longman Guide to English Usage.* Harlow, England: Longman.

Hornby, A.S. 2000. *Oxford Advanced Learner's Dictionary* 6th Edition. Oxford: Oxford University Press.

Inman, C. 1994. *The Financial Times Style Guide.* London: Pitman Publishing.

Oxford University Press 1999. *Hart's Rules for Compositors and Readers at the University Press Oxford* 39th edition. Oxford: Oxford University Press.

Oxford University Press 1998. *The New Oxford Dictionary of English.* Oxford: Oxford University Press.

Oxford University Press 1993. *The New Shorter Oxford English Dictionary* 4th edition. Oxford: Oxford University Press, Oxford.

Oxford University Press 2002. *Oxford Collocations Dictionary.* Oxford: Oxford University Press.

Oxford University Press 1996. *The Oxford Companion to the English Language.* Oxford: Oxford University Press.

Oxford University Press. 2000. *Oxford Dictionary for Writers and Editors* 2nd edition. Oxford: Oxford University Press.

Oxford University Press 2001. *Oxford Idioms Dictionary.* Oxford: Oxford University Press

Pointon, G.E. (ed.) 1983. *BBC Pronouncing Dictionary of British Names* 2nd edition. Oxford: Oxford University Press.

Roach, P. and **J. Hartman** (eds.) 1997. *English Pronouncing Dictionary* 15th edition. Cambridge: Cambridge University Press.

Room, A. 1979. *Room's Dictionary of Confusibles.* London: Routledge and Kegan Paul.

Swan, M. 1995. *Practical English Usage* 2nd edition. Oxford: Oxford University Press

Trask, R.L. 2001. *Mind the Gaffe.* Harmondsworth, England: Penguin Books.

University of Chicago Press 1982. *Chicago Manual of Style* 13th edition Chicago: The University of Chicago Press.

Upton, C., W.A. Kretzschmar Jr, and **R. Konopka** 2001. *The Oxford Dictionary of Pronunciation for Current English.* Oxford: Oxford University Press.

Urdang, L. 1989. *Dictionary of Differences.* London: Bloomsbury Press.

Webster, M. 1989. *Webster's Encyclopedic Unabridged Dictionary of the English Language.* New York: Gramercy Books.

Wells, J.C. 2000. *Longman Pronunciation Dictionary* 2nd edition. Harlow, England: Pearson Education.

Standardization organization
International Organization for Standardization (ISO), Geneva, Switzerland. (www.iso.ch)

Index

The list below refers you to all the words that are defined in this book, as well as to the topics in the language and culture boxes.

boulder ⇨ 27, 182
boulevard ⇨ 181
boundary ⇨ 28
Boxing Day ⇨ 43
boyfriend ⇨ 151
boyish ⇨ 29
braces ({...}) ⇨ 29
brackets ((...), [...], <...>) ⇨ 29
brake ⇨ 29
brand name ⇨ 211
bread ⇨ 125
break ⇨ 29
break down ⇨ 29
breakdown ⇨ 29
breakfast ⇨ 30
breaktime ⇨ 98
breast ⇨ 30
breath ⇨ 30
breathalyser ⇨ 27
breathe ⇨ 30
brethren ⇨ 33
brew ⇨ 81
bring ⇨ 30
bring up ⇨ 30
Brit ⇨ 31
Britain ⇨ 31
British ⇨ 31
British English (BE) ⇨ 29, 31–3
British Isles ⇨ 31
British place names ⇨ 33
Britisher ⇨ 31
Briton ⇨ 31
broach ⇨ 31
broad ⇨ 226
broadcast ⇨ 211
broil ⇨ 181
brother ⇨ 33
brotherhood ⇨ 33
brought ⇨ 33
brown ⇨ 27
brunch ⇨ 30
brunette ⇨ 27
BSc ⇨ 21
buffet ⇨ 33
building ⇨ 99
bull market ⇨ 23
burglar ⇨ 182
burglarize ⇨ 182
burgle ⇨ 182
burial ⇨ 33
bury ⇨ 25
bus ⇨ 34
business ⇨ 34
bust ⇨ 30
buy ⇨ 34
by ⇨ 34, 219, 227
by- ⇨ 35
bye ⇨ 35

c, ca ⇨ 35
cabin ⇨ 35
cafe ⇨ 178
call ⇨ 158
call on/call in ⇨ 220
calm ⇨ 35–6

camper ⇨ 211
campus ⇨ 36
can ⇨ 36
canal ⇨ 37
cancel ⇨ 37
cannot ⇨ 36
can't ⇨ 36
capacity ⇨ 1
capital ⇨ 37
capital letters ⇨ 37–8
capitol ⇨ 37
car park ⇨ 151
caravan ⇨ 211
cardinal numbers ⇨ 143
care about ⇨ 38
care for ⇨ 38
careful ⇨ 38
careless ⇨ 38
cargo ⇨ 88
carriageway ⇨ 117
carry ⇨ 23
carry out ⇨ 105
cash card ⇨ 21
cash machine ⇨ 39
cast ⇨ 39
caste ⇨ 39
casual ⇨ 38–9
casualty ⇨ 219
catastrophe ⇨ 3
cause ⇨ 39
cautious ⇨ 38
–cede ⇨ 39
–ceed ⇨ 39
cellar ⇨ 39
Celsius ⇨ 39
Celt ⇨ 40
Celtic ⇨ 40
cement ⇨ 40
censer ⇨ 40
censor ⇨ 40
censure ⇨ 40
census ⇨ 40
centenary ⇨ 40
centennial ⇨ 40
centigrade ⇨ 39
centre ⇨ 40
centre in ⇨ 41
centre on ⇨ 41
century ⇨ 132
CEO (Chief Executive Officer) ⇨ 128
cereal ⇨ 41
certain ⇨ 41
certificate ⇨ 62
certified ⇨ 41
cf. ⇨ 41
chair ⇨ 41–2
chairman ⇨ 42
chairwoman ⇨ 42
chalet ⇨ 35
chamber ⇨ 182
championship ⇨ 50
chance ⇨ 147
change ⇨ 42
channel ⇨ 37
chapter ⇨ 42

in character ⇨ 219
characteristic ⇨ 214
charge card ⇨ 22
chart ⇨ 129
charted ⇨ 41
chartered ⇨ 41
chat ⇨ 54
cheap ⇨ 42
check ⇨ 42
check-up ⇨ 42
cheers ⇨ 91
cheeseburger ⇨ 27
cheque ⇨ 42
chest ⇨ 30
childish ⇨ 42–3
childlike ⇨ 42
Chinaman ⇨ 43
Chinese ⇨ 43
chips ⇨ 43
choose ⇨ 43
Christian name ⇨ 83
Christmas ⇨ 43
chronic ⇨ 5
circa ⇨ 16, 35
cite ⇨ 43
citizen ⇨ 108
city ⇨ 44
civic ⇨ 44
civics ⇨ 44
civil ⇨ 44
claim ⇨ 63
classic ⇨ 44
classical ⇨ 44
clean ⇨ 44
cleanse ⇨ 44
clerk ⇨ 146
cliché ⇨ 44–5
client ⇨ 58
clientele ⇨ 58
climactic ⇨ 45
climatic ⇨ 45
cloakroom ⇨ 45
clock ⇨ 45
close ⇨ 139
cloth ⇨ 46
clothes ⇨ 45
clothing ⇨ 45
co, co- ⇨ 46
coach ⇨ 34
coast ⇨ 46
cohabit ⇨ 125
coincide ⇨ 52
cold ⇨ 206
collaborate ⇨ 54
collect ⇨ 46
collective nouns ⇨ 46
college ⇨ 186
Junior College ⇨ 97
Sixth-Form College ⇨ 97
collude ⇨ 54
collusion ⇨ 54
colon (:) ⇨ 47
coloured ⇨ 27
colours ⇨ 47, 101
come ⇨ 85

Thematic guide to usage notes

Below is a list of the usage notes in *Word for Word* which appear in tinted boxes. These give guidance on British and American English style and usage, as well as offering practical tips on how to speak and write English successfully.

Acknowledgements

Without the understanding and support from our respective families this book would not have been written. What is now the Norwegian University of Science and Technology in Trondheim, Norway is to be acknowledged for bringing the authors together a long time ago and also being flexible enough in the past 18 months to allow this book to be finished. The European Commission's Leonardo da Vinci programme is to be acknowledged for a scholarship that gave us the opportunity to plan the book. David Baker and his staff and especially our editor Eileen Flannigan at Oxford University Press are to be thanked for their professional assistance. Finally, the thousands of students, academics and business people who made the very mistakes that *Word for Word* is based on are to be thanked for their invaluable input.

Word for Word was developed from material originally used in Stewart Clark's *Getting Your English Right* (Tapir Academic Press, Trondheim, Norway, 2001). The authors and publisher are grateful to Tapir Academic Press for their cooperation in the preparation of this book.